BOOK
WORD/INFORMATION PROCESSING
AUTHOR   - CASADY SA...
PUBLISHER - SOUTH WESTER...

D1792094

WORD/ INFORMATION PROCESSING

A System Approach

Mona J. Casady, Ph. D.
*Professor,
Department of Office Administration
and Business Education
Southwest Missouri State University
Springfield, Missouri*

Dorothy C. Sandburg
*Office Systems Manager
Farm Credit Services
St. Paul, Minnesota*

Published by
SOUTH-WESTERN PUBLISHING CO.

W85

CINCINNATI   WEST CHICAGO, IL   DALLAS   PELHAM MANOR, NY   PALO ALTO, CA

Copyright © 1985

by SOUTH-WESTERN PUBLISHING CO.

Cincinnati, Ohio

ALL RIGHTS RESERVED

The text of this publication, or any part thereof, may not be reproduced or transmitted in any form or by any means, electronic or mechanical, including photocopying, recording, storage in an information retrieval system, or otherwise, without the prior written permission of the publisher.

ISBN: 0-538-23850-X
Library of Congress Catalog Card Number: 84-51929

2 3 4 5 6 7 D 1 0 9 8 7 6 5

Printed in the United States of America

Preface

Word/Information Processing: A System Approach is designed for students and instructors who already have some familiarity with word processing but who want a system approach. The system approach covers the basic concepts of word processing not as an isolated system but as one of several office automation systems that can connect for a totally integrated information processing system.

Who Should Read It? The content of the text is pertinent to those who aspire to being word processing and/or administrative support personnel, marketing support representatives for vendors, users of word processing services, salespersons, system managers, consultants/system analysts, and business instructors. All of these important occupations require a solid understanding of word processing concepts as they relate to an information processing system.

Authors' Backgrounds The combined expertise of an educator and a consultant/system manager of word/information processing provides an up-to-date, realistic textbook that is organized for the proper sequence of learning as well as effective teaching. The instructor is facilitated by the many helpful supplementary materials given in the *Instructor's Manual* and in the *Student's Reference Guide*.

Instructor's Manual The *Instructor's Manual* aids the instructor by guiding the lecture and discussion of meaningful class periods. The "Points to Emphasize and Discuss" help to direct the lecture and discussion to coordinate the end-of-chapter discussion questions and the transparencies. By following these guidelines, the instructor will see that there is continuity with the objectives, the outline, and the discussion questions to prepare the students adequately for the examinations, including the essay questions. The case problems are composed to challenge students to make the kind of decisions that system managers often face in modern business. Should the instructor have the time and wish to present additional information that is not in the textbook, there is "Supplementary Information" to enrich the presentations. Students generally are impressed with instructors who add to textbook content.

Examinations For each chapter there is an examination that includes true or false, multiple choice, and essay questions. In addition, there are two major examinations (over Chapters 1-7 and over Chapters 8-15) that can be used at midterm and at the end of the term. Both the examinations and the keys are given only in the *Instructor's Manual* so that the instructor can control the confidential nature of the instruments.

Student's Reference Guide The *Student's Reference Guide* is designed to assist students in organizing their notes, in preparing to respond to the discussion questions and case problems, in learning new terminology, and in performing related activities. The related activities enable students to apply the concepts of the chapter and become familiar with word/information processing as it exists in their communities. By maintaining this booklet in a systematic fashion, the student will have begun the development of a professional file that can be expanded throughout that person's career.

Staying on Course Both the students and the instructors are presented the objectives and an outline of each chapter. These guides enable the reader to focus on the basic points. As new vocabulary words are first encountered in the text, the terms and short definitions appear in the margin. In addition, a glossary of complete definitions is provided at the end of the text.

Visual Aids The illustrations, figures, and transparencies were carefully selected from other experts (as referenced) or creatively designed by the authors. They enhance the understanding of concepts and applications in exciting ways. The many attractive color illustrations add to the visual stimuli that will motivate students and instructors. Reading the text is both educational and enjoyable.

Chapter Highlights Here are some highlights about various chapters within *Word/Information Processing: A System Approach:*

Chapter 1 Word Processing as a Part of Information Processing To get an overall view of the major technologies that can interface for a total information processing system the students read the script of a film. Then they analyze the film by identifying the four basic forms of information and nine subsystems as they interact.

Chapter 2 Steps Toward Office Improvement This chapter describes the problems of the traditional office from a system perspective. Many internal and external pressures are placed upon the business which prompt changes. Using participative management techniques (team building), company professionals analyze needs, investigate methods for improvement, then determine the best plan to upgrade their flow of information. The investigation process uncovers specific benefits that can be derived from installing a word/information processing system based on real life experiences. The chapter closes by comparing the basic concepts of a word processing system against its traditional office counterparts in an effort to establish an improving, evolving office environment.

Chapter 3 Input Authors (users) of word processing applications have many methods of originating text from which to choose. Each method is appropriate for certain types of tasks, and each has some limitations of which system personnel should be aware. The successful system guides the users to select the best method according to the task, for evidence proves that the quality of output is contingent upon the quality of input.

Chapter 4 Output This chapter focuses on the hardware and software that make word processing a tangible experience. The reader is presented: (1) a capsulized equipment history; (2) an excellent reference guide which describes capabilities, functionalities, and features in easy-to-understand terms; and (3) a flavor for the way in which business views, analyzes, and determines equipment decisions.

Chapter 5 Reproducing Text In a continuing effort to provide the reader with practical business insight, this chapter discusses the process of reproducing text from an analytical approach. Various reprographic options are described, charts and selection graphs are illustrated—all techniques which closely resemble the process a business professional would investigate before recommending a solution to management.

Chapter 6 Storing and Retrieving Text Chapter 6 logically escorts the reader into the realms of storing and retrieving information. Rather than simply relating detailed data on the various methods and tools for storing information, the reader is challenged to view the available techniques through a cost and efficiency approach. The chapter attempts to impress its audience with the scope of the nation's paper problem and then closes after convincing arguments that the goals of business should be to prevent waste, confusion, and costly inefficiencies.

Chapter 7 Distributing Text Distributing text is another way of saying "communicating information." Communicating with others is the main activity of company professionals. Communicating effectively and easily in business today has become a very real problem. The "need to know" has become a vital part of our business life. This chapter deals with the communication or distribution of this information. It offers solutions to information communication problems in two ways: (1) understanding the company's needs and (2) analyzing the tools and methods that address these needs.

Chapter 8 Determining the Need for a System Everyone talks about it but no one tells you how to begin. Finally! We have a book containing a reference guide that explains how to determine the need for a system. The chapter guides the reader through the changes in business climate which contribute to the evitable progression of an information processing system. No make-believe fantasies—real business life experiences abound. The two most common approaches used by companies in determining their needs are discussed. Their advantages and disadvantages are listed. Selection process guides are illustrated to assist a project leader in selecting team members, developing planning functions, measuring results, selling the concept, and recommending a solution to management. Each step has been logically designed and well formatted to allow for easy instruction.

Chapter 9 Selecting and Implementing the System Chapter 9 completes the project plan begun in the previous chapter. Now that management has agreed to the recommendation, the proposed system needs must be committed to paper so that eligible vendors can offer a bid. This chapter offers an actual Request for Proposal (RFP) as an illustration. Steps must now be taken to select the vendor, ready the environment, prepare the users, develop the staff, and plan the procedures. The reader is offered examples for site layout, guidelines for installations, practical suggestions for qualifying staff, and proven recommendations for training users.

Chapter 10 Preparing the Environment The environment provided for office personnel is instrumental in affecting the performance of human beings as well as electronic equipment. The various factors that must be considered include (1) warnings about problems that can occur from inadequate planning and control; (2) guidelines for meeting minimum requirements; and (3) examples of model environments—those that are comfortable, attractive, and conducive to maximum production and job satisfaction.

Chapter 11 Developing the System Controls Intelligent people and sophisticated machines should be guided by efficient procedures that enhance the performance of office support personnel, impress users with quality work, and result in a professional and progressive company image. Many functional ideas are presented in a way that does more than tell the reader *what* should be done. Emphasis is on the *why* and the *how to* of controlling a cost-effective and pleasing system.

Chapter 12 Managing the System Once implemented, the development of a word/information processing system has only begun. Effort to modify and improve the procedures, equipment, and environment continue. The word processing manager has the delicate role of being a liaison person who can communicate effectively with users, office support personnel, and top management. Human relations ability is necessary to motivate people, provide job enrichment, and overcome resistance to change.

Chapter 13 Staffing a Word Processing Department The manager of a word processing department helps design career paths, interview and screen applicants, provide orientation for new employees, and evaluate personnel. For each of these responsibilities there are ample forms and examples that could guide a novice through these strategic steps.

Chapter 14 Integrating Technologies for Information Processing Following the unique introduction of systems in Chapter 1, the subsystems of an information processing system are identified and the relationship of each subsystem is discussed as it relates to a totally integrated information processing system.

Chapter 15 Participating in a Total Information Processing System The word/information processing system did not evolve without its share of crises. In every change people are affected positively and negatively. In order to present the most objective viewpoints, both sides of the argument for and against automation are presented for the viewer. Office automation deals with human needs and it is expected that the users encountered by careerists in this profession will raise some negative issues of their own. This chapter hopes to prepare the potential professional for those situations. As an additional preparation step, new roles and organizational structures are presented in order to provide a taste for the responsibilities and career potentials within this field. To prepare this same individual for tomorrow's job, the chapter concludes with sources and suggestions that will continue an education in office automation after the last page is turned.

The authors and the publisher wish to thank the educators who reviewed this manuscript and added their individual expertise to this test: Ronald Kapper, College of DuPage, Glen Ellyn, Illinois; Patricia Murranka, Arizona State University, Tempe, Arizona; Mary A. Myers, ITT Educational Services, Inc., Indianapolis, Indiana; Carol Swinney, Macon Area Vocational Technical School, Macon, Georgia; and, Suzanne Wegman, Nazareth College, Rochester, New York.

Mona Casady

Dorothy Sandburg

Contents

PART 1 Introduction to Word Processing

Chapter 1/Word Processing as a Part of Information Processing

Information Processing on Film, 2
Evaluation of the Film, 5
The Impact of Information, 8
Forms of Information, 9
Changes in Information Processing, 9
Subsystems of Information Processing, 11
Word Processing, 12
Data Processing, 12
Optical Character Recognition, 15
Intelligent Copiers/Printers, 16
Phototypesetting, 16
Micrographics, 18
Teleconferencing, 20
Electronic Mail, 21
Telecommunications, 22
Voice Message System, 22
Linking Information Processing Machines, 23
How Information Processing Affects Word Processing Careers, 24

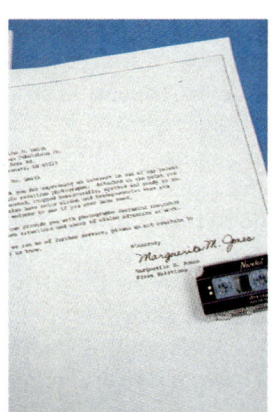

Chapter 2/Steps Toward Office Improvement

Problems of the Traditional Office, 26
Personnel, 27
The Cost of Doing Business, 28
Marketplace Competition, 28
Objectives to be Accomplished, 29
Improved Document Turnaround Time, 32
Efficient Paper Flow Without Duplicated Effort, 33
Accuracy in Keyboarding and Proofreading, 34
Minimal Mental and Physical Effort, 35
Quality Output to Enhance Company Image, 35
Economical Costs, 36
Compatibility With Other Information Processing Systems, 36
Satisfaction to Secretaries, Professionals, and Managers, 38
Trends in Other Companies, 38
Composition of a Word Processing System, 41
People, 41
Machines, 43
Procedures, 45
Environment, 45

PART 2 Information Processing Cycle

Chapter 3/Input

Word Processing Cycle, 50
Types of Input, 53
Longhand, 53
Rough Draft, 54
Shorthand, 56
Machine Dictation, 58
Work Request, 66
Communicating Workstation, 68
Optical Character Recognition, 69
Voice Recognition, 72
Determining the Best Type of Input, 74

Chapter 4/Output

Types of Equipment, 76
Standalone Word Processors, 77
Multiterminal Systems, 84
Time-Sharing Word Processors, 87
Recording/Storage Media, 88
Magnetic Card, 88
Cassette, 89
Flexible Diskette, 89
Hard Disk, 89
Bubble Memory, 91
Optical (Laser) Disk, 91
Printing Devices, 92
Impact Printer, 92
Nonimpact Printers, 95
Software, 97
Applications Software, 98
Operating System Software, 98

Chapter 5/Reproducing Text

Options Available for Reproduction, 103
Photocopying, 103
Offset Duplication, 106
Phototypesetting, 108
Commercial Printing, 111
Factors to Consider When Selecting the Option, 113
Physical Characteristics of the Job, 113
Quality, 116
Speed and Volume, 116
Cost, 119

Chapter 6/Storing and Retrieving Text

Scope of the Problem, 125
Objectives of a Records Management System, 128
Methods of Storing Information, 128
Manual Retrieval Methods, 130
Electronic Retrieval Methods, 140

Chapter 7/Distributing Text

Distribution Problems, 151
Company Mail and Delivery Systems, 154
Guidelines, 154
Internal Mail Handling Equipment, 155
Public and Private Mail Services, 159
Special Delivery, 161
Special Handling, 161
Certified Mail, 161
Registered Mail, 162
Insured Mail, 162
Business Reply Mail, 162
Collect on Delivery, 163
Mailgram, 163
Express Mail, 164
E-COM Service, 165
Electronic Mail Systems, 165
Benefits, 166
Basic Characteristics, 168
Electronic Message Systems, 168
Computer-Based Message Systems, 171
Teletypewriter Systems, 173
Communicating Word Processors, 174
Facsimile (FAX) Systems, 175
Linking for Communications, 177
Language, 179
Speed, 180
Transmission Type, 182
Protocol, 182

PART 3 Implementing Change in the Office

Chapter 8/Determining the Need for a System

Factors Contributing to the Changes in Information Processing, 187
Availability of People, 187
Energy Shortage, 188
Availability of Resource Products, 190
Competitive Position, 190
Economic Position, 191
Preliminary Steps in Planning, 192
Defining Objectives, 192
Gaining the Support of Top Management, 194
Team Analysis Approach, 196
Work Plan Development, 201
Psychological Considerations, 201
Preparing Users for Change, 203
Involving Users in the Implementation Process, 205
Providing Users With Review and Training, 205
Restructuring Jobs for Greater Fulfillment, 205
The Feasibility Study, 206
Designing the Study Plan, 206
Collecting Data, 207
Interviewing, 210
Analyzing the Survey Forms, 211
Cost of Doing Business, 212
Analyzing Work Flow, 215
Summarizing Findings, 217
Reporting Results, 217

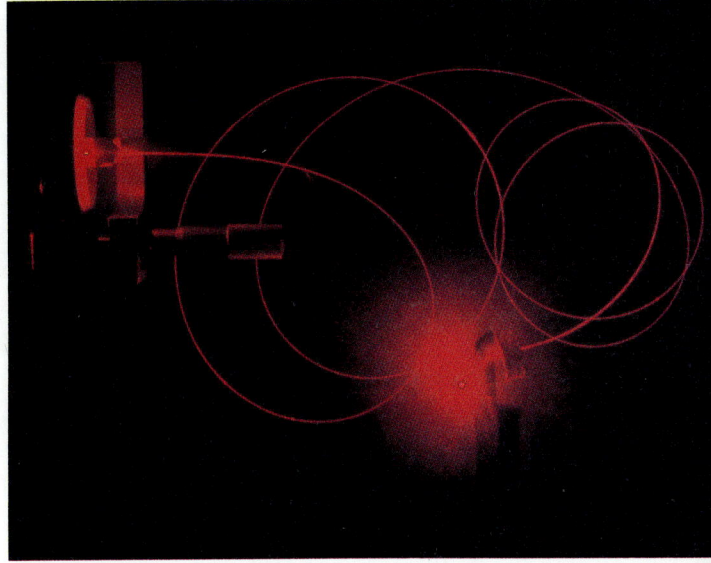

Chapter 9/Selecting and Implementing the System

Equipment Selection, 223
Design Specifications, 223
Request for Proposal, 225
Equipment Evaluation, 235
Implementation Planning, 241
Site Preparation and Layout, 241
Environmental Considerations, 250
Organization of Personnel, 254
Procedures for Efficient Work Flow, 258
Orientation Programs, 260

Chapter 10/Preparing the Environment

Why the Environment is Important, 266
Problems of a Poor Environment, 267
Effect of Environment on Productivity, 267
How Environment Changes, 267
Involvement of Personnel, 267
Work Areas, 268
Open-Office Plan, 269
Individual Work Stations, 271
Visual Display Terminals, 275
Climate of the Work Area, 277
Temperature, 278
Humidity, 278
Air Circulation and Cleanliness, 278
Electrical Power, 279
Basic Recommendations, 279
Power Disturbances, 280
Static Electricity, 280
Lighting, 283
Quantity and Quality of Light, 283
Types of Artificial Lighting, 283
Direction and Location of Lighting, 285
Color Treatment, 287
Effects of Color, 287
Choosing Colors, 288
Acoustical Control, 289
Measuring Sound, 289
How Noise Affects People, 290
Ways to Reduce Noise, 290
Office Covering Ratings, 292

Chapter 11/Developing the System Controls

Logging Work, 298
Log Sheet, 298
Work Request, 300
Why Work is Logged, 300
Measuring Production, 301
Reasons for Measuring Production, 302
Methods of Measuring Production, 305
Setting Standards, 307
Establishing Priorities, 308
Scheduling Turnaround, 309
Maintaining Quality Printout, 311
Proofreading, 311
Monitoring the Printer, 313
Standardizing Formats of Documents, 314
Benefits of Standardization, 315
Objectives of Standardizing Formats, 316
Managing Media Files, 319
Diskette Media, 320
Disk Media, 321
File Management Functions, 322
Proper Care of Magnetic Media, 323
Writing Office Manuals, 325
Types of Manuals, 325
Purposes of Office Manuals, 325
Techniques for Producing Effective Office Manuals, 326
Training Personnel, 326
Types of Training Programs, 328
The Trainees and Trainers of In-Service Programs, 328
How to Train, 328

PART 4 Information Processing in Action

Chapter 12/Managing the System

Responsibilities of the Manager, 334
Developing and Modifying Procedures, 335
Selecting and Maintaining Machines and Software, 339
Designing and Improving the Environment, 341
Supervising Word Processing Specialists, 341
Assisting Users, 347
Reporting to Upper Management, 349
Psychology of Working With People, 353
Personnel Who Are Supervised, 353
Users of Word Processing Services, 356
Upper Management, 357

Chapter 13/Staffing a Word Processing Department

Designing Open Career Paths, 360
Describing Jobs, 362
Analyzing the Jobs, 363
Determining Job Titles, 363
Writing Job Descriptions, 364
Establishing a Salary Scale, 367
Problems of Which to be Aware, 367
Facts to Justify Equitable Salaries, 368
Hiring New Employees, 370
Recruiting Qualified Applicants, 370
Screening Applicants, 372
Scheduling Interviews, 375
Testing for Employment Skills, 376
Interviewing Applicants, 379
Evaluating Applicants and Making the Selection, 382
Providing Orientation for New Employees, 383
Orientation to the Company, 384
Orientation to the Job, 386
Evaluating Employee Performance, 386
The Evaluation Form, 388
Conference With the Employee, 388

Chapter 14/Integrating Technologies for Information Processing

Information Processing, 393
Systems Which Integrate, 393
Word Processing, 393
Data Processing, 394
Electronic Mail, 397
Micrographics, 400
Optical Character Recognition, 402
Typesetting, 405
Reprographics, 408
Teleconferencing, 409
Voice Processing, 412
Linking Subsystems, 415
Local Area Networks, 415
Switch and Access Networks, 416
Wide Area Networks, 417

Chapter 15/Participating in a Total Information Processing System

Problems Involved With Merging the New Technologies, 423
Human Issues, 424
Health Issues, 425
Job Enhancement Issues, 426
Job Loss Issues, 428
Training and Support Issues, 428
Organizational Issues, 429
Technical Issues, 430
Responsibilities of the Manager of Word Processing, 431
New Roles, 433
New Operations, 435
Preparing for the Future, 438
Periodicals and Publications, 439
Clubs, Groups, and Associations, 440
Seminars, Conferences, and Trade Shows, 441
Talking to Others, 442

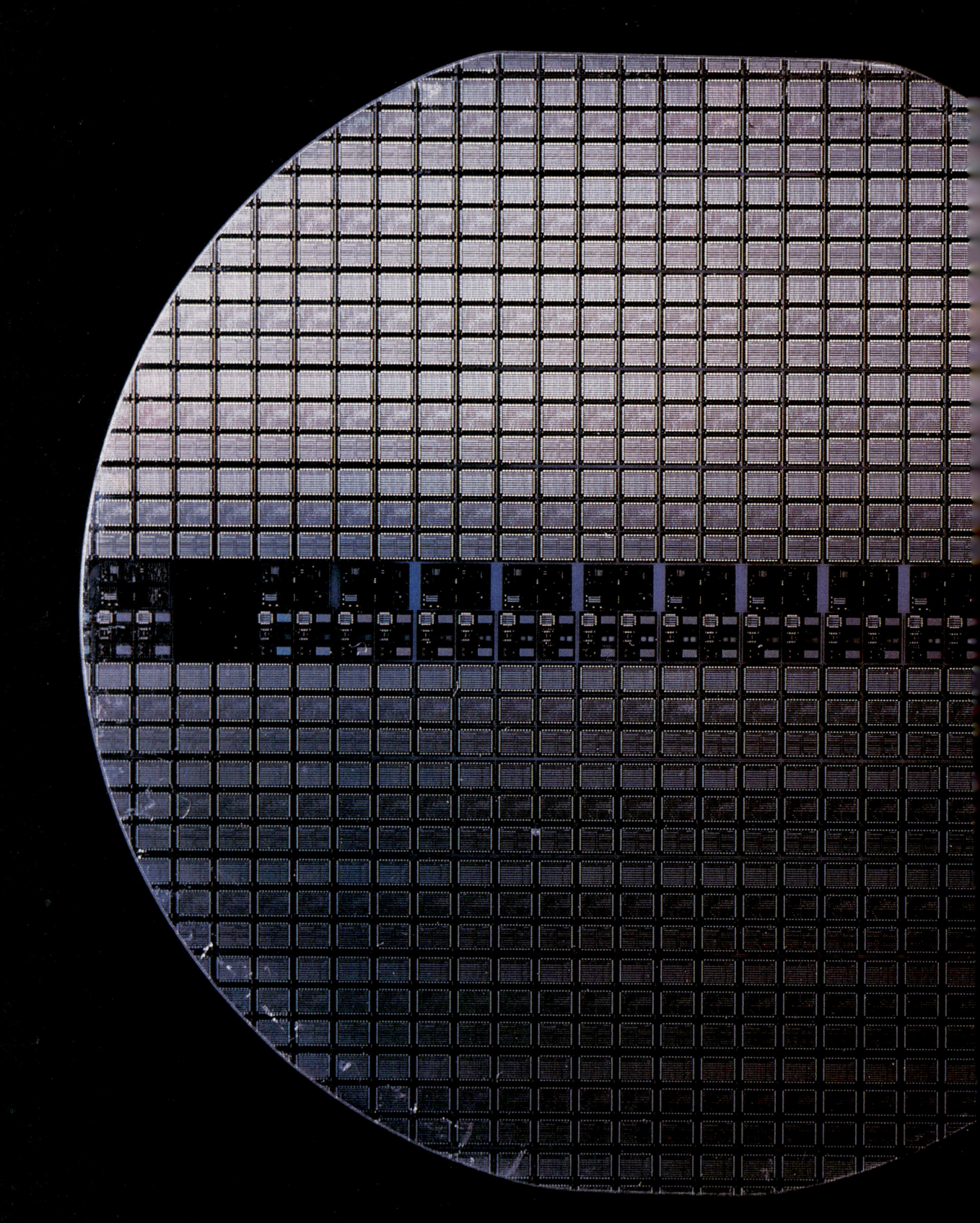

Part 1
INTRODUCTION TO WORD PROCESSING

Chapter 1 Word Processing as a Part of Information Processing

CHAPTER OBJECTIVES:

Identify the four basic forms of information.

Explain the main function(s) of each subsystem of an information processing system.

Describe some problems that occur when subsystems cannot communicate with each other or when the components within a subsystem are not compatible.

Identify the basic goals or principles of information processing for an economical and efficient system.

Name some basic ways by which machines are linked to other machines for a total information processing system.

Welcome to the exciting world of information processing! What is information processing? How does word processing relate to this new concept of office automation? As an introduction, you will be "shown a film" (in narrative form). By analyzing the "film," you will become acquainted with basic concepts of information processing.

INFORMATION PROCESSING ON FILM

Imagine yourself viewing a film entitled "Information Processing by Automation." You are visiting Acute Visions, Incorporated, to learn more about its office structure and means of communication in preparation to apply for a word processing position. Prior to escorting you on a

CHAPTER 1 Word Processing as a Part of Information Processing

tour of the company, the host invites you to see this film as a preview of their total information processing system.

Acute Visions manufactures and wholesales eyeglasses, contact lenses, and other optical products. Each product begins with a technician's idea in terms of an illustration on paper as well as specifications that are keyboarded on a computer terminal.

A conference is arranged with the managers located in the five regional divisions so that the proposed product can be discussed. The executive in charge merely depresses the appropriate keys of the terminal to check the appointment calendars of the regional managers. The executive wants to schedule the conference at a time when all six individuals are available.

To announce the meeting and include an agenda, the executive uses a terminal to send the information to the electronic mailbox (computer file) of each of the recipients. When each of the five regional managers accesses the computer for messages (by keying in the respective code), the meeting announcement and agenda appear on the screen. Should a paper copy be desired, one can be printed at the recipient's printer.

This conference is not one that involves traveling across the country to one location for a person-to-person meeting. Instead, participants remain at their workstations and exchange ideas by telephone and other equipment. To share the drawing of the proposed new product, the sender inserts the drawing into a facsimile device. Within a minute the other managers receive the copy at their facsimile devices (located within arm's reach). As one of the participants suggests altering the illustration, the sketch is entered and sent by facsimile to the other five participants.

Once the product is manufactured, it is assigned a product identification number. The label of the product's container includes the product identification number. This information is keyed into the computer system along with the price of the product.

The sales representatives and potential customers throughout the country are made aware of the new product by an attractive brochure. To produce the brochure the executive in charge brings to a terminal screen the information that was recorded onto computer storage by the participants of the conference. The executive creates the text on a word processing terminal by selecting specific data from the computer and by keying in the new descriptive text. The text can be rearranged and edited easily on the word processor, which records onto a floppy diskette.

As soon as the document is ready to be sent to the phototypesetter, the word processing specialist dials the telephone and tells the phototypesetting operator to prepare that equipment to accept the recording. The entire document is then received by the recording device of the phototypesetter. The phototypesetting operator needs only to add the

appropriate commands that arrange the text in the type style and size desired for the most attractive and readable form. None of the text from the word processor has to be rekeyed. Space is allocated for pictures to be added. What would have taken four typed pages has been reduced to one sheet with print on both sides. The phototypeset copy is then duplicated.

To retain a record of the brochure along with all of the other product brochures that have been created by the company, the document is converted to microfilm. This two-sided, one-page brochure becomes two tiny frames along with more than 90 other frames on just one microfiche card. Later company officials can access the brochure quickly by keying in the respective address of the microfiche. Upon viewing it on the screen, one could have a copy printed if needed.

As orders are processed for shipment, each item's label is passed across an optical character recognition (OCR) scanner. The scanner reads the product identification (ID) number to get the information required to check the computer file for its price and to update inventory. The price is automatically entered by the computer system on the sales invoice form; the operator needs to press only a few keys to complete the sales invoice. At the same time, the inventory of that product is automatically reduced by the number of items sold. If inventory gets too low, a signal suggests reordering. The computer system keeps an up-to-date record of sales by product ID number, sales representative, customer, and region. In addition, it keeps a running balance of each customer's account (accounts receivable).

At the end of the year a physical inventory is taken to check the accuracy of the computer inventory in case of possible theft. This is done by the worker's speaking into the computer system two numbers for each product—the product number and the number of items on the shelf. In conclusion, a printout is prepared by the computer system.

Sales for each region, each salesperson, and each product are summarized every three months as well as at the end of the year. Instead of reading long computer printouts, each employee who needs this information can get a better picture by having the summaries illustrated in charts or graphs. The chart or graph appears in three dimensions and with various colors right on the screen of the terminal. Should the user need a paper copy, one can be made on the nearest printer.

To promote goodwill the executive officers request that letters of appreciation be sent to all customers. The name and address as well as the amount of sales for each customer are on computer disk. The form letter is prepared on the word processor by merging the information in the computer with the text recorded on the word processor. The diskette is then placed in an intelligent copier/printer (IC/P) that prints the letters as well as the author's signature a page at a time. The quality is excellent for a first-class letter to an important person.

CHAPTER 1 Word Processing as a Part of Information Processing

EVALUATION OF THE FILM

Now view a rerun of the "film" and study the entire system more carefully. First, note that information in each of its four basic forms—data, text, voice, and image—is shown.

Second, the film shows various advanced technologies that process information—word processing (WP), data processing (DP), optical character recognition (OCR), intelligent copier/printer (IC/P), photo-typesetting, micrographics, teleconferencing, electronic mail, telecommunications, and voice recognition. Identify the functions of each. These various technologies interface to form a total information processing system as shown in Figure 1-1.

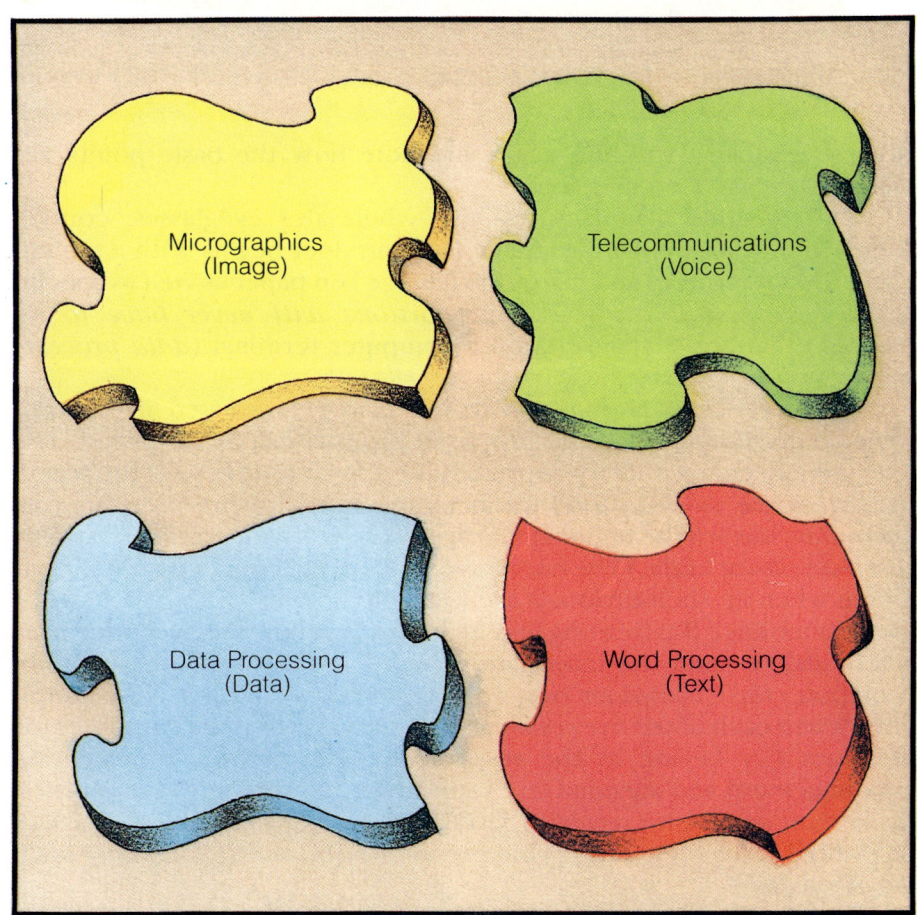

FIG. 1-1
INTEGRATION OF TECHNOLOGIES
Various information processing technologies integrate to form a total information processing system.

Third, some basic principles of processing information are represented:

1 Information once captured by one machine can be further processed by another machine without rekeying the correct portions.

2 The amount of information that is produced on paper is kept to a minimum.

3 Information that eventually must be produced on paper is not transferred to paper until it needs to be, which is at the recipient's end.

4 Information is transferred much faster than one typically could place a phone call and find the recipient at a work station or send a document by the postal system. Information can be exchanged at a conference without the expenses of travel and time away from the office.

5 Workers at all levels are affected by and involved in the processing of information.

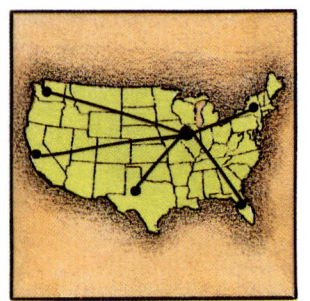

Now let's look at the film again and note how the basic points are marked for easy identification.

Acute Visions manufactures and wholesales eyeglasses, contact lenses, and other optical products. Each product begins with a technician's idea in terms of an illustration (*image*) on paper as well as specifications (*data and text*) (*correct portions will never have to be rekeyed*) that are keyboarded on a computer terminal (*data processing*).

A conference is arranged with the managers located in the five regional divisions so that the proposed product can be discussed. The executive in charge merely depresses the appropriate keys of the terminal (*executive workstation*) to check the appointment calendars (*on computer files*) of the regional managers. (*This is faster and less expensive than phone calls.*) The executive wants to schedule a conference at a time when all six individuals are available.

To announce the meeting and include an agenda, the executive uses a terminal to send the information (*text*) to the electronic mailbox (computer file) (*computer-based message system*) of each of the recipients. When each of the five regional managers accesses the computer for messages (by keying in the respective code) (*data*), the meeting announcement and agenda (*text*) appear on the screen. (*This is much faster than any postal service.*) Should a paper copy be desired, one can be printed at the recipient's printer (*commit information to paper only when needed*).

This conference is not one that involves traveling across the country to one location for a person-to-person meeting. Instead, participants remain at their workstations (*teleconference*) and exchange ideas by telephone (*voice information*) and other equipment. To share the drawing (*image*) of the proposed new product, the sender inserts the drawing into a facsimile device (*electronic mail*). Within a minute the other managers receive the copy at their facsimile devices (located within arm's reach) (*paper copy made at receiver's end*). As one of the participants suggests altering the illustration, the sketch is entered and sent by facsimile to the other five participants. (*This conference involved neither travel expense nor time away from the office for any participant.*)

Once the product is manufactured, it is assigned a product identification number (*data*). The label of the product's container includes the product identification number. This information (*data*) is keyed into the computer system (*data processing*) along with the price (*data*) of the product. (*The computer system stores the master file of product name, ID number, and price. The only time the price will have to be rekeyed will be when the price changes.*)

The sales representatives and potential customers throughout the country are made aware of the new product by an attractive brochure (*text, data, and image information*). To produce the brochure the executive in charge brings to a terminal screen the information (*data and text*) that was recorded onto computer storage by the participants of the conference. The executive creates the text on a word processing terminal (*word processing*) by selecting specific data from the computer and by keying in the new descriptive text (*merging DP and WP*). The text can be rearranged and edited easily on the word processor, which records onto a floppy diskette.

As soon as the document is ready to be sent to the phototypesetter (*phototypesetting*), the word processing specialist dials the telephone and tells the phototypesetting operator to prepare that equipment to accept the recording. The entire document is then received by the recording device of the phototypesetter (*merging WP and phototypesetting*) (*no rekeying of correct text*). The phototypesetting operator needs only to add the appropriate commands that arrange the text in the type style and size desired for the most attractive and readable form. None of the text from the word processor has to be rekeyed (*keystroking is kept to a minimum*). Space is allocated for pictures (*images*) to be added. What would have taken four typed pages has been reduced to one sheet with print on both sides (*paper use is kept to a minimum*). The phototypeset copy is then duplicated.

To retain a record of the brochure along with all of the other product brochures that have been created by the company, the document is converted to microfilm (*micrographics*). This two-sided, one-page brochure becomes two tiny frames (*text, data, and image*) along with more than 90 other frames on just one microfiche card (*reduce amount of paper files*). Later company officials can access the brochure quickly by keying in the respective address of the microfiche (*computer-assisted retrieval—CAR*). Upon viewing it on the screen, one could have a copy printed if needed.

As orders are processed for shipment, each item's label is passed across an optical character recognition (OCR) scanner (*OCR and DP application*). The scanner reads the product identification (ID) number (*data*) to get the information required to check the computer file (*data base*) for its price (*data*) and to update inventory (*data*). The price is automatically entered by the computer system (*reduces keystrokes*) on the sales invoice form; the operator needs to press only a few keys to complete the invoice. At the same time, the inventory of that product is automatically reduced by the number of items sold. If inventory gets too low, a signal suggests reordering. The computer system (*data processing*) keeps an up-to-date record of sales by product ID number, sales representative, customer, and region. In addition, it keeps a running balance of each customer's account (accounts receivable).

At the end of the year a physical inventory is taken to check the accuracy of the computer inventory in case of possible theft. This is done by the worker's speaking into the computer system two numbers for each product—the product number and the number of the items on the shelf (*voice recognition—data processing application*). In conclusion, a printout is prepared by the computer system.

Sales (*data*) for each region, each salesperson, and each product are summarized (*data processing*) every three months as well as at the end of the year. Instead of reading long computer printouts, each employee who needs this information (*data*) can get a better picture by having the summaries illustrated in charts or graphs (*images/graphics*). The chart or graph appears in three dimensions and with various colors right on the screen of the terminal (*graphic terminal*). Should the user need a paper copy (*commit information to paper only if needed*), one can be made on the nearest printer. (*Paper is printed at recipient's end—reduces paper handling for distribution.*)

To promote goodwill the executive officers request that letters of appreciation be sent to all customers. The name and address (*data and text*) as well as the amount of sales (*data*) for each customer are on computer disk (*data does not have to be rekeyed*). The form letter (*text*) is prepared on the word processor by merging the information in the computer with the text recorded on the word processor (*DP and WP merge*). The diskette is then placed in an intelligent copier/printer (IC/P) that prints the letters (*text*) as well as the author's signature (*image*) a page at a time. The quality is excellent for a first-class letter to an important person.

THE IMPACT OF INFORMATION

Why is information processing a major concern to businesses and professions? At least half of the employees in the work force are white-collar workers. Every white-collar worker handles information, much of

CHAPTER 1 Word Processing as a Part of Information Processing

which is not yet processed as quickly and smoothly as presented in the film. Instead, many companies rekey the same information over and over; most output is typed or printed on paper before it is sent. As population increases, businesses develop, and government expands, offices seek relief from the continual eruption of information overflow. In fact, this inefficient, costly condition is often dubbed a paperwork explosion or information explosion.

Forms of Information

Any information being processed is in the form of data, text, image, or voice. Here are some familiar examples: Your grades are recorded as numbers and calculated to determine your final average; this is *data* that can be processed by a computer. A research paper involves *text* that can be processed by using a word processor. An X-ray of your teeth could be sent from your dentist's office to a specialist in another city by facsimile; the X-ray is an *image*. When you talk with a friend by telephone, you are exchanging *voice* information.

Changes in Information Processing

When administrative and office operation costs grew to 50 percent of business costs, managers became alarmed. Soon technology came to the rescue with electronic tools that could help. Computers, word processors, and photocopiers are examples of electronic tools. These electronic tools were built with **microprocessors** (wafers of silicon on which integrated circuits are built; these 'chips' contain the basic logical circuits of a computer) that increased their capabilities. At the same time both the size and cost of these machines became smaller and they became more attractive to the buyer. The use of electronic tools to increase office productivity and reduce costs has been called **office automation**.

microprocessor chips containing circuits with logic for a computer

office automation use of electronics to increase productivity

Throughout the 1970s the emphasis seemed to be on helping the clerical workers become more efficient. Both data processing and word processing systems became more highly developed. However, each system worked independently to perform a single function and had its own supervision. When information needed to be sent from one place to another, it was printed on a piece of paper and physically moved. If information had to be transformed (for example, a list of accounts overdue into a summary report), the report was recreated. If a report on a word processing disk of the home office was needed by a branch office equipped with only TWX equipment (teletypewriter—not a word processor), it had to be rekeyed on TWX equipment of the sender and sent via that system. Delays are caused when executives have to wait for information to be processed by the postal service or to be recreated or rekeyed. The result of the delay is known as **information float,** another communication problem.

information float delay in receipt of information

PART ONE Introduction to Word Processing

Information can be processed in four forms: text, voice, data, and image.

CHAPTER 1 Word Processing as a Part of Information Processing

A closer look at costs reveals that labor and fringe benefits amount to about 75 percent of total office costs. Of total labor costs, less than 30 percent goes to clerical workers. The largest portion, about 70 percent, goes to managers and professionals. If technology could help to improve the productivity of clerical workers, could it not also improve the productivity of those who comprise two thirds of labor costs? Since 1980 a concerted effort has been made to improve the efficiency of all employee levels, but especially that of managers and professionals.

Most studies of managers' work reveal that over 50 percent of their time is spent communicating or preparing to communicate by attending meetings, making phone calls, writing, and traveling. Communication often involves the transfer of information from one form to another. For communication to be effective, the processing of all types of information (data, text, image, and voice) must be efficient. Executives need information to make decisions. Those who can obtain it in a rapid and usable format have the competitive edge.

A total information processing system is one in which all types of business information are easily accessible to any level of worker (within the required security restrictions). A user should be able to access any file instantly from any point on that system regardless of where the user might be at a given time.

SUBSYSTEMS OF INFORMATION PROCESSING

A total information processing system is like a family of technologies. Each one has its own types of machines, its own manufacturers, and its own language—a system of its own. The roll call of systems includes word processing, data processing, optical character recognition (OCR), reprographics (intelligent copiers/printers and offset duplicators), phototypesetting, micrographics, teleconferencing, electronic mail, telecommunications, and voice processing.

With each system having its own language and its own manufacturers, there is a lack of efficient communication. A word processing machine of one brand cannot talk directly with a word processor of another brand. Even two models of the same brand may not be able to talk to each other. For example, a disk containing a report that was recorded by a word processor may not be able to be accessed and printed by either the data processing equipment or by the phototypesetter of that same vendor. The equipment is said to be incompatible. When information that exists in one format cannot be reused without being re-entered into another separate system, the time and cost of processing the information is high. New technology is being developed to overcome these problems.

For information to be processed most efficiently, the various systems must be able to work together as a team. They must be able to "talk to" (be compatible with) each other and perform as a total information processing system. This means that each technology then becomes a subsystem of an integrated system. To remove the problem of incompatibility and to build a team effort, the various technologies are being connected by networks. Also, some manufacturers are moving toward standardizing parts. The following overview of each subsystem explains the basic function(s) of that technology in processing information.

Word Processing

word processing efficient processing of text

As the rest of the textbook explains and illustrates, a word processing system specializes in the efficient processing of text. Common types of documents include letters, memorandums, reports, manuscripts, brochures, legal documents, medical records, and financial statements. In most cases the text is eventually printed on paper. A word processing system requires the careful coordination of people, machines, procedures, and environment.

Data Processing

data processing manipulation of numbers by a computer

The computer, an electronic tool, was invented to process numbers (data). The basic functions of data processing include calculating, sorting, and merging data. Popular applications in business include accounting, keeping a record of inventory, and processing the payroll. The huge

A word processing system requires careful coordination of people, machines, procedures, and environment.

CHAPTER 1 Word Processing as a Part of Information Processing 13

Users of a computer system must be able to access the right information at the proper time from their individual terminals.

storage capacity within the computer system enables important information about customers, sales, employees, and so forth, to be stored. Users can access this large file, called a **data base**, by keying in the sequence of instructions at their terminals. Access to the right information at the right time is important for operating businesses successfully.

Managers and professionals are being confronted with vast amounts of data from computer systems. The miles of printout are impossible for

data base computer information storage file

most people to wade through and comprehend. Before this information can be used to improve decision making, it must be in a readily accessible form that is easily understood. Charts and graphs summarize large amounts of data in patterns. Patterns, rather than individual numbers, enable the viewer to see more quickly the significance of data and note relevant changes.

Many computer systems have software which converts data to graphic displays (charts or graphs on a screen) at a visual display terminal or on paper. The charts or graphs shown on the graphic terminal can be in two or three dimensions as well as in various colors. Also, the graphic display can be duplicated, routed to another machine, and/or filed. The use of graphics both clarifies information and adds eye appeal to written reports and oral presentations.

A computer system can be greatly enhanced by the addition of software packages that convert text and data to graphic displays.

Optical Character Recognition

Optical character recognition (OCR) involves reading (scanning) typed or printed data and/or text and converting it to the recording medium of another machine so that it can be further processed. The imaginary film presented earlier in the chapter gave an example of a data processing application of OCR—scanning a product label for the product identification number that was needed by the computer system for pricing and inventory control. For word processing systems, the OCR device reads text that has been keyboarded on a typewriter and transfers it to the magnetic recording medium of the word processor as shown in Figure 1-2. Once recorded on a diskette, the document can be read, edited, and printed. Thus, information that was once typed on a typewriter does not have to be rekeyed on the word processor.

optical character recognition reading typed data and converting it to a recording medium

FIG. 1-2
OPTICAL CHARACTER RECOGNITION
The OCR device reads typed text and transfers it to magnetic recording media.

Here is a quick review of the process: A document that was typed by a secretary using a typewriter is copied so that the author can mark the revisions on the photocopy. The original, unedited text is scanned by the OCR page reader and converted to the magnetic medium of the word processor, usually a diskette. As many as 250 to 300 pages can be read in an hour. The word processing operator inserts that diskette into the disk drive and brings a page to the screen. The operator revises the document as the author indicated on the edited photocopy. The text is then ready to be printed.

OCR manufacturers are developing machines that will be able to read anything (typewritten or printed text, computer printout data, charts, or drawings) on paper. The information converted to recording media would then be input to text editors, computers, phototypesetters, and communication devices such as facsimile equipment. Other new trends will be in the design of scanners to read only areas highlighted with a special marker—allowing only certain portions of text to be selected. Also, the ability to read a variety of paper sizes, colors, and thicknesses is being developed.

Intelligent Copiers/Printers

As the name implies, an intelligent copier/printer (IC/P) has some logic and can perform printing functions. As microprocessors have been introduced to photocopiers, the result has been faster copying speed, finer quality, fewer mechanical parts, and more functions.

Unlike plain paper copiers that require paper as the input, IC/Ps can print from **digital data** (such as a recorded diskette) as well as from paper. At the time the text is processed, it is stored in the IC/P's large buffer memory. When a page is ready for printing, the processor takes the data from memory and translates the digital information into patterns required for print. The output print on hard copy can be in a variety of type styles and in high-quality print. Digitized input can be stored directly on various types of output media, including magnetic tape, disks, and microfiche as shown in Figure 1-3.

Graphic material such as signatures, company logos, and charts can be reproduced. Should a large document (for example a computer printout sheet) need to be squeezed onto an 8 1/2-inch by 11-inch sheet, the image can be reduced photographically. Print can be on one or both sides of the paper. Forms and the text to be inserted can be customized to print at the same time. Once the documents have been printed, they can be automatically collated, stapled, addressed, and distributed. IC/Ps can be programmed to send or to receive documents via telecommunications (over a distance by electronic means).

Phototypesetting

The professional type that you see in books, brochures, forms, directories, advertisements, and newspapers is typically the result of phototypesetting. Many sizes and styles of type help create attractive, easy-to-read information. Spacing between words and lines can be adjusted to compress or expand characters for special effects. **Proportional spacing** (for example, *W* takes more space than *i*) allows each line to have more words than would be possible with regular typewriting (each character takes the same amount of space). The right margins are justified, as shown in this text.

---

intelligent copier/printer has logic; performs printing and copying functions

digital data data in discrete on/off pulses

phototypesetting creating type by exposing characters to light-sensitive material

proportional spacing varied character widths and spaces between words

CHAPTER 1 Word Processing as a Part of Information Processing

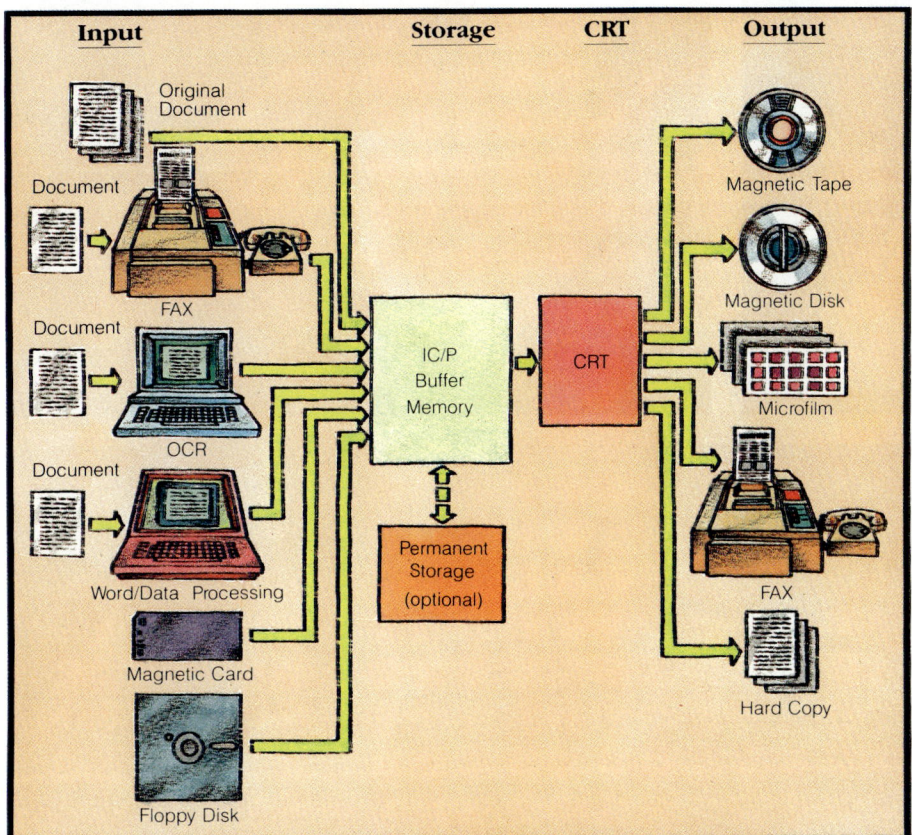

FIG. 1-3
INTELLIGENT COPIER/PRINTER
IC/Ps can receive information from many types of input and store it on various types of media.

A document that is phototypeset can be condensed to use only half of the space that it would use if it were typewritten. In turn, the costs of printing, collating, binding, and mailing are reduced. These costs are especially important when documents must be sent to many people. Also, the amount of filing space is kept to a minimum.

The machine looks much like a visual display text editor. In addition to the characters used on a typewriter, there are composition command keys that code in specifications (type style, type size, line length, etc.). Years ago text that was to be typeset had to be rekeyed, but now input can be accepted directly from computers and word processors so that only the commands have to be keyed. Phototypesetting is a photographic process. Once the original document has been phototypeset, it is generally reproduced by offset printing. Should all the steps be performed within the company (rather than by a commercial printer) the process is called **in-house printing**.

in-house printing within a company

Above Left: Text to be typeset is keyboarded and displayed on a screen.

Above Right: Typeset text is produced to the originator's specifications.

Right: The first proof of the typeset text is compared to the specifications for type style and size.

micrographics the science of reducing documents onto film photographically

microfilming the act of photographically reducing documents

Micrographics

As the volume of information mounts, so grow the problems of storing records. Rather than use only paper form, many companies are turning to a more compact form—microfilm. Micrographics, a function of records processing, is the science of photographically reducing documents to a fraction of their original size onto film. The process is called microfilming. Microfilm can be packaged in several ways. Common forms are cartridges, aperture cards, and microfiche (as presented in Chapter 6).

CHAPTER 1 Word Processing as a Part of Information Processing 19

Computer Output to Microfilm. Instead of filming paper documents, some companies have turned to a technology that bypasses that step. Computer output to microfilm (COM) is the process of converting documents recorded on computer media directly to microfilm. The documents may contain data, text, and/or graphic information.

computer output to microfilm converting documents on magnetic media directly to film

Computer-Assisted Retrieval. The partner of COM is CAR. A method of indexing microfilm images by a computer for rapid retrieval is known as computer-assisted retrieval (CAR). Another way to describe CAR is computer aid in indexing and retrieving microfilm.

computer-assisted retrieval rapid retrieval of indexed microfilm by computer

As each page is filmed, it is assigned an address (sequential location number) that corresponds to the location of its filmed image in the film magazine. The address, film roll and frame number, and other reference information relating to the document are entered in computer memory. Each document might be indexed with a number of key words or numbers—type of document, name of author, name of client, etc. These stored documents become part of a data base.

Left: COM allows documents recorded on computer media to be converted directly to microfilm.
Right: CAR allows microfilm images to be indexed for rapid retrieval.

To retrieve a document and bring it to the display terminal, the operator merely types the appropriate address and key words or numbers that are part of the reference information. Within a few seconds the microfilm image is displayed on the terminal's screen. Should a paper copy of the document be needed, the operator just presses the print button on the retrieval device.

Combining micrographics and computer systems (COM and CAR) to capture, index, store, and retrieve information is sometimes called **electronic filing**. The huge data base, an alternative to paper records, is called an **electronic file cabinet**. The link between word processing and COM is being developed.

electronic filing capturing, indexing, storing, and retrieving information by computer

electronic file cabinet a data base

Teleconferencing

Most businesses must have regular meetings to conduct business, exchange information, inform, and solve problems. For companies that have officers, sales representatives, and other personnel dispersed throughout the country, it becomes costly to have face-to-face meetings. Because of the high cost of air travel, lodging, food, and executive time away from the office, other choices are sought. With the use of the telephone and other electronic means, people can attend a conference without traveling to it.

Teleconferencing involves the meeting of at least three persons at two or more locations. The participants are connected by telephones and other electronic devices. A teleconference can be in several forms.

The least expensive form uses only computer terminals, all of which are connected to the computer mainframe. This form is sometimes called **computer conferencing**. Each person participates by keying in questions, comments, and other information on a visual display terminal. Should there need to be a record of the conference, a verbatim transcript can be printed by the computer system.

Most common for businesses is **audio (voice) teleconferencing**. In this form, each member of the conference is connected by and participates by telephone. The telephone device might be a speaker-phone, which leaves hands free to take notes or access a file. The members do not see each other and do not exchange data, text, or graphics by electronic means. Should visual aids be used, they must be distributed in advance by mail.

Another type of conference, an **audiographic conference**, combines the use of the telephone with an electronic means for exchanging data, text, or graphics. As in the aforementioned film, each participant

teleconferencing three people at two or more locations connected electronically

computer conferencing teleconference connected by computers

audio teleconferencing teleconference connected by telephones

audiographic conference teleconference connected by phones and computers

In this teleconference, participants in one location can see and hear participants in another location.

would speak through the telephone and might have a facsimile unit within arm's reach to exchange drawings for the design of a new product. Should each member have a graphic terminal, information in the computer's data base (such as gross sales by region) could be summarized in a chart or graph for each participant to see.

The most costly form of teleconferencing is a **full-motion video conference**. As though two televisions were talking to each other, a full-motion video conference gives the members at distant points the ability to see and hear each other. You have no doubt seen this type of conference on your television set when a news reporter interviews a person in another place.

full-motion video conference teleconference members see and hear each other

Electronic Mail

Electronic mail involves sending information over a distance by electronic means. The information is sent without the physical movement of paper or recording media (such as through the postal service) or of people (as in a face-to-face meeting).

electronic mail sending information over a distance electronically

Electronic mail involves machine-to-machine communication. The three basic parts involve a sending unit, a connecting device, and a receiving unit—all made of electronic parts and circuitry. The connecting device traditionally has been telephone lines. New methods of transmission include satellites, microwaves, and fiber optics (glass fibers).

The output can be in the form of a display on a screen (soft copy), paper (hard copy), or microfilm (from COM recorders). Electronic mail systems promise same-day or, in some cases, immediate delivery of the message. Common devices used to send information by electronic mail include teletypewriters, facsimile, communicating word processors, and computer-based message systems.

Teletypewriter. A teletypewriter can "talk to" another teletypewriter by typed words. The sender types the message, which is typically recorded on punched paper tape, and dials the special code number of the recipient. The message travels to the receiving teletypewriter, where it can be printed automatically without help from an operator. Telex and TWX are the common teletypewriter exchange systems.

teletypewriters typewriters that can communicate by typed words

Facsimile. Abbreviated FAX, facsimile involves sending a copy of a page. The units that can either send or receive, called transceivers, talk to each other by exchanging photocopies. The image can be in the form of a photograph, drawing, chart, graph, and in longhand as well as typed words and numbers.

facsimile transmits images electronically

Computer-Based Message System. With a computer-based message system (CBMS) the sender and receiver do not have to talk at the same time as in telephone conversation. Instead, the computer system is the message sender, carrier, receiver, and filer. Using a terminal, the sender

computer-based message system form of electronic mail

keys in the message and directs the computer system to file it in the file space within the computer storage (the electronic mailbox) of the recipient. The recipient periodically checks his or her mailbox by keying in the appropriate instructions and codes on a terminal. The message is brought to the screen for reading. Should a hard copy be needed, a printed copy can be made.

Communicating Word Processors. Word processing machines can also talk to each other by exchanging typed words; they are then called communicating word processors. Words that have been recorded on a diskette are in the form of electronic impulses. These impulses travel over the telephone lines and are recorded onto the diskette of the receiving word processor, where the text may be stored, brought to the screen for viewing, or printed on paper. Text can be transmitted without an operator being at hand. Thus, companies can take advantage of the lowest telephone rates by sending documents in batches at night. Word processors can also communicate with other machines, such as computer systems and phototypesetting machines.

Telecommunications

The term *telecommunications* is often used in the discussion of electronic mail systems in such a way that one could assume the two terms mean the same. Actually, telecommunications means communicating electronically over a distance. A telecommunications system provides the link that enables people as well as machines in separate locations to connect so that information can be sent, received, or exchanged as shown in Figure 1-4. The information might be in the form of data, text, image, and/or voice. Thus, it may involve any of the information technologies.

Voice Message System

Another way to send a message is by a voice message system (VMS), also known as **voice mail** and **voice store-and-forward**. Here is how it works: The caller picks up the telephone receiver and dials the number of the person to receive the call. The message is spoken into the phone in the natural voice of the caller. The message is recorded and stored in the recipient's audio mailbox. The recipient obtains the message at that person's convenience by accessing the computer and giving personal identification.

A further advancement in voice technology is **voice recognition**, which involves the conversion of the spoken word to a printed page. So far voice recognition systems have been limited to speaking distinct numbers, such as in the previously mentioned film—the worker spoke only two numbers for each item of inventory being taken. However, this technology is improving.

FIG. 1-4
TELECOMMUNICATIONS
Telecommunications provides the link that allows people and machines in separate locations to exchange information.

LINKING INFORMATION PROCESSING MACHINES

How can a word processor of one brand link to a word processor of a different brand or to a computer? How can word processors connect to other types of information processing machines—such as OCR scanners, phototypesetters, facsimile units—represented by many manufacturers? Could all types of information processing machines be linked so that any one could talk to any other? The first and most common method of connecting machines separated by distance has been telephone lines. However, technology continues to offer new and better ways for offices to communicate.

The problem of incompatibility is a big hurdle to jump. One way that companies are solving the problem is by a **local area network (LAN)**. A local area network is a means of linking various types of machines within a building or within several buildings that are close to each other. Designed to bring together various machines that have distinct functions in processing information, the LAN enables the machines to work together as a team. Then information that exists in one system can be reused without being re-entered into another separate system. To accomplish this feat there are various technologies and strategies used, some of which include telephone wires, radio waves, coaxial cables, and fiber optics (glass fibers).

local area network links machines that are geographically close

wide area network links machines that are geographically distant

Local networks can be expanded into larger networks that enable companies to send information from city to city, across the nation, and to other countries throughout the world. These larger telecommunication networks (called **wide area networks** or **global networks**) make use of combinations of telephone lines, microwave radio links, and satellites to send information.

HOW INFORMATION PROCESSING AFFECTS WORD PROCESSING CAREERS

For executives of a company to be effective in managing, they must have the necessary information for strategic planning and decision making. More important, the information must be pertinent to the task at hand, accurate, quickly accessible, economical, and in a form that is easy to understand. That is a challenge. It is complicated by the fact that the various technologies involved are so diverse and advanced that hardly anyone could be an expert in all fields. Yet there must be someone in the company who controls and manages the entire package. This person is commonly given the job title of information manager or information processing manager.

Those who are engaged in word processing careers—specialists, operators, supervisors, teachers/trainers, managers, consultants, marketing support representatives—must have a basic understanding of

Wide area networks make use of satellites to relay information.

CHAPTER 1 Word Processing as a Part of Information Processing

what information processing involves and how word processing fits into the total system of integrating technologies. This textbook presents the concepts of word processing that are needed for a thorough understanding of the word processing function within an information processing system.

DISCUSSION QUESTIONS AND CASE PROBLEM

DISCUSSION QUESTIONS

1. What are the four basic forms of information that are processed by businesses and professions?
2. What are some of the problems of various subsystems operating independently that are being overcome by a fully integrated information processing system? Describe five.
3. What are four of the common goals or principles of a modern information processing system?
4. How can unlike machines or machines with different languages connect in order to communicate?

CASE PROBLEM

Chris Hensely is a student in your college. With aspirations of becoming an information processing manager, Chris comes to you for academic advice. How would you answer Chris in terms of the following?

1. With which technologies (subsystems of information processing) should one be familiar?
2. From the list of courses and respective course descriptions of the bulletin/catalog of your college, which existing courses would be recommended?
3. What new courses or units within existing courses would you add to your school's curriculum to fill any void (determined from Question 2 above)?
4. Without specific courses to teach the needed information about the various technologies, how could one acquire the information?
5. Is work experience important? If so, describe the type and amount of experience that you feel would be needed.

Chapter 2 Steps Toward Office Improvement

CHAPTER OBJECTIVES:

Describe the function of an office, its principal players, and the activities performed by each.

Explain problems that are experienced in traditional offices.

List the objectives to be accomplished by a word processing system.

Name the four basic elements of a word processing system, and explain how each differs from a traditional office.

What prompts companies to change their information processing methods? How are decisions to investigate changes determined? What are the benefits a company can derive from installing a word/information processing system? What is the basic concept of word processing—its plan and its principal ingredients? These are some questions this chapter will attempt to answer in the search for a better way to do business within the office.

PROBLEMS OF THE TRADITIONAL OFFICE

office where administrative functions are performed for an organization

An **office** is a place where administrative functions, such as consulting, recordkeeping, and clerical work, are performed for an enterprise or an organization. These functions are performed by office people—managers, professionals, and clericals. The basic role of these people is to process information. The various steps in this information processing are performed by these groups according to their abilities and their levels of responsibility. Generally managers request and make decisions on information; professionals create and manipulate information; and clericals prepare, distribute, and store information.

CHAPTER 2 Steps Toward Office Improvement

The term *clericals* as used in the preceding paragraph is a general term used for all traditional office employees who perform functions pertaining to the preparation, distribution, and storage of information. Specifically, this work is performed by secretaries, administrative support personnel, and other general support staff. Typically, in a traditional office setting the secretary is a generalist. In contrast, the clerical operation within a word processing system is comprised of two distinct specialists:

- Those responsible for keyboarding text (typing) are referred to as (1) word processing specialists, (2) document preparation specialists, or (3) correspondence specialists.

- Those responsible for administrative activities other than typing, such as filing, proofreading, scheduling, and research, are referred to as (1) administrative support specialists, or (2) administrative secretaries.

This general processing of information is called **work flow**. The flow of work can be affected by the attitude of the employees and the methods and equipment used in processing the information. When employees view their jobs as rewarding and satisfying, they are more likely to contribute their best effort. Then they are more effective and productive. When the methods and equipment best fit the process, the resulting work flow is smoother and more efficient.

As a rule, most offices start small with a smooth work flow. As businesses grow, their administrative functions also grow, and processing information becomes more complicated. It becomes difficult to control the great volumes of information, to satisfy the growing needs of employees, and to compete effectively in a rapidly changing marketplace. Offices that do not adjust to these changes are called **traditional offices**.

The descriptor "traditional" was actually coined by word processing professionals as a means of distinguishing these offices from those which adopted the word processing concept. A traditional office is described in many ways. It is sometimes called unproductive, often called inefficient, and many times referred to as ineffective. Generally a traditional office is one that has not kept pace with the latest enhancements for its people, to its procedures, and in its equipment.

A company that is not up to date will have difficulty competing with progressive companies. The problems arising from these difficulties span the areas of personnel, the cost of doing business, and marketplace competition.

work flow general processing of information

traditional office many operations done manually instead of electronically

Personnel

An out-of-date office provides employees with a limited outlook for career growth. Without gradual improvements, the office retains a small number of career choices within a narrow management structure. Employees interested in career advancements and promotions will search out firms offering challenging opportunities. As a result, the outmoded office will have difficulty attracting or maintaining an ambitious, innovative staff.

The Cost of Doing Business

A company which responds to growing business needs by adding staff, increasing overtime hours, or expanding its facilities increases the cost of doing business. However, if the company makes changes in equipment or procedures that increase individual productivity, the cost of doing business will decrease.

For example, consider a lemonade stand where the product is produced and sold by one person who squeezes the lemons by hand. When warmer weather nears, more customers become interested in buying the product. The business objective is to service the expanding need. If more staff were added to prepare the product in the same way, not only would larger facilities be needed to accommodate the increased staff, but also the profits would have to be divided among more workers. The cost of doing business would increase. However, if an emulsifier (automatic juicer) were used to produce the lemonade faster, one person could service the increased number of customers. The cost of the emulsifier eventually could be justified by the increased business profits. Costs would decrease and the business could expand comfortably and effectively. In this example, equipment and procedures were changed to respond to a growing business demand.

Marketplace Competition

Some companies respond to expanding business needs by delaying service to the customers. Their product grows in popularity, but they are not equipped to handle the increased business. As a result, customers may find other avenues to satisfy their needs. The company that refuses to change not only loses the new customers to competitors, but in doing so, also places its existing business in jeopardy.

If in the previous example the lemonade business were to make no staff or operational changes, the customers would become impatient and dissatisfied. They would find other lemonade stands which would satisfy their needs immediately. In addition, these former customers would encourage others to frequent the new business which provided them with faster and/or better service.

In effect, an office system, as the administrative heart of the company, must continually have its information processing techniques reassessed, refreshed, and renewed in order for the business to grow profitably. As part of this assessment, the specific needs of employees must be satisfied to obtain their commitment and dedication to their jobs. All

The office environment should be designed to promote a smooth and efficient work flow.

office staff should be provided with the proper tools to perform their jobs in the most cost-effective and efficient manner. Employees should be provided with a comfortable working atmosphere that will instill in them a sense of company pride and the motivation to improve.

OBJECTIVES TO BE ACCOMPLISHED

To achieve a successful office system, the entire office staff should operate as a team. Management, professionals, and secretarial/administrative staff should be committed to the same goals. Each member of the team should be aware of the important part each other member plays in the performance of his or her job. An office team is like a football team in that individual members may have to carry the ball at times, but their effort is backed up by the entire team. Just as a single team member cannot win a football game without total team cooperation, a single office group cannot assume sole credit for a company's success. Often, the larger the company, the more difficult it is to develop and maintain this total team awareness and appreciation. Upper management can be the focal point for directing this team-building and providing the role model for successful employee attitudes. Office system strategies begin with this group.

Ideally the upper management group (sometimes referred to as the corporate management team) is kept abreast of work flow problems and suggestions for improvements through regular subordinate-management communications. This form of communication should be encouraged within all office ranks through periodically scheduled meetings with each rank's immediate management. When work flow problems and suggestions are filtered upward, the corporate management team can make more appropriate decisions. Several benefits can be derived from a team approach to decision making:

1 Upper management is able to make decisions based on more relevant and comprehensive information.

2 Changes resulting from these decisions will be more readily accepted by all employees.

3 The solutions are apt to satisfy existing problems without creating new problems in other office areas.

The corporate management team should obtain input from all levels of employees.

CHAPTER 2   Steps Toward Office Improvement

4 Implementation of the change will be more successful since employees that share in the decision process also have a share in its success.

5 Success breeds success; thus, new ideas and team progress will be fostered.

The upper management group begins its strategy planning based upon this team information. After recognizing the existence of a work flow problem, this group will determine the need for further action. They will establish a priority in meeting that need. This priority will be described in general terms as a company **mission statement**. The need for improvement of office information processing may be presented to the office staff as follows:

> "Research and determine a method by which our office and administrative areas can realize increased productivity, improved personnel efficiencies, and cost-effectiveness."

Subordinate (middle) management should now develop specific objectives to respond to this mission statement. These middle managers, working with their immediate staffs, will detail ways in which they can contribute to the overall company goal. Earlier staff meetings have identified specific work flow problems and suggestions for improvement. Armed with this information, the department teams should outline plans that satisfy their individual problems and trace the effects of these plans on other groups.

The individual department plans are then presented to the affected groups to identify potential problems which could result from the planned implementation. A secondary purpose of the presentation would be to share ideas and uncover new needs that may result in refining or modifying the plan. The overall goal in a team approach to setting objectives is to provide the best solutions for the company's goals. Sharing information with other departments before setting individual department objectives saves costly time and effort. Moreover, advance exchange of information stimulates interdepartmental cooperation for attaining the company's goals.

Exchanged information often includes knowledge gained through employees' associations with other companies, professional organizations, and specialized publications. In this manner, the middle management team is able to learn how others are handling their information processing problems. This may, in turn, provide the team with possible solutions.

The presentations and meetings enable middle management teams to understand that there are common objectives that need to be accomplished in order to meet the mission statement. Satisfying these objectives may increase productivity and improve efficiencies. The team can then decide whether the company should investigate office automation

mission statement
strategy planning team's main goal for solving a recognized problem

tools to determine which tools can solve their information processing problems in a cost-effective manner. They can specifically identify the objectives they plan to accomplish with a new office system. Some common objectives, their anticipated benefits, and their specific problems follow.

Sharing information between departments before developing individual department objectives saves valuable time and effort.

Improved Document Turnaround Time

An office system should provide a means of automating or eliminating the time-consuming activities required for the processing of information. Processing includes those activities performed from the creation of information all the way through to the production of the document. The results of these modifications would speed up the flow of information from author to correspondence specialist to author. The author (manager or professional) would benefit from the improved services through a reduction in the present wait time experienced for a completed document. The typing staff would benefit from the improved services through a reduction in their manual activities, an improvement in the quality of document input, and a decrease in their backlog of work. The company would benefit from an increase in productivity and efficiency among all staff members.

The team managers must develop the above objective based on the experiences of their staff and their peers. Several of the departments may have secretaries who support as many as four to six principals each. The secretary-to-principal relationship is adequate until a business grows. Then conflicts can occur. Some common conflicts are as follows:

- Many principals do not receive typed documents in a timely fashion. It is not unusual for urgent work to be delayed while the secretary completes a rush report for another professional. Sometimes one principal's typed requests are set aside (reprioritized) while the secretary completes a task for another boss.

- Secretaries often are away from their desks gathering information, delivering messages, or making photocopies. When they are at their desks, they are interrupted by phone calls and office visitors as they try to finish the typing requests. More time is then needed for the secretaries to redirect their thoughts back to their previous tasks after each interruption.

- Many authors submit their typing requests in longhand—often written in pencil on colored paper. Another person's handwriting is often illegible, and the penciled notes may be difficult to discern.

- Everything seems to be "rush" work. The secretaries are constantly reprioritizing their daily work and adding to their backlog.

- Due to delays in document production, the company may be too slow at times in formally responding to customer requests. As a result, the company may lose potential business to competitors.

Efficient Paper Flow Without Duplicated Effort

An office system should provide an automated means of producing repetitive documents without an office worker having to rekey the duplicated information. Many of the typing requests within a single department are often quite similar. In addition, much of a company's new correspondence includes material from previously typed correspondence. Many members of the secretarial staff may need the same name and address listings for customers. In a traditional office, these repetitive applications are keyed as original documents by each secretary. All personnel can achieve increased productivity with improved efficiencies if this repetitive information is captured and then reproduced automatically.

The secretarial staff often spend too much time manually typing documents that require revisions or repetitions to already-typed text. Consequently, typing activities and correspondence requests are delayed for the principals, and secretarial backlogs are increased. Duplication of effort occurs each time a staff member rehandles mail that has been keyboarded in-house. This rehandling is caused by a lack of tracking methods (an inability to locate the original document), rush requests, or photocopying material for mail preparation.

Unaccountable delays occur when mail is distributed through public and private mail carriers—sources other than the company's own mailing facilities. In addition, mail delays often occur internally because of misdirection and/or inadvertent loss. These delays compound management's ability to make decisions or react in a timely fashion.

Accuracy in Keyboarding and Proofreading

An office system should improve the quality of keyboarding so that errors and proofreading activities can be minimized. The resulting benefit would be increased secretarial productivity due to a reduction in retyping time caused by errors. In addition, productivity would increase because the time spent on proofreading would be reduced to only that of reading the revised text.

Telephone interruptions lower production rates and increase the chances for error.

Secretarial personnel have a wide variety of administrative duties in addition to their typing tasks. They are frequently interrupted while they are typing. These interruptions lower the production rate and increase the chance of error. The principals spend considerable time proofreading documents for errors. When errors are returned for correction, the secretary must retype the entire document. This retyping increases the chances for errors to occur in text that was previously error-free. Continual retyping and proofreading are time consuming to secretaries and principals alike.

Minimal Mental and Physical Effort

An office system should provide a means of reducing the mental fatigue associated with finding and correcting errors. This can be accomplished by automating the manual detection of errors and their corrections. With these automated efficiencies, employees will be more mentally alert, physically comfortable, and eager to participate in company growth plans.

Secretaries spend many additional overtime hours attempting to reduce the backlog of work. Because the secretaries do not have any extra time, the principals must spend time performing administrative duties that should have been delegated to the secretarial staff. As a result, principals are unable to spend enough time planning and preparing for new business activities. The company, then, is unable to grow and become more profitable.

Quality Output To Enhance Company Image

An office plan should introduce methods and equipment that produce quality documents and encourage customer business and support. A poorly presented document has a negative impact on the customer. Presentation materials that include blemishes and errors convey the message that the company producing the documents has careless business practices. A quality document influences the customer in a positive way and results in increased business.

Within a given company there often is a variety of equipment and supplies used by the secretarial staff. When changes need to be made to a completed document, a number of products, such as correction fluid, are used to make quick corrections. Sometimes typewriters other than the one on which the original document was typed are used to make corrections. The resulting product has inconsistent type and blemishes.

Presentation materials must either be sent out for typesetting or be prepared in-house without adequate equipment. Some departments use the facilities of a typesetter, but rekeyboarding the material is very time consuming. The chances for errors occur frequently during this process. In addition, the typesetting schedule for requested work can be inappropriate for customer deadlines.

Economical Costs

A company's automated system should be cost-effective and should decrease present administrative expenses. The system is cost-justified by the reduction of unnecessary equipment purchases, supplies, space, outside services, and increased payroll costs. Reducing or maintaining administrative expenses allows the company to recognize more net profits and growth.

Additional copying costs are incurred because secretarial personnel find copying material less frustrating and time-consuming than continually retyping documents or making carbon copies. Frequently additional amounts of document preparation are performed for company personnel by outside services, such as secretarial temporary agencies. These services add to the initial administrative costs. At the same time, these services offer only temporary relief and do not solve the problems of text revision or the rekeying of the finished documents that may be required by the in-house secretarial staff.

Many companies use a variety of typing equipment. No single department or individual has responsibility for supervising or cost-justifying the purchase of the equipment. As a result, much of the equipment has incompatible type and functions. Some machines have limited expansion potential and many have limited capabilities. Also, cross-training staff members becomes very difficult, time consuming, and costly.

There should be standard procedures for logging, measuring, or filing documents. Secretarial and management staff often design their own methods. Unnecessary time is spent searching for or retrieving previously filed material, which causes inconvenient delays in work flow at all staff levels. The resulting accumulation of paper eventually has a negative impact on the company's space plans or storage facility needs.

In addition, inconsistent company filing systems add to the cross-training difficulties caused by the incompatibility of typing equipment. It becomes difficult to identify a single filing system within the company that permits easy backup or solves existing problems.

Compatibility With Other Information Processing Systems

An office system should meet the company's needs of today and allow for easy adjustment to tomorrow's needs. The system should be configured for present work flow needs. However, as these needs expand, the equipment should also be easily expandable. In addition, as branch offices implement information processing systems, these systems must be compatible with the home office's system.

Home office personnel should assist the branch office staff in identifying their word processing needs. Correspondence is exchanged with

Opposite: Before buying equipment, departmental personnel should ensure the compatibility of the new equipment with the present system.

these offices on a daily basis. Postage costs are high. Employees often make quick trips to the airport to get an important document on the last mail flight. Regular postal service has an unpredictable delivery schedule. All of these conditions indicate a good potential for electronic mail application.

Satisfaction to Secretaries, Professionals, and Managers

An office system should provide an implementation plan that will appeal to employees in terms of equipment operation, design, methods, and procedures. A determination should be made as to how work load can be more equally distributed among the secretaries. A method should be developed wherein the professionals and managers can find adequate administrative support and quicker access to information. Work areas should be redesigned to blend more effectively with the new work tools and methods.

In a traditional office, the secretarial staff have inequitable work loads and pay scales. Often, upper-management secretaries are paid more and yet are less busy than middle-management secretaries. In addition, there generally is a continual turnover within the secretarial ranks because there is often no opportunity for advancement to management careers.

In a traditional system, each secretary is supervised by the immediate principal, who in most cases has not been educated about secretarial procedures, office management, or word processing concepts. The personnel department often has difficulty locating replacement personnel. Many of the professionals then voice complaints about the delay or lack of support. They feel they are performing duties better delegated to the support staff.

TRENDS IN OTHER COMPANIES

Information received by middle management teams through associates, meetings, and publications often provides them with some appreciation for office automation equipment and methods. Members are able to develop achievable objectives based on the experiences of other companies that have implemented systems which accomplished similar goals.

Several team members might visit these companies. A tour of the facilities can show how personnel are using the equipment. The information processing manager at the visited site usually is delighted to explain how the equipment and new procedures accomplish that company's increased productivity objectives. The presentation might go as follows:

CHAPTER 2 Steps Toward Office Improvement

The company wanted to achieve faster document production. The word processing system has helped the company do this in the following ways:

- Function keys (i.e., center, search, replace) ease initial keyboarding by automating multiple-action steps.
- Proofreading can be done on the display screen, which enables existing text to be modified before final printout.
- Printing one document occurs while another document is being keyed.
- High-speed printers are used to print out the documents.

The use of magnetic media for capturing keystrokes helps employees achieve efficiencies by avoiding duplicated effort. For example, the specialist is able to delay printing the document until the final document is needed. Another valuable time-saver is that magnetic media are shared between project users when the document requires additions or revisions to the already-keyboarded text. By sharing the media among several specialists, different portions of the same project can be completed simultaneously. In addition, sharing the media can increase work flow flexibility. Any specialist can prepare revisions to keyboarded (recorded) text if the originating specialist is busy on another project.

By using the dictionary features available on the system, the specialist can verify spelling accuracy before printing the document. Proofreading is greatly reduced by limiting the reading effort to only that of the revised text. This enables the staff to be more accurate and to increase input speed.

A tour of a similar company's facilities may provide the corporate management team with insights as to some possible uses for the new equipment.

The information processing manager might show the visiting team members the production and measurement records developed for the department. The records may indicate that the company has greater document productivity than before. Heavy revisions of documents which previously took hours of concentrated effort now take mere minutes. The correspondence staff experience less pressure and fatigue with the new system. They are proud of the quality of the final product—it presents a good company image.

The records may also indicate that the company actually has produced more work with fewer staff members. If it takes fewer staff members to produce the documents in less time, outside temporary agencies will not be needed, nor will vacant secretarial/support positions need to be filled as quickly. Increased productivity will not only improve efficiencies and reduce administrative time and costs, but it will also cut expenses in other areas. For example, floor space presently used for paper files could be reduced by filing information on magnetic media, and paper costs could be reduced because of the revision capabilities of the machine.

The information manager might show the team members the various administrative support centers. Here the administrative specialists perform a variety of duties. The information manager explains how the administrative specialists who now work within the administrative support areas do not have to perform tedious, repetitive typing and editing tasks and are able to work on more administrative duties. Professionals now have two teams, both comprised of specialists, to handle their information needs in a faster, more equitable manner.

The administrative specialists who prefer interactive, diversified duties perform better because they work in areas that are of more interest to them; and the company benefits from their enthusiasm and increased productivity. These specialists are supervised by a professional who has education and experience in secretarial procedures, office management, and/or word processing concepts. The visiting managers see that it is possible to attain satisfaction for support personnel, professionals, and managers.

The last area the team members might visit is the communications room. Here they watch an administrative specialist communicating with a branch office. By using a facsimile machine, the specialist sends a copy of an advertisement layout to the branch manager for review and approval. The branch manager makes the suggested changes on the copy and reroutes the copy to the home office. Last-minute changes are possible, and costly errors are averted with this fast communications method.

The information manager notes that plans are under way to install a document transfer system between communicating word processing equipment. With this equipment in place, it will be possible for the company to improve communications by reducing outside distribution costs and time between customers and branch offices. At the same time, it will provide the company with the ability to respond to change more rapidly. The company, then, will enjoy a competitive edge and will expand its organizational flexibility to its maximum potential.

The visiting team managers express their appreciation for the tour and the information. They leave convinced that their objectives are attainable through a properly tailored information processing system. When they return to their company, they complete the objectives and forward them to upper management with a recommendation for a formal system study. The management team recognizes that a thorough feasibility study is required which will identify the specific needs of the company and outline the direction that best serves those needs.

The management team realizes that the best approach to a system implementation would be to satisfy the urgent needs first, and then slowly phase in other applications. The team may recommend that corporate management consider implementing word processing as the first phase of the implementation program.

COMPOSITION OF A WORD PROCESSING SYSTEM

The concept of word processing includes four elements—*people, procedures, machines,* and *environment*. These elements are combined in a certain organized manner to form an efficient, effective, and satisfying office system. Many definitions have been formed describing word processing as being "the right combination of people, equipment, and environment, using revised office procedures to produce more information of a higher quality and in a faster manner." Yet these same elements exist within traditional office systems. What makes these elements different in word processing office systems?

People

In word processing office systems, secretaries are specialists—individuals who are specially trained in the art of document production or administrative support. For example, in a word processing center, specialists produce documents on electronic equipment. This equipment is specially designed to increase document production. In an administrative support center, specialists perform other administrative functions of a nontyping nature (answering phones, filing, etc.).

Instead of performing multiple support functions for only one or two principals as do traditional secretaries, word processing specialists perform a single support function for many principals. Since the function performed is specialized, the performance skill can be maximized, and increased productivity results.

CHAPTER 2 Steps Toward Office Improvement

Individuals aspiring to the job of document production enjoy concentrated keyboarding, have excellent language arts skills, find satisfaction in high-quality output, are comfortable with computerized equipment, and prefer to work without frequent interruption. Their motivation is productivity, and these individuals usually work to achieve high performance records. They are competitors who consistently look for better and easier ways to improve their performance.

On the other hand, administrative specialists usually prefer nontyping activities. They may gather data for their principals; schedule and arrange meetings and conferences; or perform a variety of telephone, calculation, and document creation routines. Administrative specialists react to the needs of the principals and are available for delegated work. They meet with customers and interact with other principals to a greater extent than do word processing specialists. Since administrative specialists work for many users, the level of the work is likely to be interesting, challenging, and comprehensive. In turn, they are valuable to the company and their service to the principals is substantial. Thus, principals share in increased productivity through two groups of specialized individuals who can more skillfully respond to their needs. When all of the employees are more productive and efficient, the company can be more profitable.

In a traditional office, it is rare to find an organization chart indicating secretarial support positions. A word processing operation often has a recognized departmental position on the company's organization chart. Word processing has been instrumental in developing career paths for correspondence and administrative support positions as shown in Figure 2-1. This situation does not exist in traditional offices.

Machines

Word processing equipment can be as simple as an electronic typewriter that captures the typist's keystrokes and replays them automatically; or it can be as complicated as a large computer system with many terminals. In a large computer system, many operators keyboard, revise, edit, and print text.

This output equipment usually is expensive in comparison to standard electric typewriters. Costs of word processing equipment range from several thousand dollars to several hundred thousand dollars. To complement the efficient work flow desired, companies must also consider the costs of installing input equipment, such as dictation systems (central or individual), communication lines, and OCR systems.

Equipment selection and its related costs are dependent upon the nature of the production desired—its quantity and its speed. Generally a study is conducted to measure this production need.

People who are selected to operate the new equipment require specialized training in procedures and in operating the equipment. This

Opposite: Selection of a word processing system must take into consideration the present mix of environment, procedures, people, and machines.

FIG. 2-1
WORD PROCESSING ORGANIZATION CHART
Word processing specialists are included in a word processing department's organization chart.

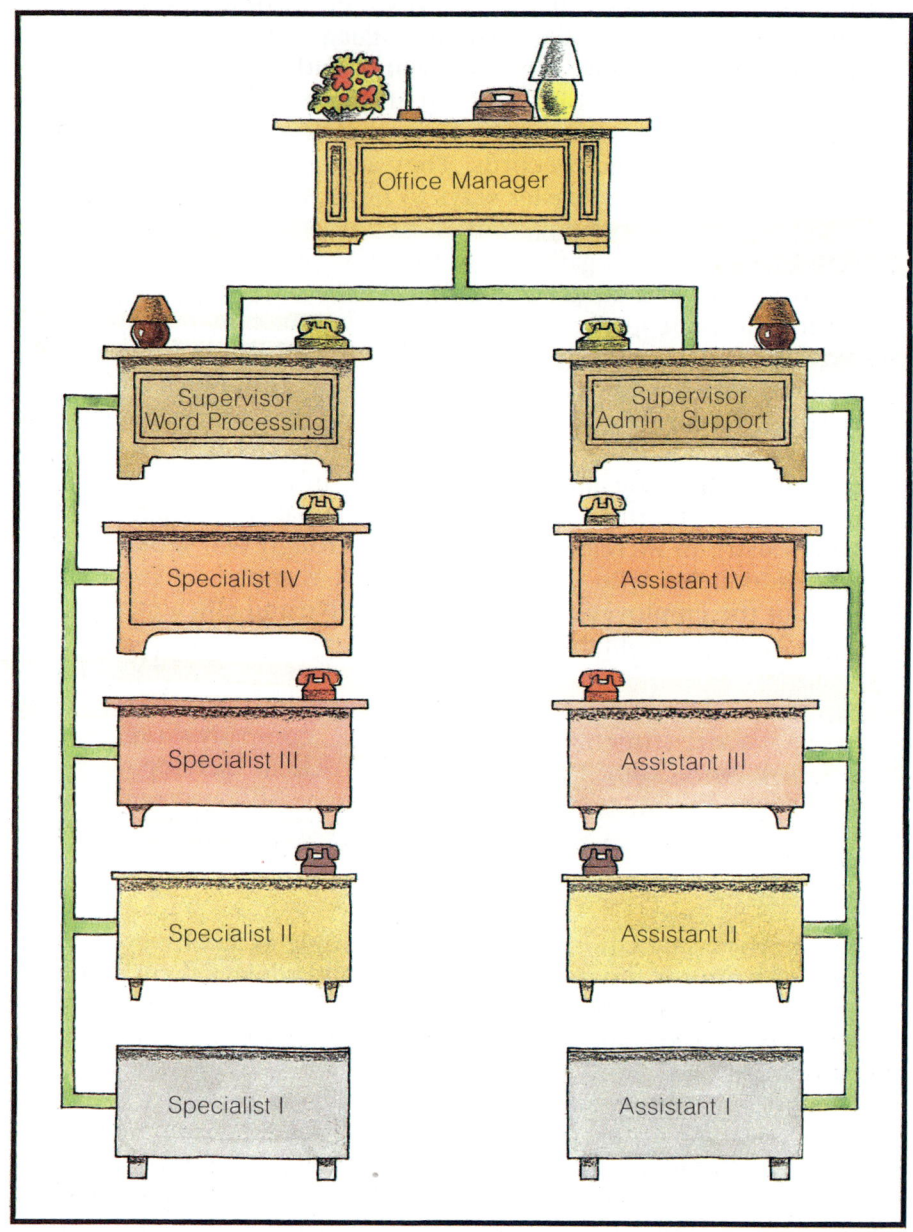

provides the company with the most efficient output. In addition to the training provided by the vendor, the company must develop an in-house training program to facilitate training in machine operation and procedures. Both training methods involve expenses for the company. Therefore, companies dedicate many hours to determine the need for training, its use, and its potential for improvements before justifying such an expense. For this reason, when many word processing operations are introduced into an office, the structure of the organization must be adjusted to complement the new equipment and its use.

Procedures

There are a variety of ways to implement a word processing system. However, in order to realize the greatest benefits of the increased productivity potential and to achieve the greatest cost savings, the equipment must be utilized by more people for longer hours in a controlled environment. It is also important that no tasks be dependent upon only one operator in the event of absences, vacations, or terminations. Training, too, is costly to the extent that improper training or lack of training could reduce the productivity performance level or even cause serious equipment malfunctions. Therefore, new procedures must be introduced to safeguard the operations, standardize the methods, schedule the activities, and track the work flow.

These new procedures not only achieve thorough control features, but also provide a basis for other company and departmental record-keeping goals. For example, the records generated by scheduling activities and tracking the flow of work can be used to develop a performance level that should be attained by new employees. Having individual performance standards, each operator within a word processing system can be rated on the exact value of the work produced. These same standards can be used by the supervisor to project new document completion dates for users. In addition, should the company decide to charge a user for the services provided by the word processing department, these records would indicate the amount of time actually devoted to the project. Thus, procedures could provide invaluable aids to other office efficiency methods.

Implementing procedures and measurements of secretarial work flow activity is unique to word processing systems. In a traditional office, where secretarial activities and controls are diversified, it is difficult and often impossible to gather such statistics or well-documented procedures. As a result of these procedures, the word processing operation can become a well-organized and well-run department.

Environment

Part of the control accomplishments are achieved by designing a new, separated work area, free from the day-to-day interruptions of the traditional office. Word processing specialists work more flexible hours, have more disciplined supervision, are free to develop a team approach to their activities, and design the flow of work in the most efficient manner.

The separated work area should include specialized acoustical and atmospheric (environmental) controls which provide the operators with comfortable and attractive surroundings. The basic environmental controls include lighting, humidity, heat, air circulation, noise control, wire management, color, layout, and surface treatment of walls and floors and ceilings. A proper environment also should permit the most ideal atmosphere for equipment operation.

After reading this chapter, you should be able to understand what prompts companies to change their information processing methods. You will understand how management teams investigate changes and determine company objectives. You will have discovered what benefits a company can derive from installing a word/information processing system. Lastly, you will become aware of the basic concept of word processing—its plan and its principal ingredients.

DISCUSSION QUESTIONS AND CASE PROBLEM

DISCUSSION QUESTIONS

1. How would you describe a traditional office?
2. In what areas of business practice or planning could a traditional office experience difficulties? Give examples.
3. Name several benefits a company can derive from a team approach to decision making.
4. What improvements would a company hope to achieve by implementing a word processing system?
5. Identify some major concerns of a management team regarding information flow.
6. Define the four basic elements of a word processing system, and explain how each differs from a traditional office.

CASE PROBLEM

Sally Armstrong was asked by her boss, the Director of Information Services, to attend a staff meeting regarding department objectives. The corporate management team had issued its mission statement—develop expense controls as a means of making each job more cost-effective. Each department was asked to respond with specific objectives that would meet these goals.

She and three other managers were then asked to review the mission statement and to develop an action plan. This plan should ensure that the

CHAPTER 2 Steps Toward Office Improvement

resulting objectives would satisfy departmental needs from a comprehensive company perspective. In addition, should any company changes be required, the changes should be accepted easily by all employees. This management group used a team approach; thus, they regularly held staff problem-solving meetings.

1. What are the three steps this team can include in an action plan before developing specific objectives?
2. What information should be included with specific objectives in order to clarify corporate management's understanding?
3. Could any of the elements of word processing contribute to meeting the company's goal? How?

Part 2
INFORMATION PROCESSING CYCLE

Chapter 3 Input

CHAPTER OBJECTIVES:

Trace the flow of words through the word processing cycle.

Describe eight types of input in terms of the following for each: (a) how it is done, (b) what tools are used, (c) what the appropriate applications are, (d) what the potential problems and disadvantages are, and (e) how to provide the highest quality.

Explain why machine dictation is preferred over longhand and shorthand dictation for most correspondence and short reports.

Discuss dictation equipment by identifying (a) dictation categories and characteristics, (b) the configuration of equipment in a central system, and (c) common types of recording media.

Give an example of an appropriate word processing application for each type of input.

As words are processed they flow through a cycle. The success of any word processing system depends upon how well each step within the cycle is performed and how well the work flow is coordinated. Each step is important, for each contributes to the accuracy, speed, and ultimate cost of the document.

WORD PROCESSING CYCLE

The word processing cycle is shown in Figure 3-1 as a pictorial flowchart. System analysts generally use symbols to write flowcharts. A flowchart is helpful in developing an efficient system and in identifying bottlenecks within the work flow.

The first step is **input**, the author's origination of text that is to be processed. Next the words are keyboarded, recorded on disk or diskette, and printed by the use of a word processor—the **output** step. The

input step first step of word processing cycle; author originates text

output step second step of word processing cycle; text is keyboarded and printed

CHAPTER 3 Input   51

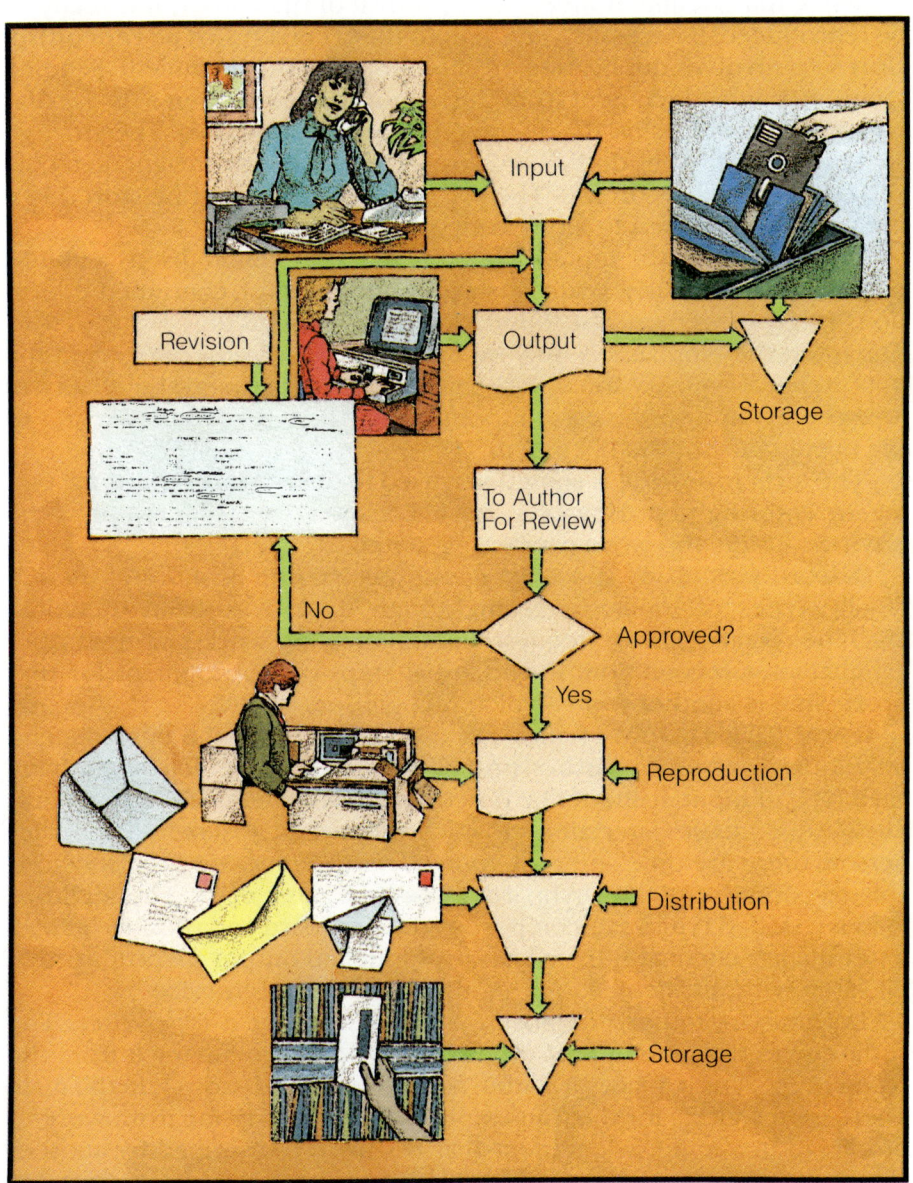

FIG. 3-1
WORD PROCESSING CYCLE
There are six major steps in the word processing cycle.

document is then returned to the author for approval or change. If changes are to be made, the author uses proofreader's marks to indicate how the text is to be revised. Correcting, inserting, or deleting text is known as editing or revising the document—the **revision** step. When the word processing specialist receives the rough draft, the diskette on which it was recorded is inserted in the disk drive and the document is brought to the screen. The correct portions of text are not rekeyed; only the revisions are keyboarded.

revision step third step of word processing cycle; text is edited

reproduction step fourth step of word processing cycle; text is duplicated

distribution step fifth step of word processing cycle; text is sent from author to recipient

storage step sixth step of word processing cycle; text is filed

Once the document meets the approval of the author, it is ready to be reproduced, if necessary, and sent to the receiver(s). The **reproduction** step involves duplicating or photocopying the document. Sending (transmitting) a document from the author to the receiver(s) is the **distribution** step. Finally, the document is ready to be filed. The **storage** step includes filing both the hard (paper) copy and the magnetic media (diskette) of the recording. The paper document might be stored in a file folder or reduced to a tiny image on microfilm.

In this chapter the input step is discussed in detail. Just as a child's education in the early years sets the foundation for continued education, the input step sets the foundation for continued processing of text. Too often the emphasis is only on output by word processors, and the importance of quality input is slighted. The method and the quality of input contribute to the ease in performing the output function and to the overall cost of the document.

The term *inputting* is sometimes used to describe keyboarding, typing, or entering text. However, in this chapter inputting refers to the way text enters the word processing system by the author.

A word processing specialist could receive one or more of the following types of input: longhand, rough draft, shorthand dictation, machine dictation, work request, communicating workstation, or optical character recognition. In the initial steps of development for text processing is another form—voice recognition.

These various types of input are used by authors who must depend on another person to further process the document. Before studying each type of input, it should be noted that whenever an author can produce a document faster alone than through the assistance of another person, there are time and cost savings. An example is a person who is able to compose at the keyboard a first-time, final copy. An individual who is a skilled typist can compose at the keyboard and produce a final, letter-quality document in one sitting. Input and output are produced in one step without the need for another person to transcribe.

Imagine an author composing a short letter at a typewriter. The author gives the letter a final proofreading before removing it from the typewriter, signs it, places it within an envelope, and drops it in the mail. There is no waiting for the transcript nor any interruption from work to proofread it. Should a document that has been transcribed by another person have to be revised, waiting time and proofreading effort are repeated. This adds to the expense of the document and slows down turnaround time.

Being able to produce first-time, final copy for short letters and memos is especially helpful. For longer documents that involve creative composition and revision, it is not likely that an author could combine all the needed skills to produce a final copy in one sitting. Recognizing the need for typewriting skill, more and more executives are acquiring

CHAPTER 3 Input

the skill in order to operate executive workstation terminals with speed and accuracy.

TYPES OF INPUT

Most authors are unable to input and output at the same time, or they have complex applications which necessitate another person's help. Thus, they must rely on various other methods. Each method of input has some value, depending upon the application and the available equipment. To have a thorough understanding of word/information processing concepts, one needs to analyze each option so that the best method of input can be recommended to users. Since 1980 there have been great strides to help executives improve their efficiency and cost effectiveness. Producing the best type of input for word processing is but one way for executives to meet these goals.

Longhand

One of the most common types of input is handwritten text. Longhand is quite appropriate for composing a creative piece of work, like a program, which may have more than three columns. Figure 3-2 is an

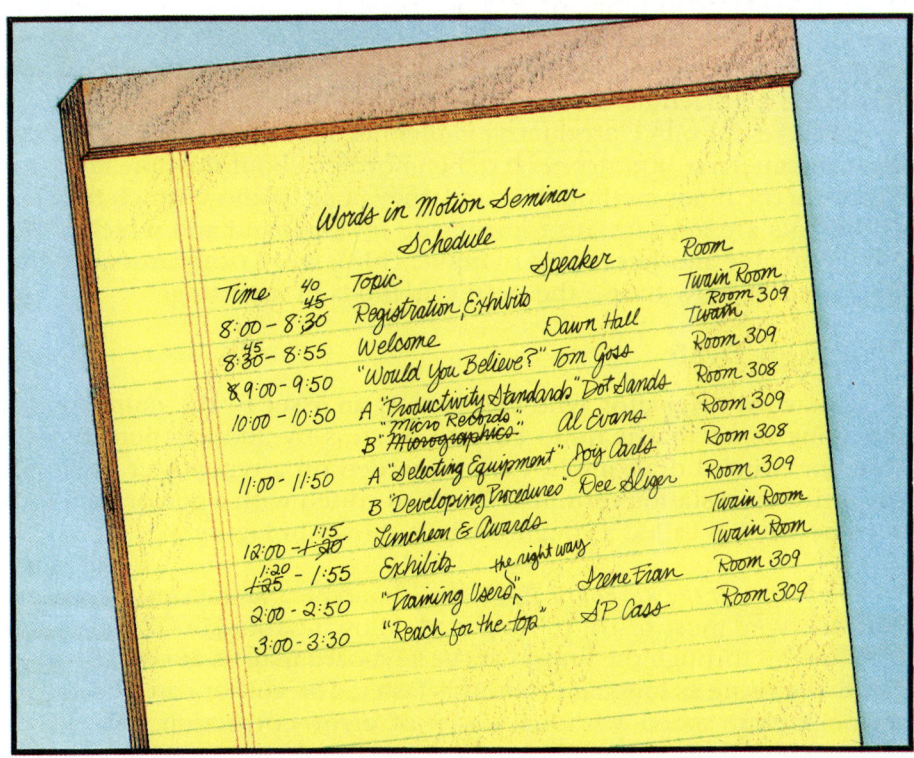

FIG. 3-2
LONGHAND
Although commonly used, longhand is a costly method of input.

example of a document written in longhand. There are both advantages and disadvantages to using longhand as a means of word processing input.

Reasons for Writing by Hand. Longhand input requires only a pen and paper for supplies. These supplies can be used easily anyplace. People are comfortable with a pen and paper, for these tools have been used regularly since childhood. Some writers claim that only by longhand can they compose with an imaginative, free-writing style. Writing by hand does not involve coordinating oneself with either a machine or another person during composition.

Using longhand as the means of input can be justified for certain creative works and for complicated tabular material. However, it must be legibly written so that anyone can easily transcribe from the script.

Why to Avoid Longhand as a Means of Input. A close analysis of all the documents that have been initiated by longhand would reveal that most of them should have been done by a more efficient means. Composing by longhand is relatively slow; it averages only about 10 to 15 words a minute (wam). The speed of transcribing from another person's handwriting is hindered by having to contend with illegible writing. Studies show that the average transcription rate is only 10 to 15 wam. Because longhand is slow in terms of writing speed and transcription rate, it is one of the most costly methods of word origination. For example, a document that originates by longhand costs about twice that of one originated by machine dictation.

To solve this office productivity dilemma requires a three-fold training program. First, authors need to be informed about the time and cost of each of the input methods. Second, they need to know which types of documents are appropriate to originate by longhand and which types should involve another means of input. Third, word originators need to be trained on how to use the better methods of inputting.

Rough Draft

Any word originator who can type is an asset to the company by providing input that is quite easy to process by another person. The typed or printed draft might be keyboarded on a typewriter or on an executive workstation terminal. It is then edited with a pen or pencil to become what is called a rough draft, as shown in Figure 3-3.

Composing at the Keyboard. One who can type a draft copy saves time over one who must resort to longhand. Allowing thoughts to flow from the brain on through the fingers at the keyboard may be as conducive to creative writing as longhand, and it is faster. The author can freely type at rough-draft speed without worry of error correction, format, or reconstruction of sentences.

CHAPTER 3 Input

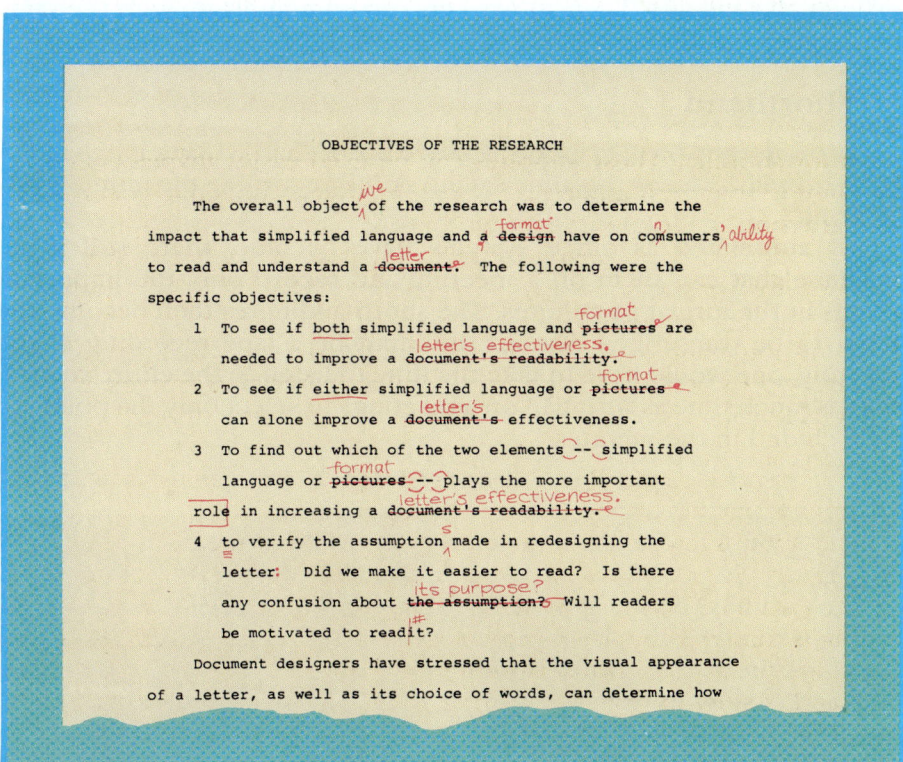

FIG. 3-3
ROUGH DRAFT
A rough draft is a typed document that has revisions marked on it in pen or pencil.

Updating Existing Documents. Once it has been typed or printed, the draft is edited. With double-spaced copy there is plenty of room to pen in proofreader's marks to edit the text. The transcriber can transcribe the final document more easily and quickly from a rough draft than from purely longhand copy.

Another form of rough draft is a document that was printed several months or a year ago and is now being updated. An example would be a financial statement, such as a balance sheet, that was printed last quarter. To update it for the current quarter, the accountant would need only to change the amounts and make minor revisions in the headings.

Potential Problems of Typed Drafts. There are potential problems that can occur with typing and then editing copy with proofreader's marks. Even though the author might be able to type from straight copy material quite well, the individual may not be able to compose at the keyboard very well. Many people compose in longhand and then type from that source to produce input for a transcriber. To first write the text in longhand only adds to the time spent for input, which is not cost effective. Another problem is the inconsistent proofreader's symbols used by various authors. All office workers should be familiar with and use standard proofreader's marks. Then all workers can communicate with the same language.

Shorthand

Writing shorthand symbols is much faster than writing longhand. A prime application for this time-saving skill is recording the minutes of a meeting.

As automated as office systems have become, there still is no machine that can sit in on a meeting and record only the important points in the format of minutes. The shorthand notes then become the input to be transcribed. Should the input be a tape recording of the meeting, one would have to take the time to listen to the entire recording (as much time as sitting in on a meeting) to select only the points to be included in the minutes.

Shorthand is a quick, convenient method to use when taking telephone messages or writing job instructions.

CHAPTER 3 Input

Advantages and Uses of Shorthand. Shorthand is normally written at speeds that range from 80 to 120 wam, whereas longhand can be written at only 30 to 40 wam maximum. These burst (straight copy) speeds for shorthand and longhand are much faster than the respective composition rates. However, even during composition a shorthand writer can produce at a faster rate than a longhand writer.

As with longhand, shorthand writing does not require more than a pen and paper. (Some companies utilize machine shorthand, but it is not commonly found outside courtrooms.)

In addition to taking the minutes of a meeting, shorthand is an efficient way to take job instructions and telephone messages. Recording messages by shorthand saves the caller's time as well as the receiver's time. At places where one does not have access to a photocopying machine, articles can be abstracted quickly in shorthand. For situations in which the secretary serves as a paraprofessional and helps the author compose documents, dictation and composition by shorthand are desirable.

Some authors prefer a personal secretary who can write shorthand as the only way to input confidential documents and rush dictation. However, in a well-supervised word processing system both situations can be accommodated.

Disadvantages of Shorthand for Correspondence Processing. For shorthand notes to be transcribed with greatest efficiency, the person who does the writing should also do the transcribing. Why? Most shorthand writers develop their own shortcuts, which are not likely to be recognized by another transcriber. Also, as the lapse of time between dictation and transcription increases, the transcription rate usually decreases. ["COLD NOTES"] For the average transcriber, the rate of transcription is only about 25 wam, which is faster than from another person's longhand but slower than from machine dictation.

Another major disadvantage of shorthand is that two people are involved during input. The author can dictate only at the office when the secretary is available. During dictation the rate of input is slowed down by normal social conversation, telephone interruptions, and rate adjustments by either the dictator waiting for the secretary to catch up or the secretary waiting for the dictator. Should 300 words (for example, two 150-word letters) have been dictated, it would take about 10 minutes for the input step. The rate of input appears to be 30 wam (300 words divided by 10 minutes). But when one considers that two people are involved in the process, the rate is only 15 wam (10 minutes × 2 people = 20 minutes; 300 words divided by 20 minutes = 15 wam). The rate is slow and the cost is high, because the company is paying for two people's time during word origination.

For the reasons just given, word processing consultants discourage shorthand dictation from being used for documents that can be dictated more efficiently by machine. Letters, memorandums, and short reports typically fall within that category of documents.

Machine Dictation

The use of machine dictation, while it has not reached its potential, has certainly made advancements in improving office productivity. It is a highly recommended form of input for many word processing applications, because it makes the best use of both the author's time and the transcriber's time. The equipment has been improved so that the process is easy and convenient for all people involved. Yet there are problems to be overcome with this form of input. Companies which are alert to and which make arrangements for avoiding such problems attain the goals of efficient word origination.

Advantages and Appropriate Uses. With dictation equipment an author can dictate anyplace (at the office, at home, in the car, on a plane) and anytime (before, during, or after office hours). One does not have to coordinate time and place with the secretary's schedule. Individually, secretaries can pace their work; and with fewer interruptions, their input productivity is maximized.

Dictation involves only the author's time; the secretary can be performing other office tasks. During the dictation process there is no time used for social conversation or waiting for either person to catch up. Any interruption, such as a telephone call, does not record on the tape; so it does not affect the transcriber's time.

Composing thoughts by machine dictation averages 60 to 80 wam, which means that the input step for two letters of 150 words each (total of 300 words) would take only 4 to 5 minutes of one individual's time. Anyone who knows how to transcribe from machine dictation can process the input; there is no need to decipher illegible longhand or shorthand. The average machine transcription rate is 20 to 35 wam, which is faster than transcribing either longhand or shorthand notes. The newer models of dictation and transcription equipment simplify the process for authors, transcribers, and supervisors. A comparison of dictation, shorthand, and longhand as input methods is shown in Figure 3-4.

The comparison of the three input methods illustrates how time is saved when a 250-word letter originates by machine dictation rather than by longhand or shorthand dictation. Time is valuable; and when time savings are converted to cost savings, the advantage of machine dictation becomes more meaningful to management.

Based on 8-hour days and 244 working days a year, the author who earns $30,000 a year is being paid $.2561 a minute, and the secretary who earns $16,000 is being paid $.1366 each minute. By plugging in these amounts to Figure 3-4, the 25-line letter that originates by longhand costs the company $8.72; by shorthand dictation, $8.99; and by machine dictation, $2.56.

CHAPTER 3 Input 59

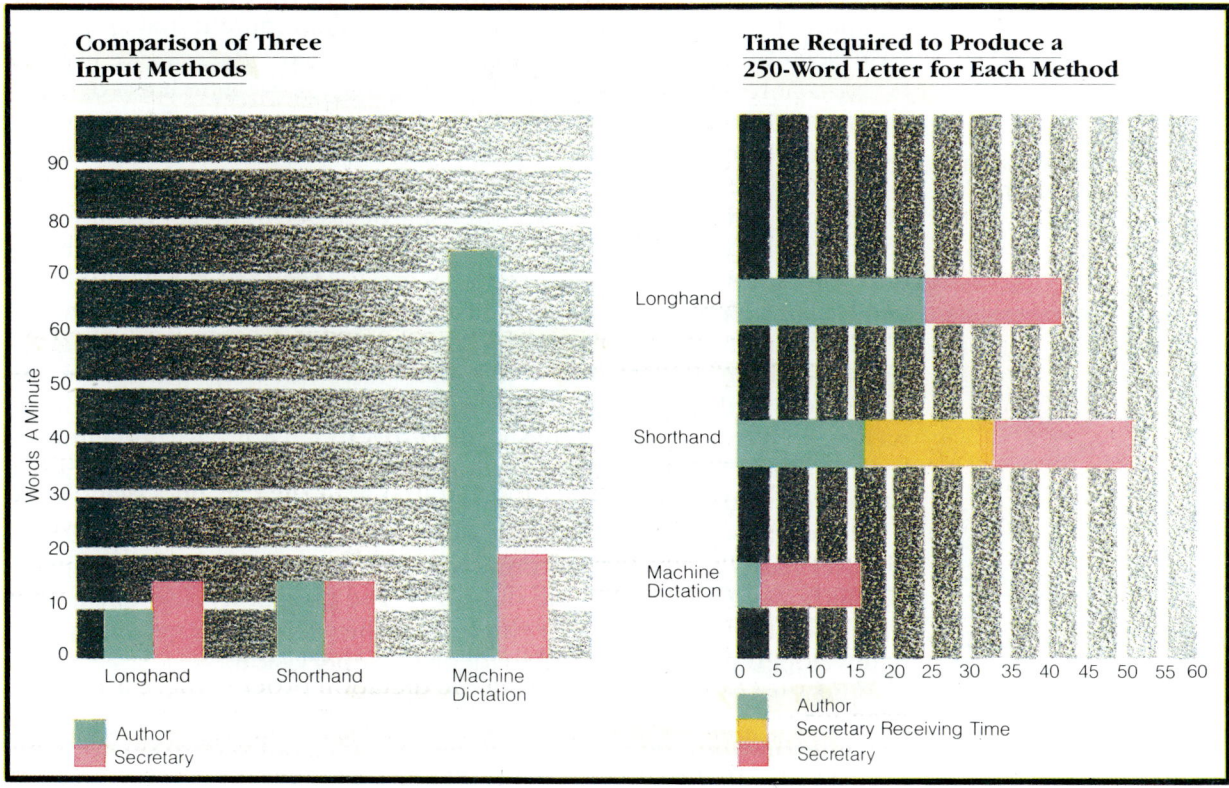

FIG. 3-4
COMPARISON OF INPUT METHODS
Dictation, as an input method, requires less time than either longhand or shorthand.

Each letter that originates by machine dictation saves $6.16 over one created by longhand and $6.43 over one dictated to a shorthand writer. This cost analysis is but one of several that have been performed by various consultants and research organizations. Individual amounts vary according to the factors (or variables) that are considered. However, all studies reveal time and cost savings of machine dictation.

Applications for which machine dictation is recommended include letters, memorandums, and short reports. Any document that does not involve complicated format or that does not require the author to see the entire document for creative composition can be dictated.

Potential Problems with Machine Dictation. Most of the problems encountered with machine dictation can be avoided. Problems result because people are not informed about input concepts (as given in this chapter), do not have efficient procedures developed, or have not been trained.

One obstacle to many companies is the initial cost of dictation equipment. Some companies allocate most of the word processing budget for text editing equipment and overlook the need for input equipment. Those that do purchase dictation equipment may not make wise selections, which can be a costly mistake. Purchasing several brands and models of equipment results in users having to learn to operate more than one kind of machine. Parts are not interchangeable. If some dictation units record on standard cassette and others on microcassette, there must be two different types of transcribing units or an **adapter** (a device that holds another size of cassette) must be used. This can hamper the even distribution of work to transcribers. Also, procedures manuals and training programs are longer than what would be needed for helping users to learn just one brand or model of equipment.

Another problem is that some authors do not use dictation equipment to its fullest potential. Why? Many have not been trained on the advantages and most appropriate applications of machine dictation, as well as on how to dictate. Thus, they resort to what is easy and familiar; but for many documents that is inefficient and costly. Poor dictation causes frustration for the transcriber and a very slow transcription rate.

If the transcription of machine dictation is not returned as quickly as or faster than that which was done for longhand or shorthand dictation, the author will regress to the old ways. The possibility also exists that some dictation will be lost. In either case, the problem stems from poorly developed procedures and inadequate supervision.

To prevent or overcome these problems, companies should:

1 Budget for and carefully select equipment that is compatible. This means that all dictation machines should record on the same type of media, so that only one type of transcribing unit is needed. Having all equipment of one brand results in more standard operation, which facilitates learning.

2 Efficient procedures for handling dictation and transcription must be developed. This assures quick turnaround and avoids any dictation from being lost.

3 Training programs need to be set up for all people involved with word processing. The best way to alleviate the fear of automated equipment and to assure its proper use is training. Even those who claim they know how to dictate may very well have developed some bad habits that should be corrected.

These carefully laid steps set the foundation for an efficient and smooth-running dictation system.

Dictation Equipment and Recording Media. Dictation equipment comes in an array of sizes, brands, and features. However, these machines are grouped into three categories according to location and use—portable units, desk top units, and central systems.

adapter allows two sizes of cassettes to be used on one machine

Three sizes of cassettes are used in dictation equipment—microcassettes (top), minicassettes (center), and standard cassettes.

Portable Units. These are designed for the convenience of an author who is away from the office. Both the microphone and the recorder are within one unit. These battery-powered, lightweight machines can be carried in one's pocket or briefcase. Newer models are made so that only one hand is needed to hold the unit and operate the controls. The author can dictate anyplace—at home, in the car, or on a plane.

Desk Top Units. These units are designed for permanent location at the executive's desk (work station). Compared to portables, desk top units generally have more operator controls and indicators. The microphone is a hand-held unit that is connected to the recorder.

Dictation equipment is grouped into three categories—portable units (left), desk top units (right), and centralized units (bottom).

Desk top equipment can be purchased as dictation units (used only for dictation), as transcription units (used only for transcription), or as combination units (used for either dictation or transcription). A combination unit becomes a dictation device when the microphone plug is inserted; it becomes a transcription device when the earphone and foot pedal plugs are inserted. The advantage of combination units is that for small offices with light dictation the cost is minimal when one machine can be used for two functions. However, the disadvantage is that the combination unit has to be moved from the author's desk to the transcriber's desk.

Central Systems. Central systems are distinguished from other types of dictation machines by the fact that the recorders are grouped in a central place within the transcription area. The dictation units, which house the microphone devices, look much like telephones. They are distributed throughout the company at authors' work stations.

Central systems are cost effective for companies that have a large number of authors with light or moderate volumes of dictation. An example would be a hospital, for the physicians spend most of their time with patients rather than with paperwork. Yet for each patient a medical report must be dictated.

To begin dictating the author merely picks up the receiver of the dictation unit and selects or is automatically connected to a free recorder. The number of authors who can dictate at one time is limited to the number of recorders within the system. For example, if there are eight recorders and twenty dictation units, a maximum of eight people can be dictating at the same time.

In a centralized system, the author can easily connect to a recorder and begin dictation.

Transcribers in a centralized system are able to work at their own pace.

Some companies provide desk top equipment for those who have a heavy volume of dictation so that they do not tie up the central recorders. It is not unusual to see all three categories of dictation equipment within one company.

Connecting Dictation Units to Recorders in a Central System. The connection between dictation units and recorders of a central system is either by direct wiring or by the telephone network. Direct wiring, also called a privately wired system, has the sole purpose of joining the various dictation units to the central recorders. There is a one-time installation charge but no monthly usage charge (since the company owns the wire connection). However, should the office later relocate, there would be another installation charge.

Wire connection by the telephone network enables any telephone on or off premises to function as a dictation unit. Thus, dictation can be phoned in from home or a hotel after office hours. Installation simply involves hooking up the recorders to the telephone network. Since the company does not own the telephone network, there is a monthly usage charge that is paid to the telephone company. During dictation from an office phone, the telephone line is busy and cannot accept incoming calls. For this reason some companies have their central dictation system wired both ways. Dictation from on premises is accommodated by the directly wired system; that which occurs off premises comes through the telephone network.

Supervisor's Console. An optional piece of equipment for central systems, the supervisor's console (monitor) aids the supervisor in managing work flow and preparing production reports. Dictation can be channeled to the word processing specialist who will provide the fastest turnaround time.

The console displays for each document the following types of information: date, time transcription begins and ends, turnaround time, author, length of document, and transcriber. Examples of summary reports that can be provided by the console include the number of documents and/or minutes dictated by each author, a list of documents transcribed by each word processing specialist, and the number of minutes each specialist has transcribed. This information can be printed as well as displayed on the console screen.

Information from work requests and from cassette tapes that have been removed from portables and desk top units can be added to the console. However, the supervisor must manually key in such information. Data is automatically recorded and computed by the console only for the documents that were dictated on the central recorders.

Recording Media. Magnetic tape, available in various sizes and packages, is the basic dictation recording medium. Unlike the older plastic belts and disks, magnetic media can be corrected by backing up and dictating on top. Once the tape has been transcribed, it can be erased and reused many times.

There are two basic kinds of recording media—discrete and endless loop. **Discrete media** must be physically loaded into the recording device prior to dictation and removed from the recorder for transcription. The transcriber then must handle the media when loading and unloading the transcription device. In contrast, an **endless loop** is a long and continuous loop that is accessible to either the dictator or the transcriber but is not physically handled. The endless loop is permanently housed within the recording unit.

discrete media must be removed from recorder for transcription

endless loop not removed from recorder for transcription

Discrete media are most commonly packaged in standard cassettes and microcassettes. Only discrete media are used for portables and desk top equipment. For central systems, there is a choice between discrete media or endless loop.

Endless loop is a long magnetic tape that moves through the "dictate" (record) head during dictation and through the "transcribe" head during transcription. The dictation unit is connected to the "dictate" head and the transcriber's unit is wired to the "transcribe" head so that neither party ever handles the tape as shown in Figure 3-5. The magnetic tape is never removed from the unit.

For central systems discrete media and endless loop tapes each have advantages as well as disadvantages. Discrete media are easier to distribute to many transcribers, whereas endless loop tapes are more limited. Dictation can be permanently stored on discrete media. However,

CHAPTER 3   Input 65

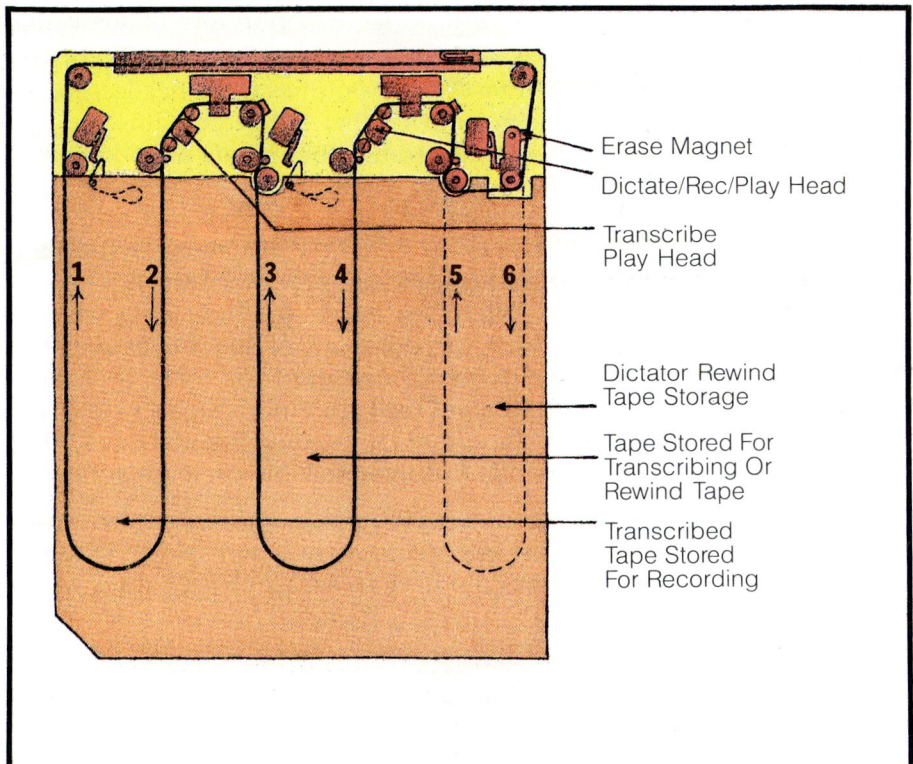

FIG. 3-5
ENDLESS LOOP
In an endless loop dictating machine, the magnetic tape does not have to be removed from the machine for transcription. (Diagram Courtesy of Dictaphone Corporation)

careless handling of tapes can result in damaged or lost dictation. Use of endless loop tapes assures that dictation cannot get lost, since there is no physical handling of the tape. Another advantage with an endless loop tape is that as soon as the tape has advanced from the "dictate" head to the "transcribe" head (about 10 to 15 seconds), the word processing specialist can begin transcribing while the author continues to dictate; this is not possible with discrete media. One disadvantage of an endless loop tape is that only one person can be transcribing the long tape at a time. (Some equipment has two transcribe heads, which allows another person to transcribe from the same tape.) Also, dictation on an endless loop tape cannot be easily stored since the tape is continually being used. Any dictation to be saved would have to be recorded onto discrete media for storage.

Transcriber's Unit. Partners to dictation units are the transcription units. Should the company have various types of dictation machines that record on more than one type of recording media, there must be that many types of transcription units. For example, a transcribing machine for standard cassettes is incompatible with dictation units that record onto microcassettes. Some brands of equipment offer an adapter, which in the case of the example enables a microcassette to be transcribed on a standard cassette transcriber. Work flow is facilitated and input costs are kept to the minimum by having all dictation equipment record on the same type of media. The transcriber's unit has (1) a headset for listening to playback, (2) a control device that either contains the tape (for discrete media) or accesses the "transcribe" head (of endless loop tape), and (3) a foot pedal.

Special Features. Standard features on dictation machines include volume, speed, tone, playback, fast-forward, and rewind controls. On most desk top and central systems there are means for indicating where a document ends and for marking the positions of special instructions. Traditionally paper index strips have been used for these indicators. Newer models replace or supplement the paper index strips with a visual display line and/or electronic queue (sometimes spelled cue) tones. In addition, there are also special features available on many models:

voice-operated relay
recording tape halts when dictator pauses and continues when talking resumes

speech compression
removing pauses from dictation as it is recorded

1 **Voice-operated relay** causes the tape to halt when the author stops talking and to start advancing again when speech resumes. The transcriber then does not have to wait for long pauses within the dictation.

2 **Speech compression** removes pauses from dictation.

3 Insertion of words can occur in the middle of a sentence without having to erase any words the author wants to retain.

4 Telephone messages can be recorded by desk top units so that the author can leave the office with the telephone unattended by a secretary. Callers leave messages on the tape, and the receiver can listen to the recording upon returning to the office.

5 Built-in speakers for group listening and supersensitive microphones for conference recordings are functional for meetings. They are features more likely found on desk top machines.

Work Request

Another way that work might be presented to a word processing specialist is by a work request form. These forms are used for input that does not originate by machine dictation, as Figure 3-6 shows.

An author might request that a standard document be merged with specific variables (for example, names, dates, and amounts that are unique to each document) and printed. As the standard document, such as a form letter, is first recorded on the word processor, it is given a document name or label. Also, at each place within the standard text where a variable will be inserted or merged the position is coded. In filling out a work request to have a form letter prepared for several

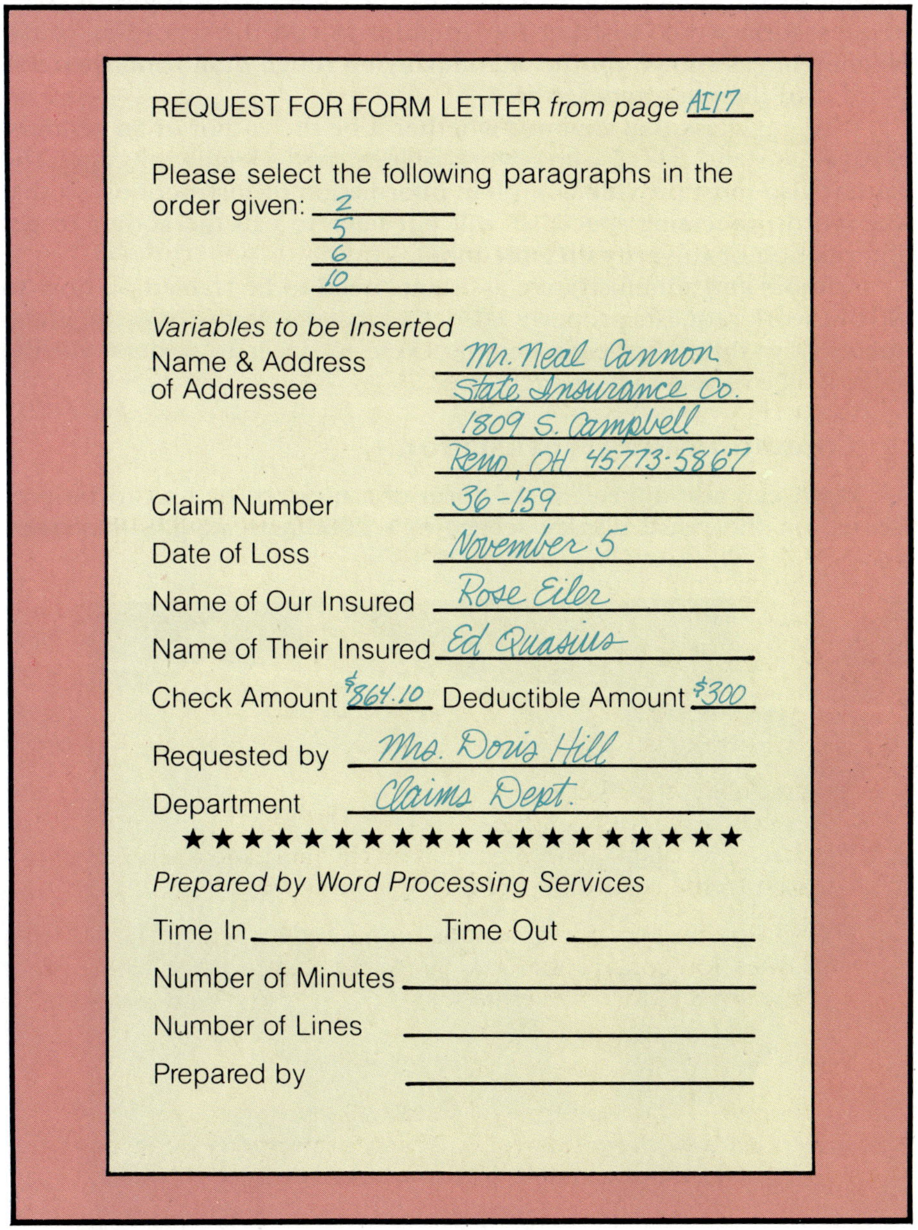

CHAPTER 3 Input   67

> REQUEST FOR FORM LETTER *from page* AI17
>
> Please select the following paragraphs in the
> order given: 2
>   5
>   6
>   10
>
> *Variables to be Inserted*
> Name & Address   Mr. Neal Cannon
> of Addressee   State Insurance Co.
>   1809 S. Campbell
>   Reno, OH 45773-5867
>
> Claim Number   36-159
> Date of Loss   November 5
> Name of Our Insured Rose Eiler
> Name of Their Insured Ed Quasius
> Check Amount $864.10 Deductible Amount $300
> Requested by   Mrs. Doris Hill
> Department   Claims Dept.
>
> ★★★★★★★★★★★★★★★★★★
>
> *Prepared by Word Processing Services*
> Time In _____ Time Out _____
> Number of Minutes _____
> Number of Lines _____
> Prepared by _____

FIG. 3-6
WORK REQUEST FORM
Work request forms are used for jobs that do not originate by machine dictation or jobs that will be further processed by another information processing system.

cases, the author gives the document name (label) of the prerecorded form letter and then lists the specific variables for each case.

Work requests are generally used for jobs that will be further processed by another information processing system. For example, an article for a brochure that has been recorded on a word processor and revised by the author would be sent back to the word processor. A work request form would instruct the operator to edit the recording of the document (as shown on the accompanying rough draft) and then forward it to the phototypesetter.

It is important that anyone (whether it be the author or an administrative assistant) filling out a work request write legibly or type. The author also must provide complete information or instructions, so that the word processing specialist will not have to call the author to get information or to verify illegible input.

Authors and administrative assistants need to be trained on how to fill out work requests properly. Also, they need to know how the documents flow through the processing cycle in order to understand the importance of accuracy at each step.

Communicating Workstation

Input can also appear in the form of a message or text to be processed on the visual display screen of a communicating workstation.

A communicating word processor can send information directly to the screen of another communicating word processor without having the information printed.

CHAPTER 3 Input

69

This input can be sent directly from another word processor without first having been printed. For situations in which several branch offices have input that is merged into one document, such as a stock catalog or a customer directory, electronic mail is beneficial. Of course, both the sending and receiving machines must be compatible so that the digital data (as discussed in Chapter 1) can be transmitted in that language. The input originates from a word processor that is located in a branch office. An author could originate text at an executive workstation and send it to a word processor within the same building.

Should a company have various brands of word processors or executive workstations that cannot communicate with the word processors, problems can occur. Text processing then requires either conversion (translation of one machine's language to another) or rekeying. Companies are encouraged to plan for input as well as output when selecting equipment for information processing.

Optical Character Recognition

Companies that have a heavy volume of typewritten or printed text (not recorded on magnetic media) to be revised can have the text further processed without rekeying the correct portions. The author uses a colored pen (not recognizable to the scanner) to mark revisions. The rough draft sheet can be read by an optical character recognition (OCR) scanner that transfers the typed text into digital information on a diskette. The document can then be edited and printed in final copy by the word processing operator. In editing the text, the operator refers to the colored pen marks of the rough draft. This sequence of events is illustrated in Figure 3-7.

FIG. 3-7
OCR AS AN INPUT TO WORD PROCESSING
If an OCR is used as an input device, revisions can be made on a document without the operator having to rekey the correct portions.

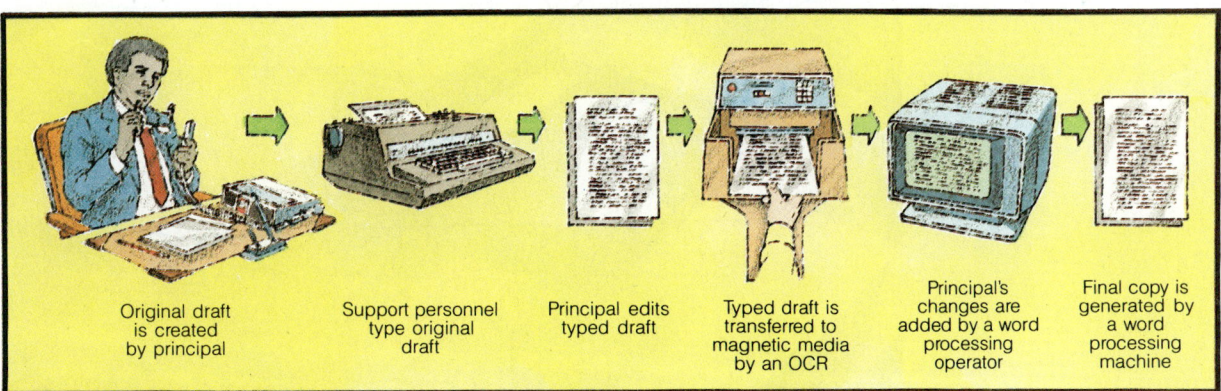

OCR scanners improve productivity by allowing initial keyboarding to be performed on less expensive machines (typewriters) and the final input stage (revision) to be performed on word processors. Although the early models of OCR page readers were limited to what they could do well, the latest models for word processing applications have greatly improved. They can now recognize both capital and lowercase letters and a wide range of different typewriter fonts. Typewriters that are used for initial input to OCR readers must have OCR-readable fonts.

Accuracy and speed in reading have also improved. The better models have been proven to make no more than one error in 300,000 characters. They can detect variations in type style, pitch, and line spacing without operator assistance. Thus, they are said to be "user friendly." The advanced machines can scan and record onto magnetic media at the

OCR readers improve productivity by allowing initial keyboarding to be done on typewriters instead of on expensive word processors.

rate of more than 300 pages an hour. However, the lower cost scanners are not as fast and do not have as many automatic features.

Benefits. A major word processing application of OCR is to enter text produced on a typewriter into a word processor for editing and distribution. Users say it is cheaper to enter text on the typewriter than on a word processor, because it frees the more expensive word processor for editing functions. In this way there is more effective use of both machines. Training costs are reduced, because not all secretaries have to be trained to operate the more sophisticated machines. Most original typing can be done by secretaries who are familiar with the author's terminology, dictation style, and handwriting.

OCR machines can interface with electronic mail devices and phototypesetters as well as with computers and word processors. Optical character recognition has long been used for data entry into the computer. An example is scanning employee time cards; the data is entered into the computer mainframe for automatic payroll processing. Now OCR can also assist in word processing and communications functions.

Companies that have Telex terminals can have typed messages read into the Telex terminal with an OCR reader. The OCR scanner eliminates the need to rekey the typed messages onto the Telex terminal. Here is another example of a communications function of an OCR machine. When information must be transmitted overseas, sending a diskette rather than a bulky package of printed paper would save a good

A typed message can be read into a Telex terminal by an OCR reader, thus eliminating rekeying of the message.

amount of postage. (The OCR scanner converts the printed word into electronic impulses on a diskette.)

Potential Problems. As with many office machines, OCR readers are sensitive to paper. Bent or wrinkled paper can cause jams. The lower the quality of the type, the more likely there will be misreads. OCR readers have difficulty reading blurred type, smudges, wavy lines, and proportionally spaced print.

To decrease the number of OCR reading errors, most input should be in a fairly standard format; this also increases the speed with which documents pass through the work cycle. The paper should be smooth, white, and of average weight. The typed characters should be black, sharp, and clear to provide good contrast to the white paper.

Readers in the upper price range are less likely to have the problems that occur in the lower price range. As with many other office machines, the features are improving and the prices are getting lower. As OCR technology improves, the machines will have greater tolerance for lower quality paper and print. One of the new features being developed is highlighting. Using a special marking pen, the user can highlight only the portions of text to be scanned, thus eliminating the scanning of excess or unneeded text.

Companies who choose to buy OCR scanners must have the volume of work and appropriate applications to justify the purchase. They must decide which configuration of equipment would be more efficient: (1) many typewriters, an OCR scanner, and a few word processors or (2) more word processors, few if any typewriters, and no OCR scanner.

Voice Recognition

Voice processing technology has several dimensions in providing input to an office system. In addition to machine dictation and telephone message systems, some input can be provided by voice recognition.

Can an author dictate a letter into a computer and receive a mailable transcript? This is not yet possible for word processing applications, but it is possible for data processing applications.

In voice recognition, a computer converts spoken words into readable form. The word originator dictates documents by using a telephone handset or an audio CRT terminal. Within a few seconds the author receives a display on the screen or a computerized printout. The document may be stored, edited, and transmitted to a secretarial workstation for letter-quality transcript. Instead of needing both dictation machines and transcribing machines, only one machine is needed to handle the creation of documents. Speech recognition and **voice input system (VIS)** are other terms used to describe this technology.

voice input system
technology that converts spoken words to print

CHAPTER 3 Input

Voice recognition equipment converts spoken words into readable form (a screen display or a printed page).

Voice recognition is a computer process. As the author speaks, the voice goes through a processor which converts the speech into digital impulses. The digital impulses are compared with the sound patterns within the computer's memory. Those that match are displayed or printed as words. Single words with distinct pauses between each (like *yes, no, off, on*, letters, and numbers) are easier to process than entire sentences without pauses.

Speaking single distinct words, known as **discrete word recognition**, is useful for handicapped people and for situations in which the author's hands and eyes are busy. For example, it would be helpful to be able to use one's hands in taking inventory of stock.

Continuous speech recognition, involving the flow of words without pauses, is more difficult to process. Voices can vary by accent of words, dialect, loudness, and pitch. Words like *than* vs. *then* and *know* vs. *no* pose problems. Also, as the vocabulary of the speakers increases faster than the vocabulary within the computer memory, more errors occur.

Although voice recognition has the potential to reduce the time and human effort of input and output, it will not eliminate the need for secretaries. Computer output of correspondence or reports, even at 95 percent accuracy (the maximum foreseeable level of accuracy for word processing applications), must be corrected and edited so that the document is letter quality and mailable.

discrete word recognition computer technology; converts single, distinct spoken words to print

continuous speech recognition computer technology; converts a flow of spoken words without pauses to print

Determining the Best Type of Input

The best type of input for further processing of text depends upon the application, the location of the originator, and the available tools. Each input form has advantages and certain applications for which it is recommended. On the other hand, disadvantages and potential problems can also be associated with any method of input.

A thorough command of word/information processing concepts requires that one have knowledge about all the types of input. Then an analysis and recommendations can be made objectively. Every effort should be made to establish efficient procedures for input, which includes emphasis on training. By submitting the highest quality input, word originators can support the most efficient and accurate processing of text.

DISCUSSION QUESTIONS AND CASE PROBLEM

Discussion Questions

1. Why should the input step of the word processing cycle be given as much emphasis as the output step?
2. Would you recommend that a secretarial student take a machine transcription course and/or a shorthand course? Why?
3. What skills enhance the quality and speed of input by an author?
4. How can most of the problems that occur with any type of input be prevented or eliminated?
5. Name seven of the eight types of input described in this chapter and for each give one example of an appropriate word processing application.

Case Problem

Martha Goodwin was the supervisor of the centralized word processing center of her company. She had ten specialists working in her department, and her two top production performers were Jim and Sally. Based on Martha's request, the company installed a central dictation system. Since most of the company's potential users had previous dictation experience, management felt additional training beyond use of the system itself was unwarranted. Martha assigned Jim and Sally the responsibility of transcribing the dictation.

CHAPTER 3 Input

At the end of the first two weeks of their new assignment, Jim's and Sally's performance levels began to drop. They were not producing as many documents as they had previously; and in addition, many of the documents they returned to their authors for approval required corrections. Martha's boss felt she should either speak to Jim and Sally about trying harder or assign someone else to process dictation for their users, since Jim and Sally apparently were having trouble with transcription techniques. Jim and Sally were unhappy, too. They felt they were performing as best they could, but they were having trouble understanding the users' needs.

Martha talked to Jim and Sally. She then recommended to her boss that what was needed was a dictation training class for the users.

1. What evidence supported Martha's recommendation to her boss? Name four of the five possible clues.
2. What bad habits could experienced dictators develop?
3. What tactful methods could be used to bring these bad habits to the attention of the dictators without alienating their ongoing use of the dictation equipment?

Chapter 4 Output

CHAPTER OBJECTIVES

Identify the three categories of word processing equipment and generic models that are included within each category.

Describe the various kinds of magnetic recording media that capture keystrokes.

Distinguish between an impact printer and a nonimpact printer, giving examples of each.

Explain the characteristics of the two basic types of word processing software.

TYPES OF EQUIPMENT

Until the early 1980s, the belief that word processors were specific pieces of hardware dedicated only to the processing of words (text) was quite common. Since that time, however, the emphasis gradually is being placed on equipment which, as part of its many applications, processes text either as its main function or as one of several functions. The word processing function may be performed by word processing machines within an office automation system, by an application added to an existing data processing system, or by a specific software package added to a personal computer. Regardless of the type of equipment used, the objective remains the same—word processing applications.

A common denominator of the many devices capable of processing words is the capturing of keystrokes to permit the easy manipulation of text before its final form. The degree to which the devices can manipulate text, the speed with which the resulting text is produced in its final form, and the cost involved in meeting those objectives efficiently are the factors which separate the various categories of word processors. The three basic categories of word processors are standalone, multiterminal, and time-sharing word processors. A variety of each type is found in companies. Each is justified on the basis of need and use.

Standalone Word Processors

A standalone word processor is a single station system with a keyboard, storage facility, and a printer that does not share the resources of a central computer system. It is basically designed to operate completely on its own; thus, *stand alone*. Some standalone systems may be configured to share resources with other systems, but this function is an enhancement to its basic design. There is a wide variety of standalone equipment. Some have display screens, disk drives, and printers. Others utilize televisions for video displays and have no external memory device. Still others perform the standalone word processing within a single typewriter-like machine.

Electronic Typewriters. An electronic typewriter is a sophisticated, electronic machine that permits limited storage and manipulation of text that is keyboarded and printed from the same device. These machines take their place at the lower price range of the word processing marketplace. They were first introduced in 1978. Since then, many vendors have entered the market. In many companies they are the first-step replacement for electric (mechanical) typewriters. Electronic typewriters generally are found in traditional office systems, where each secretary performs all secretarial services for one or two principals.

The amount of text that can be temporarily stored (allowing the operator to go back to make a correction) in an electronic typewriter is minimal. This temporary storage, called **buffer storage**, is usually a few lines or less. Buffer storage is internal to the device, and on many models the captured text is not saved if the machine loses power.

standalone word processor does not share resources of a central computer

electronic typewriter allows limited storage and manipulation of text

buffer storage temporary storage of a few lines of text within a machine

Electronic typewriters can store a limited amount of text temporarily.

Some electronic typewriters have permanent storage areas with the capacity to hold up to 100 pages. Once sent to storage, these pages are saved when the power goes off. However, to store more pages than the capacity of the storage area, the operator must erase old documents.

Many models have a display window (visual display) that shows anywhere from a few characters to two lines of text. This thin window enables the operator to see the text as it is being edited.

Time-saving features on electronic typewriters include automatic centering, automatic underlining, automatic numeric alignment, and automatic carrier return. With fewer moving parts than electric typewriters, electronic typewriters typically require fewer service calls. For first-time-final documents (those that will not be revised or printed again) copy can be produced without the blemishes of correction fluid or erasures. However, should the author require a revision to text that has already been printed, the entire document needs to be rekeyed just as if the typist had used an electric typewriter. Appropriate applications would be short documents (usually one page) that involve only light revision during keyboarding and that do not require further editing after being printed.

Mechanical Standalones. Mechanical standalones generally are electric typewriters that are modified by another vendor to include some computerized edit and logic capabilities. In addition, the modified typewriter has an auxiliary magnetic media recorder which allows the operator to store the completed text. This storage recorder is designed for the use of magnetic cards, cassettes, and cartridges.

The keyboard has a dual function. It is used for the initial keyboarding and editing as well as for printing. Many models attained popularity in the early 1970s.

In 1974 an auxiliary attachment was developed that was advertised as having the ability to convert any electric typewriter into a convenient word processor. A buffer memory stored the keyboarded text. Then when the final copy was printed, the information was placed on magnetic cassette tape and retained for storage. Service identity problems originated with this equipment and eventually caused its withdrawal from the market. Because the typewriter and the attachment were products of two different vendors, the problems were never easily resolved.

Other mechanical standalones were the true forerunners of word processing. They, along with their manufacturers, achieved fame in the early creation days of the industry. With a name that was soon shortened to **MTST**, the **Magnetic Tape Selectic Typewriter** was introduced in 1964. The recording medium onto which keystrokes could be stored was unique; it was magnetic. Unlike punched paper tape (used on the automatic repetitive typewriters that were introduced in the 1930s), magnetic tape could be corrected, erased, and reused. The MTST

---

mechanical standalone
electronic typewriter that has edit and logic capabilities

Magnetic Tape Selectric Typewriter (MTST) first electronic typewriter to use magnetic storage media

CHAPTER 4 Output

Magnetic card word processing machines are a type of mechanical standalone.

recorded onto magnetic tape cartridges that were larger than a standard cassette tape.

Shortly thereafter, three magnetic card models were introduced—Mag Card I, Mag Card II, and Mag Card A. The first magnetic card model, **Mag Card I**, captured text on a single magnetic card which could store about one page of text. On these magnetic cards, revisions were limited to changes that could be made within a single line (called a track) on the card. If the changes required using more space on the card than was originally allocated, the text following the changes would be overlaid by the inserts. Thus, the remaining text had to be rekeyed in order to maintain an accurate magnetic copy.

The **Mag Card II** improved this limitation by providing a buffer storage for editing. Once revised, text was transferred to the card and could be printed. The Mag Card II enabled automatic letters to be generated by merging the names and addresses recorded on one card with a letter recorded on the other.

The **Mag Card A** word processor was positioned as a balance between the Mag Card I and the Mag Card II. It had an internal memory into which keyboarded text was placed and manipulated. When final storage was required, the data was transferred to a single magnetic card. The Mag Card A increased the text revisional power of the Mag Card I, but could not perform the dual-card merge capabilities of the Mag Card II. Its cost also was positioned between the two machines; thus, users found the Mag Card A an attractive alternative to the Mag Card II.

Many vendors introduced a mag card word processing model. Though no longer considered state of the art, these types of systems are still used and are reliable. The major drawbacks to these mechanical

Mag Card I stores text on a single magnetic card; revisions limited to one line on the card

Mag Card II provides buffer storage for editing; has dual-card merge capabilities

Mag Card A stores text on a single magnetic card; has better text revision capabilities than Mag Card I

The one-line display on this standalone word processor allows the operator to see the typed line before it is printed.

display standalone allows material to be keyed at the same time that previously keyed material is being printed

standalones are: (1) learning to operate them is difficult; (2) coding the input requires intense concentration; and (3) editing text is difficult without a screen to see the text as it is being changed. Mechanical standalones are best suited for automatic letter writing and other single-page applications.

Display Standalones. Display standalones are popular in the word processing marketplace. Various components make up the system: a keyboard; a screen (video display that shows a full page or partial page); a media drive (called a disk drive if housing floppy diskettes); and a printer. Although some components may be combined in one unit, the printer is always a separate piece of equipment and is connected to the terminal by a cable. The combination of the keyboard and the screen is often called a terminal or a workstation.

On display standalones, text can be keyed, proofread, and edited before being printed. In addition, a new document can be created and manipulated at the terminal as the previous document is being printed. In contrast, electronic typewriters and mechanical standalones (keyboard/printer devices) do not permit keyboarding and printing to occur at the same time. Thus, the operators of those machines have to wait for the machine to print the text, which is nonproductive.

The full or partial display enhances the proofing and formatting functions by allowing the operator to see the document before having it

CHAPTER 4 Output

printed. A full-page screen most commonly displays 54 or 66 lines of text, whereas a partial page is generally limited to 24 lines of text.

The internal or buffer memory of a display standalone system is capable of holding more than a page of text. The capacity of the buffer memory determines the extent of text manipulation and the amount of new text that can be added after a document is filed (recorded).

It is not unusual to find that display standalone printers have limited-line buffer memories. When the command to print is issued from the terminal, only a small portion of the captured text is fed to the printer at a time. The printer is kept busy interacting with the drive until the completed text has emptied into the buffer. The terminal is then free to engage in another task when the printer interaction ceases.

A few exceptions to this printer limitation exist. Larger capacity buffers or free-standing devices (those that have their own logic/intelligence and do not have to depend on the connecting workstation) allow the media to be removed from the disk drive of the workstation and inserted into the printer to provide standalone printing. This situation removes the unproductive nature of waiting for the machine to finish printing.

Disk drives can be either single driven (holding only one diskette) or dual driven (allowing the use of two diskettes). Much more flexibility can be attained for the operator with a dual disk drive. For example, the operator can duplicate from one diskette onto another, perform certain operations more easily than with a single disk drive, and manipulate text more extensively.

There are advantages to using a dual disk drive. Some specific advantages are:

Both of these standalone word processors allow the operator to see a full-page screen of text.

- New or revised text can be keyboarded and merged with previously recorded files. These existing files can be developed on two workstations by two operators working on different parts of the same long document. The entire document can be printed at one workstation.

- Dual disk drives can produce boilerplate documents. **Boilerplate documents** are created by combining address lists and other variables on one diskette with standard text that is stored on another diskette to generate customized form letters. The automatic playback requires little operator intervention. The process of creating boilerplate documents is also known as document assembly or merging text.

> **boilerplate document**
> created by merging information from two separate disks

- Standardized documents that have been recorded on one diskette can be duplicated onto diskettes for other operators to eliminate rekeying the same text.

Other applications in addition to word processing can be performed by obtaining appropriate software diskettes. These diskettes program (instruct) the system to perform other functions. The system then becomes multifunctional. Examples of these application diskettes, which can be purchased in addition to word processing software, are:

- Graphics—a program that provides the user with the ability to make bar charts, line graphs, or pie charts.

- Spread sheet—a program that provides the user with the ability to make columnar calculations such as monthly accountings and budgets.

- Financial modeling—a program that allows the user to input mathematical calculations based on certain sets of circumstances and tables. Some accountants use these programs for calculating tax returns.

- Programming or personal computing—a large variety of diskettes which offer the user training in computer language programming such as BASIC or COBOL.

- Telecommunications—diskettes that provide a means for the user to talk to other computer devices, attach to other systems and use their applications, or to transfer information from their system to another system. These packages require the use of other hardware such as modems or couplers to connect telephone lines to the other systems. These telecommunication devices and their methods are discussed in Chapter 7.

Models which are identified as display standalones and which are sold primarily as word processors are manufactured by many vendors.

CHAPTER 4 Output

Higher priced models usually offer more applications in addition to word processing. Of the various categories of word processors, display standalones are the most popular among businesses and private users. In large cities there are more vendors from which to choose than in small cities. Whether purchased for the home or the office, most standalones can be expanded to provide greater flexibility and compatibility when needed. Display standalones become inappropriate only when the cost of many independent terminals exceeds the ability of the users to share resources or information easily.

Personal Computers. As the private sector became involved with the use of small computers that could be customized (or personalized) by the purchase of various software packages, the small computer became known as the personal computer. The major word processing manufacturers were intrigued by the success of these personal computers and the new marketplace in the private sector. Several word processing manufacturers began competing heavily for a share of this private sector.

personal computer can be customized to users' needs by purchasing software packages

Personal computers are common both in the home and at the office.

The major reason many businesses entered the personal computer market initially may have been to share in the sales of the private sector. A secondary purpose was to maintain a business familiarity with the product when the field began expanding. The strategy was to motivate users to attain a comfort level with personal computers within the privacy of their own homes. At their homes, users could be free from the stigma associated with learning difficulty that is often imposed at the office. With some realization of the personal computer's potential, users began introducing personal computers into the office. The goal was to improve the efficiencies of many office routines by the use of this machine. The strategy worked, and personal computers became popular in offices as well as in homes.

In the early 1980s, the world of personal computers took a giant leap forward. Many vendors entered the market. These vendors, as experts in the word processing field, did much to develop the friendliness and ease of use that has become associated with these models. More so, they were able to incorporate long-term objectives for their personal computers by designing them to be compatible with their existing products as a communication device or as an extension of their more complex office systems. This compatibility allowed private users the flexibility of transporting their personal computers between home and the office. In either place, users could share in the total information processing system.

Until recently, office system terminals were used primarily by specialists in the word processing or data processing areas. Management and/or professional staff had been reluctant to learn to operate what they thought was a complicated tool, and they had not envisioned how the personal computer could serve their needs. Thus, projections about the cost and time savings that could result from automating the office fell on deaf ears. The very people who could benefit most from the new tools were unprepared to use them. The personal computer created an atmosphere of acceptability which minimized these objections and heightened the interest of management use.

Multiterminal Systems

multiterminal word processing system has two or more workstations that share resources

A multiterminal word processing system is a configuration of equipment which includes at least two workstations. In addition, the stations share one or more resources; they cannot "stand alone." Multiterminal systems are designed for large word processing installations that require work files and printers to be shared among many workstations. When sharing occurs, it maximizes the potential use of these devices and minimizes the cost of resource duplication (for example, having a printer for each workstation). Multiterminal systems can be further described as either a shared-logic or a shared resource system.

Multiterminal word processing systems share one or more resources.

Shared-Logic System. Shared-logic systems are quite similar to computer systems maintained for the EDP (electronic data processing) industry. Their similarity begins with the use of a single central processing unit (CPU) that is shared by many terminals. This CPU is the central source for word processing logic (intelligence) and the storage of keystrokes. The CPU, shared by all users, is connected directly to the back of each workstation by cables. Similar to a telephone installation within a building, shared-logic systems have cables that run above ceilings and under floors to their destinations. Shared-logic equipment is able to support from 2 to 30 terminals depending on the manufacturer. Most models limit the distance a terminal can be supported from the CPU; usually this distance does not exceed 2,000 feet.

In addition to housing the logic and storage facilities, the CPU also controls and manages both information and operations. Thus, multiple tasks can occur simultaneously. The "brain" of the system, the CPU, remembers who the user is, what applications can be accessed, and where the user's information is stored. It can reference, control, and manage the information needs of many users. Storage facilities (internal memory and hard disks) do not require daily handling by individual users. Sharing the logic of the CPU among a number of users reduces the desk space requirements of the users to that of a terminal (integral display/keyboard). Printout may be performed while text is being keyed or edited.

Terminals that depend on the CPU for logic are sometimes called **dumb** (or unintelligent) **terminals**. However, there are some terminals that receive a portion of the CPU logic and store it in internal memory. These are then called **smart terminals**. These terminals not only

shared-logic system one CPU is shared by many terminals

dumb terminal depends on CPU for logic

smart terminal stores some logic in memory; does not depend entirely on CPU for logic

share the logic but also share the cost of the entire system with the other keyboard stations. Thus, the average cost of a workstation in a multiterminal system of eight stations (CPU + printers + terminals ÷ number of terminals) would likely be less than that of a standalone system (terminals + printers ÷ number of terminals).

Sharing central logic has both advantages and disadvantages. For instance, a single terminal or printer can be inoperative without noticeably affecting the other users. The user of a faulty terminal can move to a free terminal and continue working. Should a printer be down (not operative), the user can redirect the printing command to another printer on the system. There is no operator downtime when only one peripheral device is inoperative.

However, if problems occur within the CPU or any of the major devices that are commonly shared by users, all user terminals and printers become inoperative. The most common example of this occurrence is a power outage. Often, if a power outage occurs without a timely warning, the system administrator will be unable to **power down** (turn off) the disk drives. In that case, the disk can be damaged and information can be lost. The situation is referred to as a **head crash** or **disk crash**. The read/write head on the disk actually scratches the disk platter, destroying information and losing the ability to reposition itself.

Generally less sophisticated than a system that completely depends on one CPU, a cluster type of shared-logic system appeals to smaller installations. It offers a less expensive approach to sharing the system logic among several smaller circles of users. The clusters are branch CPUs **down loaded** (have some information loaded into memory) with their own intelligence from the main CPU with the added capability of supporting only terminals and printers clustered within a single area. For several small circles of users within the company, the cluster approach may be less expensive than the full-blown shared-logic approach.

power down turn system off

head crash disk read/write head malfunctions and is unable to access information on a disk

down loaded limited information is loaded into a branch CPU's memory

The major advantage of a clustered type of word processing system is its ability to remain independent of the CPU.

CHAPTER 4 Output

One advantage of clusters is their ability to remain independent from the main power source, the CPU. In the event of a major system failure, each cluster can continue operations that support the terminals and printers within its circle for any applications that have been previously loaded into the branch CPU (down loaded). Each cluster user may or may not be able to share any information with other cluster users. Also, cluster users cannot access information that may have been stored on the central disk storage. Thus, the capabilities of clusters are somewhat limited.

A clustered system works well in a company that chooses to start small. However, when that company's needs require sharing with other groups, the cluster can become an expensive and cumbersome system to maintain and upgrade.

Shared Resource System. Shared resource systems offer a single advantage over the shared-logic system: The multiple terminals contain their own logic (intelligence) and processing power. A malfunction of one station will not affect any other station, nor would failure of the main CPU affect any user. The resources that are shared are peripheral devices such as disk storage and/or printers. The concept of shared resource systems was added to the standalone systems to reduce the cost of expansion. Many of the personal computers also support this type of modular upgradability.

It is difficult to quote prices on shared systems because the cost is the grand total of all the devices, including processing power and software applications. Sharing printers reduces the cost per station somewhat, but the cost per station is still similar to that of a standalone system.

Distributed Logic System. Shared systems which have terminals scattered throughout the building, rather than in a centralized environment, are sometimes referred to as being distributed. Specifically, a distributed logic system is a multiterminal system that distributes the logic (computing power) of the central computer to individual workstations. In addition, those workstations share the peripherals, and sometimes the storage facilities, of the central system.

Time-Sharing Word Processors

A number of vendors provide an alternative to user-owned equipment. They make word processing services available on a time-shared basis. These services can be provided two ways; but to use a word processor for time-sharing services, the word processing equipment would need to have the communications feature.

The first method of making word processing services available on a time-shared basis provides the user with coded access into a remote

shared resource system each terminal has its own logic; resources are shared

distributed logic system terminals share the resources of a central computer and are scattered throughout the building—not clustered

time-sharing word processor many users access central computer for word processing through a communications device

computer for on-line use via a telephone network. The user is charged on the basis of a flat access rate and the clock time spent within the process. In addition to these costs paid to the time-sharing supplier, there is the cost for placing the long distance telephone call that initiates the access to the computer. An example of a user would be an attorney who needs to access a national law library facility.

The second method is employed through a continuation of the same company's service to its branch offices located in remote locations. In this situation, corporate headquarters may have a large, sophisticated word processing system and the branch offices may have standalone models. For most applications, a branch office can perform routine word processing operations using its own system. Occasionally the branch office may require more sophisticated or shared applications residing on the large, central office system. In these instances, the offices perform a communication connection that enables the standalone terminal to work off of the large system. All activity can be performed as if the user were actually on-site and operating a local terminal.

Time-shared services are cost effective for companies that cannot afford to buy or lease their own equipment. The amount of work may not justify the expenditure. Or perhaps a specific task cannot be done on the company's own equipment. For example, the user might need to access a large mailing list.

RECORDING/STORAGE MEDIA

Word processing equipment uses a variety of magnetically coated materials for the storage of text and programs. Usually this medium is inserted into a separate device which activates the recording action of the word processor. The **storage capacity** of the media is the total amount of text which may be accessed by the system without changing media. Main types of magnetic media include magnetic cards, cassettes, flexible diskettes, and hard disks.

storage capacity total amount of text that may be accessed by a system without changing media

Magnetic Card

Often called a "mag card," a magnetic card is the size of a computer card and is coated with magnetic material. Between 50 and 100 lines of text and codes can be stored on each card. Each line holds approximately 100 characters (20 standard typing words). Dual-sided cards allow recording on both sides of the card, thus doubling the card storage from 5,000 characters to 10,000 characters of storage.

Cards are inserted into a slot in the console similar to the process of accessing a 24-hour banking terminal. Word processors, such as the Mag Card II, allow a stack of cards to be read by the device with the text being placed into a buffer storage. When the completed text is to be

CHAPTER 4 Output

read onto the media, the cards are again fed into the machine. Upon completion of the task, the cards are dispelled in a lower slot.

Cassette

Some word processors use a magnetic tape that is packaged as a reel-to-reel cassette with a capacity of approximately 40 text pages. These cassettes (called digital cassettes) are similar to those used with other common recording devices such as tape recorders, tape players, and stereos.

cassette reel-to-reel magnetic tape in a plastic case used to record and store data

Flexible Diskette

Flexible diskettes (floppy disks) are the most widely used magnetic medium in the industry. They are used by personal computing equipment dealers, and almost every word processing manufacturer has a model which supports this medium. Flexible diskettes are described as continuously rotating, magnetic-coated Mylar (a type of plastic) disks enclosed in a protective envelope. Their extensive storage capacity and their ability to be handled easily without damage to the contents contribute to their popularity.

flexible diskette magnetic-coated Mylar disk in a protective envelope used to record and store data

There are three basic sizes of flexible diskettes. They are:

- Standard diskette: 8-inch diameter, capacity of approximately 75 text pages (assuming a page contains 4,000 characters, single-spaced)

- Minidiskette: 5 1/4-inch diameter, capacity of approximately 15 to 20 text pages

- Microdiskette: 3 1/2-inch diameter, capacity to store 278,000 characters or 60 pages, enclosed in a plastic case

Storage capacity of a flexible diskette can be increased through the use of a double density diskette, a double sided diskette, or a double density, double sided diskette. A **double density diskette** has a Mylar (or other chemical coating) that is altered in such a way that the diskette can store twice the amount of data as that stored on a single density diskette. A **double sided diskette** simply uses both sides of the diskette for storing data. A **double density, double sided diskette** is a diskette on which twice the amount of data can be stored on both sides of the diskette. It is important to note both the capacity and the cost of the medium itself when evaluating the overall cost of storage requirements.

double density diskette can store twice the data as a regular diskette

double sided diskette both sides used for storage

double density, double sided diskette uses both sides; stores twice the data on each side

Hard Disk

Usually available with large computer-type or shared-logic systems, a hard disk medium is described as a rigid, random-access, high-capacity magnetic storage medium. **Random access** describes the manner in

hard disk rigid, random-access, high-capacity magnetic storage medium

random access text on a disk can be accessed at random

There are many forms of recording/storage media.

serial access text on a disk must be accessed in sequential order

Volume Table of Contents identifies the location of each stored document on a disk

megabyte one million bits of storage

Winchester disk hard disk; allows dense data storage

which text is placed on the disk—in a random order. Random access allows text to be stored and retrieved faster than does **serial access** (text is stored in sequential order, as on tape). The disk contains a table of contents, which identifies the location of each document that has been stored. In many disks, this is called **VTOC—Volume Table of Contents**. The VTOC points to the position where the text can be found. If the VTOC is damaged, the information stored on the disk becomes inaccessible. Though the text will still be there, the pointers are no longer operational. As mentioned earlier, damage to a disk is referred to as a head crash.

Disks may be removable (cartridges), may provide off-line archival storage, or may be nonremovable (fixed). Storage capacity is measured in megabytes. A **megabyte**, usually represented by the symbol Mb immediately following the number, is one million bits of storage. Storage capacities for hard disks range from 1Mb (1 million bits or 250 pages of storage) to well over 300Mb (300 million bits or 750,000 pages of storage) per disk.

The **Winchester disk**, a type of hard disk, is a popular, rigid, nonremovable, magnetic oxide-coated, random access disk. Sealed within a filtered enclosure, the disk and the read/write head of the disk drive are protected from foreign elements and physical handling. Winchester disks allow dense data storage. Of the four basic sizes (5 1/4 inch, 8 inch, 10 1/2 inch, and 14 inch), the most commonly used sizes are the 8-inch and the 14-inch disks. The 5 1/4-inch disk is rapidly gaining popularity, however.

Storage capacities for Winchester disks range from 2.1Mb to 64Mb (325 to 16,000 pages) for the 8-inch disk and 6.5Mb to 635Mb (1,625 to 158,750 pages) for the 14-inch disk. Compared to an 8-inch flexible diskette (which can store only 75 text pages), the Winchester 8-inch disk has a much larger storage capacity.

A head is the small device similar to a phonograph needle that reads or writes the information to the disk. Most heads are wrapped in a magnetic oxide material which enables the head to read and write. The wrapping also strengthens the delicate head as it speeds over the surface of the disk. More recently, disk heads have been developed using a silicon chip that is layered with thin films of magnetic oxide. Their microscopic size allows them to slide 11 millionths of an inch from the surface of the disk. To illustrate how minute this is, the film caused by oil from a fingerprint on a disk will be slightly removed by the flying head. The finer the head that can slide over the disk, the denser the data that can be packed on the disk. In other words, the storage medium can contain more information if the head can write and read the information in smaller areas. A silicon chip provides eight times the data density packing of a wrapped head's disk space. As this method becomes more common, storage costs will decrease accordingly.

Bubble Memory

Bubble memory is a storage technique which uses magnetic fields to create regions of magnetization on a crystal sheet. When information is stored in these regions, small bubbles appear to skim over the surface of the crystal sheet. Each bubble represents digital information (bits).

bubble memory uses magnetic fields to create regions of magnetization in which data is stored

Electromagnetic fields manipulate the (bubble) information past the read/write locations within the memory of the system. This process can be compared to the motion of the read/write heads in either disk or tape storage devices. Bubble devices are very tiny, and the information stored within them remains intact when there is a power loss. Because the bubble devices remain intact, they are considered to be **nonvolatile**. The small size and reliability of bubble devices offer an attractive storage possibility for many terminal devices.

nonvolatile stored information is not lost in the event of a power loss

Optical (Laser) Disk

A laser storage technology called optical disk storage is being developed. In this technology, a laser beam scans the information and then lays the image onto the disk platter. The optical disk is a **"read only" storage**. This means that the disk surface cannot be reused or written over. The disk is designed to hold massive amounts of information beginning at storage levels of 4 **gigabytes**. (1 gigabyte, 1Gb, is 1 billion bits of storage, whereas 1Mb is 1 million bits of storage.) An example of a user might be the U.S. government. The government needs a great deal of storage capacity for tax returns and other paper-intensive records.

optical disk laser beam scans the information and lays the image onto a disk

read only storage cannot be reused or written over

gigabyte one billion bits of storage

Optical disks have several advantages. These advantages are: (1) they are small, taking up less physical room than magnetic disk drives; (2) they are more accurate and more reliable than other storage media since they have fewer mechanical parts; and (3) the laser can pack more information in less space than can other disk heads. The main disadvantage, however, is that the cost of the optical disk is extremely high.

PRINTING DEVICES

The variety of printing devices used for word processing can be put into two main categories of printers. All types of printers fit into one of these two categories: impact or nonimpact.

✕ Impact Printer

An impact printer is one that generates characters by stamping or inking an impression through a ribbon with a character slug, element, or hammer needle. The most commonly used impact printers use type balls, daisy wheels, or thimbles as printing devices.

Type Ball. Printers with ball-shaped elements have proven to be the most reliable and durable printers intended for the heavy-duty output demanded by word processing operations. These printers usually can attain output speeds of 150-180 wam (words a minute), which is about 15 cps (characters per second). The ball-shaped element (sometimes referred to as the "golfball") contains 88 characters. It rotates to the position of the proper character, impacts against the ribbon, and forms that character image on the paper.

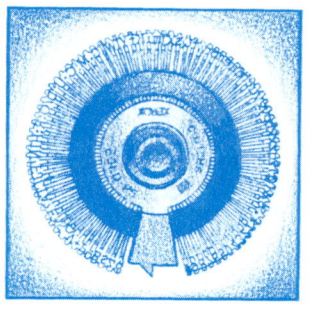

Daisy Wheel. Daisy wheel printers use three-inch wheels which have up to 96 print characters extended on the outer edge of the wheel in a petal fashion, hence the name daisy wheel. Some printwheels have two rows of 96 characters, for a total of 192 characters. The wheel can be made of a plastic or metal substance. Once rotated to position, the character impacts against the ribbon and leaves an impression. Daisy wheel printers operate more quietly and at faster rates than do single-element printers. Printing rates generally vary from 30 to 55 cps (or 360 to 669 wam); the highest rate is 75 cps. The costs of the wheels differ with the material used in the design. The plastic wheels are less expensive, but also less durable, than the metal ones.

Thimble. A thimble element also receives its name from its appearance. It is a small, thumb-sized device containing a 128-character set, which can be obtained in three sizes— 10 pitch, 12 pitch, or proportional spacing. The product was developed in Japan but is used quite commonly on many American-made printers. Printing speeds vary from 30 to 55 cps (or 360 to 669 wam), similar to those of the daisy wheel printer.

Dot Matrix Printer. Dot matrix printers can, from all outward appearances, resemble a conventional impact printer. It is only when one removes the print head that the unique mechanism is detected. The print head is a series of fine pins—18 or 32 pins in total, depending upon the manufacturer. The pins are arranged in a matrix fashion and impact the paper through a ribbon. Each printed character is developed through the series of different pin positionings. The pin positioning is controlled by programmed instructions within the system. The print head is suitable for many different character sets (sizes and type styles) and is limited to the programmable instructions available. It is possible for a system to have eight or more type styles available for an operator to use. The dot matrix printer is quite versatile (has many print styles), is easy to use (the operator simply requests the desired style in a print request), and does not require the operator to change the print head to access other type styles.

dot matrix printer strategically places dots to form specific characters

Dot matrix printers are used in both draft-quality and letter-quality applications. The print quality is dependent upon the number of sweeps the print mechanism makes across a single line. A single sweep produces draft-quality print, whereas repeated sweeps clarify the dot images and can produce an acceptable letter-quality print. Letter-quality print speeds are usually between 40 and 60 cps, while draft-quality speeds are must faster—between 160 and 192 cps. The speed varies depending upon which type size is being used. The larger the type size (10 pitch), the slower the print speed. The smaller the type size (15 pitch), the faster the print speed.

Print heads for the dot matrix printer are very long lived. Replacement is required only when the pins become damaged. In contrast, printing elements can be changed by the operator as frequently as needed. Different elements are kept on hand for different type sizes (10 pitch, 12 pitch, 15 pitch, or proportional spacing) and/or different type styles (italic, letter gothic, prestige elite, etc.). When the operator needs to print in a different style, the front cover of the printer is opened, the ribbon is removed to expose the print shaft, the element is released, and a new element is replaced. The ribbon is again reinserted, the cover is closed, and the printer is readied for printing. Replacement of elements is an easy process.

Other Impact Printers. Other common impact printers used primarily for fast, uppercase output include band printers, chain printers, cylinder printers, drum printers, element printers, and dot matrix printers. These types of printers are equipped with a programmable read-only (PROM) chip, which controls the character sequence. A **PROM chip** is a small computer chip placed within a machine that contains preprogrammed operating instructions.

PROM chip contains programmed operating instructions

94   PART TWO   Information Processing Cycle

Right: A laser printer is a high-speed nonimpact printer.
Below Left: A telecopier is a type of facsimile.
Below Right: The printing element of an impact printer is easy to replace.

Computer dot matrix printers have only four small pins which strike the ribbon to form the pattern of the characters. Chain printers have electromagnetically activated print hammers that push a small area of the form against the ribbon for each printed character. Often this output is generated by the system itself; thus, the characters are not created by keystrokes.

Most of these printers have extraordinary output speeds. For example, the speed of a dot matrix printer may be 50 to 600 cps (600 to 7,200 wam). Chain printers have speeds that range from 600 to 2,250 lpm (lines per minute). These printers are used primarily for data processing applications or rough-draft word processing output. However, they lack the high-quality correspondence output of the ball-shaped element or the daisy wheel printers. Thus, in word processing operations where letter-quality output is required, one rarely finds these types of high-speed impact printers used on a regular basis.

Nonimpact Printers

Nonimpact printers were first introduced in 1976. Unlike the impact printers, the nonimpact printers form images onto paper without impact or ribbon. The shapes of the characters are stored in the system memory and are released by a special imaging mechanism onto the paper itself.

nonimpact printer forms images without impact or a ribbon; shapes of characters are stored in the system memory

Compared to impact printers that offer high-quality legibility, nonimpact printers cannot duplicate this quality output. However, the system memory in a nonimpact printer is not limited by actual character slugs on an element. (An exception to this is the dot matrix printer discussed earlier.) Thus, it is able to store and produce a greater variety of print styles and fonts than can an impact printer. Because the print heads do not need to be repositioned each time a different character is required, they lend themselves to high-speed printing. Nonimpact printers offer average correspondence quality as well as high-speed output. They can achieve rates of 1,200 to 1,500 wam (92 to 184 cps) or better. By 1980 the output speeds of newer models had doubled the output speeds of the first models.

Two nonimpact technologies are currently being offered: ink jet and electrostatic printers. Each of these technologies was developed by a manufacturer other than the word processing vendor that marketed the product and coined the name. Since then, many vendors have offered a nonimpact printer using laser technology—another kind of electrostatic process.

Ink Jet Printer. In the ink jet technology, characters can be produced in one of two ways: as solid characters or as a pattern of strategically placed dots arranged to form the shape of specific characters (dot matrix printing). The ink jet printer does not use ribbons but actually sprays the ink onto the paper into a dot matrix format. The basic process

ink jet printer ink is sprayed onto paper in a dot matrix format to form characters

of creating characters includes translating digital character data into character dot patterns or into a digital bit code, which drives the imaging device. The printers read the bit codes in the data stream of the word processor from either (1) a removable diskette or card or (2) a buffer storage, called read only memory that resides within the system. **Read only memory (ROM)** is a solid-state memory for programs that is inflexible and cannot be altered.

> **read only memory** contains instructions that can never be altered

The characters are created as a series of dots laid down in curves and straight lines. The output quality of each printer depends on the number of dot positions available in the character matrix, the size of the dots, and the pattern in which the dots are arranged. The quality of the printout is similar to that of typewriter print.

The print mechanism is sensitive to handling and requires protection from the elements, so the printer has been designed as a free-standing unit. Since it had to be built larger for more durability, time-saving features (such as paper and envelope feeding and stacking) were added.

Electrostatic printer. Electrostatic printing equipment looks more like photocopiers than typewriters. The finished output is no longer an actual "printed" document. The process that places text onto the paper is produced by a light source and reproduced much like a copier method. This process is called **photoconductivity**. The light sources used in these instances are either lasers or CRTs (cathode-ray tubes). Images are generated on the surface of the photoconductor by dot patterns, which are produced according to coded instructions in the form of light signals. The signals control the light source by switching it on and off to form the coded characters.

> **electrostatic printer** uses a light source and static charges to form an image

> **photoconductivity** the process that electrostatic printers use to form images

There are different methods of producing an image electrostatically. In a laser configuration, the beam is stationary and is directed across the surface of the photoconductor by a rotating surface of mirrors, as shown in Figure 4-1. Each scan of the laser produces a line of dots, and the process continues until an entire page has been imaged. The second method creates images through fiber optics with each fiber representing one dot. The light in this method emanates from a CRT, and the process continues much like the laser method.

Electrostatically charged images are also formed when toner particles of an opposite charge are attracted to the image areas and cling to the surface of the belt or drum. The drum transfers the image to plain paper, and it is fused with heat or pressure to produce the printed result.

The advantages of these electrostatic processes include high output speed, the ability to use plain, inexpensive paper, and the availability of a variety of type styles and graphics. Also, every copy produced is an original. The major disadvantages of electrostatic processes include the relatively high costs for the equipment, the frequent maintenance, and the supplies.

CHAPTER 4 Output

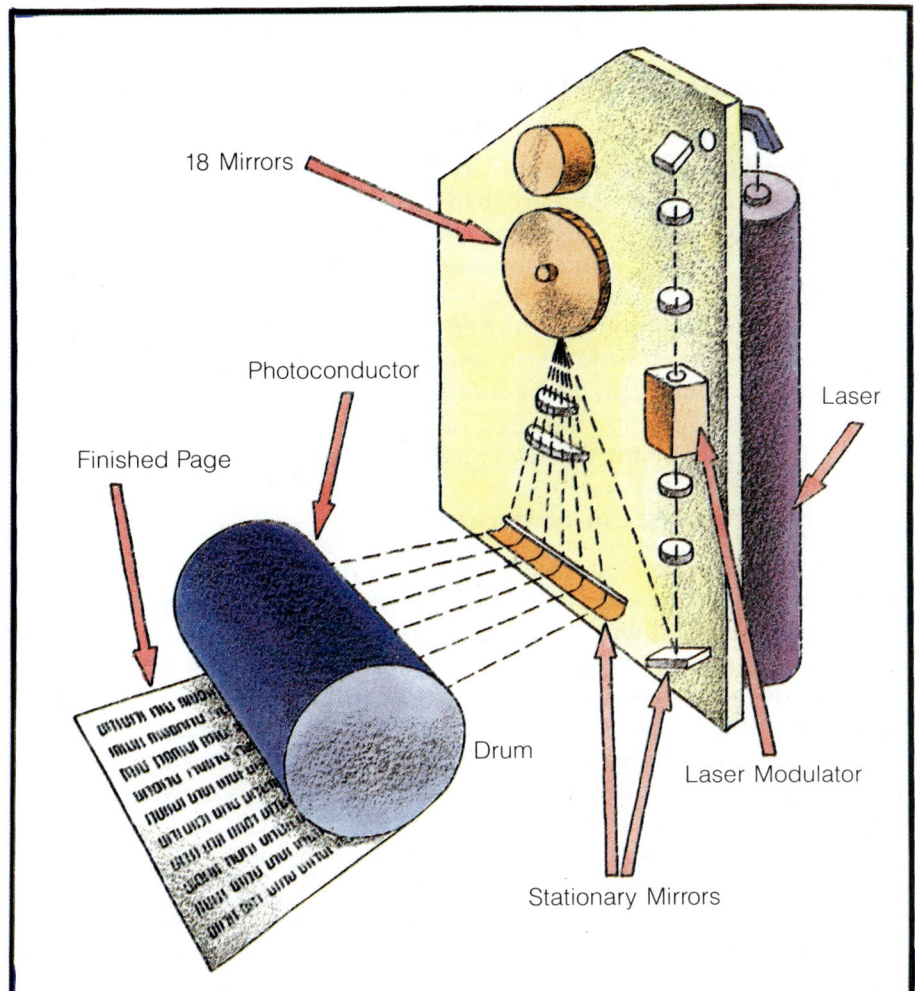

FIG. 4-1
LASER PRINTER
An image is produced by a laser printer when a rotating surface of mirrors directs the laser beam across the surface of the photoconductor.

SOFTWARE

Until now, the discussion in this chapter has been on the **hardware** of word processing equipment—the terminals, the CPU, the disk drives, and the printers. These components can be easily touched, felt, and seen. With electronic equipment, the hardware is only the window dressing. A better measure of the value of the equipment resides within the software that guides the physical operations. **Software** is commonly referred to as a program or as written instructions. There are two distinctive types of software which drive all electronic equipment: the

hardware   actual equipment that makes up a system

software   instructions used to run the hardware

operating system software and the applications software. Neither one can function effectively without the other.

Applications Software

applications software programs provided by vendor designed to perform specific tasks for users

Programs provided by the vendor, which allow users to perform tasks without having to write the programs themselves, are called applications software. The software can have standard programming languages such as BASIC, COBOL, or FORTRAN, yet can be tailored to run only on the operating system for which it was designed. For example, a BASIC application package written for the MS/DOS operating system might not be understood by another operating system device. Additionally, should the user require an applications software that runs word processing, graphics, spreadsheet (the financial "what if" programs), or other business packages, the user needs to ensure that the package is designed specifically for the user's equipment.

Operating System Software

operating system software engages equipment to accept instructions of applications software

Operating system software is commonly referred to as the instructions that command the various electronic parts of the equipment to function in a certain way. It can be unique to the equipment manufacturer, and usually is, in the cases of specialized word processing equipment vendors. Since compatibility between equipment plays such an important role in determining how applications software can be used between equipment, many personal computers use one of several popular packages in their design. Two common systems are the MS/DOS (Microsoft Disk Operating System) and CP/M 80 (Control Program for Microcomputers). The operating systems' acronyms usually reflect the names of the software manufacturers.

The operating system software engages the different mechanisms of the device to accept the instructions of the applications software. Working together, the two programs provide the specific results the operator desires. For example, the main operating part of an automobile is the engine, which powers all other mechanical parts. Yet the car would not operate without the driver, who provides the instructions for actual operation. In our example, the *hardware* is the physical part of the car; the way by which the engine directs parts to interact with each other is the *operating system software*; and the manner in which the car moves or operates is the *applications software* provided by the driver. It follows, then, that the *media* used to enhance these operations are the gas, water, oil, and lubrication.

Operating system software packages are included with the equipment when one purchases a system, but the applications software is a separate purchase made by the user to fill individual needs. Although it is routine for a user to purchase a new applications package after the

equipment purchase, it is quite rare for that user to change the operating system software. On the other hand, it is common for users to upgrade their system software to support other more sophisticated application programs. When operating system software is upgraded, a physical change in the electronic equipment is made. Usually this involves adding a new board or electronic circuit. Applications software is added to equipment simply by loading the disk/diskette into the disk drive; no physical change is made to the equipment.

Software plays an important part of the equipment selection process. The company should perform a thorough investigation of the different software programs available with the equipment in order to determine how the equipment will satisfy the company's needs. The selection of equipment with limited software will lessen the long-term effectiveness of the equipment and discourage user involvement.

After reading this chapter, you should be able to identify various categories of word processing equipment and determine how those categories could fit specific environments. You should become familiar with the media that capture the keystrokes, recognize the variety of devices that are available with each system that can print captured text, and understand the basics of the software that operate the different systems.

DISCUSSION QUESTIONS AND CASE PROBLEM

DISCUSSION QUESTIONS

1. Explain the basic differences among the three categories of word processing equipment.
2. Identify two ways that time-sharing may be configured.
3. Name three varieties of storage media. Indicate the differences in storage capacity of each type.
4. Describe the basic differences between impact and nonimpact printers.
5. Point out the differences between operating system software and applications software.

CASE PROBLEM

Isabel Morales is a salesperson for WPS Information Systems. This company manufactures a wide variety of word processing systems. One morning while she was planning her daily activity list, Isabel received a phone call from the office manager of a company in her territory. The office manager wanted to purchase a word processing system and requested cost and delivery information. Isabel was unfamiliar with the company but wanted to place an order that provided the customer with the best and most satisfying system for the company's needs.

1 What additional information does Isabel need before she can provide answers to the office manager's questions?
2 List a series of questions that Isabel should ask the office manager.
3 Next to each question, indicate the impact that the answer would have on equipment selection.

Chapter 5 Reproducing Text

CHAPTER OBJECTIVES:

Identify the four basic options for reproducing text in business offices.

Distinguish between the use of in-house typesetting and commercial printing services.

Describe four main factors to consider in selecting a reproduction option.

Select the appropriate reproduction device or option according to the circumstances given.

Companies and individuals have numerous ways to obtain copies of printed material. In this chapter, you will learn about the four most practiced methods of reproducing text. Moreover, you will discover the circumstances under which these different options are selected.

After a document has been produced on a word processor, but prior to its distribution, the document may need to be reproduced. **Reprographics** is the name assigned to the reproduction or duplication of documents. The documents might contain typed text, handwriting, graphs, or pictures. This process may be performed by photocopiers, offset duplicators or printers, phototypesetters, or commercial printers. The complete reprographic process also includes the collating and the binding of the finished product. This chapter reviews the products or processes available for reproduction as applied to the finished word processing product.

reprographics duplicating documents

OPTIONS AVAILABLE FOR REPRODUCTION

In looking at the options available for the reproduction of a word processing document, one must first examine the purpose of its creation and weigh that against its intended audience. Consider, for example, a document that both informs and suggests improvement. If its distribution is to remain within the company as an internal information source, the word processing printer output could be acceptable for copying. However, if the document is intended to influence company management to change a policy, perhaps a more attractive printing layout could stimulate a responsive action. Additionally, if that document were to be distributed to customers or to other outside contacts, the need for an impressive printed layout becomes increasingly important in order for the company to convey the best possible image. One needs to know, then, not only the value of the document and its contents but also the kind of results that are anticipated by its reading in order to make good reproduction decisions.

As you learn about the four methods of reproduction, try to distinguish how each process can most appropriately fit a document's purpose and its audience. These four methods are photocopying, offset duplication, phototypesetting, and commercial printing.

Photocopying

Copiers play an important role in nearly every business office. They have become so commonplace that many are referred to as "convenience copiers." Copiers appear in convenient public places such as banks, shopping centers, and libraries. Some are coin-operated for private individual use. Many copiers have been offered at such low prices that it is not unusual for the consumer to purchase them for home use.

Prior to the development of the xerographic process in 1937, it was uncommon to have multiple document distribution lists. Today it is common practice. An article by Donald P. Haspel indicated that each day American offices generate 600 million pages of computer printouts, 234 million photocopies, and 76 million letters. The article suggested that this amounts to about 45 pages of new paper for each individual each day—an overwhelming amount of information that is not only difficult to absorb but also expensive for companies to maintain.[1]

Locating convenience copiers close to users and providing copiers that operate at high speeds causes copy waste problems for businesses. Copying expands to the capacity of the equipment. Many users are guilty of making more copies than needed, copying items to see how

---

[1]Donald P. Haspel, "Feeding the 'Office of the Future'," *A Guide to Office Automation*, published by the International Information/Word Processing Association (June, 1982), p. 127.

they appear copied, copying personal items, or simply wasting time while standing in line waiting to use the copier. Though these practices are not deliberate, they are costly. The misuse of photocopiers is an example of modern technology increasing production levels but diminishing productivity.

Plain-paper copiers are the most popular of the four categories of copiers.

There are four categories of copiers used in businesses. The first two categories are the thermal and dual-spectrum copiers, which are used primarily by companies which have low-volume copying requirements. The two most popular copying methods employ the electrostatic process that was described in Chapter 4. This process uses either plain or coated paper. Plain-paper copiers are becoming more popular each year, and are far outdistancing their nearest competitor, the coated-paper copiers.

Thermal Copier. Thermal copiers operate by exposing infrared-sensitive paper to radiation. The original document and the special copy set

thermal copier exposes infrared-sensitive paper to radiation; heated areas darken special paper to form images

are inserted into the machine face-to-face. The image areas of the original document absorb the light and convert it to heat. The heated areas then darken the specially coated paper to form an image.

These machines are relatively inexpensive and require little maintenance. However, there are disadvantages: (1) the copying process is extremely slow; (2) the special paper is expensive; (3) each piece of paper requires individualized handling; (4) the paper turns brown and becomes brittle with age; (5) the images fade with age; and (6) the machines copy only metallic-based inks. Various characters made with nonmetallic inks will not be reproduced by a thermal copier.

Dual-Spectrum Copier. Dual-spectrum copiers also require a labor-intensive paper handling process. In this process, the image from the original document is produced onto the first sensitive paper and then transferred onto the second copy paper via a heat method. Although in a few machines the paper handling process is automatic, most often it is the user who manually assembles the different form sets.

dual-spectrum copier
image is produced on one sheet of paper and transferred to a second sheet by a heat method

Coated-Paper Copier. Coated-paper copiers use a special zinc oxide charge-sensitive paper in producing their images. They use an electrostatic process in which light is focused on the original document to form reflective positive/negative images. An electric charge is then applied to the copy paper. This magnetizes the images, which are then reproduced through heat or pressure. Finally, a dry or liquid toner is added for image development. The coated paper can be marked easily but cannot be reused. Thus, two-sided copies are not possible with this process. In addition, the paper has an unusual slippery texture, is very white, and is quite costly as compared to plain paper.

coated-paper copier
electrostatic process; uses special charge-sensitive paper to produce images

Plain-Paper Copier. Plain-paper copiers also use the electrostatic process for imaging. Instead of using specially coated paper, the machine forms the image on a rotating drum or belt and then transfers it onto plain paper for the toning process. Because the mechanism is more complex than that of coated-paper copiers, service and maintenance are required more often. Machine repair often requires replacement of parts. However, the expense of equipment maintenance is offset somewhat by the ease of operating the plain-paper copier. Since the paper itself is not subjected to the charging process, it can be reused in a two-sided copy process.

plain-paper copier
electrostatic process; forms images on a rotating drum or belt and transfers them to plain paper

Fiber Optics Copier. There are several manufacturers successfully producing compact convenience copiers which use a light rod technique called fiber optics. The medical and telecommunications industries have been performing practical experiments with this technology for several years. Replacing heavy cabling with lightweight glass or plastic

fiber optics copier a compact convenience copier that uses a light rod technique to form images

hair-like filaments that are not affected by electrical storms, echoing, or static has greatly improved the reliability and quality of transmissions. In the copier industry, the use of fiber optics reduces the need for many of the conventional copier's movable parts. Because these copiers have fewer movable parts, they are compact in size, require less upkeep and maintenance, and cost less to purchase.

Intelligent Copier/Printer. Creating images by programmed instructions or copying from an original can be performed by printers or copiers. However, an intelligent copier/printer (IC/P) can create images from many sources either as a printer or as a copier. An IC/P is called intelligent because it contains microprocessors that automate many of its functions. It can produce single copies of text from instructions transmitted by computers, word processors, magnetic media, and through communications lines from distant IC/Ps or word processors. In addition, the IC/P can be used as a convenience copier; creating copies from originals or reproducing multiple copies from a single instruction. An IC/P usually is configured to include enlargement and reduction options, two-sided printing cost efficiencies, and time-saving collating and stapling functions.

Offset Duplication

offset duplication uses an intermediate to produce images

Offset duplication is a duplicating technique that uses an intermediate medium to produce images. The copy/duplicating system processes are geared toward the high-volume reprographics market. These systems are generally used when there is a need for large quantities of output with each copy being of perfect quality. Related paper-handling functions (such as collating, sorting, and binding) are generally included in a reprographic system. Some common examples of duplicated and bound documents are training manuals, product reports, and curriculum booklets. The roller ink system of an offset duplicator is illustrated in Figure 5-1.

Duplicators are frequently used in businesses or departments requiring high volumes—500,000 to over a million copies each month. These high-volume figures contrast with the low- to medium-volume output of copiers producing 50,000 to 150,000 copies each month. There are three types of technology used in duplicating—offset lithography, direct lithography, and electrostatic copying.

offset lithography images made from a plate, to an intermediate, and to the page

Offset Lithography. This is a process in which impressions are made "offset" from a plate to an intermediate and then to a page. Offset lithography requires an operator to perform a series of steps. These steps fall into three processes. The first process involves the development of the plate. The operator exposes the original document in a platemaker, processes the exposed plate, etches the plate, and then mounts it on the

CHAPTER 5 Reproducing Text

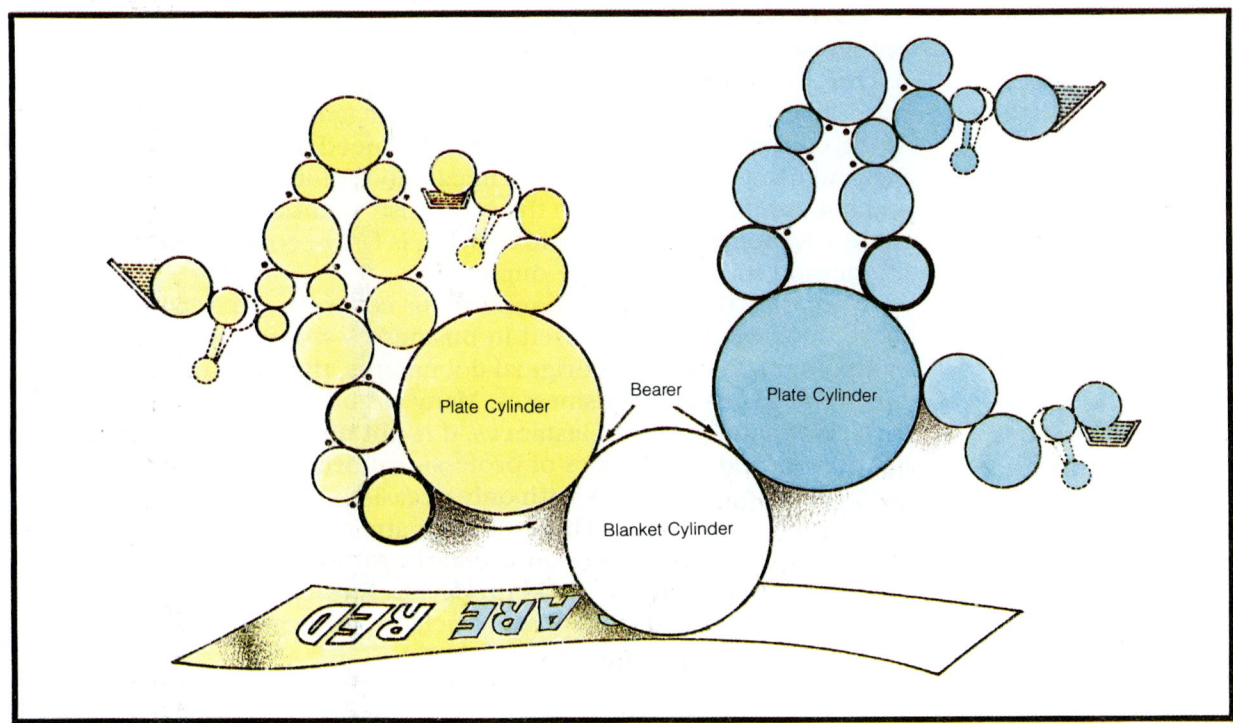

FIG. 5-1
OFFSET DUPLICATOR
In this offset duplicator, two colors of ink are offset from the plate cylinders to the blanket cylinder (intermediate) and then onto the paper to form an image. (Artwork Courtesy of Multigraphics)

duplicator's cylinder. The second process is the actual operation of the duplicator which produces the copies. The third process is the "cleanup." The operator disposes of the plate and cleans the duplicator for the next job.

Most of these steps can be performed automatically by the copy/duplicator with the exception of feeding the original document and selecting the number of copies desired. Some operations use an automatic feeder or sorter, which reduces operator intervention.

Direct Lithography. Direct lithography is a two-cylinder system which images the copy paper directly from the plate cylinder. Compared to offset lithography, it is a more automated method of lithography. Direct lithography also contains an on-line platemaker and features automatic plate mounting. Both lithographic systems require skilled maintenance and an experienced key operator. The lifetime of an on-line plate in the direct method is approximately 1,000 impressions. In contrast, the offset method provides the option of using metal plates produced off-line. The life of a metal plate and its copy range exceed that of the direct platemaker.

direct lithography a process which images the paper between a plate cylinder and an impression cylinder

electrostatic copying uses statically charged particles to form an image

Electrostatic Copying. This copy method uses all of the techniques previously described in the process of a statically charged photoconductor. The reflected image of the original document is converted into a static charge that is used to attract toner-imaging material to the surface of the copying paper. This eliminates the need for platemaking, mounting, and using the associated chemicals and solutions. Cleanup is simple and not as messy as it is with the previously mentioned methods. Due to these advantages, electrostatic copying is fast becoming the most popular method for high-volume duplication.

Although this chapter confines its coverage on reproduction to those devices commonly used in businesses wherein word processing equipment produces the original documents, there are other reproduction methods used by businesses. Many sizable businesses employ their own print shop. In these instances, it is not unusual to find offset printing presses and other types of professional printing equipment. In contrast, there are small firms with only occasional needs that still use spirit and stencil duplicators. These devices attained popularity many years ago, especially in churches and schools. Although still functional, they are rarely offered on the market today. Regardless of which duplicating method is selected, the purpose of each is to achieve the highest volume of production with the greatest speed.

Phototypesetting

In-house typesetting is becoming more and more practical as well as economical. As mentioned in Chapter 1, in-house typesetting is printing that is done within the company, rather than by an outside vendor. Either operating independently or interfaced with a word processing system, the typesetter can produce professional-looking documents. Reports, proposals, newsletters, and forms can be reproduced without the company incurring the time and expense of an outside vendor.

first-generation typesetting mechanical typesetting; mechanized the manual process

First-Generation Typesetting. Mechanical typesetting equipment originated with the Linotype machine that was developed in 1885 by Ottmar Mergenthaler. Prior to the development of this equipment, all typesetting was a manual operation. This new process mechanized the manual methods of pouring molten lead into type slugs and then casting the slugs onto a line of type. Mechanical typesetting came to be known as **hot type casting.**

Two factors influenced the development of photographic techniques. The first was the noise and heat associated with the hot operation. The second was the introduction of platemaking by lithographic processes to which the hot lead operation could not adapt.

second-generation typesetting electromechanical typesetting; uses movable optics assemblies and flash lamps

Second-Generation Typesetting. The second-generation typesetters compose text on film through the use of movable optic assemblies and

CHAPTER 5 Reproducing Text 109

Right: Due to technological advances, the fluid duplicator is not used nearly so much as it once was.

Below: Plain-paper convenience copiers are now dominating the market.

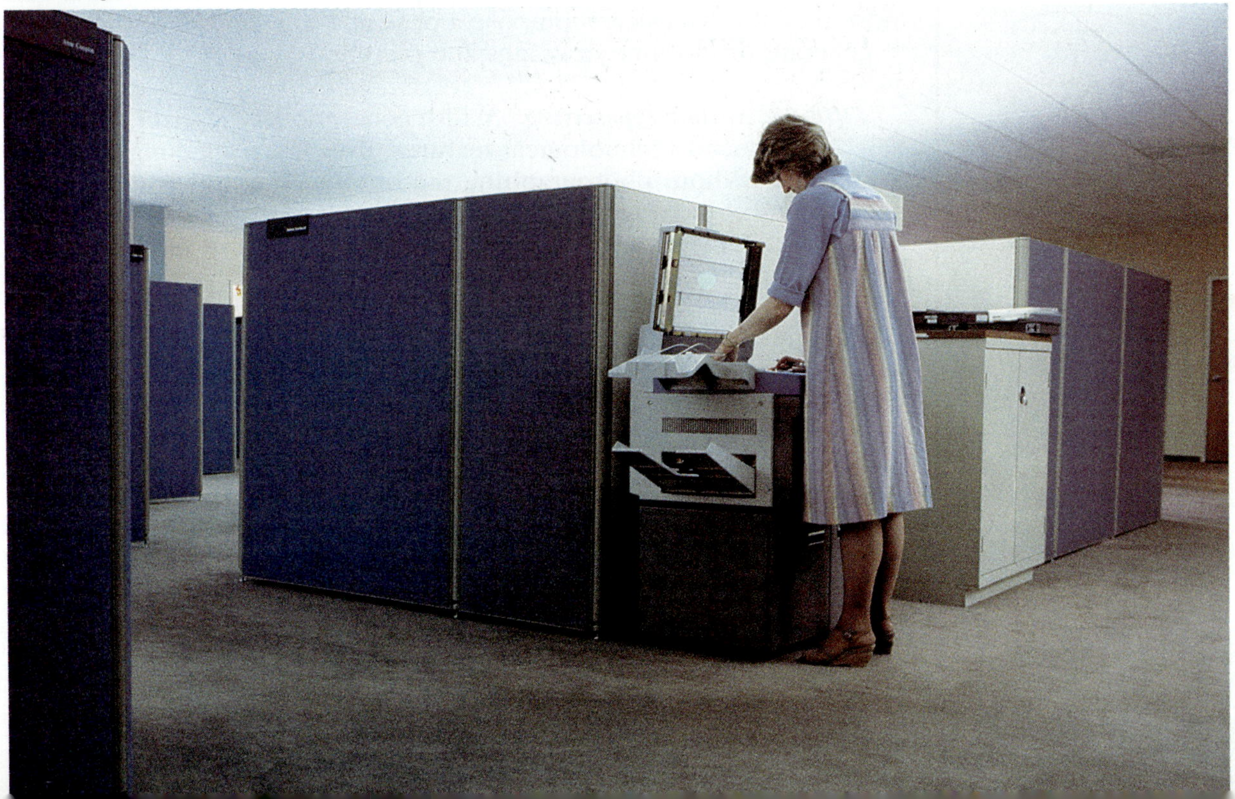

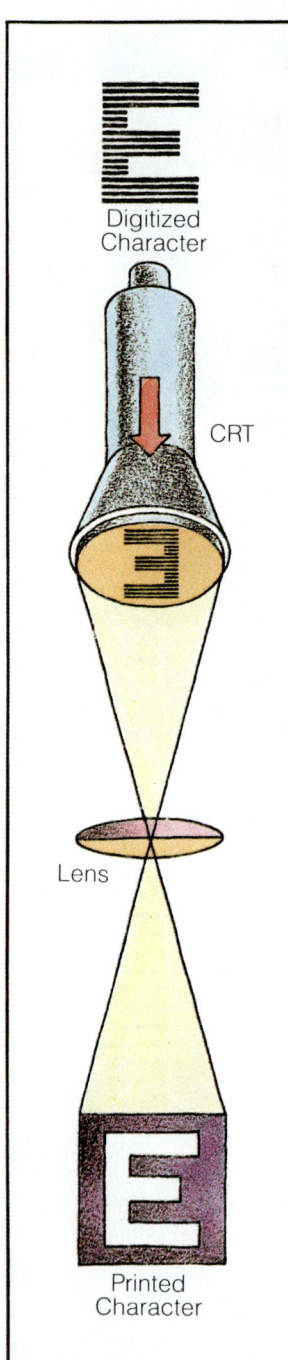

flash lamps. The character is exposed onto the photographic material by the pulses of light reflected by mirrors or passing through a prism. The size of the reproduced image is determined by the lens power and the master matrix format. Some typesetters may have predetermined master matrixes but can make a variety of type sizes through the use of multiple lens turrets. The lenses must move back and forth slowly. Optics can produce a wider or narrower character. The equipment has many moving parts, which add complexity to maintenance and service. These electromechanical devices often contain internal logic (programmed software) to perform their typesetting functions.

Third-Generation Typesetting. The third-generation typesetters are electronic and generate characters via internal logic within the CRT display terminals. Electromechanical devices have a difficult time competing with the rapid speed of an electronic device—often, 10 to 20 times faster. They offer the ultimate in speed and capabilities but are also higher priced.

Fourth-Generation Typesetting. Fourth-generation devices use laser scanning to interpret character size and to generate images. The laser process is known as digitized typesetting, for it reproduces type by means of digital mathematical information stored on a computer hard disk. It produces the image by painting the character on the photographic material. With fewer moving parts and no lenses, the laser typesetter is faster than the third-generation typesetter. The print is finer and the gray areas inherent with the photographic process are eliminated. The more recent devices can compose a page at a time and have the ability to generate or plot line drawings and pictures.

Fifth-Generation Typesetting. A fifth-generation typesetter, with the help of advanced technological features, uses laser scanning and digitized fonts without photographing the output. The unit is more compact, has fewer moving parts, and thus, is easier to maintain and operate.

Typeset copy is less expensive than typewritten copy because it uses less space. In fact, one typeset page can contain two typewritten pages of information as shown in Figure 5-2. Thus, it reduces the cost of paper, printing, and storage.

Typesetting can provide a finished copy with justified, flush-left and -right lines of text, proportionately (differentially) spaced characters, and various point sizes and type styles on the same line or page. In-house typesetting allows for a more flexible turnaround schedule. Since all jobs processed are company-requested, priorities can be established and modified based on the changing needs of the business. Customer conflict that exists in outside services is replaced by negotiable employee deadlines. Typeset copy is often easier to read than typewritten copy.

CHAPTER 5 Reproducing Text

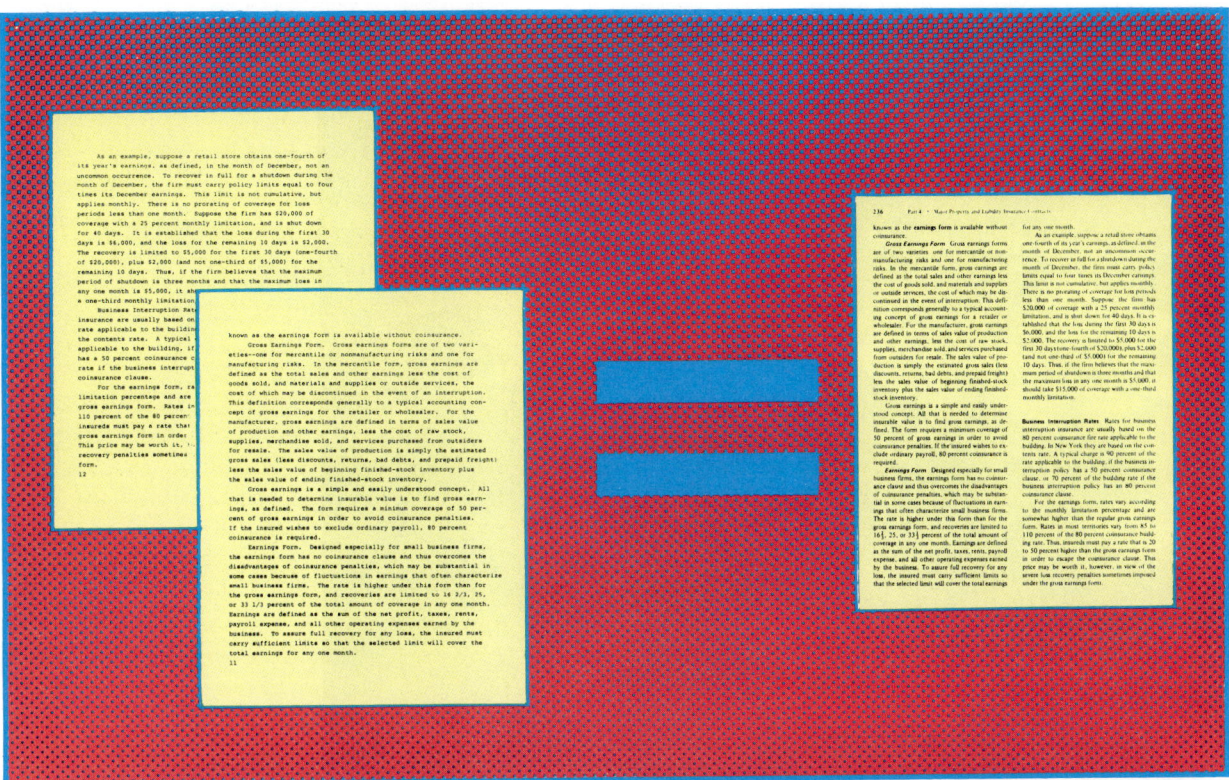

FIG. 5-2
TYPESET VERSUS TYPEWRITTEN PAGE
The use of typeset material reduces costs because less paper and less storage space are required.

Input to typesetters may come from keyboard media, such as floppy diskettes or tape cassettes. Occasionally punched paper tape is still used. Computers can generate source input through magnetic tape media or specially marked printed tape. Input can be directly keyboarded, or word processors can serve as a keyboarding means for preparing typesetting input. Some typesetting models input the magnetic media that were originally keyboarded on a word processor. Linked with word processors by way of a communication interface, typesetters can accept input directly from word processors.

Commercial Printing

There are certain advantages to using outside typesetting services. The costs of equipment, salaries, space, and supplies are not incurred because only a limited amount of equipment is required in the office. No activity downtime is experienced because of system failures; therefore, deadlines can be met. Without on-site equipment, the problem of equipment obsolescence due to technological advances is avoided. When a company uses outside typesetting services, it has no need to hire and

commercial printing
done outside a company

In-house typesetting is a viable option for larger firms.

train skilled operators. This is an advantage because competition for qualified typesetters is quite high in the business marketplace.

Outside services need only limited information from users—usually a rough draft idea of the finished product. The service is very helpful in providing suggestions for type styles, sizes, and general art layouts. Users should, however, proof the composed copy for final approval. Commercial printing establishments normally have expensive and sophisticated equipment that is capable of producing highly specialized work. These establishments use color, type styles, and layouts for the ultimate in professional quality. Outside vendors can provide excellent visuals as well as typeset copy for magazines, brochures, and books.

The use of a commercial printer also has some disadvantages. Because printing is done totally outside a user's facility, security and control of the work are not possible. All materials to leave an in-house facility must be copied for reference. Thorough instructions about the desired end product must be written for the printer. Also, the work must be transported to and from the printer.

Specialty work is generally very costly. However, it would be more costly and inefficient for an in-house operation to include little-used and seldom-requested specialty items. One way to decide whether to install an in-house typesetting operation rather than to use outside services would be to review the annual monies spent on the process. A good rule of thumb is this: When the costs of outside services approach what could be spent on purchasing, staffing, and equipping a system, then in-house printing becomes a viable consideration.

FACTORS TO CONSIDER IN SELECTING THE OPTION

Reprographics as an office function is quickly reaching maturity. Reprographic equipment presently offered on the market is being enhanced by the speed and scope of document communications and records management. Each year vendors are offering an increasing number of reproduction devices for different volumes and different applications. Although some copiers are able to reproduce color, the user pays a considerable cost for the luxury. Becoming more commonplace are dry toner, plain-paper copiers that offer the user a choice of black or brown color reproductions as well as reductions and enlargements of the original document.

Just as the numbers and types of equipment multiply, so does the complexity of the selection for the business user. As a result, the practical choice of a new machine requires careful analysis. A machine which is equipped with features that are not used can increase the storage, maintenance, and handling costs (overhead) of the company. On the other hand, a reproduction device that is inadequate for the needs of a company's jobs reduces office productivity and causes unnecessary user dissatisfaction. Users must consider their needs carefully, compare what is available in the market, and then merge the need with the availability in the most efficient and cost-effective manner.

There are four factors to consider in selecting any duplicating device. They are (1) the physical characteristics of the job; (2) the copy quality; (3) the speed with which the job needs to be completed; and (4) the cost associated with either the job itself or the equipment needed to complete it.

Physical Characteristics of the Job

Before deciding which method of reproduction to use, one must be aware of some additional information that could play an important role in the decision. For instance, the maximum size of the originals to be copied determines the desirability of oversized original copying and the

114   **PART TWO**   Information Processing Cycle

Color copiers are presently available; however, the cost of the machine prohibits its use in many businesses.

need for reduction capabilities. Many reproduction machines offer an 11-inch x 17-inch ledger-size copying option. This option is especially common on low-volume (one to five copies at a time) convenience copiers.

    Special machines also are available for the large one-to-one copying tasks (making one copy from a one-page original) of engineers and other technically oriented workers. Reduction and magnification copying, semiautomatic or automatic duplexing (two-sided copying), and job interruption functions (resuming the operation after an interruption, such as refilling the paper tray) are also features which may be desirable in a copying installation. However, depending upon the purpose for which the document is intended, oversized or undersized printouts could easily be tailored with typesetting equipment.

CHAPTER 5 Reproducing Text 115

If one were to look closely at the physical characteristics of the job in order to make a reprographics equipment selection, a simple chart could be used to direct users to the best option. A large percentage of daily business copying is performed for internal use and thus, requires limited guidelines for the users. The chart in Figure 5-3 illustrates the reprographic requirements of different types of word processing documents. The chart directs users to the process best suited for their needs.

	SELECTION PROCESS			
Conditions	**Photo-copier**	**Offset Duplicator**	**In-house Typesetter**	**Commercial Typesetter**
Word processing document:				
single page/25 copies Purpose: internal use	X			
over 25 copies/rush	X	X		
over 50 copies		X		
multiple page/25 copies collate, staple, bind		X		
		X		
single page/25 copies Purpose: obtain management approval for action	X		X	
over 25 copies/rush	X	X	X	
over 50 copies		X	X	
multiple page/25 copies collate, staple, bind		X	X	
		X	X	
enlarge/reduce need (selection dependent upon purpose)	X	X	X	X
Any of the above for outside use; i.e., customer, stockholder				X

FIG. 5-3
SELECTION OF A
REPRODUCTION OPTION
The reprographic requirements of word processing documents differ with the physical characteristics of the documents.

In reviewing Figure 5-3, one can easily see that the selection options are determined by three major conditions. These conditions are: (1) the number of copies needed; (2) the assembly requirements for documents that have multiple pages; and (3) the purpose for which the document is intended.

Quality

Although a copy is not intended to be identical to the original document, the quality level required varies with the purpose for which the document is intended. Copies of letters or records for internal use as backups or spare reproductions need only to be readable. However, companies that generate form letters for executives or multipage reports for wide distribution require more nearly perfect copies.

Copy quality is a prime factor in choosing plain-paper copiers rather than coated-paper copiers. Although it may seem to be a minor problem, the unnatural feel and whiteness of coated paper is still a major deterrent to the selection of this copier process.

Other copy-quality factors to consider when choosing a method of reproduction include the ability of the copier to reproduce photographs, colors, and text. Such considerations may or may not be important to every installation, but the copy quality should be rated on image sharpness and copy uniformity across the page.

The quality of the finished product is a distinguishing factor between in-house typesetting operations and commercial typesetters. Normally color setting, texture of the paper, photographic insertions, and specialty items are characteristics that earmark a product for commercial preparation. The commercial typesetter must meet the strict quality specifications of the user to obtain approval for payment. If the work is done in-house, these same revisions required for quality approval could be quite time-consuming, which is costly to the company. If delays occurred because of typesetting revisions, not only could the scheduled deadline of the document being typeset be postponed but also the deadlines of those jobs awaiting typesetting. Juggling priorities poses tremendous burdens on an in-house typesetting operation where quality is a prime consideration for user approval.

Speed and Volume

Copier volumes and applications are also important. Decisions such as where the copier will be placed, how fast it should operate, and how many users or departments should have access to the service need to be made. Other factors to consider when selecting the right reproduction method include: (1) the correct rate of copier speed and the number of copiers required; (2) whether the copier should be staffed by a full-time operator; and (3) when the copier should be replaced or augmented by an offset press or a duplicator.

First of all, not all copiers produce copies at the same speed. The volume of copying needed should determine the speed of copier that is required. The personnel within a copy center should be able to quote machine run time based on the number of copies required. Copying machines can produce from 600 to 3,600 copies an hour for single-sided

CHAPTER 5 Reproducing Text

117

copying. Some larger, more sophisticated copiers can produce 1,600 two-sided copies per hour. The speed and volume statistics change based upon the nature of the job, the volume required, and the equipment specifications. Vendors have brochures which describe various product performances.

Only the individual business office can set the policy and standards that will determine where the equipment will be placed within the company and the number of copies permitted. However, there are some suggestions that are normally used in efficient work flow studies. For runs up to 5 copies per original and with volumes in excess of 1,000 copies per month, a business should use a dedicated on-site copier. Higher run lengths should be forwarded to a larger in-house copy center. Many centralized copy centers schedule their own jobs based upon machine speed, volume of copies required, potential paper jams, and replenishment of supplies. They refer to this scheduling as **turnaround time**.

turnaround time time required to complete a job and return to originator

A collator is an important option for a high-volume, high-speed copier.

For widely distributed multidepartment uses, unattended copiers should be positioned within a four-minute walking distance from any user groups. For run lengths of up to 10 copies per original and volumes of over 15,000 copies per month on each machine, several unattended copiers can be used quite effectively. When the volume reaches or exceeds 70,000 copies per month, copiers should be staffed by personnel to ensure users' time savings and copy control.

In a centralized copying facility, a company should employ a staffed high-speed copier for runs of up to 10 to 15 copies per original and volumes in excess of 70,000 copies per month. The copier should include an automatic sorter and feeder. Should the volume exceed 100,000 copies per month, the company should consider buying offset equipment.

It is difficult to state when one should sacrifice user convenience for good copying control. When it is important to have immediate turnaround on high-volume work, the staffed, centralized copier is the best option. However, if user convenience is important, the distributed (convenience) copier is the best choice.

Because users requiring few copies will not object to a short wait, speed differences become important only for multicopy runs—usually in excess of 5 to 10 copies per original. Should the wait increase, the level of user patience declines, frustration results, and valuable work time can be lost. Due to this problem, copy limitations often are placed upon distributed copiers in a well-managed facility. In a staffed, high-speed copier center, greater efficiencies in control and management can be obtained. The slower speed and lower cost copier is usually preferred when user demands are for easy self-access and quick low-volume turnaround. These suggestions also apply for existing facilities that are experiencing delays in meeting copy demands. Unless the copying operation is centralized and controlled, little advantage is gained by using a high-speed copier in place of a low-speed copier.

In addition to speed and volume relationships, special features and attachments also must be considered. A copying machine could have an adequate speed rating and yet may not be durable enough to withstand the constant copying required to meet volume demands. Also, the time it takes to make the first copy could be so long that the runs of one copy per original would take more time to complete on a high-speed copier than they would on a slower speed machine with a fast first-copy time. A copier equipped with a semiautomatic single-sheet feed may be able to compete with the copying ability of a higher speed model, especially when monthly volumes and the number of originals copied approach a one-to-one ratio. Other features that increase productivity include the automatic stack document feeder, the recirculating document handler, and sorters. A **recirculating document handler** cycles a set of originals for exposure and then produces one complete collated set of copies at a time.

recirculating document handler cycles a set of originals for duplication; produces one complete set of collated copies at a time

Cost

There is a bewildering array of financial options available for purchasing reproduction equipment. Available purchase plans include: lease with purchase options, annual rental plans, monthly rental plans, and extended usage rental plans for any prospective buyer. The decision to rent or to purchase a unit is made by comparing the purchase price of the machine to the terms of the rental plans offered by several vendors. Copiers can be broken down into three cost categories: low-, medium-, and high-cost copiers.

The options available on a particular copier greatly impact on the price of the machine.

Low-Cost Copiers. The lowest priced copiers are usually the dual-spectrum copiers, thermal copiers, and coated-paper copiers. More recently, plain-paper copiers are falling into this category. These machines are generally purchased instead of rented because rental is either unavailable or costs more over the year than the purchase price of the machine.

Companies should consider purchasing thermal or dual-spectrum paper models when copying volumes are very low (under 500 copies per month) or when making transparencies is a prime requirement.

Otherwise selection of copying equipment should be based on intended use for the equipment and on budget allocations.

Medium-Cost Copiers. Coated- and plain-paper copiers are priced slightly higher than the thermal and dual-spectrum models, thus requiring a detailed rent/purchase analysis to determine the most economical choice. If one is planning on purchasing the equipment, the quality of service and the scheduled delivery date should be considered carefully.

Plain-paper copiers are more expensive to purchase or rent than are coated-paper copiers. However, the costs of materials and supplies are higher for coated-paper copiers. The copy paper, toner, and concentrate costs for a coated-paper copier should be compared against the paper toner and developer charges plus the original cost of the drum or photoconductor (usually covered under the rental agreement) on a plain-paper model. These costs should be included when analyzing copier models.

High-Cost Copiers. When copying usage exceeds 25,000 copies per month, the use of a high-priced plain-paper copier should be considered. However, a careful analysis should be made before purchasing the unit. Provisions for vendor service and maintenance cause users to favor renting the equipment. Purchased copiers seem to have a slower vendor service response than do rented machines. An irate rental user experiencing poor service may cancel a contract; however, irate customers who own their machines have little recourse other than to register complaints with their vendors.

There are several factors a company must consider when renting a copier. The first factor is the cost-per-copy figures of the various plans available. The longer the rental plan, the more advantageous is the cost-per-copy figure, but the more difficult it could be to cancel the contract. In contrast, a monthly rental plan allows short-term notice for cancellation but the cost-per-copy figures are the highest of all plans.

After selection of the basic type of copier and determination of the payment plan (renting versus purchasing), specific brands and models must be evaluated. Visits to local sales offices allow company representatives to observe demonstrations and to operate the equipment.

The following checklist should be used when evaluating specific brands and models of reproduction equipment:

- Evaluate image quality.
- Check the ease of use and ease of paper replacement.
- Listen for the noise level.
- Check on the length of time and difficulty with which paper jams and other minor problems are corrected. How "friendly" is the

equipment in guiding the operator through these steps?

- See if the machine requires special wiring, voltage, or special power regulators.
- Determine the effect of humidity and other environmental factors on the machine's operation.
- Ask for historical literature on the machine's use and service problems.
- Request references (names of other users) in order to candidly seek other opinions.

Remember that demonstrations at the vendor's site usually have ideal conditions (environment, operation, etc.) that result in perfect performances.

After the selection of a brand and model is finalized and the machine is on the premises, a thorough record of its performance problems and service calls should be kept. The key operator should design a log book in which to write the nature of the trouble, the time of the call, the time of service, the time of correction, and the remedy used. Over a period of time, this information will prove invaluable in pinpointing recurring problems. An accurate and complete log also becomes a testimonial document for possible equipment replacement should the problems be frequent and severe.

If cost becomes a serious consideration in determining whether staffed or unstaffed copiers are used, companies should investigate the use of monitor and control devices. These devices provide an element of security as well as accurate counting. Therefore, it becomes possible to develop a charge-back system and provide the user with accounting information. This will enable each department to more wisely analyze and predict copier use. Of the various devices that are available, most include either a cartridge or a **keypad meter**. Once inserted into the copier, a keypad meter activates the system and provides the user with a copy count. Since each department has its own identification number on the meter, these devices can diminish copier misuse. Some companies require users to record the number of copies run and the purpose of the job for each use of the copier control device.

keypad meter device used to monitor copier usage

After reading this chapter, you should have discovered how to select an appropriate reproduction process for your word processing document from the four basic options available in business today. If the option for phototypesetting is selected, you should be able to determine whether in-house typesetting is preferred over commercial printing. Whichever reprographics method is ultimately selected, your choice should be the most appropriate, since you will have approached the selection from a thorough analysis of the four main factors affecting the desired results.

A keypad meter is a small device that monitors copier usage.

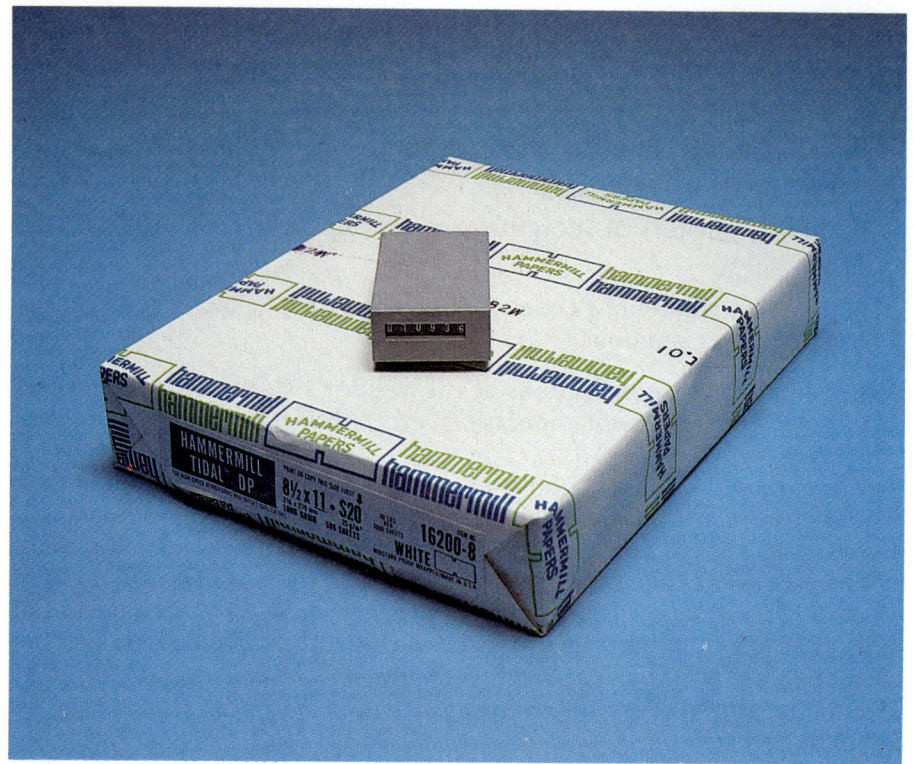

DISCUSSION QUESTIONS AND CASE PROBLEM

DISCUSSION QUESTIONS

1. What makes a copier "convenient?"
2. Name the four kinds of convenience copiers and describe their processing differences.
3. What differentiates offset duplication devices from electrostatic duplication devices?
4. When would you select an in-house typesetting operation over an outside commercial operation? Give some job examples appropriate for each.
5. How is a copier selection process determined? What factors influence the selection?

CHAPTER 5 Reproducing Text

CASE PROBLEM

Jane works in a successful real estate office. She is solely responsible for the secretarial and administrative activities. She does frequent copying for the 20 salespeople assigned to her office. Most of these copying jobs are contracts, sales forms, and letters requiring two-sided copy options. Her copy volume exceeds 6,000 copies per month. Jane cannot spend much time with her copying duties since she is interrupted frequently by her telephone activities.

1. What type of copier would you recommend for Jane to use?
2. List the office conditions that influenced your selection.
3. List three alternate copier choices and indicate a factor that disqualified each from being selected.

Chapter 6 Storing and Retrieving Text

CHAPTER OBJECTIVES:

Identify the scope of the nation's paper problem.

Name the four objectives of a records management system.

Identify the basic methods of information storage and retrieval.

Cite the advantages of a centralized filing system and a decentralized filing system.

Describe three controls for hard disk storage.

Explain at least five advantages of storing information on a microform.

Suggest ways to prevent wasteful duplication, wasted space, filing confusion, and costly inefficiencies.

Information is only as useful as one's ability to recall it when needed. When the need to use the information no longer exists, the information itself becomes useless and should be discarded.

The human memory is said to be an excellent storage and retrieval system. A vast amount of information can be stored within it. Yet added capacity never alters its physical size. When the information stored within the human memory is not frequently accessed, the ability to recall that information is lost. It still remains stored, but the link which allows the person to retrieve it easily has become rusty with disuse. Most often, memory retains its sharpness and accuracy with information it relates to on a daily basis. When stored information is seldom referenced, the memory becomes dim and specific facts become distorted. For example, many childhood memories fade because the individual ceases to dwell on them. One could say that those memories have been filed away to make room for current information needs.

CHAPTER 6 Storing and Retrieving Text

125

The storage and retrieval systems of businesses have information activities that both parallel and contrast with the human memory system. Information not referenced on a daily basis is filed away and often forgotten. However, even when business information has lost its usefulness, too often it is not discarded.

Unfortunately business information is usually created on paper. As new information replaces the old, the paper filing activities and storage requirements increase at insurmountable rates. Control and maintenance of a paper storage and retrieval system are labor intensive and require a vast amount of storage space. Both of these requirements are fast becoming limited commodities as well as costly overheads for companies. Information vital to the needs of a business has become an excessive paper problem and an urgent concern of good management.

In this chapter, the scope of the paper problem is discussed, and ways to deal with it are presented. Also, the various methods available to companies for their information storage and retrieval needs are given. Finally, you will learn techniques that can be used to file information and to organize an effective records management function. The goal of a storage and retrieval system is the prevention of wasteful duplication, wasted space, filing confusion, and costly inefficiencies.

SCOPE OF THE PROBLEM

Datapro Research Corporation in its Automated Office Solutions publication on records management provided the following information on the quantity of paperwork produced within the United States:

The storage and maintenance of paper records is a major problem for U.S. businesses.

"Fifteen hundred trillion pieces of paper are on file in the nation's offices and storerooms. Two million file clerks are kept busy servicing them.... the growth continues at a rate of 62 million file drawers each year. The annual dollar loss from unnecessary paperwork alone is well over the billion-dollar mark."[1]

The article referenced only the formal filing facilities of U.S. businesses in its measurement statistics. There still remains an unaccountable number of personal file drawers not included within this count. Every individual working within an office has approximately four file drawers of information in addition to the company's formal filing system. Quite often the information stored within these private/personal file drawers duplicates the information stored within a company's formal records facility.

The article goes on to state that of all of this information making its way into file drawers each day, only 3 to 10 percent is ever referenced again. Many statistics show that 35 percent of all filed documents are never retrieved. Ninety to 95 percent of the remaining documents are never accessed after the first year. Twenty percent of these documents are equally useless but are interfiled with useful papers, making them difficult to sort out. Fifty percent of this bulk can be kept in low-cost storage rather than in the office's storage space. Only 1 percent must be kept permanently. Office studies also reveal that 1 to 5 percent of all documents are misfiled.[2] The pie chart in Figure 6-1 graphically illustrates these filing percentages.

By relating these percentages to cost figures, one can get a clearer picture of the staggering cost/space/time problem facing businesses today in their paper retention. The National Records Management Council of New York indicates that the 1983 Eastman Kodak Study revealed that the cost for filing a single page of documentation over a year's time amounts to 25 cents. The costs are based upon a composite of labor dollars, equipment, supplies, and floor space.[3] This cost does not include the preparation of the business document—over $8.00 per letter as annually projected by the Dartnell Institute of Business Research.

In addition to the filing cost, misfiling a document adds another 9 cents per page to the base cost. A single four-drawer file cabinet holds approximately 16,000 pieces of paper—4,000 papers per drawer or $4,000 per cabinet. By destroying the 35 percent of the nation's documents that would never be missed, over $500 million dollars could be saved each year. If a way to avoid misfiling documents could be found,

---

[1] *Automated Office Solutions* (Delran, New Jersey: Datapro Research Corporation, June, 1978), page A41-10-101.
[2] *Ibid.*
[3] Information collected for a 1983 Eastman Kodak study (National Records Management Council: New York, 1983).

CHAPTER 6 Storing and Retrieving Text   127

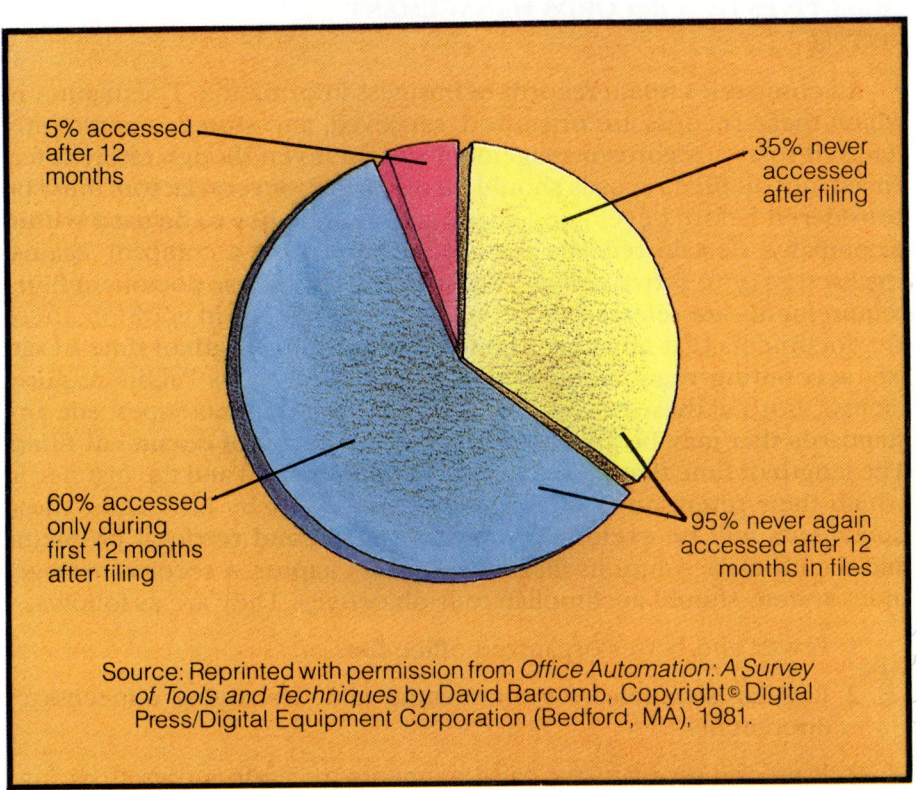

FIG. 6-1
SCOPE OF THE FILING PROBLEM
Only 5 percent of all stored documents are accessed after having been filed for 12 months.

Source: Reprinted with permission from *Office Automation: A Survey of Tools and Techniques* by David Barcomb, Copyright© Digital Press/Digital Equipment Corporation (Bedford, MA), 1981.

that 1 percent a year at a rate of 9 cents per copy would amount to another $500 million saved.

Another way to look at the problem is from a single-company approach. If an average small business has 250,000 filed documents in 10,000 file folders which are stored in 20 four-drawer cabinets, the company probably spends $80,000 (20 cabinets × $4,000) annually for the filing of these documents. However, if these files become inactive or archival, the annual cost to the company to maintain this file space is approximately $15 per lineal foot per year or approximately $1,800.00.[4] Misfiling about 1 percent of those filed documents at a rate of 9 cents per item, adds another $225 [(250,000 documents × 1%) × $.09] to that expense. Thus, if specific studies are correct in the assumption that 35 percent of these filed documents could be reduced to archive and the misfiling be eliminated, the firm could save approximately $28,000 a year.

---

[4]Information from a study conducted by the Association of Records Managers and Administrators: St. Louis, 1983.

OBJECTIVES OF A RECORDS MANAGEMENT SYSTEM

records management system how business records are organized, retrieved, and stored

All companies retain records of business information. The manner in which these records are organized, retrieved, and stored is commonly referred to as a records management system. Even though rarely referenced, not all filed records should be discarded. Several factors must be considered before developing a standard filing policy to be used within a company. Certain records are needed to protect a company against legal action or to prove compliance with the law. These document filing requirements are referred to as "legal requirements." In addition, there are documents that must be retained for a certain length of time to satisfy accounting regulations, which are referred to as "audit requirements." Both of these document retention requirements supercede any standards that may be appropriate for the majority of document filing. The length of time that these documents are retained and the manner in which their retention is directed are spelled out by law. Thus, these documents will be excluded from the storage and retrieval problems and the ultimate solutions discussed in this chapter. A records management system should accomplish four objectives. They are as follows:

1. Fewer and better organized office files
2. Regular schedules for eliminating and destroying unnecessary documents
3. Preservation of historical documents, records required by law, and vital company information
4. Efficient and effective retrieval methods

METHODS OF STORING INFORMATION

There are several methods of storing information that have originated from word processing input. The documentation (text) resulting from the work flow assumes three types of records:

1. The input record from the author (either a source document—handwritten paper or rough draft—or dictation recorded on magnetic media)
2. The paper document produced by the printer
3. The magnetic media which captured the keystrokes of the operator when the document was keyed

The initial input from the author usually is returned to that person with the completed documents. The author normally reviews the processed work and, if satisfied, discards the paper input or reuses the tape

In many businesses, handwritten records are typed and then stored in the filing system. Often these records are never referenced again.

for another item. If there are discrepancies in the final document, the author may review the initial input to verify which information is accurate. In any case, the original input is rarely reused for the revision.

If the author had used a central dictation system, the word processing center would have stored the dictation for a prescribed period of time that coincided with a normal revision cycle. After this period had passed, the dictated tape would have been erased for reuse. Storage of original input, therefore, has little impact on storage and retrieval problems.

The primary concern is with the forms in which text can be stored. The most problematic form is that of **hard copy**—the completed paper document. The problem arises when the amount of storage space necessary for paper filing simply requires too much room. To help solve this dilemma, an increasing number of businesses are turning to magnetic media, hard disks, and microforms in order to maintain the most information in the least space. Each of these storage methods can be classified as belonging to either of two retrieval techniques: manual or electronic (computer-assisted). Hard copy and magnetic media that are individually processed belong to the manual retrieval category. Hard disk storage and microforms have electronic retrieval capabilities; thus, they fall under the latter category. Let's investigate each method to determine its practicality in given situations.

hard copy the completed paper document

Manual Retrieval Methods

This category focuses on those storage methods used for traditional paper files (hard copy) and individually handled recording media systems (such as diskettes). Information is physically handled in the storage and retrieval cycles.

Hard Copy. There are two methods used in the filing of paper: centralized filing methods and decentralized filing methods (sometimes called distributed filing methods). Many large organizations have centralized file rooms that are managed by a filing supervisor and that can be accessed only by filing personnel. At the same time, each department may have its own files that are maintained by a secretary or an administrative specialist. In either case, executives and other personnel often prefer to keep important current files in their own offices. There are advantages to both methods, as shown in Figure 6-2.

FIG. 6-2
FILING METHODS
Regardless of which filing method is used, the main objective should be accessibility to the data.

ADVANTAGES TO THE CENTRALIZED METHOD	ADVANTAGES TO THE DECENTRALIZED METHOD
1 Duplication of equipment and records is minimized.	1 The confidentiality of the information can be protected effectively.
2 There is full-time supervision for maximum control.	2 Records are handy, convenient, and near persons who need them.
3 Filing personnel develop specialized skills and efficiencies.	3 Systems best suited for the individual material, its use, and its user can be established.
4 The cost of the system is relatively low.	4 Departmental team filing effort can be enhanced.

The question of which method is better is purely arbitrary. The key to a successful and efficient filing system is its ability to become easily accessible to the users. Therefore, how the information is filed—its order and its accuracy—is of prime importance.

As a student, you can personally relate to the convenience of a good filing system when you accumulate your research notes, exam papers, class notes, and reports. If your papers are properly stored, identified, and in good repair, they will be more valuable to you when they are needed. If, on the other hand, they are left to accumulate and are not put in sequential order, they will be difficult to reference or locate when the need arises. In fact, you will waste precious time sorting through a

CHAPTER 6 Storing and Retrieving Text

131

semester's accumulation of paper in a last-minute effort to study for exams or to prepare your term reports.

Offices experience similar panic on a larger scale when a letter or document is needed in a hurry and cannot be found. A major problem businesses have is the careless or improper assignment of personnel to store and retrieve information. In too many instances, filing duties are assigned to untrained office employees who cannot be placed elsewhere because of lack of skills. In truth, the selection of personnel to store and retrieve information can be more effective when companies choose personnel who possess certain attributes. Such attributes include a sense of orderliness, accuracy, manual dexterity, quick reading comprehension, and a liking for detail.

Prefiling. There is always a chance that something will be filed away prematurely—before necessary action has been taken. This can be avoided by standardizing prefiling procedures as well as filing procedures.

Before preparing a paper for filing, the first step is to devise a work form that indicates that the necessary action has been taken and that the information is ready to be filed. Many businesses use a sign-off sheet. For instance, in a case where reference material needs to be distributed to several employees within a department for their review, the sign-off sheet provides blanks for initials and dates, which are then filled in by the reviewers. An example of such a sign-off sheet, called a routing slip, is shown in Figure 6-3.

When all reviewers have acknowledged its release, the information can be filed. To be efficiently designed, the sign-off record should list

Please review, initial, date and circulate.

Name	Date
✓ B. Clark	BC 3/14
✓ C. Stone	CS 3-17
___ D. Woods	
___ B. Lopez	
___ R. Worthington	

Return to H. Overton, when completed.

FIG. 6-3
ROUTING SLIP
A routing slip is used to send a document to designated people.

the recipients' names and provide spaces for initials and dates to be written. This promotes faster turnaround by eliminating the amount of information the user must provide to acknowledge the document. Prior to circulating the information, it is wise to date the article, indicating the time of initial receipt. In this manner, information can be either filed for historical reference or discarded if its date indicates obsolescence.

Material to be filed should be reviewed for its condition, and the papers should be mended where appropriate. Unnecessary attachments and paper clips should be removed. Often misfiling occurs when paper clips inadvertently are attached to other papers, which then become filed with inappropriate material.

Preparation for Filing. After the material is returned from routing, the next step is to decide the caption or title under which the paper would most likely be found in a filing system. This may be the name of the subject matter, the name of the writer, the firm that is associated with the material, an assigned number for a numeric file, a location for a geographical file, or a key word. For example, a paper that discusses a particular brand of word processing equipment purchased by the office systems department for a branch office of the company could be filed under any one of the following headings and cross-referenced under the other headings:

1 **Name of the firm**—vendor of equipment

2 **Subject matter**—word processing equipment

3 **Name of the author/group**—office systems department

4 **Geographical name**—location of the branch office

5 **Assigned number**—purchase order number

indexing   deciding under what title to file a document

coding   marking the indexing decision on a document

Making this filing decision is called **indexing**. Marking that decision on the document by highlighting or writing is called **coding**. Both of these activities are of major importance in maintaining an efficient, well-organized filing system.

Cross-referencing, another important filing activity, enables one to retrieve a paper that logically could be filed under any of two or three captions. Some companies make a copy for each of the logical files for reference. Of course, if the ultimate goal is paper reduction, then a good cross-referencing index is more cost effective and can be just as efficient. The choice reflects specific standards set by a company based on its measure of paper importance.

When creating files, a folder should be prepared when five or more pieces of correspondence exist for a particular caption. A miscellaneous folder behind each file section is a good place to store the incomplete files until the needed quantity is reached. Files should be kept neat, and

CHAPTER 6 Storing and Retrieving Text 133

damaged folders should be repaired regularly. A good filing system is rated by the ease with which one person can locate information from another person's files even when that person is away from the office.

Filing activities should be a top priority of office activities. When filing chores are delayed, the accumulation of papers to be filed can add to the problem of misfiled documents. No one cares to be involved in a frenzied search for an important document only to discover that it lies on a desk waiting to be filed.

Retrieval From Files. When material is needed from a file, the usual procedure is to fill out a requisition slip. Figure 6-4 illustrates the type of information commonly found on a requisition slip. If someone else requires the filed material in a hurry or has higher priority to the information, it can be traced easily.

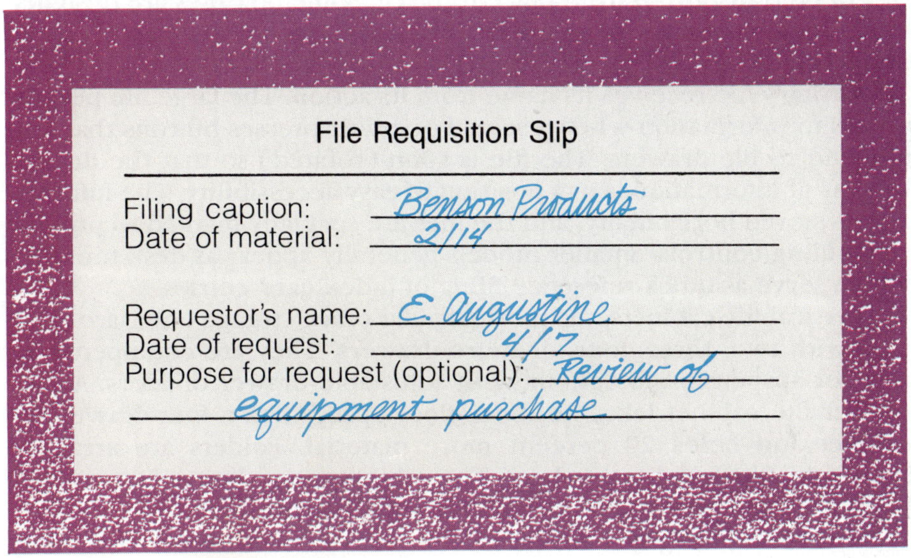

File Requisition Slip

Filing caption: Benson Products
Date of material: 2/14

Requestor's name: E. Augustine
Date of request: 4/7
Purpose for request (optional): Review of equipment purchase

FIG. 6-4
FILE REQUISITION SLIP
File requisition slips aid companies in keeping track of frequently accessed information.

Some companies never permit the original documents to leave the file, but provide copies of the material instead. This method of material retrieval ensures the integrity of the original file but does not contribute to paper reduction. The method of material retrieval to be used must be based upon the nature of the document and its importance to the company.

Storage Devices. There is a variety of filing equipment available for paper storage. Equipment selection is determined by several factors: (1) the size and quantity of documents, (2) space requirements, (3) the access convenience, and (4) the desired office decor. For example, management personnel may prefer to have their readily accessible files placed in desk drawers or credenzas in order to maintain an attractive office environment. Administrative support personnel may require larger, more frequently accessed files. Many of these employees have two or more two-drawer file cabinets positioned conveniently within their immediate work area.

Equipment within a centralized area should be designed for frequent access by many users. Box files generally are used for documents that are rarely, if ever, accessed but have a required retention period. Automatic rotating devices or floor-to-ceiling lateral suspension files usually are reserved for a central records library. Regardless, all filing equipment should be selected with an eye towards growth and expansion.

Box filing equipment is constructed of steel-reinforced boxes or of fiberboard for heavy-duty handling. Box filing equipment can be stacked or can be transported from place to place. Some box files are designed with drawers; others open from the front or top to permit easy access to stored material.

A rotary file receives its name from its action. The large file permits access to information when a seated operator presses buttons that correspond to file drawers. The file is spun (rotated) so that the desired drawer of information is in a position of easy accessibility. The information is stored horizontally, and the files are specially marked to provide strict filing controls. Smaller models generally appear as desk top units which serve as quick reference filing of index card entries.

Vertical file cabinets, the most popular office storage units, are available with two, three, four, or more drawers. They are equipped with rails for suspension folders or with adjustable drawer dividers. A five-drawer file cabinet takes no more floor space than a four-drawer file cabinet and holds 20 percent more material. Folders are arranged within the file from front to back. The cabinets come in a wide variety of colors and textures to blend with any office environment.

Open-shelf filing systems are often used for centralized access. They resemble bookshelves in appearance and have dividers or supports for file folders. They offer the greatest overall capacity and economy for filing either legal- or letter-sized documents. They are flexible and easily adjust to differing needs and sizes.

Files in a suspension system are hung from rails or clips in an open framework. They are similar to an open shelf filing system because the material is not contained within drawers. These systems are commonly customized to fit into an area; thus, they have a finished, well-organized appearance.

Tub files more commonly appear in centralized word processing centers. The tub stand can have sides that are either open or closed. File folders are suspended from the top of the stand. Word processing centers use tub files for prioritizing incoming work from authors. The

CHAPTER 6 Storing and Retrieving Text 135

design allows easy retrieval of any work file and permits the supervisor to view the backlog of work at a glance. These files are often mobile and can be positioned close to the needed work area.

Material within lateral filing cabinets is stored lengthwise. These cabinets are usually wider than, but not as deep as, vertical files. Access to the cabinet is not by a drawer but by a pull-up shelf that slides into the cabinet exposing the entire width of the file space. The shelf can be rolled out for full access but, when closed, takes up a minimal amount of space. These types of filing cabinets are commonly used as dividers between work stations in an open landscape environment.

Most popular is vertical

Lateral filing cabinets are widely used by businesses for storage.

Left: Open filing systems are commonly used for centralized access.

Right: Automated filing systems allow easy retrieval of material.

Floppy Diskettes. Special storage problems for the office have been created by the use of magnetic media (such as floppy diskettes) in word processing operations. One of the basic reasons for justifying the use of magnetic media is the equipment's ability to reduce the amount of paperwork generated by other nonmagnetic methods. The theory is that once the keystrokes are captured, the revisions that would occur on paper by conventional means would not have to be generated until the final copy is approved. Thus, the amount of paper output would be controlled.

Convenience. Each diskette can hold numerous documents—all within an arm's reach. Each document can be recalled quickly and displayed on the screen for easy viewing or revision. In addition, a single diskette with its many documents requires only a fraction of the storage space compared to its paper document counterparts. However, the ability of word processors to generate output more easily has increased the paper proliferation problem.

Cost. As you will recall from the earlier part of this chapter, the cost to file a single page of paper over a year's time is 25 cents. Let's compare that to the cost of filing a page of text on a magnetic medium, such as an 8-inch floppy diskette. The cost to store that single page of information on this medium costs 30 cents. If the costs of storage cases and special files are added to this base figure, the cost increases to 41 cents per page.

To be practical, the justification of this increased cost for using magnetic media storage must be offset by the elimination or reduction of paper storage facilities. However, business has added these media storage methods to paper storage methods instead of replacing paper files; thus, duplicate files exist. The full impact of the combined costs of duplicate files against the initial financial expectations is seldom weighed. Without the proper controls, this new technology can result in unexpected administrative costs and real economic setbacks to the profit goals of the enterprise.

Type of Files. The surfaces of magnetic media must be protected from dust, fingerprints, the elements, and defacement. Magnetic cards, for example, have plastic jackets that protect the media surface. Some magnetic media containers also include provisions for identifying the data contained on the medium itself. This identification assists the operator in retrieving the information stored on the media.

Special drawers or trays are fitted into conventional vertical or lateral filing cabinets to accommodate magnetic cards. Some users prefer to use special notebooks with plastic-jacket inserts to contain magnetic cards. Others use rotary carousel files which provide freestanding easy access.

Cassette tape files are stored in specially designed drawer files or in notebook cases. The cassettes snap into the notebooks, and the entire file can be positioned upright on an operator's desk for easy retrieval. Rotary files are also made to support the storage of cassette tapes, providing another easy access and storage of such media.

A floppy diskette can be stored in a tub, box, or tray; placed in a notebook binder; or used in a rotary configuration. A protective envelope surrounds the diskette to prevent damage to its magnetic surface. Like the magnetic card, the jacket of the diskette also is used for labeling and filing the diskette in proper sequence.

A magnetic medium, though more costly than paper, has a redeeming factor. It can be erased when its usefulness has been terminated; and, it can be reused. Thus, the actual cost for storing that single page of text on a magnetic medium can be reduced somewhat. Its ability to be reused many times is relative to the quality of the medium. Normally, the medium should last through ten erasures and reuses. The life span of a magnetic medium is contingent upon the number of revisions and its ability to withstand physical handling. Quality and durability are reflected in the cost of the medium itself.

Quality Control. For a truly cost-effective and efficient operation, the manager of word/information services must ensure that there are specific standards for media storage as well as procedures to control its retention cycle. Procedures should designate who is responsible for maintaining the media copy.

Consider a 20-page financial report authored by the accounting department and prepared by word processing personnel. The entire report has been finalized and has been distributed to the readers. Having been acted upon, the report will not need to be revised. In this case the retention requirements of the media within the word processing center have been satisfied. The responsibility of the decision to maintain the report on magnetic media has transferred to the accounting department.

Should the report contain information which could be reused for future reports or should there be a need to reduce the amount of storage space appropriated, the media should be retained by the accounting department. If there is no need to retain the recording, the media should be erased and prepared for reuse by the word processing department. Decisions such as these cannot be made haphazardly and should be reviewed with participating authors.

All procedures for magnetic storage should be designed with original record management objectives in mind. Here is a review of those objectives:

1 Fewer and better organized office files

CHAPTER 6 Storing and Retrieving Text

Left: Floppy diskettes are often stored in binders.

Below: Tub files prevent dust and dirt from accumulating on diskettes.

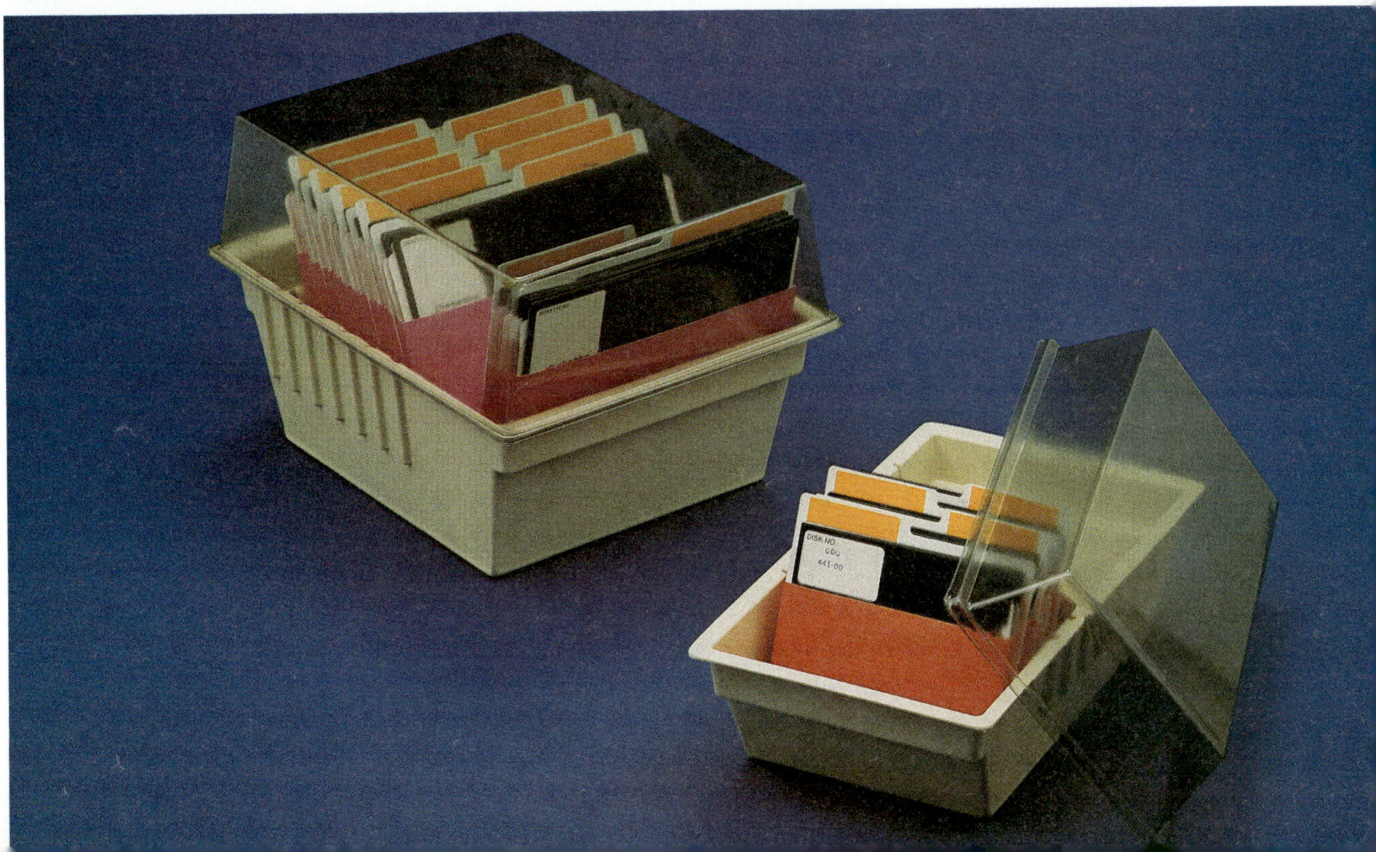

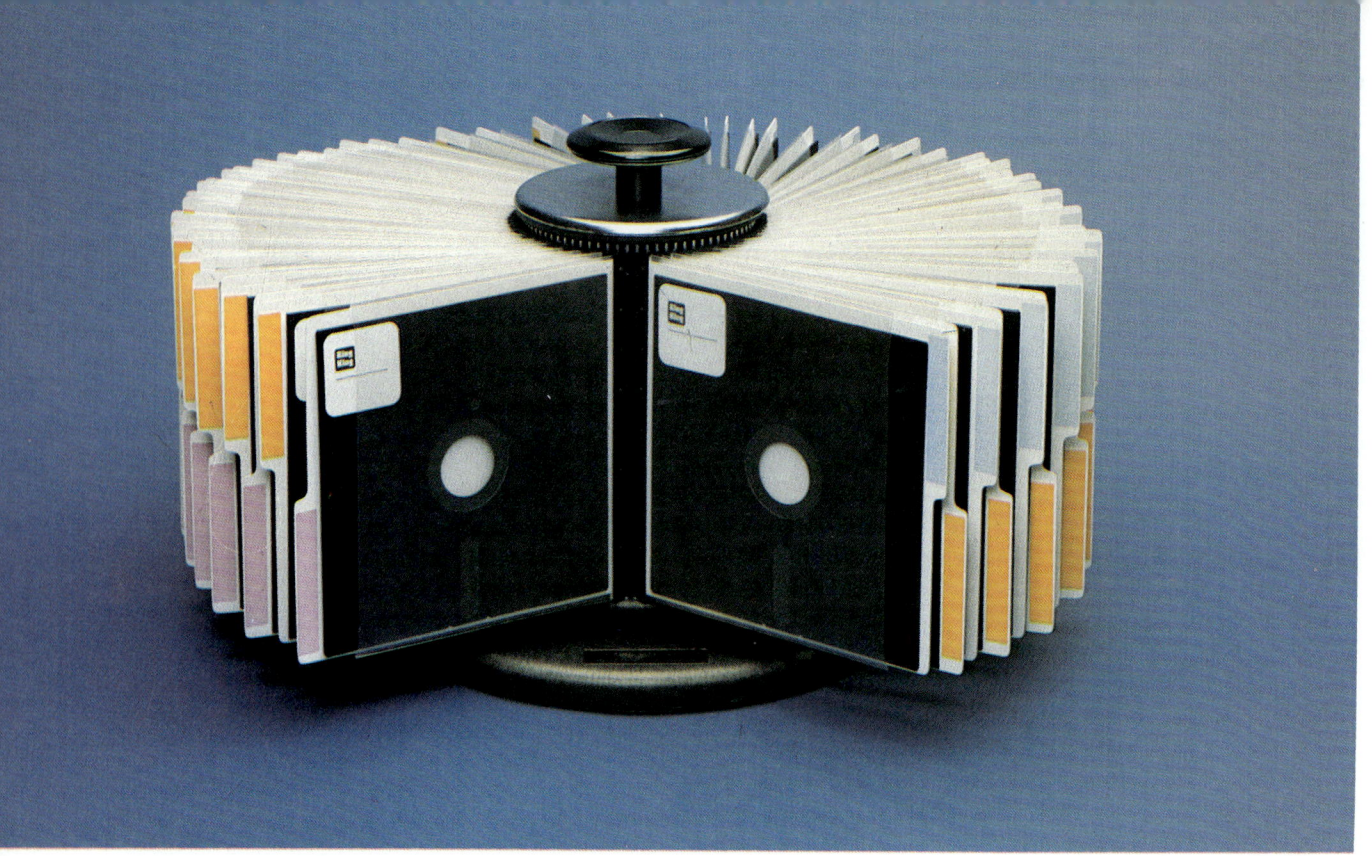

Rotary storage devices are commonly used for diskettes that must be kept within easy reach.

2 Regular schedules for eliminating and destroying unnecessary documents

3 Preservation of historical documents, records required by law, and vital company information

4 Efficient and effective retrieval methods

Electronic Retrieval Methods

Electronic (or computer-assisted) methods of information retrieval are becoming much more common as companies strive to respond to space problems caused by excessive paper storage. The two most popular systems use hard disks or microfilms for storing and retrieving. These two electronic retrieval systems are capable of storing vast quantities of information in a substantially reduced space compared to their manual system counterparts. Another reason for the increasing popularity of these systems is the ability of qualified individuals to access the information in these systems easily and quickly without (in many cases) leaving their work stations.

Disk Storage. Hard disk storage is used by multiterminal word/information processing equipment. In this equipment configuration, users of

CHAPTER 6 Storing and Retrieving Text

the terminals share the storage facilities of the centralized computer system. The information captured by keystrokes is placed on hard disks, which have a storage capacity predefined by their disk size.

Capacity. Some hard disks do not allow document storage to exceed 25,000 blocks of information, such as the 75Mb disk. For example, this disk reserves two blocks of information for every page of text. The system allocates two blocks of information for even a portion of a page. Most documents average from two to two and one-half pages in length (four to six blocks). This means that there is storage capacity on each disk for approximately 5,000 documents.

However, there are study statistics which indicate that an average document has a minimum of two revision cycles. When the editing function is requested on this type of system, two additional blocks of space are allocated the user. These space allocations cannot be reused by the system for any other purpose even though the user may not have used the entire block. In this example, the capacity for available documentation storage is then reduced to fewer than 3,000 documents.

Cost. Going a step further, one can determine what it costs to store the system document in the previous example. A 75Mb disk drive has a purchase price of approximately $17,000. This means that each block of available storage is worth approximately 68 cents. A document that is two and one-half pages in length and requires two revisions uses 10 blocks of space and costs approximately $6.80 to store. This appears to be a very expensive storage medium when one considers that paper storage costs are 25 cents a page.

Storage Problems and Resolutions. There are methods that will reduce the amount of space that is unused but not free. The methods generally are referred to as **system utilities**, but they may be referred to by various names on different systems.

The function of system utilities is space reorganization. Files can be reorganized by the user or the system administrator. The purpose of the reorganization is to better define the pointers to the fragmented parts of the revised document so that the disk head can position itself more easily. A secondary utility program reallocates the space on the disk, freeing the unused portions and returning them for system use. This program is called *Restore*, and operation of the program generally is restricted to that of the system administrator.

Only one third of the used space will be recovered with these system utility programs. The only other way to free additional disk space is to remove the documents from disk storage. Documents that are stored on hard disks can be transferred to floppy diskettes or magnetic tape—a process known as **archiving**.

system utilities special system programs under which methods that reduce the unused storage space on a disk are located

archiving transferring documents from hard disk storage to floppy disk or magnetic tape storage

Users of these systems have difficulty coping with the removal of their documents from disk storage. Removal from storage does not have to be a permanent deletion of file records. Important documents can be archived into diskettes or magnetic tape for interim storage until the need to access them recurs. Users should be encouraged to have unnecessary or useless information permanently deleted.

Allowing disk capacity to be maximized is not only costly but is also an ineffective use of the equipment. Machine response time slowly erodes, and the operator is faced with seconds of screen inactivity between keystrokes. Waiting for the machine to respond can be frustrating, especially when deadlines increase the pressure to produce.

The disk drive itself cannot function as well when it is at full capacity. It has difficulty searching for a document because it must wade through the voluminous table of contents to find the location. If multiple disk drives are being used on the system, users' files may be located on any of these devices, each having its own VTOC. Such a configuration only complicates an already difficult locating problem.

Some companies ease the disk storage problem by purchasing additional disk drives or by expanding the storage capacity of their present model. Either decision incurs increased costs for the company. The paradox of disk storage problems is that most often the user has a hard copy file of this same document. In these instances, the cost of space and paper proliferation cannot be justified.

Quality Control. Can something be done about this problem? Proper controls and procedures could establish regular house cleanings. What do you do with your closets that get too full and messy? You discard any items that are no longer needed. You rearrange the most necessary items and place into permanent storage those that you will not be using on a daily basis.

A disk storage system is similar except for one big difference. In the home, users' personal storage habits affect no one but their own household. In the office, full libraries affect all other users on the system. Many of the files that experience no activity and are quite old need to be removed. Here is how it can be done.

1 Delete those documents no longer needed.

2 Archive those documents that are important but may not be requested for revision for some time. The system administrator should provide a tape copy of those items. Upon being needed again, they can be read back onto the system. They will regain their position for changes as before. Better than that, having the copies on tape will avoid accidental damage to their content should the system ever crash (fail) because of power or equipment problems. Their value and historical importance will be preserved. Additionally, their confidences will be guaranteed

CHAPTER 6 Storing and Retrieving Text

because no one will be able to access them inadvertently.

3 Keep those documents on disk storage that are fresh and current or require frequent revisions.

At the time a document is originated, the author should designate how long the recording needs to be retained on magnetic media. The procedures of most word processing systems provide that unless otherwise specified, correspondence is retained only three to five days. Then the stored documents are automatically deleted without notifying the author. Other documents require instructions from the author at the time of origination and at periodic intervals of document deletion and archiving. Figure 6-5 shows how one company controls document storage on magnetic media. The work request form requires that the author designate how long the document should be retained on media. Then prior to deleting the document at the end of that designated period, the word processing personnel ask the author to give final approval for deletion.

Storage Devices. Storage devices for hard disks and magnetic tape come in a variety of racks and cabinets that either suspend or support the

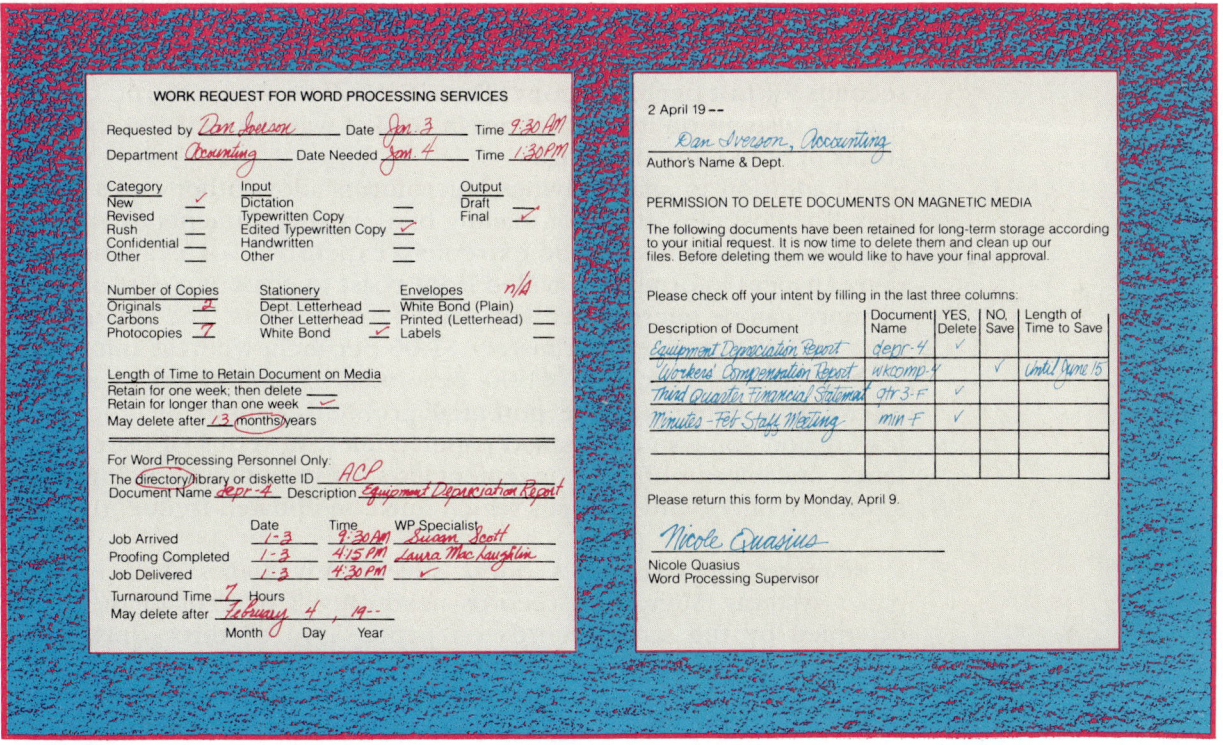

FIG. 6-5
DELETING DOCUMENTS STORED ON MAGNETIC MEDIA
In many word processing centers, authors must give final approval before documents stored on magnetic media can be deleted.

media. The units can be kept in large storage facilities, such as a computer room, or in a specially designed safe for special data security. Units also can be freestanding to accommodate individuals who need storage at their work stations.

Micrographics Storage. As you will recall from Chapter 1, micrographics is a photographic method of filing information in reduced form onto film. The process of filming the information into its miniaturized form is called microfilming. The end products produced by this microfilming process are called **microforms**. The microfilming of documents has provided a tangible solution for retaining and retrieving the increasing amounts of knowledge needed to conduct business. Microforms, alone or as part of a total information processing system, can provide secure, compact, reproducible, accessible, and economical information storage and retrieval. This process may be linked to a computer, facsimile, word processor, and any other information processing technique to form a part of the total system. Examples of documents that are microfilmed include checks, financial records, population statistics, accounting records, and billing records. Micrographics is widely used by financial institutions, public utilities, insurance companies, and government agencies.

Microforms, in a few square feet of space, duplicate original documents that previously required several thousand square feet. Users have found that they can retrieve, display, and reproduce microforms in seconds for just pennies a copy. The U.S. Navy uses microforms of engineering systems on its submarines instead of wasting valuable space for stacks of books and drawings.

In addition to space savings, microforms allow other types of savings. The cost of postage for mailing hard copy documents by the hundreds and thousands can be extremely expensive. For example, hard copy (paper) information mailed from coast to coast at a cost of $7.00 or more can be microfilmed and mailed for 20 cents. The storage cost for a reel of film is approximately $1.06 per inch; whereas microform storage is approximately $1.00 per inch.[5] The archival quality of microforms eliminates the potential problems caused by dog-eared, frayed, and sometimes misfiled paper copies. In terms of user acceptance, microforms offer a convenient alternative to bulky catalogs, odd-sized brochures, and manuals which must be updated frequently.

Advantages. Micrographics offers several advantages over existing paper systems. Microform records need only 2 percent of the space occupied by the same records on paper. Two or three drawers of

microform the end product produced by microfilming documents

---

[5]Information from a study conducted by the Association of Records Managers and Administrators: St. Louis, 1983.

microforms are the equivalent of 100 drawers of paper records. Another comparison is that microforms stacked one inch high contain the same information as 26,000 pages of computer output.[6] Another advantage is that, regardless of the size of the original document, images are reduced to fit standard microform dimensions for convenient handling. If needed, paper copies can be produced in seconds from the microform images.

Duplicate microform records can be prepared at a nominal cost and sent to other locations to provide a backup set should the first set be destroyed. Information on microforms is recorded in a fixed sequence, which decreases the possibility of misfiling, mislaying, altering, or losing the information. Information can be retrieved in seconds, even from a data base of millions of documents. Valuable work hours spent sorting and filing paper records can be eliminated and channeled into more productive work.

Microforms are protected from possible wear and tear by the nature of their design. Information is secure since the film easily can be stored in smaller, less obvious areas. Fire hazard is reduced because the film is noncombustible. Also, microforms are not vulnerable to erasure or memory loss caused by power failure or computer downtime. Since information cannot be altered or easily damaged, microform records are legally accepted in virtually all 50 states. The federal government also accepts microforms on the same basis as paper documents. Some users predict that microforms will provide an archival record of historical significance to future researchers.

Disadvantages. There are, however, a few disadvantages of the microfilming process. Updating information is not easy on most microforms. The information would need to be revised in its computer form and then remicrofilmed for a new copy. This limits the use of microforms to unrevised copy. Another major disadvantage of microforms is that information can be accessed only by those who have a terminal (reader).

Common Microforms. One common type of microform is microfilm. Microfilm can be packaged in a number of ways. Roll film resembles 16mm or 35mm movie film with the pictures in sequence along the roll. Roll film commonly is used for relatively inactive records. Microfilm also can be packaged in a cartridge or cassette. This form of microfilm is more portable than roll film and the film image is smaller. Cartridges or cassettes commonly are used when automatic retrieval is an option.

The micro-thin jacket accommodates 16mm and/or 35mm film in several rows across the jacket. Jackets both protect the microfilm and facilitate organization of the material. Jackets can be viewed with the

---

[6]Information from a study conducted by the AIIM, 1983.

naked eye for quick, easy reference; updated with new microfilm at any time; and duplicated as microfiche.

Microfiche is a transparent sheet of film containing multiple rows of microimages. A 6-inch by 4-inch microfiche is equivalent to 98 pages of data. Microfiche is a popular, economical, and highly practical record storage medium.

The **aperture (tab) card** contains one or more microfiche frames. Each frame is near an identifying code (printed or keypunched) which permits rapid access to the information.

A new microfiche technology is called **ultrafiche**. One 6-inch by 4-inch ultrafiche may contain 4,000 or more pages of data or text. This means that one million pages of material can be contained in a stack of film cards about six inches high. Imagine the total contents of over 50,000 books being stored in one drawer of a filing cabinet.

As you can see, microfilmed documents are packaged in a number of forms. Which form to use in any application depends primarily on the type of input, the characteristics of the information stored, and how the information is to be used. However, additional factors are important. They include: (1) the speed and ease of retrieval, (2) the capabilities of handling the volume of work and supplying hard copies as desired, (3) the frequency of updates or file changes, (4) the security of the material files, (5) compatibility with existing office machines and equipment, and (6) the overall system cost.

Microfilming is a technology that easily can be made compatible with computer systems. Computer-recorded data can be transferred from the computer to film in a fraction of the time required to print the same data on paper. In fact, microfilm can be created and retrieved through a computer. These processes are referred to as COM (computer output to microfilm) and CAR (computer-assisted retrieval).

microfiche a card or a sheet of film with multiple microimages

aperture card contains microfiche frames with identifying codes

ultrafiche can hold much more data than a microfiche

A COM recorder can produce microfilm or microfiche directly from computer data.

CHAPTER 6 Storing and Retrieving Text

CAR assists users in retrieving stored microfilm for review.

COM. A COM recorder is capable of producing microfilm or microfiche directly from computer data (or word processing data) via industry standard interfacing. (The most common interfacing is known as RS232 connecting ribbon cabling. The front cover of the textbook is illustrated with this industry standard interface ribbon.) The COM recorder is connected to the computer in much the same way that a standard printer would be connected. To the computer, the COM recorder also acts in the same manner as a printer would. The COM is programmed to accept the same page formatting and printing type commands as would normally be sent to the printer. However, instead of the data appearing as paper output, it appears as film. The film is protected by a reloadable cassette. This cassette allows all filming and processing functions to be carried out in daylight.

CAR. The information that is processed through the COM recorder will have precoded indexes recorded in a special file within the computer. With this file, a user can access the information bank and query the film location. The file (data base) will identify the coded cassette pattern which enables the user to locate the cassette more easily. This assists the user in retrieving the film for review; hence, the name computer-assisted retrieval.

Some systems permit random-access selection by several users with the use of display monitors connected via terminal-activated TV circuits. Microform libraries can store upwards of 5 million frames of reference material. Some sophisticated systems include an electrical lockout, which prevents unauthorized viewing of confidential information.

Equipment and Storage Devices. Most microfilming storage equipment devices are designed around the microform media used by the company. The type of film, the quantity of the storage, and the retention cycle of the copy determine the style and capacity of the cabinetry. With the exception of computer-stored devices, most equipment has **smart drawer storage facilities**. These devices provide controlled filing for sequential coding and promote easy retrieval. There is a wide range of microform storage and retrieval equipment available. The equipment ranges from a simple file drawer to systems involving computers, local and remote data transmission, and high-speed, automatic display/printing capabilities which provide enlargements, indexed data, and selected retrieval.

A variety of devices are available for viewing microforms. The choice depends on the environment in which they will be used, personal needs, the specific microform system in use, and cost. Basic types of readers include: stationary readers, portable readers, and reader/printers. Reader/printers are designed both for viewing and producing hard copy reproductions from a microform. The film can be retrieved and displayed in a relatively inexpensive reader, which requires little operational training. Should a hard copy be needed, it can be made easily and inexpensively.

It is a relatively simple process to operate a reader. Generally the documents are fed by hand through the unit in much the same manner as one would feed a copier. The cassette or strip is loaded into the machine prior to feeding the original documents. Many machines have control devices that alert the operator of the filming and loading steps. The strips of film or cassettes are exposed during the feeding cycle. The COM process is normally performed through an automatic software application program within the computer system. The operator simply accesses the program and directs the documents to this automatic process for filming.

Micrographics is well established as the most cost-effective way to store large files of inactive information. As the technology advances and users become more comfortable with it, micrographics will play an increasingly important role in everyday active communications.

After reading this chapter, you should be acquainted with the growing paper storage problems facing many companies. You should recognize the need for those information records to be well organized and managed in order for companies to easily retrieve, reference, and reproduce them. You should have developed a familiarity with various

---

smart drawer storage
controlled filing for sequential coding; promotes easy retrieval

techniques for filing information and organizing an effective records management system. Lastly, you should have learned about the many different methods of storage and retrieval which are available to companies. You should be able to sense the mechanics of each method's operation and weigh its cost effectiveness.

This chapter has discussed the scope of the paper problem and how to deal with it. In doing so, it has attempted to illustrate that the goal of business should be to prevent wasteful duplication, wasted space, filing confusion, and costly inefficiencies.

DISCUSSION QUESTIONS AND CASE PROBLEM

DISCUSSION QUESTIONS

1. What universal problem faces many businesses today? Quote some statistics that would indicate the scope of the problem.
2. Name the two classifications of document retrieval. Define their differences. Give an example of each classification.
3. Name any two objectives of a good records management system.
4. What is the most cost- and space-effective method of storing large files of inactive information?
5. List two types of companies that could effectively use micrographics for storage. Explain your choices.

CASE PROBLEM

Mark is responsible for the administration and daily operation of the shared logic multiterminal office system in the company at which he works. Most of his users make daily use of word processing applications. He encourages all users to clean their libraries weekly. He suspects, however, that the users are not as diligent as they could be about this duty. He has noticed that the system response time is degrading. When he checked the system's space availability, he discovered that there was very little room left for expansion.

1. What are Mark's alternatives in providing additional space for the users of the system?
2. Which alternative is the most cost-effective approach to use?
3. Which alternative will bring about the quickest results?
4. Which alternative is the costliest to the company?

Chapter 7 Distributing Text

CHAPTER OBJECTIVES:

Understand problems that are associated with the distribution of information within the office.

Describe various methods and equipment available to companies for their internal and external distribution of information.

View distribution from a cost and time/benefit analysis.

Determine delivery methods based on appropriate company needs.

Explain the basic characteristics of compatible data communications.

One can easily forget one of the basic purposes of an office after spending considerable time organizing the work flow, selecting the equipment, establishing procedures, performing analyses, and designing the environment. One basic purpose of offices is to produce information in the form of documents. If everything is done correctly, the office operates quite efficiently. In order to maintain this level of quality, there must be an effective means of controlling the way that information is channeled into, through, and out of the office. This controlled handling must assure that the recipient will receive the information in a timely and cost-effective manner.

Just as certain factors influence the choice of reproducing copies (as described in Chapter 5), similar factors help determine the best distribution method. The means of distribution must meet established criteria to ensure that the delivery choice is appropriate. In considering the time and cost of various distribution options, one must examine three relative factors: (1) the nature of the message—its importance, (2) the resulting action required, and (3) the size or quantity of the information.

CHAPTER 7 Distributing Text

For example, a postcard with a few written lines from a vacationing friend requires no action on the part of the recipient, is rather small in size, and has no urgency connected with its message. The cost of mailing the postcard is less than 25 cents, and the time it takes to transmit and deliver the card is about a week. Regardless of its low cost and its delayed receipt, the recipient enjoys the news. However, if it had been sent by overnight express mail (costing about $10), it would be viewed as a foolish extravagance—an inappropriate delivery method based on cost.

In contrast, should those few written lines be a notice that your name had been selected in a cash award contest requiring an immediate reply to ensure eligibility, the personal priorities for delivery would dramatically change. No doubt it would be sent by either registered mail or telegram. Although these methods are more costly, both assure receipt and provide ample opportunity for response. Should this notice have been delivered through normal first-class mail service, it would be viewed as an inappropriate delivery method based on time.

From the examples, you can see that information (a document) requiring distribution from an office must be weighed for the value of the contents and the results anticipated by its use. In addition, the quantity and size of the document influences the delivery method. Bulky packages requiring delivery could be sent via truck or air depending on their urgency. Massive mailings of letter-size documents could be sent by bulk mail methods (slow), first-class mailing methods (faster), expressed deliveries (still faster), or electronic methods (immediate). The method selected is determined by the priorities and controlled by the distribution standards of the company.

This chapter discusses the problems that offices encounter in distributing information. Various methods and types of equipment are available for the distribution of internal and external mail. By viewing distribution from a cost and time/benefit analysis, you will learn how to determine appropriate delivery methods based on company needs.

DISTRIBUTION PROBLEMS

Numerous studies about office correspondence have been conducted over the past 15 years. Many of these studies state that between 75 and 90 percent of all paper business documents consist of internal correspondence, and 90 percent of that amount involves only textual material.[1] A great need exists for improved efficiency in generating and communicating messages within the same company.

---

[1] John J. Connell, "Office of the 80s, Productivity Impact," *Business Week* (February 18, 1980), page 4.

Of course, information is distributed in ways other than by mailing paper documents. A considerable amount of office information is gathered or dispatched through telephone calls. Thus, it is important to consider the quantity and quality of this method of information delivery. Historically, telephone calls have proven to be a tremendous bottleneck to the smooth flow of information processing. Except for the myriad of phone message slips, the paperwork explosion is unaffected by this information process.

The ease of telephoning for information has created its own statistical problems. Independent studies conducted by local Bell Telephone companies and as referenced in Harry Newton's *Communication Lines* column have shown that:

- Approximately three fourths of all business calls do not reach the intended recipient on the first try.

- Two thirds of all office calls made are intracompany—to other employees.

- Over half of these intracompany calls are then returned only to find the caller unavailable.[2]

A tremendous amount of office information is dispersed by telephone.

---

[2]Harry Newton, "Communication Lines," *Business Communications Review* (May-June, 1980).

CHAPTER 7 Distributing Text

Business refers to this phenomenon as telephone tag. Telephone tag is one of the most criticized time wasters in the daily office routine. Few employees are immune to its irritating effects.

To lend further credibility to the staggering problems connected with the flow of information, the chart shown in Figure 7-1 was obtained from a study conducted by Comserv Corporation in 1982. The chart shows actual work time converted to annual cost figures for both support and managerial positions. The intent behind the illustration was to expose the current information handling methods to the close scrutiny of company management. In reviewing the figures, management was encouraged to assess the value of a voice/electronic mail system and consider better ways of distributing information. The study assumed that all traditional information handling methods were to be replaced by electronic methods. This illustrated the full impact of cost- and time-saving results. Of course, not all traditional methods can be replaced by electronic methods.

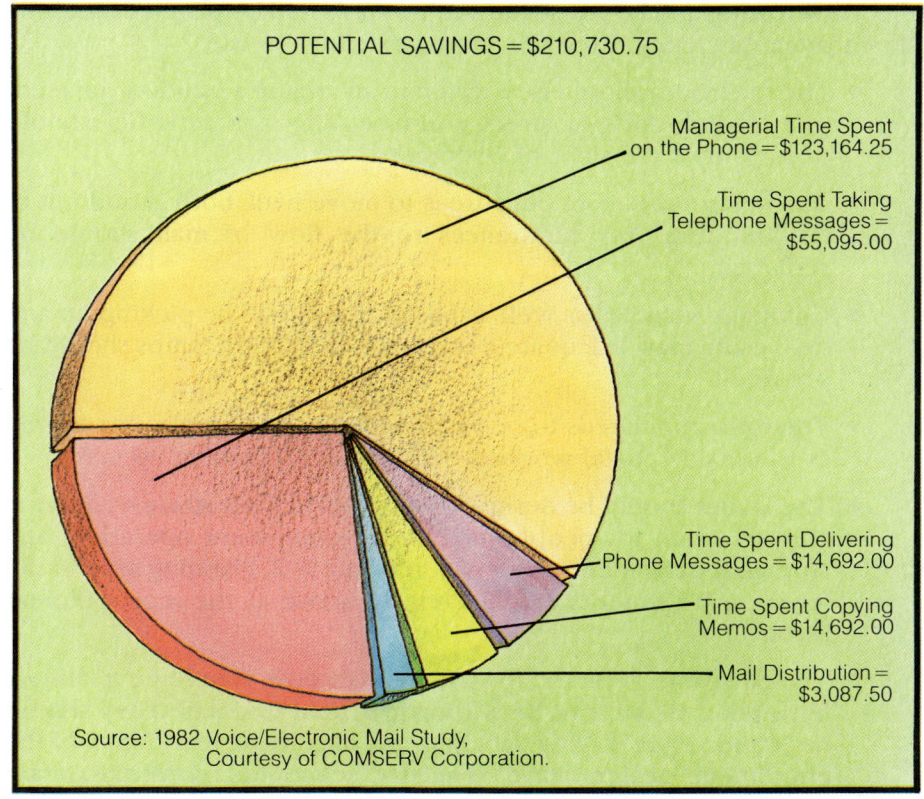

FIG. 7-1
VOICE/ELECTRONIC MAIL
The implementation of a voice/electronic mail system potentially could save a company a great deal of money.

This chapter reviews the common traditional and electronic methods that are alternatives to first-class mail and telephone calls. Each is described in terms of its practicality or appropriateness for general situations. How an individual company chooses to regulate its distribution methods must be determined by its specific needs and objectives.

COMPANY MAIL AND DELIVERY SYSTEMS

There are no standard procedures which designate the location of a company mailroom. In fact, many mailrooms are secluded in lower rooms of a building. Often, employees are unfamiliar with the location of their mailroom unless an urgent matter requires their personal attention. The mail facility is a department that is not often visited by company executives, which is likely to be distressing to the mailroom supervisor. Management's lack of awareness makes the mailroom supervisor's job of gaining approval for efficiency improvements difficult.

Guidelines

The location and layout of the mailroom should be planned carefully to enhance efficiency. Here are some guidelines to use:

- The mailroom should be located in an area of a building adjacent to a loading dock or street entrance. The mail activities should occur out of the sight of customers.

- The mailroom's main purpose is to move mail, both in and out of the building. Any hindrances to the flow of mail should be removed.

- Company vehicles as well as postal trucks will be picking up and delivering mail. Adequate dock space or loading ramps should be provided.

- The mailroom needs to be easily accessible to employees as well as to outside postal workers delivering and picking up mail.

- The layout should be designed to conserve floor space—allowing enough room for people movement, equipment operation, and storage requirements as shown in Figure 7-2. Planning several different arrangements enables one to arrive at the most efficient layout.

- The personnel selected to staff the mailroom should be qualified, have good vision, and be willing to attend to detail. They should be trained in packaging, labeling, and classifying mail. Many of the equipment dealers have regularly scheduled classes to train mailroom staff.

For example, one vendor opened a training center devoted exclusively to improving the efficiency and economy of internal mail handling and the use of the U.S. Postal Service. The training sessions cover

CHAPTER 7   Distributing Text   155

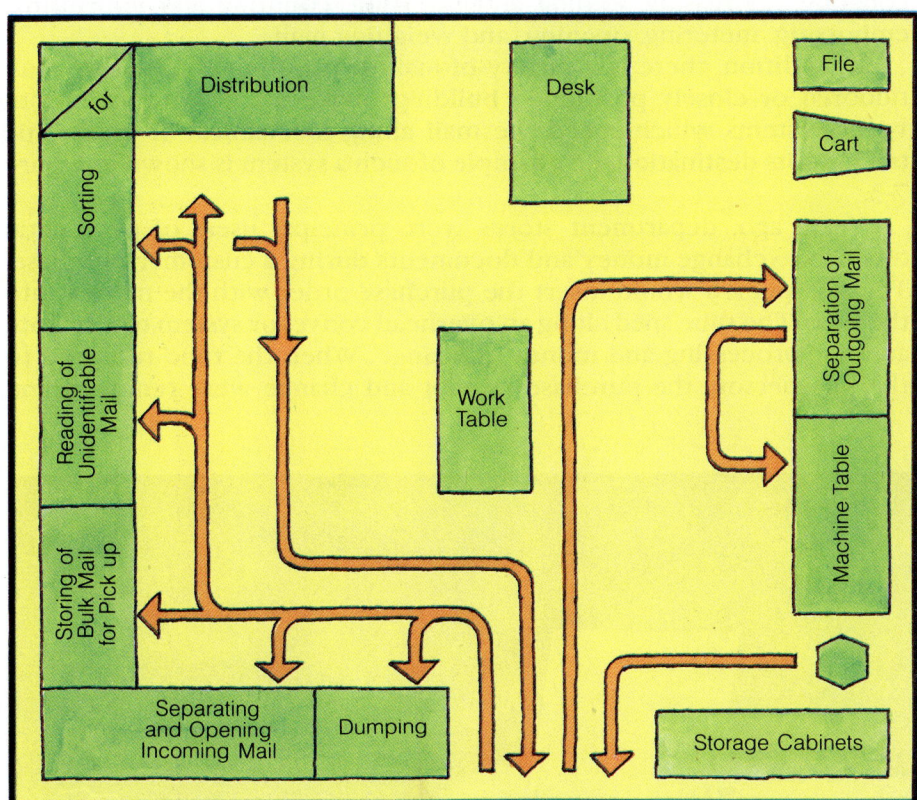

FIG. 7-2
WORK FLOW DESIGN
A good work flow design allows work to be done smoothly and efficiently.
(Courtesy of the U.S. Postal Service)

all aspects of mailing operations in a two-day class. It is also possible to develop training orientation classes that are tailored for specific company situations. Training is the key to effective and efficiently run mailroom operations. The experience can be rewarding and beneficial to the staff.

Internal Mail Handling Equipment

Many of the mail handling processes can be performed manually, which is usually the method used by small firms. Many large firms with ever increasing mail volumes use equipment designed to speed the preparation of this handling without having to increase staff.

Automatic equipment can ease the burden of folding, inserting, labeling, and metering. To determine the practicality of adding such equipment, companies weigh the cost of the equipment against the cost of doing the job manually to see where the greatest economies are gained. A full line of automated equipment is available that specializes in various mail handling activities. This equipment is capable of copying, collating, addressing, folding and inserting, counting and imprinting, embossing, metering, opening, and weighing mail.

In addition, there is a variety of mail distribution equipment. Multifloored or closely positioned buildings make use of automatic conveyor systems which speed the mail along mechanical or electronic tracks to its destination. An example of such a system is shown in Figure 7-3.

Years ago, department stores were principal users of pneumatic tubes to exchange money and documents during a customer purchase. The salesperson would insert the purchase order with the money into the tube. The tube sped along an overhead conveyor system to a remote area for processing and money exchange. When the tube returned to the salesperson, the purchase receipt and change were removed and

An addressing machine is used by many large businesses.

FIG. 7-3   ELECTRIC TRACK DELIVERY SYSTEM

handed to the customer. The salespeople did not have to operate a cash register for each transaction as they do today.

Pneumatic tube methods have been replaced with speedier processes in today's shopping centers. However, their use is still being sought in many businesses for the distribution of documents and parcels. Conveyor systems of all sizes are commonly used to relay bulk packages or large volumes of mail.

A popular delivery system of large, single-level offices is the electronic mobile mail unit. The first mobile mail unit was introduced commercially in July, 1980. A bank was one of the first users of the system.

The mobile mail unit is a self-propelled delivery cart guided by an invisible fluorescent path painted on the floor or carpeting. An ultraviolet light and a photoelectric tracking system are used to detect the path and keep the cart on course. The path can be erased and altered when necessary. Although the paint does not affect the carpeting, the carpet can become route-worn by the continual tracking of the wheels.

The cart makes regular rounds, stopping at points along the way in predetermined intervals. These stops allow the employees to remove

The mobile mail unit is an automated means of delivering mail in single-level offices.

mail addressed to them and to insert mail that will be forwarded to others on the line. The cart can be manually held for longer periods of time by a touch control. It is also equipped with a front bumper that is touch sensitive to obstacles and will stop if impeded. If the obstacle remains in its path for a predetermined interval, the cart will make periodic nudges until its pathway is free. It "beeps" its presence while making its rounds and will return to the mailroom to deactivate itself. Mail delivery carts can be recharged every eight hours to ensure successful delivery rounds. The latest models are programmed for elevator use to increase the delivery distance.

Many companies experience high employee turnover rates in the areas of mail and message delivery since these jobs are usually low salaried and considered to be entry-level positions. Thus, the use of automatic equipment is justified primarily through reduced staffing.

PUBLIC AND PRIVATE MAIL SERVICES

The distribution of material through the public mail system can be frustrating to business managers, for they have no control over the entire handling process. However, the U.S. Postal Service (USPS) is committed to aiding the business person and provides many special services that can be utilized effectively by business.

In recent years, private mail services have become more competitive with the special delivery methods of the public mail system. These new options permit the business user to explore various means of distributing information in a cost-conscious and timely manner.

The USPS is often under criticism by the press and other media for not meeting rigid standards of mail delivery. To place its position in perspective, one should understand the difference between public and private services. The USPS is solely in the business of information distribution—unlike some of its competitors that operate delivery services in addition to other business activities.

By the early Eighties, the USPS employed over 700,000 employees. The chances for human error are proportionate to the numbers of people working on the mail. The amount of mail processed daily is staggering. Consider that if the postal service met its published standards for delivery of mail 99 percent of the time, there would be 900 million pieces of mail not delivered on time. Less than 1 percent of the mail is sent by private carriers. The chances for error based on the amount of mail delivered is greatly reduced for private services. If a customer of the USPS is dissatisfied, the local postmaster is available for assistance. A publication that is available free of charge from the post office is entitled *A Consumer's Guide to Postal Services and Products*. This pamphlet contains information on all products and services offered by the USPS.

The special services offered by public and private carriers give the business customer a wide variety of services from which to choose,

PART TWO Information Processing Cycle

Left: A staggering amount of mail is processed daily by both public and private mail services.

Right: The delivery of packages has created its own unique problems.

depending on particular mailing requirements. Of course, these special services cost more than regular first-class mail. Since the rates and charges change from time to time, costs of these services are not included in the descriptions that follow.

Special Delivery

Special delivery services provide delivery for an item soon after it arrives at the addressee's post office. Delivery is assured on the day the item is received by that post office. However, the transportation time from the point of origination is not speeded up. Special messengers, rather than the normal mail carriers, usually handle special delivery mail. The cost of this service is added to the cost of regular postage.

Special Handling

Special handling is a preferential dispatch and transportation that is available for third-class (advertising) and fourth-class (parcels or bulk packages) mail. The fee for this service is about one half of the cost of special delivery.

Private carriers use a similar method for transporting bulk packages (such as word processing equipment). In these cases, the transportation usually is provided by trucks, and the package will reach its destination within 10 days. The truck makes several scheduled stops to deliver packages from many different users. Common trucking firms, such as moving and storage companies, subsidize their regular return trips with this service. In addition, there is often an insurance fee based on the value of the goods. A popular special handling service which provides specific attention to delivery routing is the United Parcel Service (UPS). As a specialized delivery service, it schedules frequent deliveries. Thus, it can usually guarantee a fast delivery cycle.

Certified Mail

Certified mail service provides a record of delivery that is maintained by the post office of the addressee. The carrier delivering the item obtains the signature of the addressee on a receipt form, which is kept for two years. Certified mail is used primarily for items that have no monetary value. There is no insurance feature. If a return receipt is requested by the sender, an additional fee is charged. Should proof of delivery be requested within the two-year period, the fee increases.

Certified mail service provides an economical and convenient way of obtaining proof of delivery for letters and other mail of no intrinsic value. All it takes to mail a certified letter is a special sticker; but if proof of delivery is desired, another sticker is required. Many companies use this service to protect themselves from customer claims, such as in the case of insurance cancellation.

Registered Mail

Domestic first-class mail, airmail, or priority mail may be registered with an indemnity limit of $10,000. This insurance protection is purchased by those who mail stocks, bonds, jewelry, and other items of value. Registered mail provides the customer with a receipt at the time of mailing, and the post office of the sender maintains a record of all registered mailings. For a small additional fee, a proof-of-delivery receipt can be returned to the sender. Other registered mail services include: (1) registered C.O.D., (2) return receipt, and (3) restricted delivery.

Registered mail is accounted for during transportation by its number. It is transported separately from other types of mail. The registry fees, added to first-class or airmail postage, are scaled according to the declared value of the piece. Registered mail cannot be deposited in collection boxes, because a receipt must be issued at the point of mailing.

Firms that mail money, negotiable securities, and other high-value articles frequently carry commercial insurance. To declare an incorrect value on the item is against postal regulations. Where such claims are found to be erroneous, the postal service can deny or reject the claim.

Insured Mail

Third-class and fourth-class mail may be insured up to $400 for protection against loss or damage. For articles insured for more than $20, recipients will be assigned a receipt of delivery which is filed through their local post office. The return receipt identifies who signed for the item and the date it was delivered. It is the proof of delivery. If it is necessary to note the exact delivery address, an additional fee is charged. It is possible to obtain a receipt for insured items under $20; however, special fees and arrangements must be made with the local post office.

Business Reply Mail

People who wish to encourage responses to the mail they send can pay postage for those responses by using the business reply service. Application for the permit is made by special form, for which no fee is charged. Business reply mail may be used in any quantity and may be distributed in any way the mailer wishes. Responses can be sent from any U.S. post office to any valid address in the United States. Using one permit, the user may provide for the return of all replies to one location or to several locations.

The mailer guarantees payment for the postage of all replies that are returned. The postage rate per piece is the regular first-class rate plus a slight fee determined by the weight. An international business reply service between the United States, Great Britain, and the Netherlands is now available.

Collect on Delivery

With collect on delivery (C.O.D.) service, a letter or parcel may be mailed with the provision for collection of both the postage and the value of the contents at the delivery point. The amount collected from the addressee is returned to the mailer by a postal money order. The fee schedule varies depending upon the amount to be collected. The maximum amount collectable is $400.

Mailgram

A Mailgram is a combination letter and telegram which is designed to provide overnight service to addresses in the continental United States. The customer presents the message to a telegraph office or phones toll free to a centralized telephone operator. The message is sent electronically to a teleprinter at a post office near its destination. There it is placed in a distinctive envelope and delivered to the addressee by a regular Postal Service letter carrier. Most Mailgrams are delivered the next business day.

Businesses can originate Mailgrams directly from their teletypewriters. Large-volume users also may originate messages by computer terminals. The unit cost of a Mailgram is reduced for companies that have an input device (such as a teletypewriter or computer terminal) that can communicate directly to the vendor's computer mainframe.

Because Mailgrams involve both manual delivery by the public postal service as well as electronic distribution, they are difficult to categorize. Some authorities on distribution methods classify Mailgrams as a special delivery method of the public postal service, and others consider it to be a form of electronic mail.

A Mailgram is a combination letter and telegram.

Express Mail

Express Mail is a high-speed, intercity delivery system designed for fast, reliable transfer of time-sensitive documents and products. This service is provided by the public postal service as well as by many private carriers. The cost for the delivery is high, but the service is guaranteed next-day turnaround. The service is customized to the user's needs. Many options are available. Some of the more common options are as follows:

- **Door-to-Door Service.** The mail is picked up at the time and place specified and goes without delay to the airport. On arrival at the destination airport, the mail immediately is delivered to its final stop.

- **Door-to-Destination Airport Service.** The mail is picked up where specified and delivered to the destination airport. The addressee will pick up the delivery at the airport.

- **Originating Airport-to-Addressee Service.** The sender takes the mail to the airport. The destination airport driver delivers it to the addressee.

- **Airport-to-Airport Service.** The sender takes the mail to the airport. The addressee picks up the mail from the destination airport.

- **Regular Express Mail Service.** The sender brings the mail to a post office by a certain time in the afternoon. It is ready for pickup by the addressee at 10:00 a.m. the next business day, or it is delivered to the addressee by 3:00 p.m.

Overnight mail service is provided by both public and private mail services.

E-COM Service

The U.S. Postal Service also provides services for messages that originate within computers. It is called E-COM (Electronic Computer Originated Mail). Twenty-five strategically located post offices have special equipment which can receive and print messages that have been transmitted electronically over private telecommunications lines. Once the post office receives the message, it is printed and trimmed so it appears much as an individually typed letter would appear. The letter is inserted into its special envelope and marked for first-class delivery. The Postal Service offers this E-COM convenience service for companies with a guaranteed two-day delivery within the continental United States.

Understanding all of the various mailing options available is only a small part of the mail distributor's job. To take advantage of the lowest cost options, the distributor must separate, sequence, meter, label, and bundle mail according to predefined directions. Getting the job done is first priority in the mailroom. Achieving a cost savings is often a second priority. In Harry Newton's column, *Communication Lines*, he said:

> "... Banks are actually the largest users of first-class mail in the United States. Remarkably, very few banks avail themselves of the post office's discount for presorting envelopes in Zip order."[3]

ELECTRONIC MAIL SYSTEMS

Electronic mail systems originated in 1837 with the telegraph that was introduced by Samuel F. B. Morse. An electronic mail system (EMS) is a person-to-person communication of information using an electronic means for the creation, transmission, delivery, and storage of the information. In its simplest form, an EMS can be the connection of two telephones. A sophisticated form would be a computer network.

Electronic mail systems can provide answers to many of the office information communication problems. In a typical week, office personnel spend approximately 4 percent of their average work week rehandling mail that has been keyboarded in-house. This rehandling is caused by:

- The absence of tracking methods—"Where is the original copy filed?"
- Rush requests—"I need it now!"
- Preparation for mail dissemination—"I want each manager to receive a personally addressed copy!"

---

[3]Harry Newton, "Communication Lines," *Business Communications Review* (November-December, 1979), page 27.

Time is also spent copying keyboarded text for distribution. Delays are apt to occur when distributing mail through sources outside of the company. These delays are often beyond the company's control. Delays also can occur internally because of misdirection or loss.

Delays hamper a company's ability to make decisions or react in a timely fashion to both internal and branch office happenings. Branch offices that are scattered far from the headquarters facility have unpredictable mailing schedules. Correspondence can be delayed for six to ten days in routing. Responses to an initial inquiry can be similarly delayed in return mail routing. In all, the information problems confronting businesses can be summarized as complaints of poor document turnaround, delayed decisions, and increased unproductive time.

Benefits

An appropriate EMS can both displace and avoid the cost accrued by these problems. For management and professionals it can mean increased productivity by providing:

- Timely information and documentation
- Increased creative time
- Better decisions
- Faster approvals
- Reduced follow-up/tracking
- Reduced telephone follow-up
- Reduced document input decisions

EMS also can identify delegable tasks which can be assigned to support staff. Support personnel can assume responsibility for routing correspondence and initiating document tracking (or follow-up) systems. For the typing staff, an EMS can provide:

- Reduced pressure and fatigue
- Reduced duplication of effort
- Reduced rekeying for/from transmission
- Reduced unproductive time

For the administrative support staff, an EMS can provide:

- Reduced hard copy distribution
- Reduced opening and logging of mail
- Reduced envelope stuffing
- Reduced envelope addressing

- Reduced copying
- Reduced telephone follow-up

In addition, an EMS can provide a potential reduction in the cost of equipment, supplies, courier (outside) services, messenger (internal) services, postage, overtime, temporary help, recruiting and hiring, and training. However, not all of the benefits are in the productivity and cost categories. There are some added values provided by EMSs. They include:

1 Improved communication due to reduced distribution time and the ability to respond to change

2 Improved customer service due to improved document quality/consistency and increased customer response

3 Increased management support due to the ability to balance the work load, track information in process, measure equipment loads, increase consistency, and improve document security

4 Increased organizational flexibility with the use of existing communication facilities, company-owned hardware and software, and existing procedures which prompt consistent and controlled use

Electronic mail systems provide same-day delivery of information.

5 Enhanced company growth by providing the capacity to add components and to broaden existing communication facilities

Basic Characteristics

Electronic mail systems come in various sizes and types. They can be simple or extremely sophisticated. They are either computerized or noncomputerized. The most sophisticated EMSs available today are those operated within a computerized environment that have display terminals or workstations. Extensive planning is required to prepare the environment, and it is necessary to have trained specialists to oversee the operation of the equipment. The actual operation from a user's standpoint is automatic and friendly. The simplest and the most widely used EMSs are facsimile units, which are relatively easy to install and require limited training.

An electronic mail system can operate in either the foreground or the background. Data communication specialists refer to these operations as (1) asynchronous or (2) synchronous modes of transmission. An **asynchronous** mode (operating in the foreground) means that the people involved must be on opposite ends of the line at the same time to complete transmission. With a **synchronous** mode (operating in the background), an unattended transmission can take place automatically. Modes of communication transmission will be detailed later in this chapter.

Electronic mail can be displayed on a terminal for viewing and/or printed on paper. A system can more easily be cost justified if the text is displayed on a terminal, because the cost and time for rehandling the document are greatly reduced. Paper output is not likely to be completely eliminated due to the importance that office personnel place on tangible copy.

Electronic Message Systems

Many public and private vendors are marketing products which are being described as electronic message systems. These products are a type of electronic transmittal of information between devices and/or locations; but they are not, in the true sense of the meaning, electronic mail systems. There are two types of electronic message systems—message switching systems and digital voice exchange.

Message Switching Systems. A message switching system is a computer storage and control device that can be attached to an on-premise telephone system. Its function is to provide a personal or human means of responding to users' incoming telephone calls when the users are not available. Its goal is to provide more thorough attention to the users' messages and prompt callers to leave more informative notes.

---

asynchronous transmission both parties must be on-line during transmission

synchronous transmission occurs automatically; both parties need not be present

message switching system computer storage and control device; can attach to on-premise telephone system

CHAPTER 7 Distributing Text

Without a message switching center, when a caller phones an employee who is unavailable, the call can be routed automatically to a central number. However, the person responding to the forwarded call does not know who the caller is seeking or which phone has been forwarded without asking the caller questions. Under these circumstances, the caller usually is uncertain of leaving a message and will try the call later. Repetitive calling and telephone tag continue to be problems with this method.

With a message switching system, the message center is equipped with a terminal that displays certain information about telephone users. For example, the system recognizes the initial phone number called and displays the employee's name, where the employee can be reached, when the employee will return, and perhaps, what to say if a select individual phones. Forwarding of the call is programmed through the telephone key pad and is initiated by the users.

The information that is offered by the message center also is provided by the telephone user. The message center personnel, armed with this information, can more intelligently answer an incoming call with the user's name and key the message onto the terminal display. The caller is greeted by a human voice—not a digitized recording. When the user returns to his or her phone, a light indicates that a message is waiting. The user can either phone the message center and have the message read or have the message printed on the nearest printer.

Some companies have all messages printed and either routed through normal delivery services to user's desks or left in a central location for their retrieval. The goal of this service is to eliminate the telephone tag problems associated with offices.

A second type of message switching system offered by private communication carriers uses remote computing equipment and has packet switching capabilities. This means that the company provides off-premises computers to store and forward messages to distant computers via privately purchased communication lines. The user who has an immediate need to prepare and distribute an occasional electronic message but who cannot justify the purchase of the needed equipment, software, and communication lines can use this resource. The cost is determined by the length of the message and is limited to hard copy output at its destination. No editing capabilities can be offered at the document receiving end.

Digital Voice Exchange. A secondary development of an on-premises switching system is a digital voice exchange (DVX). A DVX is a separate computer voice storage device. The caller has the option of leaving the message with the message center or (if the contents are confidential) asking to be connected to the voice storage device.

The digital voice exchange system records voice messages, converts

digital voice exchange
computerized voice storage device

A digital voice exchange system converts voice messages to digital pulses and stores the messages in an audio mailbox for the recipient.

them to a digital format, and stores them in an audio mailbox for subsequent access by designated recipients. The voice system automates distribution of these messages among users of the system.

Any individual with an appropriate identification code entered into the voice directory can both send and receive messages on the system. The user presses a single key on the telephone key pad for each function. Access is guided by voice prompts to enter a user ID and an optional password.

After the user enters a destination address or telephone number, the system verifies the intended recipient's name for the user. The user then creates a message of up to six minutes in length and specifies either immediate delivery or the time and date of delivery, within a 31-day period. The user can then review, rerecord, cancel, or send each message. A message can be sent to a single recipient or to several recipients. The user can even establish regular distribution lists of recipients.

Users who travel often are able to keep in touch with the office by picking up the phone from remote locations and having their office messages spoken to them. The voice device also can place calls to others for the system user. One executive missed his plane, called his voice system, and had it phone his wife at regular intervals to alert her by digital voice of his change in flight schedules. Although there are several vendors specializing in digital voice exchange devices, the market for them is limited to companies with a high volume of traveling users. The cost of the voice equipment is extremely high, and few companies can justify the expense.

The voice system can deliver messages to both system and nonsystem users in audio format only. No printed copies are available yet. All messages are stored until accessed, at which time the user has the option of saving the message for later retrieval, responding to the message immediately, or deleting the message. The theory behind the development of the system is to reduce unanswered calls, provide more informative messages, and automate the process.

Computer-Based Message Systems

The ultimate in electronic mail systems is the user-owned, computerized mail system. Few organizations recognize the benefits that could be derived from using such a system. Neither rain nor snow nor dark of night can keep a computer-based message system (CBMS) from its appointed rounds. As you will recall from Chapter 1, the sender and the receiver do not have to talk at the same time. The computer stores the message until the receiver accesses it. An installed CBMS is readily accepted and appreciated by office employees who need to distribute information to other workers and branch office employees within a short time.

As part of a computerized office system, a CBMS offers the ultimate in efficiency. By encouraging the use of soft copy output (viewing the document on a display screen), companies can reduce the cost of unnecessary paper output. The mainframe of the system generally is situated at a company's corporate headquarters with distribution points extending via communication lines to the branch offices. Branch offices can be either national or worldwide, but they must be able to be dialed directly. In other words, a call placed to another office must not be intercepted by an operator, but be assured of direct access.

Routing schedules and times are determined by the mail administrator. When properly programmed, the CBMS can check in at each branch office to pick up and deliver messages, data files, and word processing documents. The system calls on each workstation at corporate headquarters at regular intervals. Pick up, delivery, and routing of messages and documents to the appropriate recipients are all fully automated. To take advantage of the system, users need only to do the electronic equivalent of dropping a letter in the mail. Tables stored in the system establish times for making the rounds and enable the CBMS software to do the mail sorting that is required to get the messages and documents to the proper recipients.

Senders of information can request reports that confirm the delivery of their items to the intended recipients by date and time. Even deliveries still pending can be listed. In addition, users can ask the system to remind them that replies to specific items were requested by a given date. Imagine the support time that is saved.

A CBMS transmits documents, data files, and messages over privately purchased communication lines (for example, WATS). The cost of the service can be as inexpensive as a WATS call if the company already uses such services for its normal telephone use. In fact, because the company pays a fixed fee for the use of these lines, the more that a CBMS is used, the less expensive is the transmission of each message.

The system works quickly, transmitting a document of up to 50 pages in less than a minute. That speed makes the system ideal for transmitting time-critical information. Any information transmitted via a CBMS can be revised, incorporated in other documents, passed along to other workstations, filed, reviewed on a CRT screen, or printed.

At many companies, the CBMS gets heavy use for the transmission of contracts, proposals, forecasts, and information for budgeting and bookings. Using the electronic mail system to send contracts and proposals back and forth saves these companies a considerable amount on facsimile and Express Mail charges. In addition, rush trips to the airport are eliminated.

Sending budget information to an accounting department via the CBMS reduces the paperwork required for the budgeting process. Accounting personnel can manipulate within the system the figures transmitted to them before having them printed. Electronic mail also can be used to send weekly time utilization reports to branch offices—some of which may be located in other countries.

A program interfacing with the CBMS can convert the time report data from another brand of mainframe computer into compatible reports. These reports can then be transmitted to each branch office where they can be printed or viewed from a workstation screen.

A CBMS has an unheralded advantage. The system's communication capabilities can help to build "a camaraderie," a real working-together spirit that crosses departmental boundaries. System users can gain a better understanding of how their individual responsibilities contribute to larger goals and thus learn to work together more cooperatively. The users will likely become very enthusiastic and be eager to learn. Implementation of new applications is easy in this working climate.

The message portion of the CBMS provides the user with an electronic convenience for taking short notes and telephone messages, calendaring and scheduling, and making quick responses. The user, prompted through each screen display, can key a short note for quick

CHAPTER 7 Distributing Text

delivery with an alert warning for the recipient. The recipient can reroute the message, distribute the message to other users, save the message for later retrieval, print it, or delete it. An example of a CBMS message screen is shown in Figure 7-4. The screen shows (1) the original message sent to Carol Chan and (2) her reply.

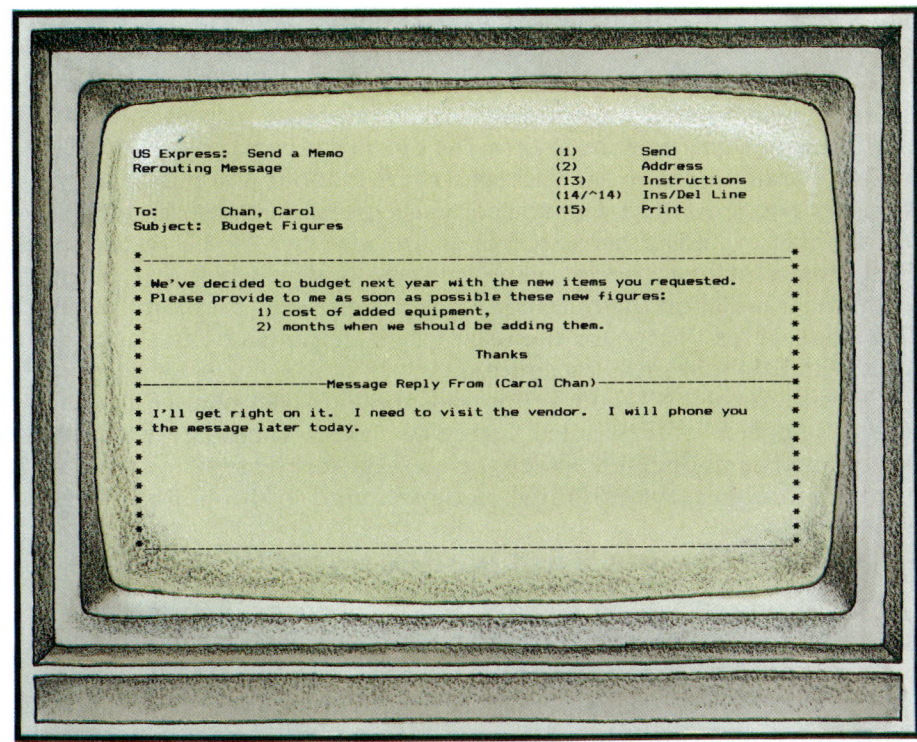

FIG. 7-4
COMPUTER-BASED MESSAGE SYSTEM
By encouraging the use of a CBMS, a company can reduce unnecessary paper output and save money.

Some CBMSs send graphic as well as text information. Examples include flowcharts, organization charts, floor plans, pie charts, and line graphs. These systems require graphic terminals with high resolution at one end and a compatible graphic terminal, printer/plotter, or intelligent copier at the receiving end. Having graphics capability can increase the cost of a CBMS operation from two sources: (1) the purchase of a specialized graphics terminal, and (2) the increased expenses resulting from the longer transmission times.

Teletypewriter Systems

The teletypewriter is the sending and receiving equipment for the telegraph wire service known as Telex. Telex was the only form of written message carried by wire until the Teletypewriter Exchange Service (TWX) was introduced.

Telex messages originally were prepared on punched paper tape and transmitted at the rate of 66 words a minute. TWX messages are sent over ordinary telephone lines at a rate of 100 words a minute.

Both TWX and Telex allow off-line preparation on either punched paper tape or, in the case of communicating word processors, magnetic media. Next, the medium is fed into the sending machine. The operator then dials the receiving terminal, and the document is transmitted at the full speed of the sending terminal. The output is in the form of hard copy.

Though it is simpler for the principal to think in terms of words a minute (wam) when transmitting text, equipment manufacturers usually speak of transmissions in terms of bits per second (bps). The speed of data communication for teletypewriters is about 300 bits of information per second (bps). Compared to the sending rates of other electronic mail systems, this speed is at the low end of the transmission spectrum. However, because the message is keyed before sending it, less time is spent on the telephone line and the cost is minimized. Both TWX and Telex charge for the use of their networks by the number of pulses and the distance transmitted.

International TWX and Telex transmissions take place through the use of selected centers called "gateway cities." These centers provide specialized personnel who place the message for the sender and route it through foreign services similar to those found in the United States.

Communicating Word Processors

Word processors can be equipped with communications capabilities, which gives them advantages over teletypewriters. Unlike teletypewriters, communicating word processors allow either the sender or the receiver to edit the document. Whereas teletypewriters provide only hard copy output, word processors enable text to be displayed on the screen (soft copy) or to be printed (hard copy). An ordinary telephone call can be placed to transmit documents to other communicating word processors. The charges are based on actual line usage, and there is no expense for network services (as in the case of Telex and TWX).

Like CBMSs, communicating word processors can transmit documents between remote locations when the normal delivery of interoffice or regular first-class mail is too slow. They may also communicate within the same building to other types of equipment and to host computers. The devices required to provide these transmissions are called modems (an acronym for a modulator/demodulator). Each sending and receiving device must be equipped with a compatible modem. In addition, each device must have compatible communications protocols (described later in this chapter) and speeds.

On some word processors, the operator can choose from various options and select a mode of transmission. The vendor provides a list of

CHAPTER 7 Distributing Text

available options, which appears on the display screen. This list permits the operator to set the rules governing the transmission in cases where multiple communication modes exist. For example, the operator can set the line speed to various rates. Some possible settings are:

- 300 bps—slow transmission, such as Telex operations
- 2,400 bps—normal communication transmission speed over telephone lines
- 9,600 bps—usually provided by specially leased lines where conditioning aids the quality of the transmission, or by satellite communication devices, which use many times the 9,600 bps speed in their communication transmissions

Some word processors have a single mode of transmission (a preset group of parameters). The vendor has taken the guesswork out of establishing the connection by indicating in menu format a single way to communicate with another device. When the transmission is in an automatic mode, the communications can be received unattended. However, if the transmission operates in the foreground, the operators of the two systems must both be present to verify the transmissions.

A word processor can be used as an electronic mail terminal. The most cost-efficient means of document or message creation is **off-line**, which means that the operator is not actually connected to the communication line while creating the document.

After the document is created, the operator establishes connection with the communicating computer and transmits the information. An operator could not key information as rapidly as even the lowest rate of transmission—300 bps. To key the document while on-line would be not only extremely costly but also very impractical. However, there are many Telex communication devices which permit only this type of on-line keying.

An off-line method reduces the connection time between the systems. Also, with some processors the off-line method keeps the entire range of editing capabilities available. After composing, the user may store the document on a diskette, edit it, and reissue it as necessary.

off-line operator is not connected to communication lines during document creation

Facsimile (FAX) Systems

Another method of sending information electronically is facsimile transmission. A FAX device will transmit either text or graphic material (such as photographs, drawings, charts, and longhand) from one point to another. The time it takes to transmit an 8 1/2-inch by 11-inch document across the country generally is less than three minutes. High-speed models can transmit a paper within 20 seconds. Formerly, facsimile equipment was impractical because of incompatibility between machines. The various vendors used different types of transmission and modulation. Most FAX devices now operate similarly and are compatible.

The FAX device consists of an optical scanner in which an electron beam from a CRT sweeps across the document and generates digitized representations of the black and white information. Signals relay this digitized information across the country, and the information is reassembled (like the original) on the receiving FAX device as shown in **Figure 7-5**. The clarity of the re-created image (its resolution) and the speed of transmission are of great importance in the use of facsimile devices. The faster the speed and the greater the resolution, the more costly the process.

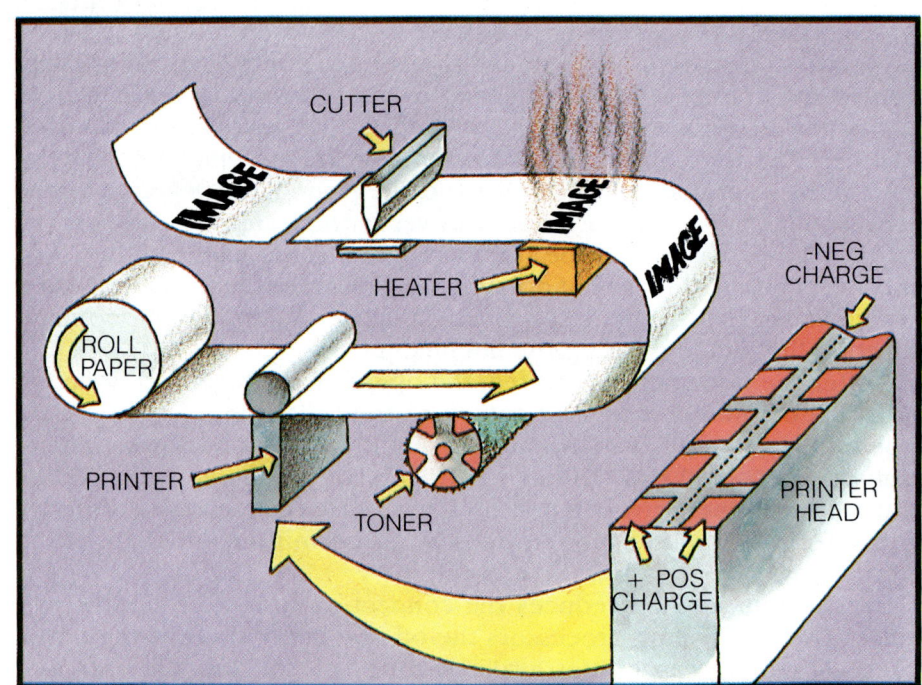

FIG. 7-5
FACSIMILE SYSTEMS
Text, as well as graphics, can be transmitted across the country by FAX systems in a manner of minutes.
(Courtesy of Panafax Corporation)

There are computerized FAX machines which store text as well as graphic images on magnetic media. The most space-efficient manner of storing graphics consists of a black design on a white background. In order to compress the stored space, the white background is removed before storing the design in its digitized form onto the disk. Ordinarily, a page of graphics requires more storage space than a page of text if one were to include the entire black/white image; however, compression reduces the amount of storage required for the design alone. Stored graphics can be printed and reproduced many times, but the image can never be altered or edited.

CHAPTER 7 Distributing Text   177

A FAX device can transmit both text and graphic material.

FAX devices are used quite heavily by companies that need to move graphic documents, such as those requiring a signature, from one remote location to another at low cost. The equipment is simple to operate and is relatively inexpensive. The length of time needed for the transmission governs the urgency of the equipment use. In the case of FAX equipment, time of transmission is the main element of expense weighed by information managers.

LINKING FOR COMMUNICATIONS

The decade of the Eighties has become known as the Information Age. As progress into the Information Age continues, communications are playing a vital role in the movement of information. This information passes through communication lines in many forms—data, voice, text, and graphics. For businesses to remain competitive in this Information Age, the provision of an information link to these communication facilities must be a corporate goal.

As word processing and data processing activities moved closer together, a certain advantage in merging the two technologies was recognized. The industry often describes this potential merge as office automation or information processing. Until this time, equipment purchases by either of the two processing groups were made independent of the other group's manager. Neither decision making nor financing was discussed jointly and shared. Once the communication barriers were broken, many companies interested in pursuing an information processing approach made some revealing discoveries. They found that they had a wide variety of equipment, each type capable of duplicating many applications of the other; yet media were incompatible. The likelihood of uncovering media-compatible equipment was rare.

Fortunately an integration of incompatible equipment for office automation can be accomplished with the use of telecommunications. But first there are some similarities and differences between word and data processing equipment that need to be understood.

Keyboarding is a common parameter of both word and data processing. However, it is communications capability that provides the link to merge these two different systems. For instance, word processors have fixed software with **Boolean logic** parameters. This means that text can be manipulated, but certain text units remain unchanged. The software itself focuses on space changes. When applying function codes, such as *insert, delete,* and *paragraph,* the software adjusts the spaces within the area to match what is recognized as a word, a sentence, or a paragraph. In this example, a word is separated by a space before and after; a sentence is followed by a punctuation symbol and two spaces; and a paragraph is separated by two carriage return symbols. Data processors, on the other hand, have software that can be modified, replaced, or added as necessary. Using a binary numbered system, the data processing machines can add, subtract, and compare. Through continuous addition and subtraction, they also can multiply and divide.

In order to ensure a workable arrangement between word and data processing equipment, communication characteristics of each terminal must be compatible. The ability for each machine to communicate is not enough. Each communicating device has a series of special, matching specifications that allow one machine to "talk" to the other machine. There currently are no standards ensuring compatibility, and the likelihood of equipment manufacturers establishing standards has not yet materialized.

Unless two identical devices are communicating, there is the problem of unlike word processing code structures. Word processing codes determine what will happen to the characters when they are printed on a page. It is unlikely that the same code from different pieces of equipment will produce the same behavior on a printout. Therefore, it is important to understand what text editing machine compatibility means, how it works, and how it can be used effectively.

In essence, **compatibility** means the ability of one machine to share with or communicate information to another machine. The first method

---

Boolean logic word processing logic; recognizes words by space changes

compatibility ability of one machine to communicate with another machine

CHAPTER 7 Distributing Text

of achieving compatibility between competing products is by interfacing them with a **black box**. This device may be a freestanding unit, or it may be a cable connected to a text editing machine. Its purpose is to translate signal flows from one message protocol to another protocol.

black box allows compatibility between two incompatible machines

Compatibility also can be achieved when one piece of equipment does not read codes and only accepts alphanumeric data. This essentially means that the receiver is receiving unformatted text and must provide formatting. In both of these cases, the method of compatibility requires either close proximity of the two machines or the manual manipulation of the magnetic media.

The second element of compatibility is achieved when one text editing machine has the ability to communicate with another machine. The transmitting and receiving machines do not have to be the same model or even have to be produced by the same manufacturer. In some cases, a text editing machine can interact with a computer. In this latter case and in order to communicate effectively, each machine must have similar characteristics. These include four elements: (1) language; (2) speed; (3) transmission type; and (4) protocol.

MACHINE INCOMPATIBILITY

Brand X *word processor* that records on *magnetic card*
    cannot communicate directly with
Brand X *word processor* that records on *diskette*.

Brand X *word processor* that records on *diskette*
    cannot communicate directly with
Brand Y *word processor* that records on *diskette*.

Brand X *word processor* that records on *diskette*
    cannot communicate directly with
Brand X *computer* that records on *diskette*.

Brand X *word processor*
    cannot communicate directly with
Brand Z *computer*.

FIG. 7-6
COMPATIBILITY
There are many types of incompatibility that must be overcome before communication can occur.

Language

The most common language or code used in the transmission of information is known as **baudot**, in which five equal length bits represent one character. A bit is an abbreviation for binary digit, either 0 or 1. This code originated in 1874 by a French inventor, J. M. E. Baudot, for a teleprinter and generally is used for telegraph transmission. It is the international standard for Telex transmission.

baudot most common code used in transmission of information

There are three languages presently used between word and data processing equipment. They are as follows:

- **ASCII (American Standard Code for Information Interchange)**—a 128-character government standard including seven bits plus a parity bit which checks for accuracy.
- **EBCDIC**—a 256-character language which has eight bits including uppercase, lowercase, and punctuation symbols.
- **EBCDIC/WP**—a 512-character language including special tab codes, symbols, Greek letters, engineering codes, and indent instructions.

There are enough characteristics included in this latter code to represent all possible code symbols by their hexidecimal value. (All computers reason with hexidecimal codes.) Therefore, if an error occurs in a display mode, one can view the hexidecimal value of the code and make an immediate correction if it is warranted. For example, if the printed material requires indenting and the final product does not indent, it is possible that the character represented on the display as *indent* has a hexidecimal code that produces another function. Changing the value of that symbol to its hexidecimal *indent* code will produce the correct results. Both systems must use the same hexidecimal value codes to reach the same conclusions.

Speed

analog signal has variable wave lengths

Voice signals may be transmitted over ordinary telephone lines at a rate of 300 to 3,000 bits per second, which is a range of 2,700 bps. This range represents low- to high-pitch voice levels. The signal resembles a wavy line during transmission and is called an **analog signal**.

data signal consists of structured pulses

Data (or digital) signals, on the other hand, are structured, digital pulses consisting of two line conditions—either a plus one (1) for *on*, or a zero (0) for *off*. These pulses contain both DC and very high frequency components.

The current telephone network, which is the backbone of our communications industry, is not designed for the transmission of digital signals. Therefore, the signals are translated through a modem or an acoustic coupler and converted to analog signals suitable for transmission on existing voice circuits as shown in Figure 7-7.

modem converts data signals to/from analog signals

Modem is an acronym for modulator/demodulator. It is a device used to convert data signals to/from analog signals for transmission over telephone lines. A modem also is known as a dataset.

modulation conversion of analog signals to data signals

In the modem, the square-edged pulse train from the computer or word processor is tailored electronically to fit between the telephone channel frequencies by a process called **modulation**. With the appropriate modulation technique, information can be sent by telephone at high speed without undue distortion. At the receiving end, the data is recovered from the transmitting signal by a process called **demodulation**. Since most data communication systems transmit and receive over the same pair of wires, the modulator and demodulator circuits are usually combined within the same package, giving rise to the name *modem*.

demodulation conversion of data signals to analog signals

An **acoustic coupler** is a small device with openings that accommodate the earpiece and microphone end of an ordinary telephone headset. It indirectly converts data signals to and/or from tones for transmission over telephone lines. This data transmission takes place in three modes.

acoustic coupler indirectly converts data signals to/from tones

1 **Simplex.** Transmits information in a single direction. A typical example of this would be a data-collecting device or an input device consistently transmitting information to a central collection point. At no time does the collection point retransmit any information to the originating terminal.

2 **Half-Duplex.** Allows two-way transmission but transmits in only one direction at a time.

3 **Full-Duplex.** Provides simultaneous two-way transmission.

The modulation technique is important since it not only tailors the data to the line characteristics, but it also determines how fast and with what protection from line noise and distortion the data can be sent.

With the advent of private telephone companies, internal use between like pieces of equipment may not require modems (datasets).

FIG. 7-7
ANALOG AND DATA SIGNALS
A modem is used to convert analog signals to and/or from data signals for voice transmission.

These private telephone suppliers are referred to as interconnect companies, because their private telephone lines within a building interconnect with the public telephone lines for outside line access. Most interconnect telephone networks within the same building have digital controllers and need no other devices, since analog signals are not used in-house.

Approximately 83 percent of all lines used within the United States are analog in design.[4] Therefore, a modem (dataset) must be used when intercepting these lines or going outside a private switching network owned by a particular company.

Transmission Type

A reference was made to "modes of transmission" earlier in this chapter. It was stated that there are two modes of transmission: asynchronous and synchronous. These are generic data communications terms. As products began interfacing more commonly with computers, vendors coined their own versions of these terms to establish personal product identity. As their products became popular, their versions of these terms also became popularly used by the industry.

Thus, today there are dual sets of terms that describe the two types of transmission. The first, known as asynchronous (nonsynchronous), is a slow transmission of eight bits of digital information with a start bit preceding and a stop bit following the eight bits. The start and stop bits are used for counting and identification purposes. This start/stop method of transmission is commonly used in teletype transmission. Its signal resembles the sound made by the telegraph system.

The second method is bisynchronous (synchronous) transmission, which includes a clock/modem transmitting digital information in blocks to a similar clock/modem. The clock records the time and thus, tracks bits of information. This usually is a faster method of transmission than asynchronous but is also more expensive.

Protocol

protocol preliminary exchange between units so transmission can occur

Protocol is the preliminary negotiation or exchange that takes place before transmission between two communicating units. The CPU must accept the type of protocol before transmission can take place. For unlike systems to communicate, each system must be able to interpret the other's system codes.

Communications technology provides a key to the door of an integrated office system. Specifically, telecommunication permits the interconnection (merging) of separate office technologies into a total information processing system. With communications it is possible to have

---

[4]Richard A. Kuehn (From a lecture to the American Management Associations, Chicago, Illinois, 1981).

CHAPTER 7 Distributing Text

incompatible equipment talk to each other, exchange information, and speed the information on its way.

Another benefit that can be derived from communications is telecommuting. Many firms are allowing employees to work at home by providing them with workstations that have communications features. The goals of these firms are reduced costs, reduced absenteeism, and increased productivity. For the employee, travel time is reduced and flexibility of working hours is made possible. The company's overhead costs for floor space and utilities are reduced. However, there can be problems with the supervision of work and less opportunity to socialize with co-workers.

In conclusion, communications technology provides an information manager with the ability to break down information barriers. Using the resource effectively can reduce costs, increase productivity, speed the flow of information, and provide equipment compatibility.

DISCUSSION QUESTIONS AND CASE PROBLEM

DISCUSSION QUESTIONS

1. What is one of the most criticized time wasters in the daily office routine as described in this chapter?
2. Name three special services provided by the USPS or private carriers. Explain what each service provides.
3. What is the oldest form of an electronic mail system? Is there any similarity between current methods of communication and this older form of electronic mail system?
4. What type of messaging allows CBMSs to operate at top efficiency? Why?
5. What are the two types of transmission? How do they differ?

CASE PROBLEM

Pedro is the mailroom supervisor for a large insurance firm. His company is planning a new structure and has asked Pedro to prepare some guidelines for the new mailroom layout.

1. List three guidelines Pedro should include in his report.
2. Explain how each guideline would effect mailroom efficiencies.

Part 3
IMPLEMENTING CHANGE IN THE OFFICE

Chapter 8 Determining the Need for a System

CHAPTER OBJECTIVES:

Understand what prompts companies to look toward new technology for solutions to their business problems.

Become familiar with the two approaches used by companies in carrying out such solutions.

Select the approach offering the greatest potential for success.

Select and develop team participation.

As a project leader or team member, be able to plan activities that: (1) produce statistics on the current cost of performing office functions; (2) encourage employees to accept the change; (3) weigh the advantages of the new technology; and (4) recommend a practical planning strategy to management.

"Why change? We've been doing it this way for many years, and we get along just fine."

Comments like these were very common in the early years of word processing implementation. As difficult as it was to overcome this early resistance to change, word processing was being implemented in many companies. The positive results of the installations were convincing arguments for many more companies to accept the new technology, reap its benefits, and pave the way for further advancements.

Data and word processing made the task of producing information easier and faster than ever before. But with large volumes of this information available to them, managers found themselves unable to easily extract, analyze, file, retrieve, and communicate decisions from this information. They literally were flooded with information that could not be refined into meaningful facts. They needed a better way to process this information.

As technology advanced, new applications were introduced to respond to these information processing problems. At the same time, companies began experiencing external pressures from different sources. Economic and social changes in the business climate complicated the slower methods of processing information. Companies were forced to look for more effective, more efficient, and less costly ways of conducting their business.

FACTORS CONTRIBUTING TO THE CHANGES IN INFORMATION PROCESSING

There are five major factors which contribute to the inevitable progression of an information processing system within companies. They are: (1) availability of people, (2) energy shortage, (3) availability of resource products, (4) competitive position, and (5) economic position. These factors exert their influence at different times and in varying degrees depending upon individual business activities and interests. In other words, not all companies are affected by the same factors at the same time. Thus, it is not unusual to discover companies throughout the nation in different stages of system development or implementation. To better understand how businesses are affected by these factors, one first needs to identify the factors and then determine when and how they become important influences.

Availability of People

The 1980 United States Census figures illustrate the lowest birthrate in recent years to be the period from 1970 to 1975. Specifically, it predicts a potential new working population ratio of 8.7 million males and 8.4 million females. If this is compared to the 1980 newly available working population of 23.4 million males and 24.5 million females, there is a pronounced declining work force. These figures are a convincing argument in predicting that there will be a work force shortage by the late 1980s. Further, in many parts of the country, schools are closing or consolidating in order to provide an economic balance to filling classrooms.

In some states, enrollment in office education classes at vocational schools has declined by 50 to 70 percent during the last decade. These percentages represent the decline in high school entrants alone. They do not consider the vocational office education enrollment emerging from those who are reentering the job market or from those who are presently employed and are seeking advanced skill training.

The availability of people is one of the four factors contributing to the changes in information processing.

Decreased enrollment in office education fields suggests that potential students are choosing careers in other fields. Prime reasons for not choosing an office career are the low to moderate salaries offered, the lack of career advancement, and the visibility of these positions to upper management. If one considers the already declining population and compounds the problem with the reduction of recent high school graduates entering office occupations, the traditional office will most certainly experience employment difficulties. However, in companies that have made strides in recognition and in better pay for the greater skills required for office system operation, many unskilled employees are acquiring the needed training to compete for these more rewarding jobs.

Energy Shortage

Though not widely publicized recently, the energy shortage is just as real as ever. Fuel is expensive because the supply is low and the demand

The energy shortage is still a very real problem, as it affects employees' travel time and expenses.

is high. This energy shortage restricts the flexibility of workers to choose the location of their jobs relative to their homes. Travel time and method of transportation become serious considerations when high gas costs are involved. In order to attract qualified staff, companies must either locate in people-intensive areas or pay higher salaries to compensate for the greater travel cost and time.

Businesses that depend on travel to conduct their activities are faced with costly increases in air fares and with reduced flight schedules. The higher costs of accommodations incurred by arriving early or staying late because of inconvenient flight schedules is a direct result of the energy shortage. These increased costs must be passed on to customers in the form of higher priced products or services in order for the company to maintain a profit. The effect on these increased costs enables local competitors who are not subjected to the same expense difficulties to attract or gain customers.

Additionally, the escalating oil prices affect the cost of mail delivery and postal rates primarily because the delivery methods rely on the airways for distribution. The last few years have recorded many such increases based upon the increased cost of oil and fuel. These increased costs impact the way in which businesses handle their mail distribution.

Thus, they simultaneously shift the increased cost to their customers. If customers can do business with a local company at a price which excludes these increased costs, they usually do so.

The energy shortage, then, challenges a company's ability to operate competitively; and it limits a customer's flexibility to shop and negotiate. Companies operating solely under traditional communication routing methods will most likely suffer business losses.

Availability of Resource Products

The whirlpool effect of the energy shortage impacts the commodities with which businesses operate on a daily basis. Lack of petroleum decreases the production of oil-based products; i.e., plastics and synthetics. A quick look around your immediate area will enlighten you to the abundant use of these materials. The notebooks you use in class, the chairs in which you sit, and the pens with which you write all are made from oil-based products. Cutting back on the manufacture of these products has an impact on timber resources. Substituting wood products for synthetics reduces the reserve supply for paper products.

Paper is becoming an expensive item to purchase. The current practice of producing business correspondence in unnecessary and wasteful quantities only hurries the potential, costly shortage of this resource. Businesses that continue to produce extensive amounts of paper for communication will have difficulty adapting to the shortage. Additionally, they will increase their paper storage and space costs unnecessarily and affect bottom-line profits.

Competitive Position

Competition is a trademark of American society. In schools, in sports, and in careers there is competition. Businesses must compete aggressively to be profitable and to be recognized in the business world.

Being "number one" means having recognition, success, growth, and profit. Achieving number-one status requires that the business provide the best product, at the best cost, to the most customers. Staying number one requires consistent quality control measures in the areas of customer satisfaction, product sales and development, company management, and employee morale.

Should any of the quality controls weaken because of lack of attention or support, the credibility of the firm's products or services will falter. The company will experience a decline in sales and may be overtaken by its competition. When a company loses its competitive edge, the struggle to regain that edge requires a double effort. The company not only must strengthen its own weaknesses, but it also must work harder and smarter to overtake its competitor. This implies finding new ways to become (1) more productive with reduced staffing, (2) more

CHAPTER 8 Determining the Need for a System 191

responsive with quicker decisions, and (3) more progressive with new technology.

Economic Position

Businesses are competing in a serious inflationary time. In order to maintain a competitive edge and economic survival, businesses are compelled to:

- Eliminate unnecessary expenses

The availability of resource products is of concern to all businesses, but especially to manufacturing businesses that use raw materials.

- Make faster decisions based on speedier and more thorough research
- Communicate these resulting policies more quickly to the staff

In order to accomplish continuing profitability with these strict measures, companies must work harder, faster, and smarter than their competitors. Information processing systems can provide these companies with the tools and procedures to assist them in their struggles.

PRELIMINARY STEPS IN PLANNING

Once it is agreed that a company needs to investigate information processing technologies and systems, a project implementation plan must be determined. What are the beginning steps? What function should be implemented first? These are the typical questions of office managers in many companies throughout the nation as they contemplate their future office automation plans. What is needed to answer these and similar questions is a blueprint for office automation that accurately reflects a company's needs and overall goals.

Defining Objectives

An opportune time to develop such a blueprint is the period when upper management is involved with budget planning, making long-range projections, and establishing corporate goals and objectives.

Company policy statements and long-range projections generally reflect the concerns of upper management about operations and new directions the company will take. As such, they are ideal for helping to establish a perspective for the two main areas of the blueprint—developmental planning and implementation planning. **Developmental planning** occurs prior to obtaining top management's approval for the project plan. It is the vehicle by which top management is convinced that there is merit to be gained in planning such an implementation. Thus, **implementation planning** of the actual project activities will occur only after receiving management's approval to begin the project.

Developmental planning must include defining objectives of the proposed plan so that top management will understand the potential benefits to the business. Using general corporate objectives as a guide, the planning effort should define company needs and suggest methods of addressing those needs. For example, corporate objectives might include such stated goals as: increased productivity, reduced expenses, restrained hiring practices, quicker access to information, and availability of information messaging.

The first goal, increased productivity, can be achieved through implementation of word processing. Also, it might form the basis for further office automation planning. The second goal, reduced expenses,

developmental planning preparing for top management's approval of a project plan

implementation planning carrying out a project plan once top management has given approval

may be attained through a number of automated office functions including:

- Teleconferencing, which will reduce travel expenses
- Electronic mail, which will eliminate messenger services
- Automated filing systems, which will eliminate redundant paper copies and storage space used for duplicate copies

Many automated functions will be interrelated—a fact that should be noted in any planning effort. New position hiring, for example, may be curbed by combining support services that result from word processing implementation and administrative support groupings. Likewise, electronic mail and automated filing systems can stimulate productive time, reduce wait time, and provide quicker access to information.

Using specific corporate goals as a guide will make the development of the planning blueprint easier. Moreover, the planning effort is more likely to obtain support from top management if it responds directly to management-stated concerns.

Developmental planning includes defining objectives and goals so that top management will understand the potential benefits of a project to the business.

Gaining the Support of Top Management

After specific objectives have been defined, they must be presented to top management in a form which includes a statement of intentions and a strategy plan with dates for completion as shown in Figure 8-1. The initial strategies presented to top management do not have to indicate the specifics of the implementation plan. How a plan is to proceed will be important only after the necessary approval has been given. However, top management must be informed of the current office problems, told how the proposed implementation will resolve those problems, and informed as to whether the plan will effect additional benefits to the company. This should be included in a textual report accompanying the strategy portion of the oral presentation. An example of a textual report is given in Figure 8-2.

FIG. 8-1
STRATEGY PLAN
The planning team should present a strategy plan to top management that summarizes their objective and the strategies to be used to attain that objective.

**OFFICE SYSTEM DEPARTMENT
SYSTEM STRATEGIES**

Objective: To provide a network for integrated office systems to facilitate word processing, remote/local computer access, data storage and manipulation, records management, telecommunications, and electronic mail.

Strategies

1. Provide and monitor an effective and cost-efficient office system (to be used as an interim solution to meet the immediate needs) with word processing, telecommunications, and limited data processing features.
   Time Required: 6 months

2. Select an effective and cost-efficient integrated office system network for the new headquarters facility.
   Time Required: 10 months

3. Facilitate initial and ongoing education.
   Time Required: Ongoing

4. Facilitate continued enhancement and maintenance of the integrated office systems network.
   Time Required: Ongoing

5. Provide ongoing and open-ended analyses and recommendations for continuing requirements of the company's integrated office systems.
   Time Required: Ongoing

6. Implement a new integrated office systems network.
   Time Required: 15 months

CHAPTER 8 Determining the Need for a System

―2―

- Delays occur beyond our control when distributing mail through sources other than our own. Often delays occur internally because of misdirection or inadvertent loss. These delays compound our inability to make decisions or react in a timely fashion. Often they prompt costly, ti[...] with emplo[...]

BENEFITS:

By adopting an in[...]
expect immediate [...]
intensive, relati[...]
scheduling, maili[...]
clerks can be lar[...]
viding many areas[...]
sional such as re[...]
are positively in[...]
higher quality de[...]
organizing and sc[...]
all design would [...]
a capacity to add[...]

BONUSES:

Professional Offi[...]
successful integr[...]

1. The ad[...] instal[...]
2. The ca[...] a leve[...] integr[...] wherei[...]
3. The gr[...] job di[...] not be[...]
4. Profes[...] area w[...] simult[...] comman[...] its in[...] servic[...]
5. An int[...] ronmen[...] less c[...]

OFFICE SYSTEMS

Primarily because of its accelerated growth rate, the once-productive office environment of Professional Office Systems, Inc. is mired in inefficient and costly information, paper, mail, and filing systems. The administrative staff is relying upon antiquated typing equipment, inappropriate tools, and "dumb" copiers to meet this rising and disproportionate demand. It is clear that an integrated office system with its synergistic effect on productivity will produce the cost-effectiveness and quality improvements needed not only for our present requirements but for future growth as well.

PROBLEMS:

- Secretarial/clerical staff account for 17.4% of the present work force within the company and approximately 8% of salary dollars. They are currently operating at about 25% of their potential with improper equipment. Too much time is spent manually typing documents requiring revisions to already-typed text.

- Typing activities and correspondence requests are delayed due to the lack of time needed to perform this increasing backlog.

- Additional copying costs are incurred because secretarial personnel find copying like-material less frustrating and time consuming than continual retyping.

- Professionals also are experiencing frustration because their creativity is restrained and often abandoned by lack of supporting resources. The professional staff account for 67.4% of the work force and approximately 69.2% of the salary dollars. Outside studies indicate that without the proper tools and support resources, this group may operate at only 46% of their potential.

- Management decisions based on this supporting documentation also are delayed due to the work flow problems in the areas of preparation and distribution. The penalty costs of late management decisions can be high.

- Additional amounts of document creation are being performed for personnel in local and field offices wherein secretarial support is provided and is being charged as "temporary" salary expense.

- Multi-vendor office equipment has proliferated company-wide, without supervision or concern for the resulting incompatibility problems, cross-training difficulties, inadequate capabilities, limited expansion, and thorough justification.

- Duplication of effort occurs each time a staff member rehandles mail that has been keyboarded in-house. This rehandling is caused by lack of tracking methods, rush requests, copying material, and preparation for dissemination of mail.

- Unnecessary time spent searching for or retrieving previously filed material casues delays within all staff levels and their convenient work flows. Concurrent with the research problems, the accumulating paper storage needs will eventually have a negative impact on our space plans. Individual filing systems offer no relief from the cross-training difficulties. As in all of the administrative activities, no systems have been implemented to permit easy backup.

FIG. 8-2 TEXTUAL REPORT The textual report should summarize current problems, tell how the proposed plan will solve those problems, and list any additional benefits the plan may provide.

Often, such a report is formally presented to top management. In this way, the presenter will be available to qualify any concerns or add verbal or visual information to the report to clarify management's understanding of the information. Additionally, the presenter has a unique opportunity to create visibility with management and establish good rapport. This opportunity may be an invaluable aid to career development even if the project does not gain approval. However, a formal presentation is more likely to gain top management's approval of a project and support during implementation. Planning a formal presentation is well worth the extra effort.

Team Analysis Approach

There are usually two methods by which decisions are made to introduce new systems to a company: (1) by top management or (2) by group participation. The first is usually implemented by edict—in other words, the employees have no say in the decision or implementation process. They must accept the decision and make the best of it. The second method is implemented after a group decision has been reached.

Careful planning and selection of team members can increase the chances for a successful planning process.

The group generally is composed of employees who will be affected by the installation. An implementation process that is made with knowledgeable acceptance is more apt to be successful.

The second method is more commonly referred to as a task force approach or team approach. Recommending an office system by means of a team approach is the preferred direction taken by many companies. Regardless of how popular and democratic this approach may be considered, there is no absolute guarantee of a successful outcome. Nor is there any assurance that all team participation will be harmonious.

The process of selecting team members is critically important to the outcome of the project. It is a very arduous and time-consuming task and should not be taken lightly. Careful planning and selection of team members can increase the chances for a successful planning process. Also, defining the criteria for individual participation may lessen the risk of delays due to misunderstandings, presumptuousness, or inexperience of the various members.

Developing the team approach method occurs only after the objectives of the planning process have been determined and approval to proceed has been obtained from top management. A team member must be an individual who can devote the necessary time to the project, has a thorough understanding and acceptance of the plan, and who can review the process from a position that is objective and benefits the company. A team member should be a respected member of the company whose judgment is valued. An ideal team should be configured from both a functional as well as a representational standpoint.

A functional standpoint implies that team members are selected for the expertise that they can add to the equipment selection and implementation process. For example, if the proposed plan includes integrating the new system with present typesetting equipment, it may be wise to have a team member with knowledge about data communications or typesetting. A representational standpoint implies that team members are selected so that each user department affected by the proposed plan is represented. A listing of potential team members may be obtained by reviewing a company's organization chart. Departments or areas directly affected by the scope of the project should be represented. The departments most likely to be affected by the implementation of a new information processing sytem are as follows:

Administrative Groups	Data Processing
Data/Telecommunications	Cost Analysis/Accounting
Human Resources	Reprographics
Office Services	Marketing
Research and Development	Training and Development
Records Management	Public Relations
Word Processing	Long-Range Planning

Next, the objectives and planning strategies that were presented to top management should be reviewed. Specific areas of the planning process that require additional assistance or expertise should be identified. For example, Steps 1, 2, and 3 of the planning strategy shown in Figure 8-1 are as follows:

1 Provide and monitor an effective and cost-efficient office system (to be used as an interim solution to meet the immediate needs) with word processing, telecommunications, and limited data processing features.

Time Required: 6 months

2 Select an effective and cost-efficient integrated office system network for the new headquarters facility.

Time Required: 10 months

3 Facilitate initial and ongoing education.

Time Required: Ongoing

From these objectives, specific activities that may require assistance can be defined. For example, in developing their project plan the team should:

- Study and document the current office system
- Define requirements of the new office system
- Evaluate offerings and select a vendor
- Develop an implementation plan
- Provide user training and ongoing public relations

It is possible that the activities which require assistance can be provided by someone other than a team member. The needed support should be analyzed. Then, performance responsibilities and their limitations can be identified. For instance, the team members may require:

- Clerical assistance to gather documentation on current work flow
- Technical advice on networking issues
- Technical advice on interfacing with the data processing areas
- Upper-management advice on company issues and plans
- Financial advice
- Skilled personnel who have experience in determining user needs and applications
- Strong analytical skills

Determining the functions and areas that will produce the most qualified team member is difficult. Therefore, it is important to qualify

CHAPTER 8 Determining the Need for a System 199

the responsibilities of the team member against the objectives of the project. This can be done in graphic form.

In the project example, there are three major categories into which all project activities can be grouped. They are (1) defining requirements, (2) evaluating offerings, and (3) selecting a vendor. These three categories have different values or degrees of importance to the outcome of the project. If the entire project can be considered as a 100 percent effort, each category must be a portion of that percentage. The value of each is determined by the project leader. In this example, category values were determined to be 25 percent, 35 percent, and 40 percent, respectively.

These categories are listed across the top of the chart shown in Figure 8-3. Represented department areas are listed down the side of the chart. The purpose of the chart is to rate potential areas according to their anticipated support. The rating should not exceed the total value that was placed on each of the categories. Totaling these ratings will produce a ranking of areas wherein there is a good potential for a team member.

TEAM MEMBER CHART

Departments	Defining Requirements	Evaluating Offerings	Selecting a Vendor	Total
Administrative Groups	20%	30%	30%	80%
Data/Telecommunications	10	20	10	40
Human Resources	10	—	—	10
Office Services	15	15	15	45
Research and Development	10	10	10	30
Records Management	10	10	10	30
Word Processing	25	20	20	65
Data Processing	25	20	20	65
Cost Analysis/Accounting	10	—	—	10
Reprographics	15	—	—	15
Marketing	10	—	—	10
Training and Development	15	15	15	45
Public Relations	—	—	—	—
Long-Range Planning	10	30	30	70

FIG. 8-3
TEAM MEMBER CHART
A team member chart helps organizers choose team members by rating departments and groups within the company on the interaction they will have with the new system.

The areas that attain the highest score and also include a ranking in each of the major function categories are the most likely departments from which to obtain team member candidates. Individual selection of a candidate within that area may be determined by the department head, regardless of the project leader's preference. However, having this chart as a guide should give support to the leader's judgment in selecting candidates.

Now that potential areas for membership have been determined, some thought must be given to the size of the group. A workable team usually is composed of an uneven number of members. With an uneven number of team members, the possibility of a tie in reaching decisions is eliminated.

The actual size of the group should be determined by the objectives and scope of the project. A small project extending over limited areas requires only a few team members. In contrast, a large project with extensive information system plans requires participants from many affected areas. A team composed of more than nine members is considered to be a large group. There are both advantages and disadvantages in creating an analysis team with many members.

One advantage of a large analysis team is that input is generated from all areas of the company. Selecting a member from each department provides the needed input and additionally, supplies a thorough feedback and public relations potential to the selected departments. Another advantage to a large analysis team is that large groups tend to regulate the work load by spreading tasks among the team members so that the total work impact is not felt by only a few. Since company needs can be so widely diversified, a larger representation on the team can more likely provide a broader-based technical expertise from which to make a decision. And, when making that decision, a larger team reduces the possibility of a deadlock in the case of a close decision. Finally, with all users being able to share equally in decisions via their own representatives, the chances for overall company satisfaction are greater.

Large groups have their negative aspects too. For example, a large group can be difficult to control since distractions are likely to occur. Further, training and/or learning becomes more difficult to manage with many team members. It also is more difficult to maximize attendance of all team members; thus, meetings can be delayed and deadlines can be missed. As a result, the effort loses impetus.

Another problem with large groups is that the members may view their needs subjectively rather than from the broad company perspective desired by a thorough analysis. Team members are more likely to become mired in personal demands rather than in overall company needs. When this occurs, it is possible that a team member's specialty may become confused with the main objectives of the project. The final outcome could prevent unanimous decision making and make the many team decision processes extremely difficult. There are no clear-cut rules for designing a team approach; however, having defined criteria will stimulate a better planning process.

Work Plan Development

Now that the team members have been identified, the first objective of the task force is to develop a comprehensive study plan. For the team to be successful and to determine the best possible solutions for the company's information processing problems, the members need to plan their work activities together. The ideal arrangement is to study the situation in depth for a minimum of three to four weeks. This will allow all team members time to familiarize themselves with all of the areas of need within the company. This also is the time when the team leader educates the group about the techniques of information processing. The team should spend this time (1) studying all user support needs; (2) estimating total study cost and defining recommended team member responsibilities; (3) defining the limits of the study; and (4) developing the study schedule with clear breakpoints, milestones, and reviews.

The resulting efforts should produce a work plan which will serve as a guide to structure the team's activities, define the length of time required for these activities, and provide a management review of the project costs and reports. Major activities should be emphasized by headings much as those found on outline formats. Details of each major heading would be listed under its respective objective, such as in the example of a work plan shown in Figure 8-4.

The first phase of the work plan contains detailed information on the following:

- Project objective and scope
- Tasks and activities
- Schedules
- Human resource requirements
- Responsibilities
- Cost estimates

Once a work plan has been developed, the team submits the plan to company management for its approval and signal to begin the study. Having obtained this approval, the team is ready to proceed with preparing the users (sometimes called the "user community") for the potential change and designing the study procedures.

PSYCHOLOGICAL CONSIDERATIONS

New technology is often met with resistance in the office. This is especially true when introducing technology which requires restructuring the office and changing traditional roles. If this new technology also requires learning new skills and/or de-emphasizing current skills, the

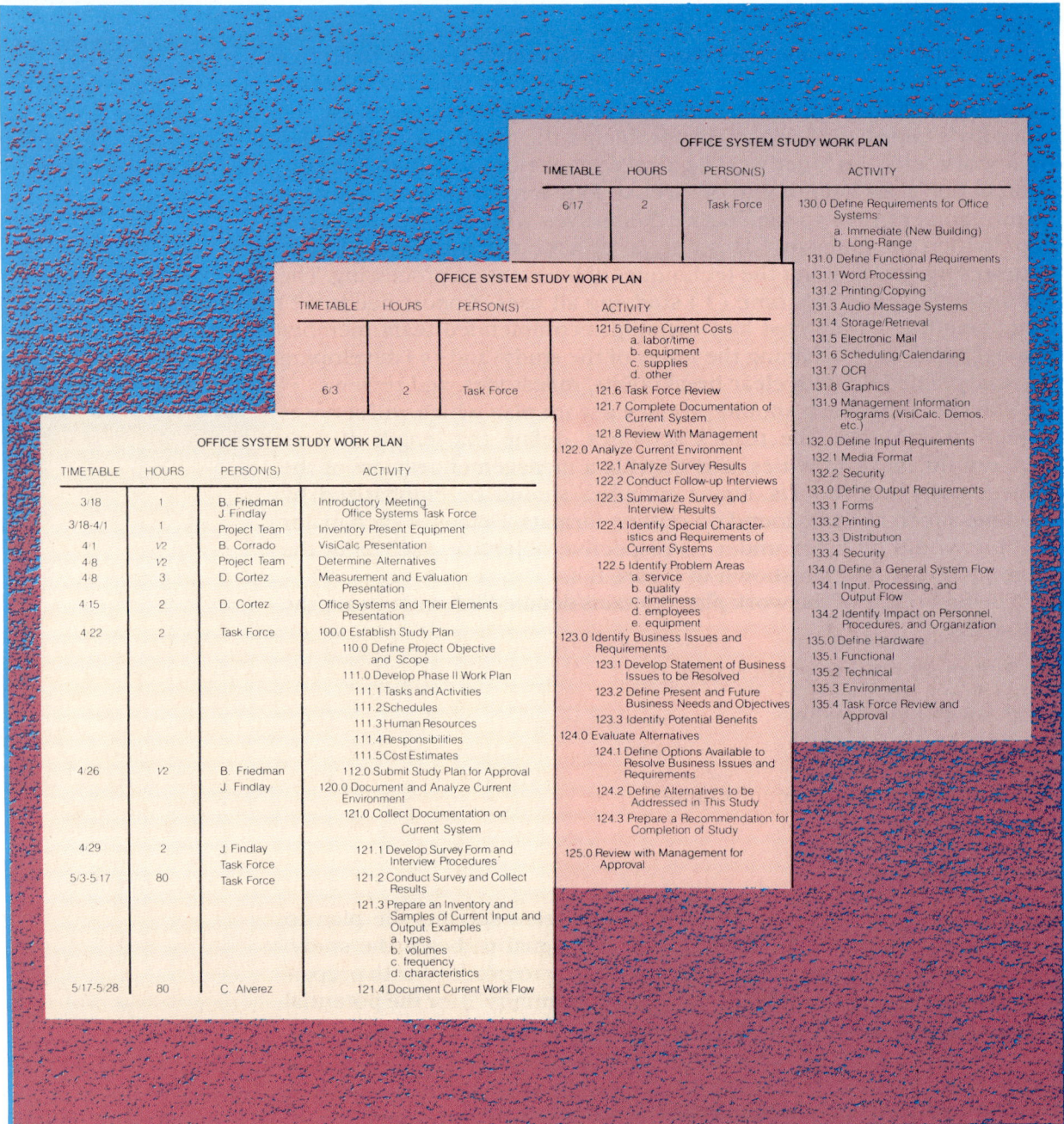

FIG. 8-4 WORK PLAN   A work plan serves as a guide for the team's activities, the time required for these activities, and a management review of the project costs and reports.

change becomes even more threatening to the employee. However, those responsible for office automation can make the transition easier if they constantly keep the human factor in mind during the various stages of the study and implementation.

Preparing Users for Change

Once the decision has been made to develop an information processing system, an analysis of the current office system begins. Its purpose is to determine needs, priorities, and procedures for implementing office automation—a complex and time-consuming process.

The team members are responsible for examining company files and records, making personal observations, conducting employee interviews, measuring correspondence production, watching product demonstrations, and conducting surveys and library research. The mere thought of such analyses and activities can be very intimidating to an employee.

At this stage it is important that office personal be informed of pending changes and be kept up to date about the study. Many word processing systems that were installed in the past were not as effective as planned because little emphasis was placed on the importance of preparing people for change.

In the future, the changes caused by office automation will affect a broader range of activities and more levels of staff than merely secretarial changes. As electronic devices become part of managerial as well as clerical job functions, preparing people for change not only should intensify but also should become a priority item.

A sharp manager in a forward-looking, modern company recognizes that people are an essential ingredient to the growth of such an operation. A manager can unpretentiously include employees in the decision-making process in the following ways:

- Prepare them for a change. Employees should understand (1) what automation the company is considering; (2) why it is necessary for the company to be looking in this direction; (3) what changes the employees can anticipate; (4) what benefits the new equipment will have on their work and on them personally (such as new skills developed through training programs); and (5) what the entire implementation schedule is.

- The staff also should be made aware that positions and organizational structure will be changed with the idea of enhancing office efficiency and exposing the benefits of information processing to all areas of the company. This exposure will later provide additional interest and spark creative ideas for new applications.

- The emphasis on cost justification in business is a product of good management. Cost analysis, cash flow, investment tax credit, lease versus buy, and a number of other factors regarding the acquisition of office equipment must be considered. In addition, these factors must be measured against the pressures of competition, inflation, and potential profit.

During the justification study, clerical and managerial job functions and performance are closely scrutinized. This can be an uneasy experience for employees who may fear that their jobs are on the line or that their office skills will no longer be relevant. To prevent such anxiety, emphasis should be placed on the positive benefits that employees will derive from the new technology. Examples would include better tools to help workers do their jobs, better career paths, and increased production.

- The decision stage requires bringing together all of the preceding reports for the purpose of making the most logical equipment choice. If input is obtained from those who will be using the equipment, the information on which equipment selection is based will more likely reflect overall company needs.

When planning the implementation of an information processing system, managers should include employees in the decision-making process.

Involving Users in the Implementation Process

Actual introduction of new equipment into the office is simpler and faster if employees have already been made familiar with the concepts involved. If employees feel that they are a part of the overall change, they will support it. Conversely, if they feel they are not directly involved or if they feel it is not going to benefit them, they may retaliate. Thus, users should be involved in the implementation.

For the greatest productivity, a work area should be arranged so that people do not have to radically change all of their traditional ways. The team chosen to design the system should invite other employees to meetings arranged for this purpose.

Participation helps employees to be more satisfied with their new working environment and encourages them to be more efficient. Because employees helped create the new system, employee turnover should be reduced. Also, it will probably be easier to attract personnel to the new office positions. Moreover, their cooperation will allow the new technology to be accepted.

Providing Users With Review and Training

Once the equipment is in place and is operating, constant review of office policies and procedures is necessary in order to maintain efficiency. Operator and user manuals must be written, tasks must be defined, and productivity must be measured. Again, operator and user feedback is essential for determining additional training needs and improving productivity.

To increase skill levels related to the new technology, training must be provided. As more electronic office equipment is installed, it is necessary to develop an ongoing training program to keep users abreast of possible applications. In addition, continual training should be provided for management and clerical employees.

Provision for specific training at an educational institution may not be feasible. Therefore, in-house programs are required to equip personnel with the proper skills. In-house training also serves to help employees accept, on a first-hand basis, the methods that have been designed to do the job.

Restructuring Jobs for Greater Fulfillment

Employees should be informed that the company will make an effort to eliminate routine and uninteresting jobs. Jobs will become more exciting and varied by encouraging creativity and directing automated tools to do the repetitious tasks. To effect these changes, the company must reassess, reevaluate, and restructure job functions. Employees should be involved in analyzing their jobs and in writing job descriptions.

Job descriptions should reflect the stronger role employees will be playing in restructuring, staffing, and equipping the new office environment. Constantly updating job descriptions, functions, and analyses ensures the credibility of the team's good intentions. Keeping the human factor in mind during the study and implementation guarantees a more successful transition into office automation.

THE FEASIBILITY STUDY

feasibility study a way of determining the practicality of implementing a study's objectives

A feasibility study, as the name implies, is a way of determining the practicality of implementing the study objectives—in this case, an information processing system. In order to check the validity of their proposal, the team members need to have background information on how the current office work flows. Their goals are to collect data on this work flow, document the current office system, help prepare users for possible changes, and then analyze the resulting information for their company's long-term needs. Only after this phase of their work plan is complete can they prepare the report and make realistic recommendations for change to upper management.

Designing the Study Plan

Team members first determine what information should be gathered in their study efforts. The following items need to be included:

- An accounting of each employee's time versus activity
- An inventory and samples of the current input and output for each activity; i.e., types, volumes, frequency, characteristics
- A determination of backlog—a means of measuring the unfinished work load
- A needs assessment—what the user needs to perform the job more efficiently
- An indicator of employee resistance to or acceptance of change

Survey forms are an easy way to gather information without spending individual time observing or tracking each item of data required for the study process. They must be designed to ensure user support, understanding, and accuracy.

Survey forms must be a vehicle to contain the information required but should not be a substitute for face-to-face communication. Thus, the survey form must be designed so that the user can easily identify the information requested without wasting valuable time asking for explanations. The design should enable the user to complete the forms easily without spending an unnecessary amount of time researching answers. Also, the form should be designed in such a way that it preserves the user's privacy and ensures that the results will be accurate without being threatening. Once the survey form design has been completed, reviewed, and approved by management, data collection begins.

Collecting Data

There are three major methods of collecting data: action paper, observation (random sample), and survey form. The following discussion considers only one collection method—the survey form (questionnaire).

Each team member selects an appropriate number of questionnaires to be completed by support personnel and managerial staff within a respective area. The approach will differ among upper-management, middle-management, and support personnel because of the nature of their functions, time, and attendance. Support personnel generally are more flexible for a meeting arrangement. The managerial staff are more elusive for group scheduling.

One popular method of collecting data is through the use of questionnaires.

Support Personnel Survey. An ideal time to provide background information on the project is after the support staff has been assembled and prior to dispersing the questionnaires. First, explain the nature of the survey and the objectives of the team. Then solicit their support by indicating some benefits that the support personnel may derive from the study. This also is an excellent time to answer any questions or concerns the support staff may have.

The questionnaires then should be distributed. Some sample questions from a support personnel survey are shown in Figure 8-5. Review the entire survey with the group and arrange to collect the questionnaires at a predetermined time. Setting a specific deadline for completion of the surveys usually encourages timely performance. Emphasize pertinent information that could be overlooked by the participant; i.e., the survey is based on one week's production. If individuals have difficulty responding to a question and a work example might clarify the problem, then encourage the individual to include the example.

After the surveys are returned, review them to ensure that all information is accurate and complete; i.e., percentages and hours are appropriately stated, totals are accurate, and all attachments are included. If any items need clarification, it is advantageous to get back to the participants while the information is still fresh in their minds.

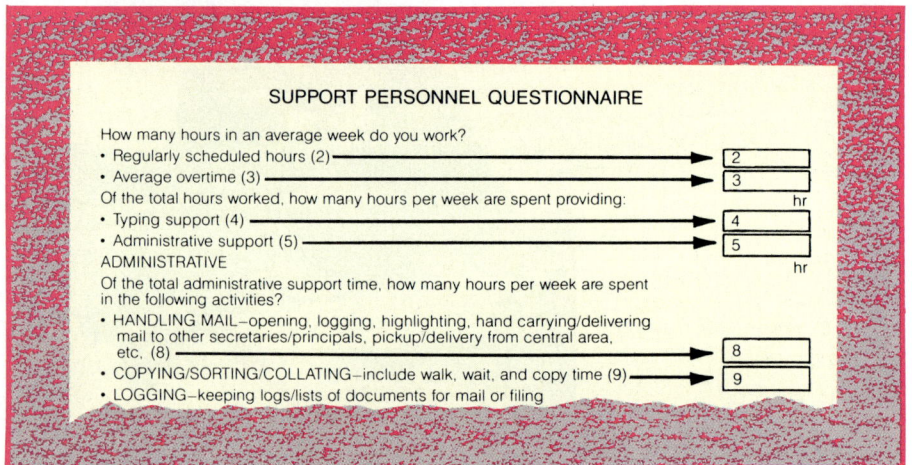

FIG. 8-5
SUPPORT PERSONNEL SURVEY
This survey gives the team some idea of the activities performed by support personnel and the time spent on those activities.

Managerial Staff Survey. Since there may be difficulty arranging a group meeting with upper-management and middle-management personnel, many single (one-on-one) meetings should be planned for the completion of the surveys. Though the meetings should cover some of the same issues and points, they should be limited to approximately 30 minutes in length. To produce good results from managerial staff surveys, explanations need to be brief, concise, and accurate. Also, survey completion should be immediate.

CHAPTER 8 Determining the Need for a System

The meetings should begin by a team member identifying the nature and scope of the questionnaires. Then, the team member should solicit the managerial staff's interest and support. The managers should complete the survey at this time, and the surveys should be collected. Some sample questions from a managerial staff survey are shown in Figure 8-6. The accuracy of the answers should be verified before the meeting is adjourned. If attachments are needed to clarify the responses, they should be secured as soon as possible. All completed surveys then are delivered to the team meeting headquarters for final review and tabulation.

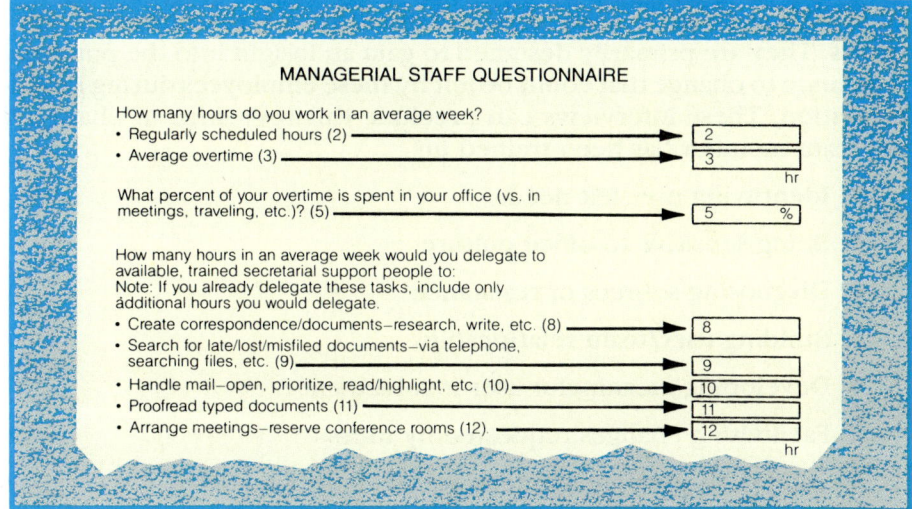

FIG. 8-6
MANAGERIAL STAFF SURVEY
Team members should require managerial staff to complete their surveys the same day that they are distributed. This gives team members immediate feedback and requires the least amount of the managerial staff's time.

Work Flows. Additionally, each of the team members should be required to submit two diagrams depicting the flow of work within a respective area. The work flows should be completed simultaneously with the questionnaires and must address both the managerial and support functions to be meaningful. To achieve certain objectives, these two work flows should illustrate repetitive activities as well as those unique to their areas. The three major objectives to be achieved are as follows:

1 Familiarize the team members with the work patterns and general flow of work through the various departments.

2 Identify any functions or work flows that are unique and require special consideration or need further analysis.

3 Identify those areas in the work flow for which automated equipment and procedures might be applied.

Work flow, as defined here, is associated with the creation and processing of documents and the flow of these documents through a department. It is not used to evaluate individual jobs or responsibilities. Correlating the work flow charts with the survey information also provides a means of validating the study results.

Interviewing

Simultaneous with the work flows and questionnaires, interviews with managerial and support staff should be planned. The intent of the interviews is to provide a comfortable setting free from the overtones of work measurement and examination wherein employees can more easily discuss all aspects of their jobs.

The interviews are used to complement the more regimented study efforts. They are primarily designed to gain an insight into the potential resistance to change that could be felt by these employees during implementation. These interviews can preclude this resistance to change if the team member has been trained in:

- Identifying user-felt needs
- Being sensitive to office culture
- Diagnosing sources of resistance
- Building user/team relationships
- Developing meaningful user involvement
- Facilitating changes requested by users

An interview allows team members to identify human factors as they analyze system users. The fear of change is associated with how people view their work world and their surroundings, and how they derive benefits from these work habits. Suggesting change that affects interpersonal relationships of this work world may be met with resistance. It is important to discover the value that people place on particular habits prior to suggesting changes.

For example, an employee has revealed to an interviewer that certain tasks require repeated trips to another employee's desk. If you suggest that a piece of technology will make the job easier and reduce those repeated trips, you expect the employee to accept this as a benefit. Rather, the employee places great value on those trips because they enable that employee to see a friend ten times a day. What you are suggesting takes on a new perspective. The employee views the new technology as having a negative impact and will resist the change.

Interviews can provide the means to learn about various reward systems of employees. It allows the team member to become sensitive to these values and to apply the human factor to the system design in order to encourage acceptance of the system by the employees.

CHAPTER 8 Determining the Need for a System

Analyzing the Survey Forms

When the completed questionnaires are returned, the team begins tabulating the results. This is a time-consuming task and requires detailed concentration. The task becomes less strenuous if each team member tabulates a portion of the survey results. Departments are grouped to consolidate time and to accumulate activities. Companies may further consolidate the task by grouping departments into divisions, which involves adding several departmental results together. The final tabulation accumulates all figures into an overall company result. A breakdown of the various groups may resemble those shown in Figure 8-7. Actual survey tabulations, however, will be more detailed and comprehensive in a search for time/activities measurements that can be improved with automation.

FIG. 8-7
TABULATING RESULTS
Survey results should be tabulated for each department, each division, and the entire company.

	Department Tabulations		Division Tabulations		Company Tabulations
Total number of employees		14		44		744
Total number of hours worked in a week		560		1,560		29,760
Time spent on typing activities		200		800		7,800
Time spent on administrative work		360		760		21,960
Time spent looking for lost mail	10.0		99.0		410.0	
Time spent addressing mail	4.5		44.5		544.5	
Time spent copying mail	10.2		75.7		290.2	
Time spent on other mail activities	65.3		70.8		745.3	
Total time spent on mail		90		290		1,990

Not all surveys will be completed within the required time frame, and the tabulations should reveal these statistics. Should the missing information be important to the accuracy of the study, attempts should be made to complete the survey. Management should be made aware of the total number of questionnaires distributed and the number of completed questionnaires received. Then the information is meaningful for all-encompassing decisions.

Analyses should be designed to include a minimum of one week's work figures to provide a good sampling of normal work activity. All cost, quantity, and time totals should be viewed from this perspective. To obtain an annual approach to figures and to reflect a full-time employee (FTE) equivalent, most studies rely on Industrial Engineering standards of 2,080 hours = 1 FTE.

The human resources department (personnel department) of the company should supply the employment/staffing statistics for the period of the measurement. If the survey favors an annual position, the salary figures must be based on the average annual salary plus the current percentage of fringe benefit allowances. The salaries can be used as differentials for supplying cost factors to the time spent on activities by each level of employment.

For example, the average annual salary for support personnel may be $15,000 plus a 23 percent fringe benefit factor (worth $3,450), which totals $18,450. Middle-management personnel may have an annual salary of $35,000 plus a 23 percent fringe benefit factor (worth $8,050), which totals $43,050. And, upper-management personnel may have an annual salary of $75,000 plus a 23 percent fringe benefit (worth $17,250), or an equivalent salary of $92,250.

Showing management the amount of time spent on activities which could be automated is rarely impressive. However, if these same time figures can be converted to cost figures, the management staff will be more easily convinced of the need to reduce these costly activities by the introduction of new methods.

Detailing specific activity steps helps to define the work flow process so that bottlenecks can be discovered and pinpointed. The time increments (steps) that could be eliminated if the process were automated can be identified. In other words, a potential for time improvement that could trigger a productivity increase can then be projected.

These time increments are translated into dollar savings by applying the appropriate salary figure into the analyses. The report will identify two potential savings:

- Hard dollars—actual cash savings; i.e., reducing the cost of intracompany distribution
- Soft dollars—productivity improvements savings

Neither savings is a tangible cost justification for an automated office system since current performance, activities, or methods must change to achieve the improvement and produce the potential savings.

Cost of Doing Business

The people study (including the questionnaires) accounts for the cost of the employees' time performing their different business activities. In addition to the people study measurement, there are often separate studies conducted to determine the entire cost of doing business in a nonautomated environment. For instance, these studies can place a value on a single sheet of paper, whether it is newly purchased, used for copying, or placed in the public mailing system.

Once all study information has been sorted and tabulated, the analysis begins. It must be noted that not all individual data can be translated

CHAPTER 8 Determining the Need for a System

into meaningful results. Some submissions will be unique and thus have no bearing on overall company objectives. Keep in mind that the study analysis is designed to illustrate: (1) how employees currently spread their time over administrative activities; (2) which administrative activities account for the majority of the time; and (3) which of these activities could be improved with new technological tools.

The analysis will produce major categories of administrative activities which meet these criteria. Information processing categories obtain their classifications from many different study activities. For example, under the study activity "Mail", the team specifically measures the time that support personnel and management staff spend locating lost mail, hand carrying documents, preparing them for routing, copying them for distribution, and transporting the documents to their destinations.

Handling Mail. When an independent study is conducted to indicate the cost of handling mail, the following information should be collected:

- The total number and amount of time spent on mail pickups and deliveries
- The frequencies of intraoffice and interoffice deliveries
- The types of mailings
- The times associated with activities (sorting, stamping, weighing, etc.)

The cost of handling mail within a company is an important aspect of the cost of doing business.

- The costs involved in salaries, vehicles, and related costs (gas, insurance, upkeep)

A combination of these measurements will produce various costs associated with specific activities. Combining these costs and then dividing the total by the average pieces of mail handled within the study time period produces the cost per item for handling mail.

Since the mail study defines types of mail, it is possible to separate the quantities of mail distributed internally. These figures can be further detailed to show internal distribution to branch offices as well as to headquarters facilities. Resulting statistics can produce an average cost for intraoffice mailing with and without postage figures. Maximizing data collection in the study provides flexible statistics which will support various strategies of implementation.

Copying. In order to derive a company's actual copier cost per item, it first is necessary to determine the annual cost of copier rental and/or depreciation, supplies, and labor expenses. Then this amount must be divided by the total number of copies made annually.

In the study, the category "Copying" is comprised of information that could be spread over several automated functions. Some examples are as follows:

- Information regarding the time spent copying material for internal distribution can be allocated to the electronic mail function for a time-saving calculation.

- Time spent copying material to serve as a reference guide can be allocated to filing systems.

- Information about the number of copies routed in-house and the growing filing requirements of each employee can be allocated to micrographics for an automated solution.

Scheduling/Calendaring. The category called "Scheduling/Calendaring" includes the amount of support personnel and management time unnecessarily spent by phone or in person arranging meetings, and sending reminder notices (ticklers). This can be compared to the time one would require if the schedules could be displayed on the screen electronically. The difference in time would be a savings generated by using electronic methods.

Filing. The "Filing" category includes a measure of the time spent by the staff manually searching for and retrieving information in filing systems. This also includes phoning or writing other employees for this type of basic information. The time savings accrued is the difference between manual filing practices and automated retrieval systems.

Typing. The category "Typing" should be viewed and measured from a nonelectronic environment, wherein each written word is originally keyboarded and revisions require retyping text. This needs to be measured against a word processing environment wherein repetitive text and revisions take less time and cost less. Several measurements should be shown for comparison.

Analyzing Work Flow

As noted before, there are three major objectives for the work flow analysis:

1. Familiarize the team members with the work patterns and general flow of work through the various departments.

2. Identify any functions or work flows that are unique and require special considerations or need further analysis.

3. Identify those areas within the work flow for which automated equipment and procedures might be applied.

Both the managerial and support functions should be considered.

Correlating the work flow charts with the survey information also provides a means of validating the survey results. The work flow charts should be consistent with the survey results.

In evaluating the work flow, the major functions should be scrutinized—input, output, revision, reproduction, distribution, and storage. Refer to the examples of common work flows shown in Figure 8-8. Work flows for general correspondence and reports are common to all departments. The special category represents the work flows that are unique to a particular department. The general correspondence and reports work flows are distinguished by certain characteristics. Also, within the two categories there are minor variations by departments and within each department itself based on the work being performed.

The work flow for general correspondence, shown in Figure 8-8, contains all normal correspondence, which generally is in the form of letters or memos. The input primarily is dictation or handwritten copy. Other forms of input include typed copies and verbal requests. Most of the input is prepared by the authors; only a small portion is originated by support personnel. Normal typing is done on the original copy and is returned to the author for review and/or signature. Changes to the original copy are limited, usually requiring only one review and change cycle. Documents for distribution are copied by support personnel and sent to the mail room for distribution. In a small number of cases, documents are delivered by the support personnel. Filing of the documents varies by department.

The reports work flow, also shown in Figure 8-8, is similar to the correspondence work flow but is characterized by a high degree of

FIG. 8-8
WORK FLOWS
Although the work flows for general correspondence, reports, and special correspondence are basically the same, there are important differences.

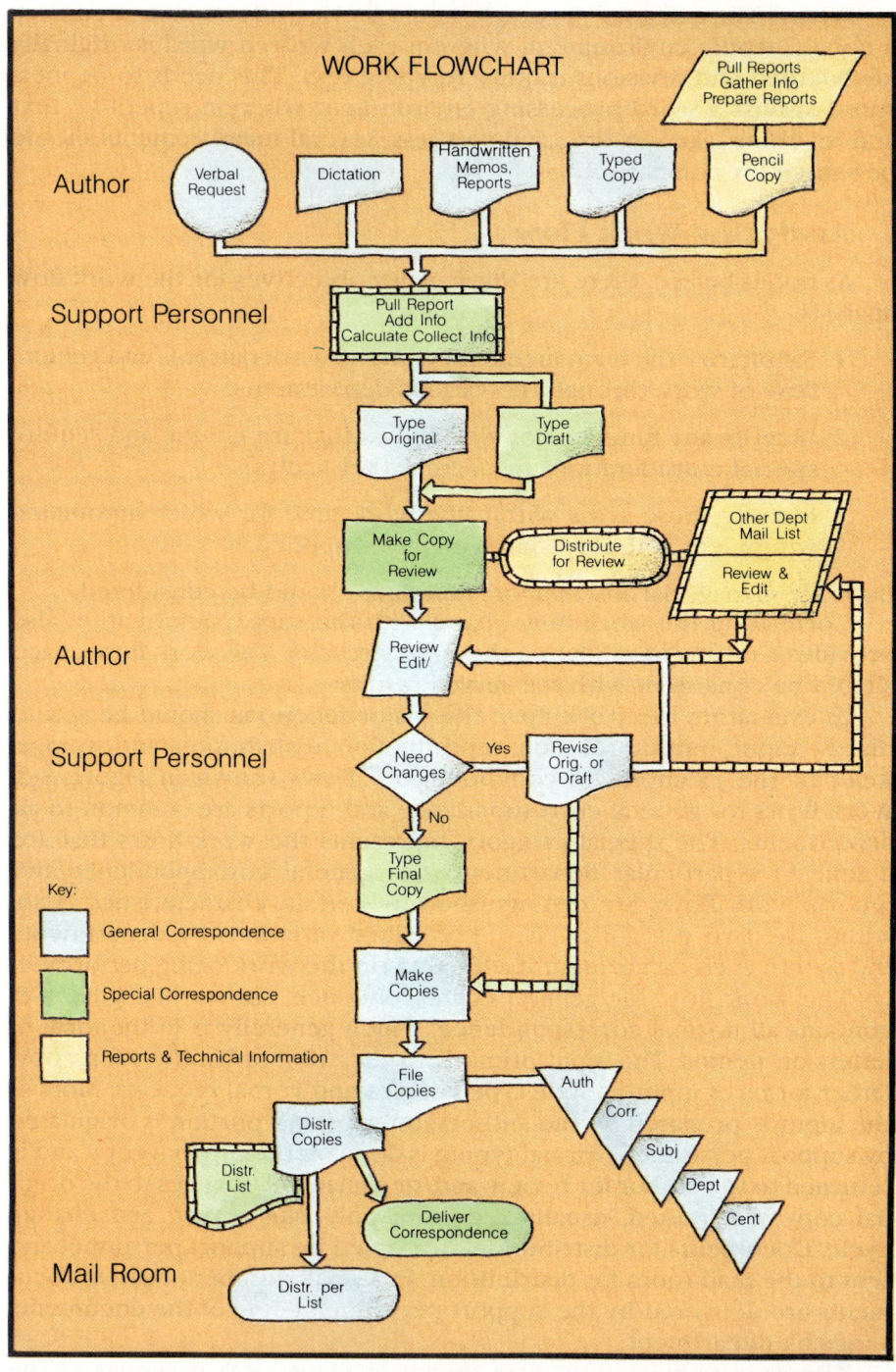

input (text/word origination) by both the authors and the support personnel. The input functions are primarily handwritten or typed copy. A significant amount of review and editing is done by both authors and support personnel. Most of the initial typing is done on draft copies, and the document can go through multiple review and change cycles before a final copy is produced. Copying of reports is done by support personnel or by a centralized copying center; and in some instances, the reports are printed. Delivery of the reports by support personnel is fairly common. The greatest variation in work flow among the three examples is in the number of review and editing cycles. In these examples, potential benefits from automated office systems exist in all areas of processing.

The flowchart for special correspondence contains those work flows that have characteristics unique to a particular department. The work flow does not follow the normal processing functions. There is extensive review of the input document before typing. The work flow involves a special typing and proofreading process. Copying and distribution are then done by support personnel. In this example, each case must be examined individually for the best application of automated office systems.

Work flow evaluation can achieve the first two objectives:

- Familiarization with the work patterns and general work flow
- Identification of unique functions and work flows

The next step is to use this information, plus the information from the questionnaires and interviews, to identify those specific areas where advanced office systems might be advantageous.

Summarizing Findings

The analyses and consolidation of categories will produce specific areas wherein the greatest potential for productivity improvement and cost savings can be applied. These categories should be presented in a format that makes major findings instantly apparent to upper management. An example of such a format style is given in Figure 8-9.

Reporting Results

Feasibility studies which identify the potential benefits of implementing a particular automated office function must focus on the tangible economic benefits to the company in order to have an impact on management. A report which merely states that implementing a certain automated office function will save employees a lot of time each week is of questionable value. Instead, a report should translate the reductions in time or work load into hard dollar savings.

A report could be given to the management of a large company with

FIG. 8-9
SUMMARIZING FINDINGS
Major study findings should be presented in a neat, concise manner that makes the results instantly apparent to upper management.

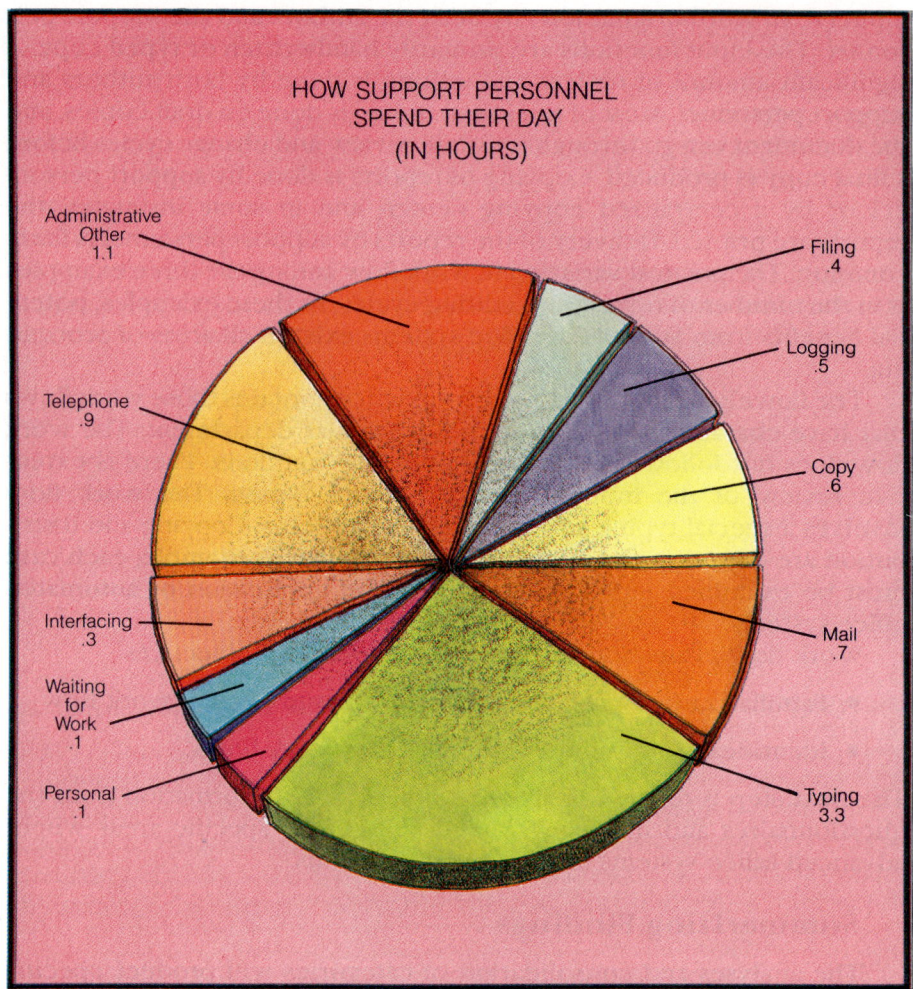

several branch offices that summarizes the favorable results of a feasibility study on electronic mail. The report, with supporting documentation attached, could be presented in three sections as follows:

1. Statement of the problem.
2. Presentation of the solution—electronic mail.
3. Discussion of potential benefits.

The Problem. The first part of the report should state the concise problem and the reasons it exists. Included would be supporting statistics to illustrate that improvements should be made. It might state, for example, that staff personnel spend 4 percent of their work week (303 hours) rehandling mail that has been keyboarded in-house. This is caused by the absence of tracking methods for the work done (177 hours), rush requests (25 hours), and preparation for mail dissemination (101 hours). An additional 122 hours are spent copying material for distribution.

Other problems that are not so easily quantified also should be included. An example might be time lost through misdirection or inadvertent loss of mail, both internally and through other sources.

The Solution. The second part of the report should present the solution, in this case electronic mail, along with the reasons why it was selected and a brief explanation of how it might be implemented. For instance, the report might state that electronic mail could eliminate most of the time spent copying or otherwise rehandling keyboarded items. This would substantially reduce delays caused by transmitting documents between branches and headquarters by conventional mail.

The report might further point out that electronic mail should be implemented first with the company's branch offices that have word processing compatibility. Then it could be implemented within the headquarters organization.

The Benefits. The third section of the report might explain additional benefits, such as cost displacement/avoidance and added value. Points that might be covered under the first category include productivity increases, more logical delegation of tasks, improvements in administrative activities, and reductions in overhead costs. Added value might include such items as improved communications, better customer service, increased management control, more organizational flexibility, and company growth.

When presenting such a report, it is important to stress that commitment to any automated office function must occur within the framework of a totally integrated office systems approach. Effort should be made to avoid the occurrence of incompatibilities with existing or future equipment. A report that is complete and can show direct cost savings is valuable in helping management make objective decisions.

After reading this chapter, you should understand what prompts companies to look towards new technology for solutions to their business problems. You should be familiar with the two approaches used by companies in carrying out such solutions and be able to select the approach offering the greatest potential for success. You will have learned how to select and develop team participation. Then, as the project leader or a team member, you should be able to plan activities that will: (1) produce statistics on the current cost of doing business, (2) encourage employees' acceptance of change, (3) weigh the advantages of the new technology, and (4) ultimately recommend a practical planning strategy to management.

The dimensions of an information processing feasibility study are threefold: directions and goals, a framework for action, and a rationale for decision making. The basis of a successful feasibility study is intense preparatory work. Preparatory work is crucial because it sets the stage for success or failure. Defining what is being done today helps to better plan how work should be done tomorrow.

DISCUSSION QUESTIONS AND CASE PROBLEM

DISCUSSION QUESTIONS

1. Name several factors that might influence companies to consider implementing one of the new office system technologies.
2. Where can you find a guide that will help you in defining objectives for your system planning process?
3. Name two methods by which systems usually are introduced into companies. Describe how they differ.
4. After you have installed your system, what can operator or user feedback provide for you?
5. What does an analysis team hope to achieve by conducting a feasibility study?

CASE PROBLEM

Paul was an administrative support secretary in a national accounts department of a large manufacturing company. One of his duties was to arrange and schedule the various conference rooms for customer presentations by the staff. In an interview with a team member, Paul expressed how this part of his job was taking up half of his workday.

The salespeople were changing times, changing rooms, or making last-minute media requests that impacted on his time considerably. He felt disorganized and frustrated but was always able to appear composed in front of customers. Fortunately he was able to squeeze his other activities into his free times during the day so that everything got done. He was certain that he was not doing his best on these duties, although no one complained.

CHAPTER 8 Determining the Need for a System 221

The interviewer suggested that conference rooms and equipment could be scheduled automatically with new technology and thus free up his time. He could assume more administrative activities and be less frustrated. Paul became quite angry and insisted that he wanted no part of such a device.

1. Why did Paul resist the apparently beneficial change?
2. What point did the team member miss in Paul's interview?
3. How could the interview have ended on a positive note?

Chapter 9 Selecting and Implementing the System

CHAPTER OBJECTIVES:

Identify important parts of a Request for Proposal.

Develop evaluation criteria and guidelines for determining equipment needs.

Understand how a thorough vendor selection can be determined.

Schedule an implementation plan.

Prepare a site layout.

Identify installation checkpoints.

Organize personnel.

Plan procedures for system operation.

Develop orientation programs.

One of the most enjoyable stages in office systems planning is designing the new system. Up to this point, the team members have been busy learning about the new technology, educating company employees, gathering data to determine their case, and convincing upper management that there is definite feasibility for implementing an automated office system.

Armed with work flow statistics, the team can begin designing a system which will respond to the needs of their company. In this chapter we will see how the team at first considers only very broad cost or technology constraints. After the ideal system has been designed (the first stage of the process), it must be refined into a feasible approach that meets the limits of cost and technology.

When the team determines the most appropriate alternative, detailed specifications are created—the next stage. If the proposed plan requires the work to flow in a certain manner, a narrative explanation should describe the logical flow for the new activities and explain what is to be gained by these flow processes. This means that the system to be selected should be able to follow a certain work flow process in order to gain the most logical efficiencies for administrative activities. File structures must be designed, and the questions of what data should be stored and what type of access is necessary have to be answered.

Input/output forms and procedures also have to be developed at this stage. The logic of the system has to be converted into programming requirements and into manual procedures to be followed by users and the operations staff in the computer department.

The last stage in the process is implementation. Here it is seen that program testing is satisfactorily completed and that the system is converted. During this stage, training for users also must be completed and any conversion activities such as file creation are finished. Finally, the new system is installed and users become dependent solely upon it for information processing.

EQUIPMENT SELECTION

The selection of equipment for an information processing system has two stages: (1) a design specification stage by which the team develops the basic design of the system in order to prepare a Request for Proposal for prospective vendors, and (2) an equipment evaluation which qualifies the bidding systems and extracts the most appropriate alternative.

Design Specifications

During this stage, the team spends its time designing model system specifications. This effort results in a narrative report which can be provided to all vendors. It contains all of the background information on the company, its work flow, and its expectations for system use. It is referred to as a Request for Proposal (RFP) since its primary purpose is to solicit bids for a system from each potential vendor.

Generally there are two different phase-in approaches a team can take in its implementation plans.

- The first approach assumes that a specific department will be the test site for system implementation. After successful testing and review of the model area, implementation is phased in slowly over the remaining departments until the entire company is dependent on the information processing system.

- The second approach assumes that the entire company will be implemented with a single information processing application (subsystem), such as word processing. Then after successful testing and review, other applications (subsystems) are phased in slowly until the entire spectrum of information processing is being used.

Either method is acceptable and can be successful. The only difference in the implementation process is in the amount of documentation and the variety of procedures that must be readied by implementation time. The first method requires the preparation of multiple documents and user procedures in order to implement a variety of applications. The second method requires only a single training preparation. The choice of a method would depend upon the size of the company, the level of user sophistication, and the length of time the team could devote to documentation and procedure writing.

The interviews and the various study results illustrate the company's administrative needs and requirements. With the analyses, the team members are able to determine the collective automated functions the office system should include. More specifically, they are able to identify the features that these functions should employ in order to gain the greatest productivity with the least amount of user resistance.

Several concerns may materialize from management and staff during the study cycle. They may question how much money the company should spend for the equipment, how long the company would have to wait for implementation, and how employees will be trained on the new equipment. These concerns should be voiced during the planning effort and prior to development of the actual design specifications. These concerns play an important part in user and/or management acceptance of the system and thus should be weighed carefully to ensure system support.

The RFP begins with the team defining the requirements for the office system from both an immediate and a long-term approach. Specifically, the team must agree upon and define:

- The functional requirements of the applications which form a part of the system—how each application must perform; i.e., word processing, printing, electronic mail, and graphics.

- The input requirements—the media format and the security of the media.

- The output requirements—forms, printing, distribution, and security of those items.

- An equipment system work flow—the impact on personnel, procedures, and the organization.

- The hardware requirements from functional, technical, and environmental standpoints.

Immediate and Long-Range Office Systems Requirements

BACKGROUND

Comserv Corporation is a leading manufacturer of applications software products for the manufacturing industry. The company's principal business is producing, marketing, implementing, and supporting its manufacturing software systems AMAPS and AMAPS/3000. Comserv also designs, produces, and markets educational products that teach AMAPS clients how to use these manufacturing systems most effectively. Comserv's Professional Services Department provides industry consulting services and systems and programming services to Comserv clients. Comserv also provides remote-batch computer processing services through a data center in its Twin Cities facilities.

In the spring of 1983, Comserv Corporation will be moving into a new corporate headquarters building in Eagan, Minnesota. The new corporate headquarters will include 191,000 square feet of office space and will house a staff of approximately 500 employees.

Comserv expects its work force to continue to grow. Thus, the plans for the company's new corporate headquarters will allow Comserv to expand its headquarters office space to 360,000 square feet through the construction of two planned additions to the main building. The new Comserv corporate headquarters will also support an expanding network of both domestic and international branch offices.

Copies of reduced floor plans for the new corporate headquarters are attached for your further information. Our new corporate structure is located across from the Blue Cross building, overlooking the Minnesota River; specifically, the intersection of Highway 13 and Yankee Doodle Road in Eagan, Minnesota.

Concurrent with its occupancy, Comserv is determined to have completed its research and evaluation and begun an aggressive implementation plan for an automated office system. This system will be a network-supported, integrated environment designed to meet the company's immediate and long-term needs and simultaneously realize increased productivity, improved efficiencies, and cost-effectiveness.

GENERAL SYSTEM FLOW & PHASE IN

Present occupancy plans anticipate moves in unison by all Comserv departments into their new quarters within a ten (10)-day interval. Therefore, the phase-in plans will be based upon specific "functional" requirements of a workstation (terminal) environment supporting the entire new corporate headquarters, rather than implementing a pilot or prototype area experimenting with full-function/integration applications.

The intent of this method is to ensure a smooth transition and offer a transparent continuity to the administrative requirements of Comserv. A secondary aim, equally as important, is to provide timely, well-organized training classes for personnel based on methodical teaching techniques of desired application plus instruction (learning, absorbing, adapting) equals mastering. New functional applications will be added as the need arises and/or as an ease-of-use comfort level has been established.

It is expected that the local area networking will be installed in conjunction with architectural requirements, now scheduled for October, 1982. This networking should be baseband installed for a plug-in workstation expandable environment. Estimations are projected to a potential ratio of 3:2 (people vs. workstations) environment. This suggests the growth potential of the original 191,000 square feet complex to be approximately three hundred (300) terminals/workstations.

Broadband networking is an acceptable consideration; however, it must have dedicated baseband widths sufficient to support the active environment being described and additionally must be cost compatible with more discriminate offerings. Comserv has no intentions of paying more for speculations.

Full video channels are presently a future projection within Comserv Corporation; however, the application's potential use as an educational tool, a cost-of-travel deterrent, and an effective employee communication vehicle are just a few of the potential benefits recognized. A video-teleconferencing application is being reserved until such time as the current costs of operation and/or technological advancements justify its implementation, thereby making it a viable resource.

Phase I Plans

Phase I plans are initially to install the "core" intelligence to support a companion base of fifty (50) workstations throughout the structure. These workstations will be operated primarily by secretarial personnel performing word processing applications.

The "core" intelligence will remain within a dedicated environment with this decentralized equipment added as cable-connected or 'shared environment' with the basic intent of maintaining centralized management control.

This base system will provide the full-spectrum, state-of-the-art word processing capabilities, shared printing options, and communications capabilities. Three units must specifically interface with a Comserv-owned phototypesetter: Merganthaler, Omnitech 2100, and Omnitech 2001. Presently, the word processing equipment is hard-wired.

> Media conversion will be a separate issue, but bidders should be aware that current work load must be converted to a new format prior to implementation.

This same system should be capable of relatively simple (turnkey) expansion as more and more of the company's information and transactions are switched from manual to automated methods.

Phase II Plans

Phase II will expand into electronic mail and distribution functions, initially within the local structure and then remotely, as expansion of workstations occurs within field offices [eleven (11) communicating word processors within eight (8) offices]. These offices are as follows: Boston, Chicago, Cleveland, Dallas, Los Angeles, Philadelphia, San Francisco, and Winston-Salem.

The eight field offices presently have light word processing requirements averaging 2,000-3,000 lines weekly. However, their office system workstation needs also include an ability a) to perform some personal computing, i.e. budgeting and spreadsheet activities, b) to communicate with corporate headquarters for daily transaction reporting, and c) to perform product demonstrations remotely for prospective customers.

CHAPTER 9 Selecting and Implementing the System

Secretarial and clerical personnel locally produce approximately 116,000 lines of typing weekly, of which 83,000 lines are copied and distributed within the local headquarters complex. Another 9,000 lines are keyboarded and mailed to our field office locations via the public mail system. Excluding reports which are multipaged and usually hand delivered, this line count equates to approximately 2,500 one-page documents that weekly could be distributed electronically.

Additionally, the nature of Comserv's business, compounded by its rapid growth and the high percentage (83%) of technical/professional staffing, is a natural inducement of no-contact telephone calls (telephone tag). In an average week, Comserv personnel reported that they make 3,584 calls to other employees who are temporarily unavailable. By similar suit, 53% of these calls are returned when they are no longer available. (Since only 82.2% of the staff contributed to the study, the results can be easily assumed as being on the low side.)

If strict automation productivity methods are adhered to, the electronic mail/message/distribution system recommended should not introduce replacement steps to the work flow process, i.e. a telephone call to ascertain an electronic message receipt or a manual keyboarding procedure alerting the originator of message receipt. Rather the system should provide automated response/status indicators; thereby eliminating an unnecessary work flow step.

Phase III Plans

Phase III will introduce intelligent copiers/duplicators designed to accelerate printing, receiving, microfilming, or duplicating options in local or remote locations.

Comserv presently has two high document production areas: software documentation manuals and customer education/training manuals. Both areas require little margin for error, multiple revision cycles, a short turnaround cycle, and many-paged, multicopy documents. The combined weekly production line effort is 150,000, of which 79% is subject to revision. These lines are not reflected in the volume statistics indicated for the Phase I plans (see Functional Requirements: Word Processing); however, the ability to interface with intelligent copiers/duplicators is a strong possibility and the bidder should be prepared to report on both aspects of the work flow.

Normal administrative functions provide multicopy report formats weekly in the amount of 37,500 lines. Not included in this volume statistic are bound multicopy reports/exhibits which may be prepared by outside vendors. Accurate inventory statistics have been difficult to derive; however, study indicates an average weekly volume is 1.9%, or approximately 2,200 lines.

Professional workstations will be added performing convenient personal computing applications of grid sheet, modeling, planning, forecasting, and budgeting. Each workstation additionally performs less-sophisticated text creation and editing, and electronic mail and filing functions. This implementation consists of an additional fifty (50) workstations. Additionally, all workstation equipment must be capable of communicating or interfacing with our AS/9000 mainframe with an operating system supporting VM/SP, OS/VS1, DOS/VSE, CICS, and a Comten communications controller.

The communication should be via a high-speed link (9,600 B). The vendors should indicate what communications facilities they have, specifying protocols and what their devices would look like to the host. Additionally, they should be prepared to respond to the following concerns:

- How do you interface with our VM operating system?
- How many similar units are placed locally?
- How many CE's support the maintenance of these units?
- How far can terminals be placed from the CPU, and how many terminals will the unit support?
- Is the software locally supported? By whom?

- What upgrades are possible?
- How much operator attention does it require from a computer-room type operation?

Final Phase

The Final Phase will expand to full central library capabilities with "authorized use" restrictions to central facilities and in-house data processing facilities via personal and central filing, storage, retrieval, and manipulation functions.

Each workstation should be able to create information; review and proof information; retrieve immediate and archival files; receive, store, and send mail and messages; and produce hard copy output when needed.

Functional Requirements

Electronic Mail Functions are potentially the most positive impact on efficiencies and cost improvements. Comserv personnel require the following specifications to guarantee productivity improvement:

- A nonsynchronous system freeing its users from time constraints; sender and recipient may be involved at different times.
- A mail system intelligence to retain messages in computerized files and permit users to receive messages on their terminals, at their convenience, and from any location.
- Must serve a community of 200 to 500 growth users, ranging from inactive to active; thereby, a system with 12-15 access lines initially, or supporting a 6-7% active on-line time relative to the number of employees (growth 34 ports).
- Must perform: message creation—input, editing, and transmission of text storage—maintains files for the originator and recipient receipt—allows reading, forwarding, and disposal of messages.

- Must use friendly and familiar notes and become "user-name" automated; yet maintain a high degree of security.
- Must display status: the number of messages unread and unsent.
- Must support an automatic log-off as a cost/quality control feature.
- Must support several levels of addressing: (a) individual; (b) group lists (personal); (c) group functional lists; (d) urgent/priority; and (e) high security.
- Must indicate, in some prompting manner to the recipient, that an urgent message is waiting.
- May be accessed remotely via any ASCII terminal.
- May access subscriber networks including information banks, TWX, and Telex.
- Must include several directory choices for identification.
- Must permit the sender to specify a time for transmission, (urgent) support priority mail, support return-receipt mails; supports both hard and soft copy requests.
- Must provide instant file creation and file maintenance, and safeguard against destruction. Must contain automatic file-search and retrieval functions.

Word Processing Functions initially will support a user staff of approximately 200. It will decentrally service a weekly work load of:

a 82,693 original keyboarding lines
b 12,563 revised lines
c 32,490 statistical lines
d 37,332 stored and/or repetitive lines

Other reports, manuals, statistical setups, and repetitive work may flow through the system occasionally.

At the final stage, provision must be made for satisfying a weekly volume of 350,000 variety lines with a growth factor of 22% applied each year until completion of the project. Work flow is rather consistent and in diverse kinds; peaks and valleys occurring approximately three times yearly.

Products must meet strict cost-effective guidelines and result in a 4:1 ratio of increased typing productivity over traditional methods.

Word processors (workstations) must share the core processor for system logic, be centrally located, and be cable-connected to satellite decentralized stations as expansion occurs.

As the automated phase in continues, existing equipment must be capable of expansion with little or no downtime to existing work activities. It should be upgraded by a turnkey system complete with required hardware/software and ready to use. Special consideration will be given to user-programmable systems; the input of which will be user-discrete authorized methods.

Workstations must be easy to learn to operate (self-teach) with a good set of operator prompts. Help function or its equivalent is mandatory. All functions basic to word processing must be available. Functions which are unavailable should be identified.

Full-page CRTs are preferable; exception would be an uncalculated numeric display of a full page. All storage media (card, tape, floppy, disc) must be compatible with all equipment, and capacity for final storage and text manipulation must be virtual.

Display Features

As a communicating word processor, the system should perform these activities in the background, enabling the operator to use the keyboard and display for other work simultaneously:

- Edited text should be highlighted.
- Character size should be enlarged or reduced at command.
- These features should be displayed and not merely coded: (a) underscores; (b) superscripts; (c) subscripts; (d) grammatical notations; (e) justified spacing.
- Line spacing of single, double and space-and-a-half is required.
- Cursor movement should be horizontal, vertical, and diagonal and should return to home

when cleared.
- Screen should have contrast and brightness controls and an angle adjustment for viewing. No flicker or glare is to be evident; all letters should be quite legibly indicated.
- Screen and keyboard should be separate components in these decentralized areas.

Editing

Words and phrases should be moved easily to new positions throughout the document rather than within a single page. Insertions, deletions, and replacement to existing text should be easily executed and easily identified.

A built-in control for error handling and safeguards for deletions should be included. Buffer memory should be large enough to facilitate transposing large blocks of information and should define a block of text in size for transposition-storage.

The following features or functions must be performed:

- hyphenation decision
- right justification
- dictionary program
- pagination
- repagination of multipage documents
- capability to merge text from unrelated documents
- global search and replace
- string search by character and mixture of all caps, all lowercase, mixture or underscore, etc.
- backward, forward, and side-to-side scrolling
- long document handling
- repetitive document merging in background
- quick system response (identify)

Document Formatting

Include the following features or functions:

- Ease of format use and selection
- Multiple format choices
- Modification to format options
- Keyboard reformatting capability
- Automatic centering
- Automatic cursor positioning
- Decimal alignment
- High-speed indenting
- Electronic carriage return
- Tabbing position options
- Form design capability
- Tabular/columnar options, i.e., vertical and then to top of page, shifting columns, and transposing.

Document Handling

Finished products are required to be:

a easily stored
b easily duplicated
c edited readily
d printed automatically
e archived for permanent storage

Indexes or tables of contents must be created automatically. There must be a batch filing/retrieving capability.

Output Options

Multichoice printers are predetermined, i.e., ball type, daisy/qume wheel, nonimpact, matrix, and intelligent copier.

Impact printer should be bidirectional and have a minimum speed of 45 cps. High-quality print is a necessity for all output, the exception being data reports. Nonimpact printers must have a minimum speed of 90 cps.

Minimum choices of type styles and sizes must be 12. Carriage width minimum is a 15″ platen.

When offering proportional spacing, identify how justification spaces are added. If added between characters, it will spoil the value of the feature and its output quality.

System logic should be geared to operate several printers at once. Queue printing positions are required, and status printed by request is a requirement. Additionally, while printing is performed, the operator can input/edit another job.

Optional feeds for twin sheets, envelopes, labels,

and continuous forms are required.

Dual printer head for mixed type style pass is a consideration only. The system should handle multilevel equations.

Links and interface identity must be indicated for communications and photocomposition units; if available—via compatible disc? interface? on-line?

Office System Features

The terminal also must serve as a device to display information stored in a data base, i.e., directory and calendars. It should also serve as a data processor for storage and retrieval function, sorting, collating, arithmetic computations, and background storage.

Security Provisions

Confidentiality and authorized access should be governed by three (3) levels of entry. Security should be a function of the master control area only.

In order to protect documents from alteration by unauthorized individuals, password security (or its equivalent) is required.

Backup Recovery Provisions

The bidding vendor should be prepared to detail extensive central system backup and recovery practices. In addition, if a file or a disc should become damaged, it is desirable to have some sort of an information recovery facility.

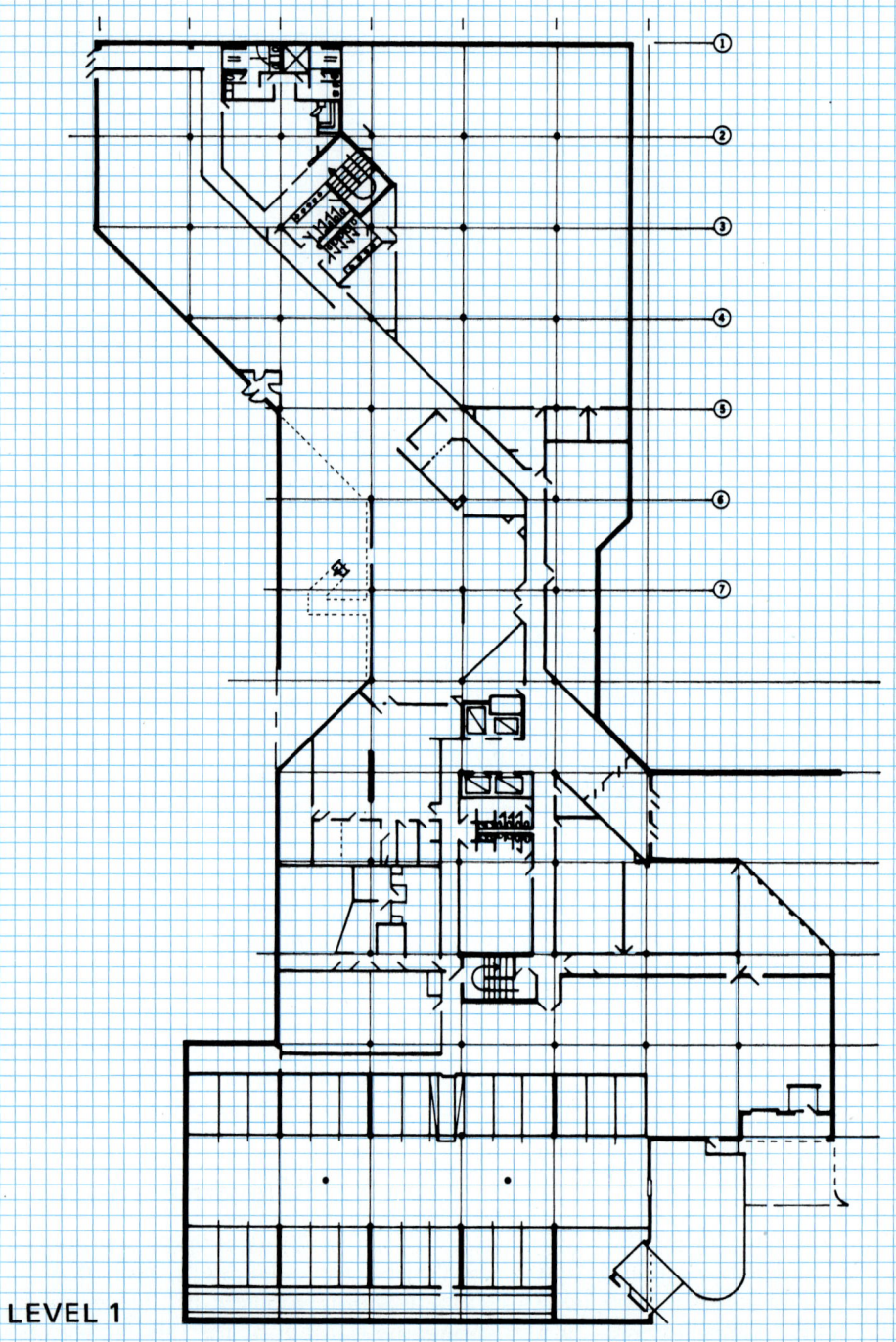

LEVEL 1

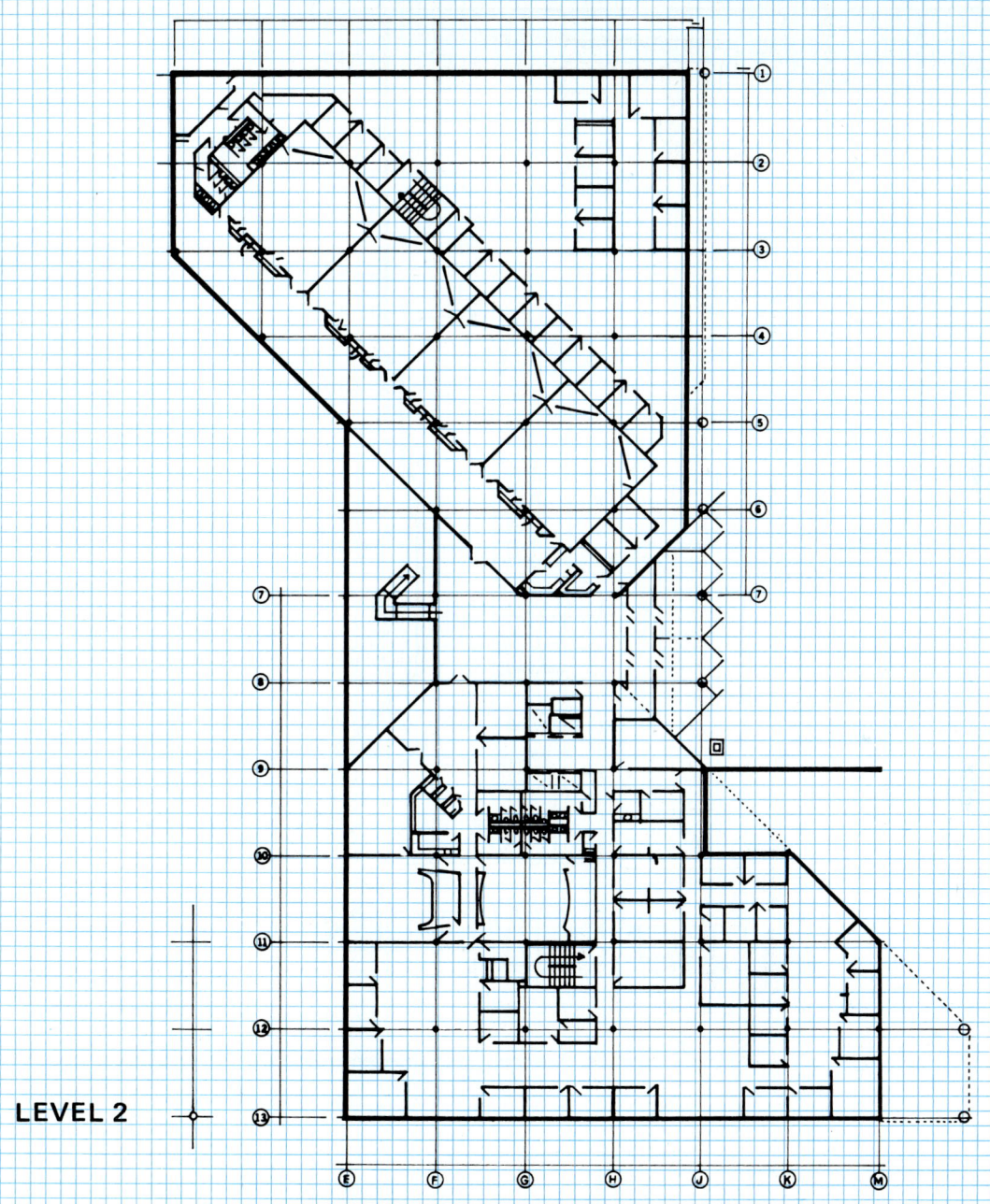

LEVEL 2

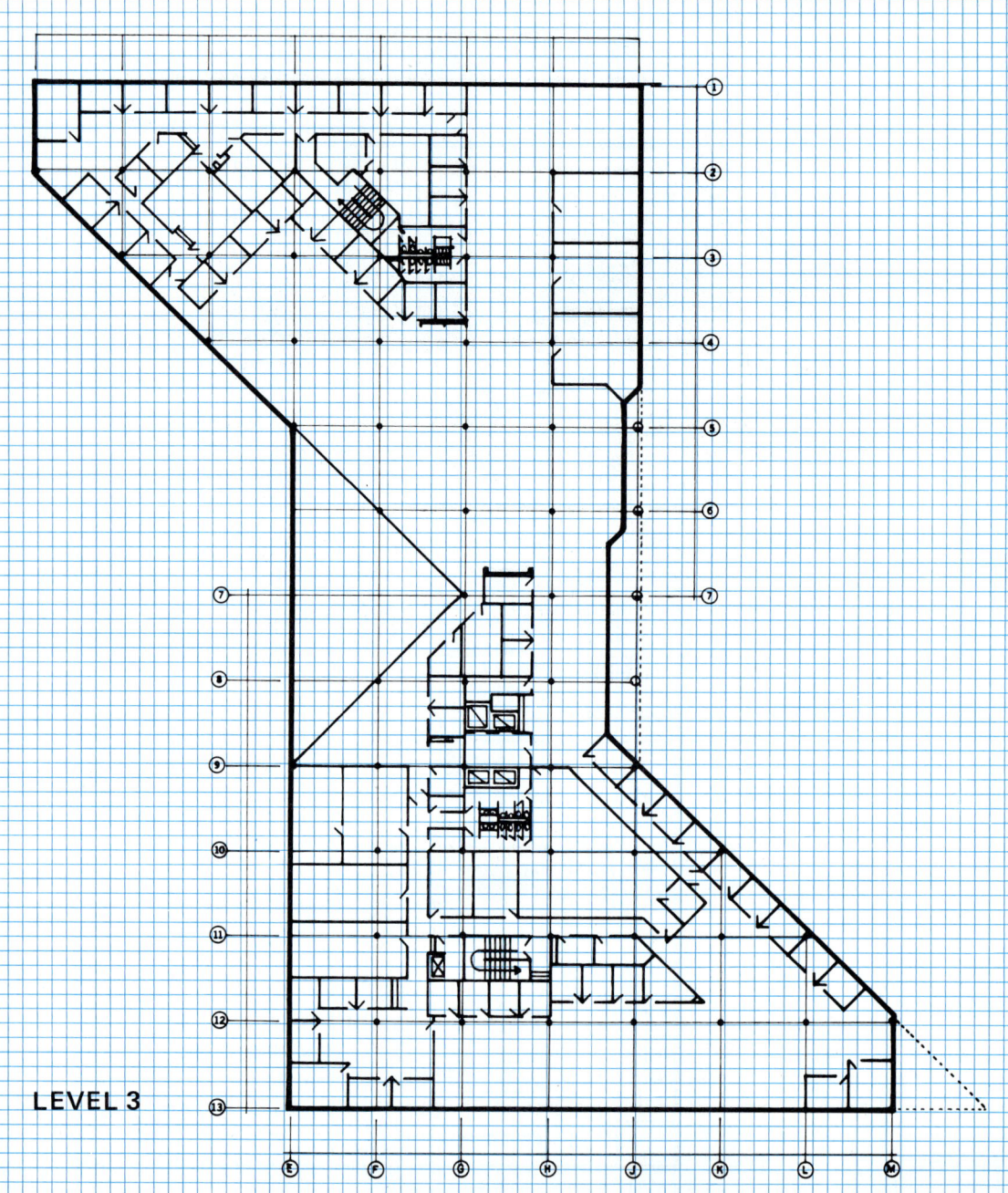

LEVEL 3

- A vendor evaluation checklist—specifications of top priority to the system design; i.e., functionality, usability, reliability, availability, expandability, compatibility, vendor support, and training.

The team members may perform an initial vendor evaluation prior to sending out the document. Some team members may be well acquainted with certain vendors and may be able to provide substantial evidence to eliminate some vendors. This may arise from personal knowledge of a vendor's lack of product availability or from historically poor support from that vendor. It might be judged appropriate to distribute the RFP to all vendors regardless of personal objections in order to maintain good customer relations. This is an area wherein management may provide some valuable insights.

The RFP is distributed with a cover letter which indicates the nature of the request and the bidding procedures. A deadline for response is necessary in order to maintain a continuity of the work plan schedules. Each vendor should be encouraged to contact a designated team member if further clarifications of the RFP are needed. In addition, each vendor who wishes to respond should be prepared to host an on-site demonstration for the entire team.

Rather than allow vendors to give their usual demonstrations, it is wise to prepare a demonstration package of applications that represent common functions required by your company. Each vendor is then given the same opportunity; and there is a sound basis upon which to make note of the time it takes to perform each application, the problems encountered in operating the equipment, and the time-saving features of the equipment. Following this part of the demonstration, the vendors could demonstrate other important features of their equipment.

Buyers and vendors each have certain responsibilities. Vendors show what their equipment can do, and they generally point out the features that are unique or that are better than those of their competitors. Buyers should not expect vendors to reveal what their equipment cannot do. It is the buyer's responsibility to research, study, and observe what each vendor's equipment can or cannot do, as well as to note the efficiency of the various features.

Equipment Evaluation

After presenting the specifications to the vendors for their bids, the team begins to schedule and attend vendor presentations and demonstrations. Usually one team member, the leader, is responsible for scheduling the times for these presentations. Times are selected so that all team members are able to attend. This aids the team in arriving at a consensus decision.

To prepare each team member for a thorough system analysis, evaluation factors and guidelines should be designed and distributed in advance of each presentation. In addition, group meetings should be scheduled immediately following each presentation. The advance preparations and group discussions tend to tailor upcoming presentations to be more practical and useful. Most importantly, these preparations develop a broadened and cohesive analysis of each vendor's offering by the entire team membership. An example of an evaluation guideline form is given in Figure 9-1. You will note that the evaluation guidelines include extremely detailed word processing capabilities.

Following the presentations, the team should meet at length to develop the final evaluation criteria which will produce the vendor selection. Team members initially can be polled to select the vendors they feel would best meet the company's needs. This polling will narrow the field down to the few select vendors satisfying the initial requirements. The vendors that have been disqualified should be informed of their status.

Often, the team may request that several vendors re-present their bids in another fashion stressing different factors and functions. Others may be asked to reconfigure their bids using different products or concepts. These requests by the team are designed to establish the best possible configuration for the company. It is also an attempt to make all of the presentations more uniform when the team begins evaluating the bids.

Evaluation criteria are developed for the categories which represent the priority concerns of the feasibility study. A point value is determined for each major category. This value indicates how critical the team feels satisfying the needs of the category is to their selection. For example, the team may develop values for each of the following categories and weight their point values accordingly:

Word Processing	100 points
Electronic Mail	80 points
Electronic Filing	50 points
Calendaring/Scheduling	20 points
Vendor Support/Training	80 points
Typesetting	40 points

This example implies that team members will consider the most detailed examination of the word processing capabilities in their evaluation process. Secondly, they will require good electronic mail capabilities and strong vendor support. Categories which require less consideration are electronic filing, typesetting, and calendaring.

Once point values are determined, the team sets out to detail the important characteristics of each category. They must list the manner in which word processing must function in order to make it an acceptable application for the company. Each item must be weighted in value on a scale from 1 to 10. The number 10 implies that the required item must be totally satisfactory, whereas a lesser number indicates that the item is necessary but is not as important to the overall goal. Example item weights might look like those shown in Figure 9-2.

CHAPTER 9 Selecting and Implementing the System   237

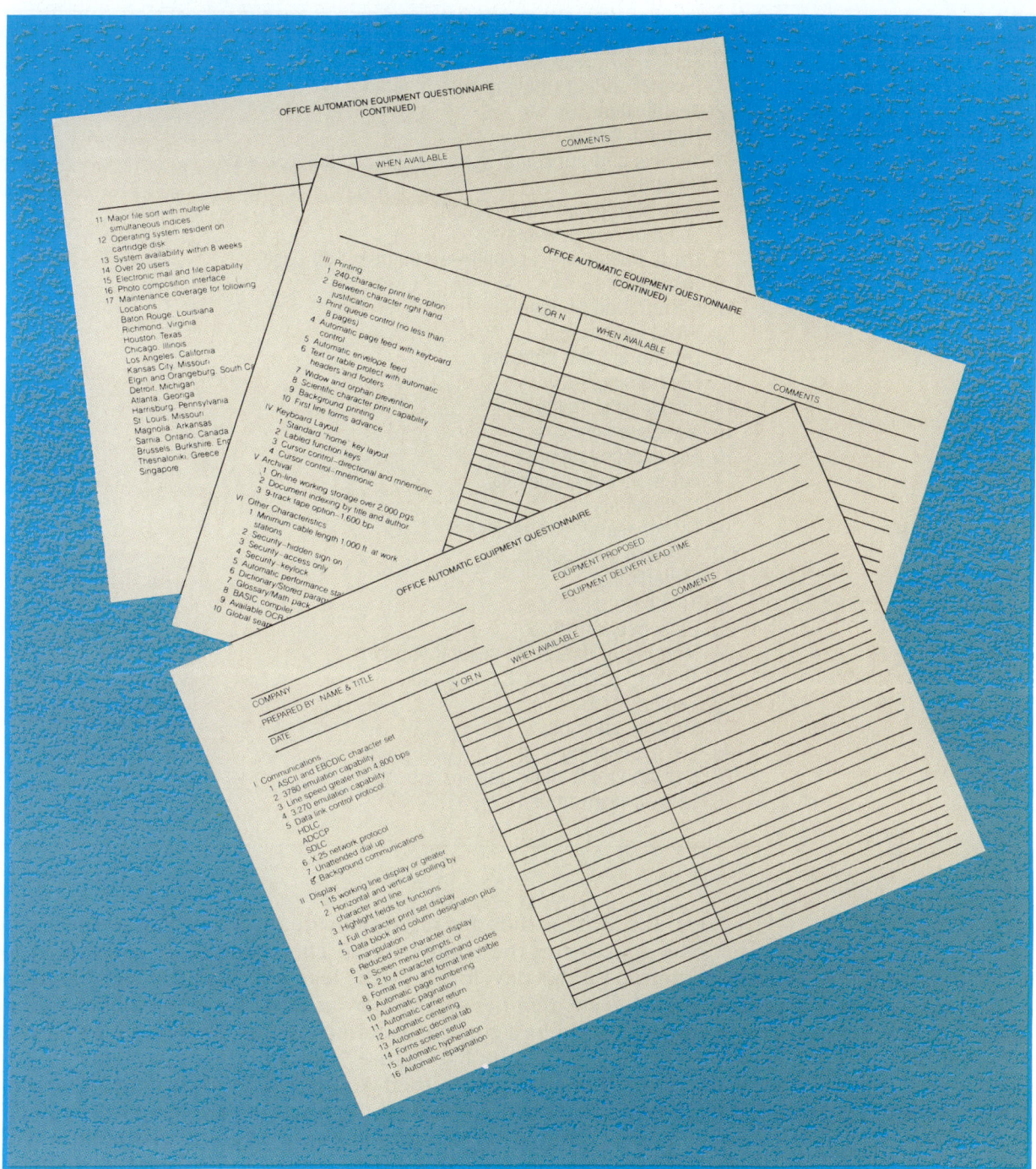

FIG. 9-1 EVALUATION FORM   Evaluation forms should be given to team members before vendor presentations. This allows team members to make more thorough analyses of the presentations.

FIG. 9-2
WEIGHING CHARACTERISTICS
Team members must weigh each characteristic of word processing systems to determine the system that is best suited for the company's needs.

WORD PROCESSING (100 POINTS)	Weight
1 Ease of editing (moving text, inserting text, deleting text, etc.)	10
2 Justification	10
3 Hyphenation	7
4 Vertical and horizontal scrolling—minimum 132 wide	10
5 Security	10
6 Easy storage and duplication	10
7 Function key oriented	9
8 Large document capability—minimum 100 pages	10
9 Pagination	10
10 Background printing	10
11 Word wraparound	10
12 Directories and indexing	10
13 File naming	8
14 Sharp clear image	10
15 Nonglare screen	5
16 File access response	5
17 Forms design capability	6
18 Dictionaries	3
19 Global search and replace	10
20 Headers and footers	10
21 Underlining	10
22 Keyboard response	10
23 Detachable keyboard	5
24 Merging of data from several sources	10
25 Tabbing position option and ease	10
26 Centering text	10
27 Moving columns	10
28 List processing	10
29 Sort and math packages	10
30 Easy to learn to use	10

Next, the vendor bids are rated individually according to how well each offering satisfies the team criteria. Their ratings are listed next to the maximum ratings developed by the team. Vendors are rated individually by each team member and then by groups of team members. In this way, each vendor gets a consensus rating. A consensus rating of various vendor offerings may look like Figure 9-3.

The individual ratings are then multiplied by the point value and added. This figure, when divided by the total point value possible, indicates the percentage of satisfaction that would be attained by this vendor for the category evaluated. A total category evaluation by vendor is shown in Figure 9-4.

CHAPTER 9 Selecting and Implementing the System 239

WORD PROCESSING (100 POINTS)		RATE			
	Weight	Advanced Concepts	Systems Unlimited	Info Systems	Systems of the Future
1 Ease of editing (moving text, inserting text, deleting text, etc.)	10	9	7	7	9
2 Justification	10	9	7	5	9
3 Hyphenation	7	10	0	7	10
4 Vertical and horizontal scrolling—minimum 132 wide	10	8	10	10	10
5 Security	10	10	10	7	7
6 Easy storage and duplication	10	10	10	10	10
7 Function key oriented	9	10	3	5	9
8 Large document capability—minimum 100 pages	10	10	10	9	9
9 Pagination	10	10	10	10	10
10 Background printing	10	10	10	8	10
11 Word wraparound	10	10	10	10	10
12 Directories and indexing	10	10	8	8	10
13 File naming	8	10	6	8	10
14 Sharp clear image	10	10	10	7	10
15 Nonglare screen	5	8	8	10	8
16 File access response	5	8	8	8	8
17 Forms design capability	6	10	0	3	10
18 Dictionaries	3	8	0	6	10
19 Global search and replace	10	9	8	8	10
20 Headers and footers	10	10	10	10	10
21 Underlining	10	10	3	3	10
22 Keyboard response	10	10	3	3	10
23 Detachable keyboard	5	10	10	10	10
24 Merging of data from several sources	10	10	10	7	7
25 Tabbing position option and ease	10	10	9	9	9
26 Centering text	10	10	8	8	10
27 Moving columns	10	10	9	7	10
28 List processing	10	10	3	3	10
29 Sort and math packages	10	10	3	3	10
30 Easy to learn to use	10	10	7	7	9

FIG. 9-3
RATING CHARACTERISTICS
After each vendor presentation, team members must rate the individual bids according to the established weights.

The evaluation form may contain many categories and be as detailed as the team determines. The highest percentage will indicate the product most likely to satisfy the requirements of the company.

The team then develops its recommendation in a report and presents it to management. The report is a composite of:

- **Vendor selection**—Who will provide the system?

		RATE				RANK			
WORD PROCESSING (100 POINTS)	Weight	Advanced Concepts	Systems Unlimited	Info Systems	Systems of the Future	Advanced Concepts	Systems Unlimited	Info Systems	Systems of the Future
1 Ease of editing (moving text, inserting text, deleting text, etc.)	10	9	7	7	9	90	70	70	90
2 Justification	10	9	7	5	9	90	70	50	90
3 Hyphenation	7	10	0	7	10	70	0	49	70
4 Vertical and horizontal scrolling—minimum 132 wide	10	8	10	10	10	80	100	100	100
5 Security	10	10	10	7	7	100	100	70	70
6 Easy storage and duplication	10	10	10	10	10	100	100	100	100
7 Function key oriented	10	10	3	5	9	90	27	45	81
8 Large document capability—minimum 100 pages	10	10	10	9	9	100	100	90	90
9 Pagination	10	10	10	10	10	100	100	100	100
PRINTING									
1 Large carriage—15″	10	10	10	10	10	100	100	100	100
2 10, 12, and proportional and required spacing	10	10	5	5	10	100	50	50	100
3 Sheet, tractor, and continuous forms feed	10	9	7	3	10	90	70	30	100
4 Font selections	5	10	5	5	10	50	25	25	50
5 Speed	5	10	10	10	10	50	50	50	50
6 Ability to print in 1, 1.5, 2, or 3 space lines	10	10	10	8	10	100	100	80	100
7 Ability to assign a printer easily	8	10	8	5	10	80	64	40	80
8 Selective page printing (ex. Page 3-6 of 20 pages)	10	10	9	7	10	100	90	70	100
9 Font loading	5	8	8	8	10	40	40	40	50
10 Redundancy	5	9	9	7	7	45	45	35	35

(Total Weight Value = 3,460)

	Total Rank	Rank %	Points
Advanced Concepts	3,359	97.1%	97.1
Systems Unlimited	2,589	74.8%	74.8
Info Systems	2,444	70.6%	70.6
Systems of the Future	3,306	95.5%	95.5

FIG. 9-4
RANKING VENDORS

CHAPTER 9   Selecting and Implementing the System   241

- **Evaluation criteria**—How was the decision made?
- **Cost justification**—How will the system benefit the company?
- **Implementation schedule**—When will the system be installed?
- **Cost analysis**—What will the system cost us now?

This information package provides management with the background needed to make a thorough and cost-effective decision.

IMPLEMENTATION PLANNING

The implementation of an information processing system requires a planned, coordinated effort. This effort involves not only the actual equipment selection but also such related factors as:

- Site location, floor plan, and preparation for equipment installation
- Environmental considerations
- Organization of personnel
- Procedures for efficient work flow
- Orientation programs

Site Preparation and Layout

A major area of concern while planning a site is selecting the location of the CPU, disk drives, disk storage, printers, and workstations. The complete system may be centralized in a single room; or workstations may extend the system throughout the building, across town, or across the country. The site may be open and readily accessible, or it may be securely restricted.

Usually the CPU, disk drives, and printers are located in one area. The workstations are placed wherever needed in open centralized areas, in several small clusters near the departments they serve, or in individual offices. Workstations may be many floors away from the CPU.

Site Layout. Figure 9-5 consists of a grid layout of a floor plan and a grid layout for equipment floor space dimensions. These types of grids usually are included in a site layout work kit provided by the vendor. A normal grid size represents each small square to be 2 inches and each block of six squares to be 1 foot.

To plan a layout, the proposed site must be measured and drawn to scale on the floor plan grid. Next, reference needs to be made to the vendor's recommendation for the floor space required for the equipment. The dimensions of the equipment pieces then must be drawn on

PART THREE Implementing Change in the Office

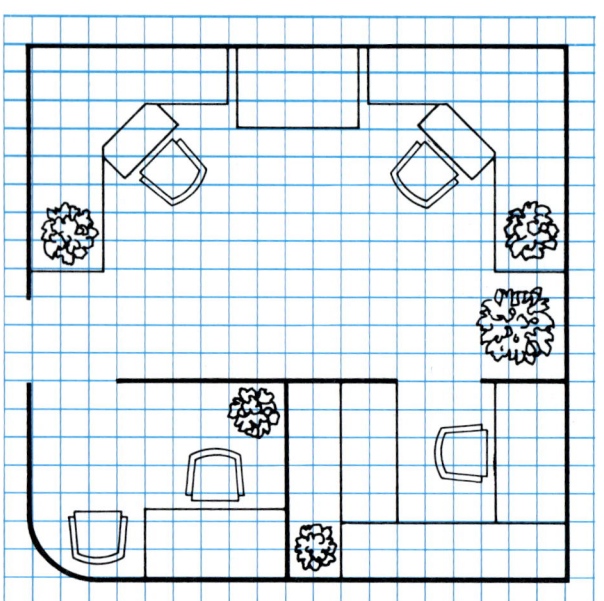
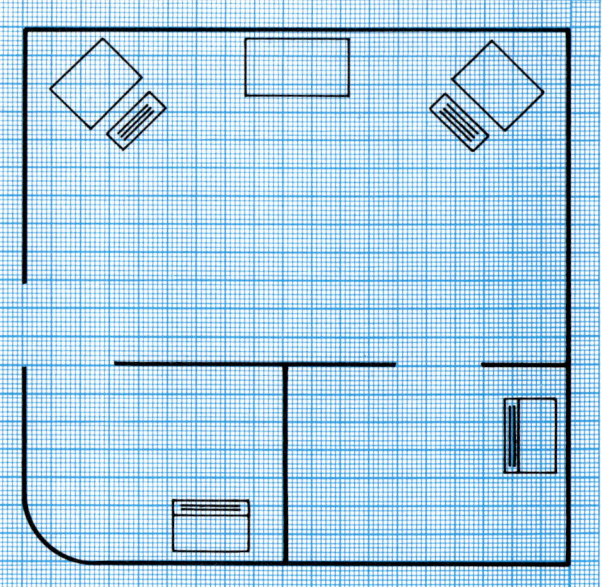

FIG. 9-5
SITE LAYOUT
This grid layout suggests an office that looks much like the one shown in the photo.

CHAPTER 9 Selecting and Implementing the System 243

the grid layout for equipment floor space dimensions. These pieces must be cut out and positioned on the floor plan grid in various ways until an optimal setup is determined.

In addition to the equipment components, items such as work stations, filing cabinets, and other furniture also should be mapped onto the floor plan grid. The cut-out pieces should be rearranged until the setup for the equipment, furniture, and storage best enhances work flow.

After a good physical setup has been composed, the electrical outlets (receptacles) and line voltages that correspond to the required equipment specifications must be designated. Separate outlets should be made available for nonsystem equipment; i.e., dictation equipment and calculators. To allow for future expansion, planners should request that extra outlets be provided.

Location of equipment and furniture should be based on the operational requirements of the system as well as the efficiency, comfort, and

Left: Electric cables can be run just under the carpeting.

Right: When the carpet squares are in place, it is not obvious that the cables are underneath them.

convenience of the people using the room. Layout of the equipment, furniture, and storage devices must be planned before furniture and equipment are moved into place and connected for operation. Two considerations affect layout: (1) individual pieces of equipment usually are interconnected by cables of limited length, and (2) clearances for access, service, and work space must be maintained. Thus, you may need to consider several tentative layouts before selecting the one best suited to your operational requirements.

To protect confidential or sensitive information, access to the CPU or master workstations should be restricted. Maximum security can be achieved by locating the CPU, operator workstations, and desk files behind locked doors. Backup programs and recorded media files should be locked in a separate, and perhaps remote, location. Fireproof storage vaults should be used for optimum protection of recorded media. Other items to consider when designing a floor plan are listed in Figure 9-6.

Storage of Disks and Supplies. Most information processing systems require certain supplies. You will need storage space for bulk paper, operations manuals, disk packs, and cleaning supplies. Equipment such as disk packs will require both (1) short-term, easily accessible storage and (2) long-term, backup storage to ensure a smooth and efficient operation of the system. Space should be reserved for operators and work produced by the system. Provisions for waste and recycling also should be made.

The amount of space allocated for the storage of diskettes, disk cartridges, disk packs, and magnetic tape depends on the volume of work to be done and the types of storage media to be used. Diskettes are easily stored on shelves in the work area or in plastic cases or plastic pockets at the operators' desks.

A disk cartridge contains one disk platter and is enclosed in a plastic case about 2 1/2 inches high and 15 inches in diameter. A disk pack contains more than one platter and may be up to 12 inches high. For short-term storage, the cartridge provides adequate protection. Cartridges may be stacked (up to five high) or stored on their sides in dust-free, fire-resistant cabinets. For long-term storage it is recommended that the disk cartridges (or disk packs) be repacked in their original cardboard shipping containers to further protect them from dust accumulation.

Ideally the storage environment for disks should be the same as that of the disk drive. If disks are stored in an environment that differs from that of the disk drive, the disk should be brought into the same room at least two hours prior to use. Highly sensitive and/or important disks (such as those containing payroll information) should be copied daily (backed up). Then the backup disk should be kept at a remote site. Daily disk backup ensures that no more than one day's work will be lost in the event of a power outage or other catastrophe.

CHAPTER 9 Selecting and Implementing the System 245

FLOOR PLAN DESIGN

CHECKLIST

Consider the following before determining the location of your office system group:

_____ What are the space requirements of the purchased system?

_____ Is there enough space allocated for servicing the equipment?

_____ Will you have to alter existing space in some way, or does your company already have a space that fulfills your requirements?

_____ Where your equipment will be installed, is there any type of strong magnetic equipment nearby?

_____ Is your office system group organized in one central location or in small clusters?

_____ Are there any remote workstations?

_____ How many people will inhabit the total work area if you are using a center?

_____ At what place do you expect the greatest amount of traffic to occur?

_____ Is your office design traditional, or do you use an office landscaping approach?

_____ Have you established work flow procedures?

Double check the following items after creating the office layout:

_____ Is there adequate room for the equipment to fit through the doors at the installation site?

_____ Is the furniture that will be used large and sturdy enough to support the equipment?

_____ Is the largest concentration of traffic in an area where it is least likely to create a disturbance?

_____ Does a work flow board exist for authors to check the status of their work?

_____ Is the location of the files convenient to the people who will use them?

_____ Is there sufficient room for each operator to move around?

_____ Do any operators have to face windows, sit in drafts, or be near heat sources?

_____ Is future expansion room available?

FIG. 9-6
FLOOR PLAN DESIGN
There are many important items to consider when designing a floor plan.

Fire Protection Equipment. Fire protection equipment should be reviewed and implemented before installing the office system. Machine rooms should be equipped with portable fire extinguishers suitable for quick, efficient use. A nonwetting fire extinguisher for electrical equipment is recommended. An insurance agent and the local fire department can advise you of applicable regulations, recommend the best type of fire prevention equipment for your needs, and advise you of the best locations for its placement.

Fire protection around the outside of the data processing and word processing rooms (in adjoining rooms, and the floor space above and below the rooms) is as important as fire protection within each room itself. Halon gas systems, fire walls, and magnetic doors are among the many fire protection methods available.

Combustible materials such as cleaning solvents should be stored in fire-resistant containers in accordance with National Fire Protection Association standards. In addition, attention should be given to protecting paper forms, reports, disk cartridges, diskettes, and tapes from destruction in the event of fire. A fire-resistant safe or file cabinet may be used for this purpose. It is always a good practice to keep a backup copy of important data and text files in a remotely located, fire-resistant container.

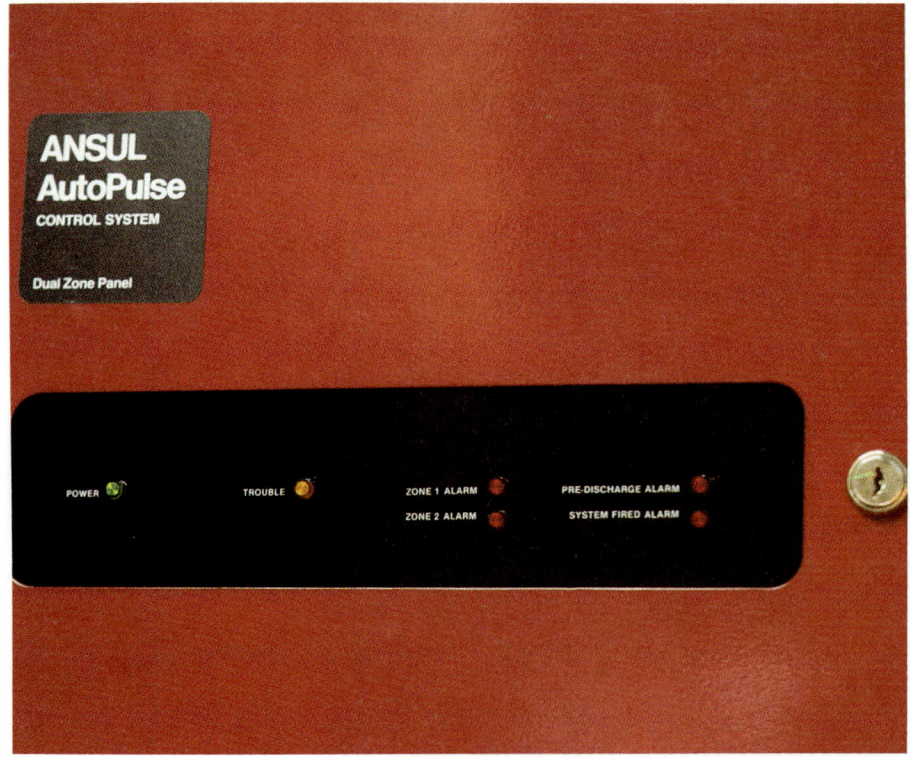

Some type of fire protection system should be used for rooms which house data processing and word processing equipment.

CHAPTER 9 Selecting and Implementing the System

Power and Cabling Considerations. All system power requirements must be discussed with a qualified electrical contractor before system installation to ensure that all wiring and electrical hookups conform to local building codes and ordinances. The equipment components and accessories must be powered from a single main source that is stable and free of noise to ensure uninterrupted operation. A checklist for power and cabling requirements is shown in Figure 9-7.

REQUIREMENTS FOR POWER AND CABLING

CHECKLIST

- Make sure that there are enough dedicated electrical outlets for the system.
- Outlets need to be close enough to the equipment.
- Be sure to ground all electrical devices and system components appropriately.
- Electrical outlets should accommodate three-prong plugs.
- Power lines must meet the recommended ampere and VAC specifications.
- Make sure standard cables that come with equipment are adequate.
- If cables are being run through conduit pipes, the pipe must be 1 1/2 inches in diameter to accommodate it. You will need a larger one if you are running more than one cable.
- Before the equipment is installed, all the electrical lines and cables should be strung.
- Cables, telephone cords, and electrical wiring should be located overhead to prevent employees from tripping on them.
- Where telecommunications is applicable, an access to telephone lines must be available.

FIG. 9-7
POWER AND CABLING REQUIREMENTS
Many offices hide electric and phone wires in the ceiling or under floor tiles to prevent employees from tripping over them.

Most vendors have strict electrical codes for their equipment, and these requirements should be closely followed. The vendor should provide you with guidelines for power and frequency tolerance ratings, system grounding techniques, and electrical noise preventatives.

There are three common methods of running cables at an installation site. The first of these methods uses cable troughs (plastic or metal). Plastic troughs are usually recommended to protect interconnecting cables routed across a large floor area. Cable troughs may be bought from suppliers in varying widths and heights to accommodate system cabling.

An alternate method is overhead cable routing. This method eliminates long cable trough runs when the equipment is installed in the center of a large floor area. The cables may be routed above the ceiling and dropped to the machine or equipment components. All interconnecting points must be firmly supported. Cables for the office machines should not be routed near any AC lines or other powered equipment (such as heating and air conditioning equipment).

A third method utilizes a raised floor. This method allows cables to be run under the floor and out of the traffic area with relative ease, as cables can be run from device to device.

Power for a system is often obtained from cables run under a raised floor.

In general, devices are connected directly to the CPU. However, some disk drives may be connected indirectly by chaining to another drive. The system must be situated close enough to a power outlet so that the power cable supplied with the CPU will reach the outlet without an extension cord. Extension cords should never be used to connect any part of the office system equipment.

Some installations require cable interconnections from building to

CHAPTER 9 Selecting and Implementing the System 249

building. In this case, they must be routed underground in a conduit to protect the cables both physically and electrically. Specific electrical codes must be adhered to in this instance, so a qualified electrical contractor should be contacted.

This portion of the implementation process requires thorough and careful planning. Cabling, electrical, and construction costs are quite high; thus, poor judgment or limited future planning can cause unnecessary expenses for the company in the future.

Preparation for Equipment Installation. The team should delegate the implementation process to a group who will be responsible not only for planning the actual equipment installation but also for providing the plans for personnel that will be affected by the installation. This group, usually three or four individuals, will be responsible for preparing the company site for the most efficient location of equipment and personnel.

With the increasing complexity in circuit and system design, now more than ever before, site preparation is critical to the overall performance of processing equipment. Location, design and construction of a site, the power source, the environmental control systems, and even the operators contribute to the effective operation of a system. From the simplest of printers to the most complex CPU, the system will not perform up to its maximum potential without care and planning in the selection or building of a suitable site.

Under normal conditions, the vendor will perform the actual installation of the system hardware. However, it is wise to develop an installation schedule with the vendor in order to ensure that the system is installed to function optimally. An example schedule may look like this:

Ten Weeks Prior to Delivery
1 Prepare a preliminary layout of the proposed installation.
2 After the site has been planned, review the equipment order.
3 Submit the equipment cabling order at this time.
4 If a telecommunications package is ordered, contact the telephone company or an approved modem vendor to prepare the installation of all telephones, modems, and telephone lines.

Six Weeks Prior to Delivery
1 Complete the plans for the equipment room and have them approved by the vendor.
2 Review cable requirements, especially for cables routed through conduits, ceilings, floors, or walls.
3 Inspect facilities for the installation of sprinkler systems, environmental control equipment, and fire extinguishers.
4 Have the electrician review the electric service, line noise, wiring, power supply, and power distribution.
5 If building alterations are required, complete these modifications before

system delivery. Include space for supplies, instructional brochures, and procedures manuals.
6. Check the loading capacity of elevators and the size limits of halls and doorways that will be used in transporting equipment to the desired site.

Two Weeks Prior to Delivery
1. Have all planned modifications for wiring, air conditioning, and communications facilities completed and tested one week before machine delivery.
2. Have all building modifications completed at this time.

Environmental Considerations

Temperature, humidity, airborne dust, and electrical noise in prospective installation sites should be evaluated during the planning stage and controlled, if necessary, before the system arrives. In general, if the room in which the system is to be installed is comfortable for operators, it will be satisfactory for the equipment.

Environmental specifications also are applicable to storage areas for magnetic media. In addition, the humidity and temperature in areas for paper storage should be maintained at the same levels as in the equipment room. Otherwise, differences in humidity may alter the size and weight of the paper when documents are moved into the work area. This rapid change can cause the paper to warp, which is the most frequent source of feeding and stacking problems. Important environmental considerations are listed in Figure 9-8.

Temperature. Excessive temperatures will cause equipment failure. Because information processing systems are cooled by the surrounding room air, temperature control is an important environmental factor. The temperature in office buildings nearly always is controlled within the allowable limits for the system through the usual heating and air conditioning units. Nevertheless, a number of factors should be considered to determine the adequacy of existing temperature controls.

- **Heat dissipated by the equipment**. All electrical equipment generates heat that is discharged into the room and will raise the temperature of the room unless the air conditioning unit can handle the additional heat.

- **Heat dissipated by other equipment**. Heat also will be generated by other machines in the room (electric typewriters, copying machines, and auxiliary processing equipment).

- **Body heat**. Individuals occupying the room will also contribute added heat. This can be an important consideration if a large number of people will occupy the office system area.

- **Air flow**. The volume, temperature, and humidity of fresh air entering the room must be taken into account. Poor ventilation will cause heat to build up near the heat-generating equipment.

CHAPTER 9 Selecting and Implementing the System 251

CONDITIONS OF THE ENVIRONMENT CHECKLIST

Humidity and Temperature
- _____ What is the number of people that will be working in your group?
- _____ How often does the air in your work space need to be changed?
- _____ Do humidity and temperature levels conform to the equipment specifications and requirements?
- _____ Have relative humidity hygrometers been installed?
- _____ Are drafts very noticeable?

Dust and Dirt
- _____ Is adequate air filtering provided by the heating, ventilating, and/or cooling equipment?

Lighting
- _____ Have your fixtures been selected and your lighting system designed?
- _____ Is there glare-free lighting in your work place?
- _____ Has a lighting maintenance schedule been established?

Static Electricity
- _____ Is humidity control properly regulated?

Aesthetics
- _____ Does natural light come into your office? If so, from what direction?
- _____ Do paintings and plants break the monotony if your office is neutrally colored?
- _____ Are you using light colors to create an illusion of space?
- _____ Are colorful banners hanging from your ceiling to identify your group?
- _____ Do you have music in your center?
- _____ Will people be allowed to smoke, eat, and drink in the office? If so, will they be required to do these activities in designated areas only?

Acoustics
- _____ Has your carpet passed the Carpet and Run Institute's "Shuffle Test"?
- _____ Your printers should be separated from the work place. Are they?
- _____ To eliminate a boxed-in feeling, have high-noise areas been enclosed with glass walls?
- _____ Did you use soundproof tile on the ceilings?
- _____ Are there drapes on the windows?
- _____ Is fabric being used on the chairs?
- _____ Are you using cork, fabric, or fiberglass wall coverings to absorb sound?

FIG. 9-8
ENVIRONMENTAL CONDITIONS When designing an information processing system, team members must consider such environmental factors as humidity, temperature, dust and dirt, lighting, static electricity, aesthetics, and acoustics.

- **Direct sunlight**. A window or glass wall provides virtually no insulation from direct sunlight. Drapes, shades, or venetian blinds should be employed to protect the equipment from direct sunlight. Sunlight can raise the temperature excessively without necessarily exceeding allowable air temperature. If a large glass area cannot be shaded, one of the commercially available glass tinting films which block heat-producing infrared rays is recommended.

Humidity. Proper humidity must be maintained in the equipment room. Humidity levels approaching the maximum limit may have an adverse effect on the overall operating efficiency and, therefore, should be avoided whenever possible. For example, high humidity may cause improper paper feeding or improper operation of the magnetic heads. In extremely humid environments, it is advisable to install a dehumidifying unit in the equipment room.

Most heating and air conditioning units have a drying effect on the environment. When the humidity is too low, a process known as oxide shed occurs. This is when the magnetic coating on the media wears off excessively on the head, causing read/write errors (I/O errors) and loss of data on the media. In addition, when the humidity is low, static electricity charges tend to build up significantly. These charges can destroy data both in memory and on the rapidly rotating magnetic disk. Grounding will minimize the static effect but will not eliminate it completely. It may be necessary to install a humidifier to add moisture to the air in very dry areas.

Dirt and Dust. The amount of contamination usually found in the air in a normal business environment will not interfere with the operation of the system equipment. However, normal precautions should be taken to keep dirt, dust, and other foreign matter away from the machines. The system should not be installed in an area having a high dust content or where there is exposure to abrasive materials or corrosive gases.

Airborne dust, dirt particles, and smoke can cause equipment operation or maintenance problems. If a film of dust or dirt accumulates on internal surfaces, excessive wear of mechanical parts may occur. Electronic components may short-circuit and malfunction. Disk storage units are especially vulnerable to damage from excessive dust.

Usually dust can be controlled effectively by the normal heating, ventilating, and cooling equipment if units are supplied with adequate filters. These filters should be cleaned at regular intervals. If the filters do not control dust effectively, an electrostatic filter should be installed.

After installing the system, floors should be cleaned regularly. These guidelines should be followed:

- Before cleaning the area, remove diskettes from drives and store them in their original containers in a cool, dry location free from magnetic or radioactive fields.

- Damp mop tile floors. Do not use dry or wet mops.
- Vacuum carpeted floors using nonconducting nozzles.
- Do not buff floors with steel wool.

Static Electricity. Static electricity not only is an annoyance to the people operating the system, but it also can cause the equipment to malfunction. Minimizing or eliminating the sources of static is important.

Select furniture with antistatic upholstery and metal wheels. Plastic upholstery builds up a charge when clothing moves over it, and rubber wheels prevent static bleed-off through the floor covering. The discharge of this buildup to the system framework when the furniture or its occupant come into contact with the equipment can cause the system to malfunction.

The installation of equipment in a carpeted area should be avoided. If carpeting must be used, it should be designed to minimize static electricity and should be treated with antistatic sprays. This problem is particularly severe during winter when buildings are heated and the air is dry.

Lighting and Acoustics. Office lighting should be evenly diffused and relatively free from glare. Brightness should be uniform and shadows should be minimized.

Glare is any brightness that interferes with vision or causes eyestrain or fatigue. Excessive glare or brightness in the work area forces a person's eyes to continually adjust as they move from light to shadow and back again. Causes of glare include light sources that are too bright or too large for their particular areas, light sources located too close to an operator, or a dramatic contrast between a source and its surroundings.

To prevent excessive glare, all lamps within the field of vision should be shielded and light sources should be placed above the normal line of vision. Light-colored ceilings should be used because they reduce the amount of contrast. Background brightness should be equal to the brightness of the work area. This lessens the amount of adjustment the eyes must make.

Background noise has no effect on computer equipment operation but may affect the operator's efficiency. Since some devices such as printers generate noise, it is advisable to consider noise output when planning the placement of equipment. For example, printers may be set up alone or with the CPU and disk drives in an isolated area. Cloth-padded modular panels may be used to surround the printers and absorb the noise.

The greatest sound reduction can be achieved by treating the ceiling. The best results are obtained from a dropped, porous ceiling. If overhead ducts exist, noise may be transmitted from room to room unless proper precautions are taken.

For large rooms, the floor is the next most effective area on which to apply sound-absorbent material. Carpeting absorbs more sound than tile, wood, or marble surfaces. Sound baffles, such as shelving or drapes, can be applied to the walls to help reduce reflected and transmitted sound.

Organization of Personnel

One of the most sensitive and critical areas of implementation planning for an information processing system involves organizing, developing, and training company personnel to use the new tools and methods. A successful implementation will sustain high morale among support personnel, generate positive interest among potential users, and reassure upper management that its decision to back the office systems effort was a good one.

The implementation project is a combination of three planning processes which should be conducted simultaneously and be complementary. The planning processes are as follows:

1 Installation of the system's hardware and software applications tailored to the company's needs.

The organization of personnel is an important aspect of implementation planning.

CHAPTER 9 Selecting and Implementing the System

2 Identification of specific needs and applications with the cooperative involvement of the users.

3 Training and development of the training staff and the user group based on their needs and available applications, and the commitment of the system's use by company staff.

The way in which an office system is planned and implemented is important in determining its success. Offices frequently are rather conservative and traditional in their working methods. Radical changes imposed from outside a working circle tend to be rejected without due regard to the potential personal benefits and productivity increases. Involvement and commitment of the users early in this design process is one way of overcoming the resistance to change and ensuring a successful implementation.

The importance of selecting the right individual to administer the user design and involvement effort of the office system project cannot be overemphasized. The person selected will be a key to the success of and smooth transition to the system. The following criteria should be used in the selection of this individual. This person should:

- Understand the company—organization structure and work flow.
- Have a product (system) knowledge; understand the impact of the product on all areas of the company.
- Have good communications skills; be a good listener.
- Be a good organizer, motivator, and supervisor.
- Perform liaison duties; therefore, be a good diplomat and negotiator.
- Be well disciplined and handle stress.
- Have imagination, an analytical ability, and decisiveness.
- Be a high achiever—dedicated and prepared to commit 100 percent of his/her time.
- Be a respected, valued member of the company.

Responsibilities. This key person in the planning and implementation process would be responsible for planning, organizing, and administering to the human factor (user) needs of the project. This person must:

- Define the operating relationships with the system installation team and the user training team.
- Analyze and define user applications.
- Develop distribution listings for mailings.

- Assist in the development of user procedures.
- Initiate progress reports, status reports, or requests for improvements to upper management.
- Oversee users' performance and strive for users' acceptance of the system.

Background. This key person should have the following credentials:

1. Background in information processing concepts and operations. One year of word processing and/or data processing experience is ideal.
2. Project and/or systems management experience in a word processing or data processing environment.
3. The ability to communicate with personnel at different levels within the company.
4. An understanding of the business including an ability to analyze applications for use on the office system.
5. The ability to plan and organize people and projects.

Ideally this person eventually should become an integral part of an office systems staff in order to ensure a continuity of user support and interest.

Earlier in this chapter the two different phase-in approaches a team can take in its implementation plans were discussed. The first assumes that a prototype area, such as a specific department, will be the test site for the implementation of all subsystems. The second assumes that the entire company will be implemented with a single information processing subsystem, such as word processing. Some points to consider before implementing a word processing subsystem are listed in Figure 9-9.

If the entire company implementation of a word processing system is being planned for a firm with no prior word processing system, major personnel reorganization may ensue. The traditional one-on-one secretarial/boss relationship can be altered by the establishment of a centralized center approach.

Secretarial and clerical personnel would be realigned to their best advantage in word processing or administrative support centers. Their job responsibilities and job descriptions would change to reflect their new duties. Many companies begin with this approach and then migrate to a decentralized approach.

Let us review for a moment a **centralized word processing approach** to information processing. A company has a word processing center—a center that has trained and dedicated word processing specialists. When the company is organized into the centralized concept of word processing, people are moved to new areas and duties are defined

centralized word processing approach
all word processing equipment is located in one area

CHAPTER 9 Selecting and Implementing the System

WORD PROCESSING—CENTRALIZED OR DECENTRALIZED

CHECKLIST

Office system groups are most often recommended for:

_____ Companies that are large and have big typing loads
_____ Companies where new office systems are supported and encouraged
_____ Companies that seek to expand their current word processing system

Work clusters are recommended in particular for the following:

_____ Companies that are small but have heavy typing loads
_____ Companies that phase in word processing by using test groups in special areas
_____ Departments that may benefit from close interaction between operator and author because of highly technical typing applications

Consider the following points if you plan to use a remote workstation:

_____ A filing time should be set up
_____ Archived diskettes should be centralized near the master unit
_____ The team should know how many people the workstation will accommodate
_____ The workstation must be located near a phone or intercom
_____ The remote area requires longer cabling
_____ The interior design should be as attractive in your remote location as in your center or cluster
_____ The size and location of remote areas may change

FIG. 9-9
WORD PROCESSING SYSTEMS
Word processing systems can be centralized or decentralized. The choice of a system depends upon the type of company and its specific requirements.

and separated into two classifications: (1) document production by using word processors and (2) administrative support tasks. The new support teams then become responsible for serving from 3 to 20 principals.

As the price of word processing equipment declines and the successful benefits of its installation are tallied, the company eventually may provide workstations for administrative support personnel. This then means that terminals (workstations) are distributed throughout the company and are no longer within one central, managed area. This approach is called a **decentralized (distributed) word processing approach**. The workstations used by these administrative support personnel are used for word processing and other administrative applications as well. The bulk of the document preparation can be (1) forwarded to the center for specialized production, (2) performed by the

decentralized word processing approach
word processing equipment is scattered throughout the company

administrative personnel at their own workstations, or (3) a combination of these two approaches.

Another approach to the implementation of a word processing system includes putting the terminals (workstations) into departments or branches where the people working on them are already familiar with certain applications. The support personnel may use them for word processing and other administrative activities. Managerial personnel served by the support personnel may need access to the system after business hours. All personnel are likely to become intrigued with a machine that makes it possible to not only originate and edit text but also provide a means of communicating with others faster and easier. Sharing begins and information processing evolves.

Actual physical restructuring of the jobs and their locations plays a lesser role in distributed systems compared to centralized systems. In either case, training of personnel assumes a critical role. The new system with its new tools and methods requires intensive training at all levels to dispel fears, ensure user satisfaction, and create system efficiencies. As information processing is phased into companies, the challenge is to have programs, training, and interfaces smoothed so that the system can match the personality and needs of the individual.

Procedures for Efficient Work Flow

The ultimate success of a word processing group is based largely on the effectiveness of its procedures. It is important to create sound procedures and to carefully document them in a manual or guide which is made available to all operators and authors. The authors who use the group's services should know and understand the group's procedures. Chapter 11 discusses the details of procedure development in a word processing center.

procedures guidelines for office activities

Procedures are guidelines for the activities performed in the office. Procedures are developed to help control the management of work flow, personnel, and the operation of the word processing equipment. The procedural activities performed in the office are based on the needs of the people using the word processing services. One of the primary objectives of word processing facilities is to process company paperwork in a professional and efficient manner. In this role, turnaround service is of primary importance. Not only must a word processing group produce high-quality output, but service must be prompt to ensure that both the operator and the users maintain a high productivity level.

To maximize use of the system and enhance efficiency, it is necessary to determine appropriate word processing procedures. Work flow, file management, system operation, personnel management, and training are all elements of procedures. A checklist of work flow procedures is given in Figure 9-10.

CHAPTER 9 Selecting and Implementing the System — 259

WORK FLOW PROCEDURES
CHECKLIST

The following questions should be answered by your work flow procedures and diagram:

Original Input and Processing

____ What methods do you use?
____ Who generates the input?
____ Who receives the input, and what actions are taken upon it?

Printing

____ If you have an attendant at the printer, what are his or her duties?
____ If you have a remote printer, what methods of communication are set up between printer and workstation?

Proofreading

____ When are documents proofread in the course of the work cycle?
____ If the office systems group does not have a proofreader, do authors know that proofreading is their responsibility?
____ When a document needs editing after proofreading, what steps are taken?

Document File Management

____ Where do you locate the files?
____ When should filing be done?
____ Who is responsible for filing?
____ What information should be contained in the file log book?

Delivery

____ When are deliveries made?
____ What are your policies regarding messengers?
____ If you do not use messengers, what are your policies for notifying authors that work has been completed?

Maintaining Work Records

____ What type of work records do you need to keep for chargeback and administrative reports?
____ What are the procedures for completing related record keeping forms?

Revision

____ Who is involved in the revision cycle?
____ What actions are taken when a document requires revision?

FIG. 9-10
WORK FLOW PROCEDURES
The ultimate success of a word processing system is based on its work flow procedures. Therefore, the team must pay particular attention to the development of sound procedures.

Work Flow. Work flow is the method by which work comes into the center, is processed, is completed, and is delivered. An analysis of current office procedures provides a good basis for charting and establishing work flow procedures for word processing. The emphasis of such an analysis is on current work flow procedures, production statistics, physical layout, potential word processing applications, and author input.

File Management. File management consists of archiving, retrieval, and backup procedures for word processing systems, as well as filing and backup procedures for the total office information system. It is important that these procedures be performed on a timely basis and that responsibility be designated to assure this. A checklist of file management procedures is given in Figure 9-11.

file management
determination of archival, retrieval, and backup procedures

System Operations. System operations allow a supervisor to automatically control the equipment operations of the system. This includes message devices, printer operation, and electronic mail monitoring.

System Maintenance. System maintenance (recordkeeping) is closely related to system operations. An accurate and up-to-date record of the equipment maintenance history should be kept. The vendor's customer service personnel will refer to this information to determine needed adjustments or repairs to avoid unnecessary and extended downtime.

Personnel Management and Training. Job responsibilities/descriptions for personnel should be documented in a procedures manual. In addition, it would be helpful to identify training paths and programs to assure proper training for each job description.

Not all offices require a full-scale analysis to determine word processing office procedures. An analysis may be accomplished with information that is readily available. It is important that all information collected be documented in a procedures guide. Futhermore, the range of applications for word processing on the information processing system have a direct bearing on the procedures established for the center.

System procedures should be implemented whether the system is a small standalone word processor or a shared resource, multiterminal information processing system. The larger the system, the more important it is to have written procedures for each operation.

Orientation Programs

Education and training are fundamental factors in the success of any planning project. Education is especially important in implementing office information systems. Employees can control the growth of office technology within their company. Their failure to accept and use the system will result in system failure. Thus, orienting employees and

CHAPTER 9 Selecting and Implementing the System 261

FILE MANAGEMENT

CHECKLIST

Consider the following points when you are filing information:
- _____ Which documents really need to be filed?
- _____ What will the filing requirements be in the future?
- _____ What is the number of people using the files?
- _____ How often will filed material have to be referenced?

Magnetic media have certain physical requirements that must be satisfied before storing:
- _____ Does the storage area have controlled temperature and humidity?
- _____ Is the area as clean and dust-free as possible?
- _____ Are smoking, eating, and drinking prohibited near the filing area?
- _____ Are storage shelves made of noncombustible material?
- _____ Is there any magnetized equipment near the storage area? If so, it should be relocated.
- _____ Do file cabinets have locks?

You may want to adopt these procedures for your documents if you have a centralized filing system:
- _____ Do not keep hard copies for storage; all documents should be stored on disk.
- _____ Establish retention dates for documents.
- _____ Determine which files contain confidential material, and decide how they should be classified.
- _____ Determine whether the files will be numerical by project number or alphabetical by author or department.
- _____ Assign a particular person to filing duties.
- _____ Publicize throughout the group the specific times for filing.
- _____ Record, either on the system or manually, all the changes made daily to the file log.
- _____ Initiate a system which advises authors when retention dates are up on their material.

You should adopt the following procedures if you are decentralized:
- _____ One person should be appointed for filing duties.
- _____ A certain filing time should be specified.
- _____ Telephones should be convenient to all remote workstations in case problems arise.

For office information systems, the following decisions for backup of information need to be made:
- _____ What information needs to be backed up.
- _____ Who should perform backup activities.
- _____ When and how often backup should be performed.
- _____ The manner in which backup disks should be rotated and maintained.
- _____ How disks or diskettes should be used for backup.

FIG. 9-11
FILE MANAGEMENT PROCEDURES
File management is a major problem for many businesses. Therefore, it is important to develop procedures to control the proliferation of paper within a company.

including them in the planning process help eliminate misconceptions people may have about computers or office systems. Employees who understand and help design the system which will serve them are more apt to make it a successful operation. Education specifically dispels two fears employees generally have about the new technology—that the arrival of the technology means a loss of jobs, and that the employees themselves will not be able to cope with the new, complex equipment.

Employees should become a part of the planning process from the beginning of the feasibility study. In the study, the team introduces them to the new technology through meetings, brochures, familiar settings, and sometimes films. Magazines indicating the various types of equipment available should be circulated throughout the planning process.

After the approval to proceed has been given by management, a more detailed education planning should begin. This orientation process should extend to all levels of employees—upper management, middle management, and support personnel. Selected equipment should be on display at the company, and employees should be encouraged to meet informally to try it out. Vendors should be present to demonstrate the products and to discuss special applications. If possible, presentations should be made to all employees in small groups to allow for easy and comfortable interaction.

As installation of the system nears, employees should be scheduled for training. The training classes should be tailored to the needs of each group or individual department. Instruction should be both written and verbalized. Each employee should be provided quiet time to seek and discover machine operation without fear of embarrassment brought on by formal training and/or supervision. Instructional training should be tailored for each level of user in easy to understand language. The reasons for strict procedural operation should be explained in order to ensure that the user understands the functions of the entire system. The select few who later will be responsible for instructing others generally are given specialized courses away from the office.

Teaching the skills required to use the new technology increasingly will be embedded in the system itself. Thus, the new technologies suggest using the successful teaching technique of the past—learn by doing. Until such time as training manuals are developed that prove adequate for user learning, the best route to take for company training includes combining in-house training with user manuals.

The systems of tomorrow can be self-teaching and self-orienting, but there really is no substitute for a trainer. A trainer not only can observe learners, gauge their rate of learning, and anticipate their needs, but also can intervene at the precise moment help is required. A trainer also can check to see that each employee enjoys a maximum level of comfort.

In-house training can benefit from these additional recommendations:

- Use an area of the office in which there will be a minimum number of interruptions.
- Have a machine for each pair of hands.
- Allot three hours in the morning.
- After a first-day introduction, have employees bring meaningful tasks to practice on.
- Allow for individual rates of learning.

After reading this chapter, you should be able to identify the important parts of a Request for Proposal. You also should be able to develop evaluation criteria and guidelines that will help you determine equipment needs and make a thorough vendor selection.

Following the vendor selection process, you should be able to plan and schedule a system implementation that includes a site layout. This implementation plan should identify specific checkpoints during the installation cycle that monitor your progress.

As equipment installation progresses, you should be able to prepare for the changes that will affect personnel. You should understand how the users should be organized to complement the new activities, how they should be oriented, and how they should be trained. Simultaneously, you should be able to develop new procedures for the actual system operation.

If handled correctly, implementation of the system will run smoothly. The information processing system which was designed, evaluated, selected, and implemented should be thoroughly administered. Only then will users discover a system which is tailored to their needs, operating efficiently, and performing smoothly.

DISCUSSION QUESTIONS AND CASE PROBLEM

DISCUSSION QUESTIONS

1. What is an RFP, and what is its purpose?
2. Name three goals of equipment evaluation criteria forms.
3. In planning your layout site on grid paper, what factors influence the location of the equipment and furniture?
4. How does centralized word processing differ from distributed word processing as it relates to document preparation?
5. What is the best route for training personnel that a company can take?

CHAPTER 9   Selecting and Implementing the System

CASE PROBLEM

Nancy and Joe worked as training and development specialists for their company prior to the installation of a new office information system. Both were trained by the office system vendor to be instructors for the employees in their firm.

Joe had an easy time learning the system operation directly from the vendor-provided manuals. Nancy, on the other hand, found her rate of learning increased with the instructor's assistance to these manuals. Nancy and Joe were told to develop an in-house training program for all personnel.

1. How can their two learning methods be compromised to attain a good training program?
2. List some recommendations to their class design that may benefit all of the different learning abilities of company personnel.
3. Explain, in your own words, the advantages of each recommendation.

Chapter 10 Preparing the Environment

CHAPTER OBJECTIVES:

Justify the importance of environment as one of the four parts of a word processing system.

Explain the characteristics, advantages, and potential problems of an open-office plan.

Recommend ways to avoid problems caused by the continuous operation of visual display terminals.

Describe the ideal climate for a word processing center.

Tell what causes power disturbances (including static electricity) and how they can be prevented or lessened.

Explain how the right quantity of light with maximum usability, efficient energy, and economical cost can be provided for word processing systems.

Describe the effect of color on employees and evaluate color treatments of offices.

Give ways by which distracting noise can be controlled in offices that have word processing centers.

When word processing systems were first developed, the emphasis was only on people, machines, and procedures. The fourth major part of the system, environment, was either ignored or not given due emphasis. **Environment** is that which surrounds a person, including air, light, color, sound, furniture, and fixtures. People spend one half of their waking hours in the working environment.

environment that which surrounds a person

WHY THE ENVIRONMENT IS IMPORTANT

As technology has evolved during the last 10 to 15 years, environmental factors have become increasingly important. The environment affects the productivity and job satisfaction of people as well as the performance of machines.

Problems of a Poor Environment

Without a proper environment people eventually suffer physical and mental health problems. They become dissatisfied workers, which causes increased absenteeism and turnover. Machines also are sensitive to an improper environment. They utterly stop working, for which users often inappropriately blame the vendor for equipment failure. The result is lowered productivity.

Effect of Environment on Productivity

A well-planned environment can result in increased productivity of managers, professionals, and technical specialists. Much can be learned by involving employees in office design and other environmental decisions. The 1980 Louis Harris survey (commissioned by Steelcase) of more than 1,000 full-time office workers revealed that 80 percent of the workers feel there is a strong connection between their comfort in the office and their job performance.[1]

The 1983 results of the Buffalo Organization for Social and Technological Innovation (BOSTI) study pinpointed four main issues that affect output. This study questioned 5,000 workers and their supervisors, all of whose offices were moved. The four main issues affecting output according to this study are lighting, visual access, control of access, and participation in design.[2]

How Environment Changes

The office environment has changed radically within the last ten years, and it continues to change. There are several reasons for the evolution. First, technology keeps advancing for all types of information processing equipment, including word processors. Also, more and more users are equipped with a visual display terminal. Some users spend only 5 percent of their time operating terminals, while others spend most of the working day at terminals. Finally, high personnel turnover rates present a need for flexible office design and furniture that can be adjusted easily for new users.

Involvement of Personnel

As technology abounds, it becomes more apparent that people want to be treated as human beings rather than as robots. There is now more concern for health and safety, personalization of work areas, and involvement of employees in planning the office design. The design of a

---

[1] David Steinbrecher, "WP/IS Furnishings Stress Comfort and Flexibility," *Word Processing and Information Systems* (March, 1982), p. 30.
[2] Stephen D. Channer, "The Case for Furniture Befitting the Human Condition," *Modern Office Procedures* (June, 1983), p. 56.

The environment of an office affects both productivity and job satisfaction.

work area where employees are grouped to perform related functions

word processing work area not only has a decorative function, but it also has an impact on employee morale and overall productivity.

This chapter describes six major environmental concerns. These environmental concerns include work areas, climate factors, electrical power, lighting, color treatment, and acoustical control.

WORK AREAS

A work area is a place where employees are grouped to perform related functions. A department, a division, a large center, or a satellite center could be treated as a work area. On the other hand, a department or a division of a company could be divided into more than one work area.

The design of a work area depends upon the space allocations, the order of work flow, and the individual needs of employees. With the cost of space increasing, companies typically allow only the minimum for each worker. A newly constructed building should allow for expansion. However, the remodeling of an old building must be contained within the already constructed outer walls. Workers should be positioned to facilitate work flow without unnecessary walking and telephoning. Supervisory personnel and machines that are shared need to be centrally located. Employees who require privacy for conferences and quiet concentration may desire an office with permanent walls and a door (a closed office or a private office). Those who share the work of projects and other office functions may best be accommodated by individual work stations that are separated by panels or partitions (an open-office plan or an open-plan system). Whether word processing services are centralized or decentralized, they should be located as near as possible to the authors.

CHAPTER 10 Preparing the Environment

Open-Office Plan

Figure 10-1 shows the layout of an office system. Without permanent walls and doors, this type of system design is known as an **open-office plan**, an **open-plan system**, or as **open-office landscaping**.

open-office plan does not have permanent walls or doors

The basic goals of this concept in office design include customizing work stations, facilitating work flow, and providing for integration of systems. The system is flexible so that it can be rearranged easily or expanded as the needs of the work area change. Flexibility is possible because each component can be taken apart easily and inserted into another component.

Various components comprise an open-plan system. Wall panels or partitions of varying heights and surface textures replace permanent walls that extend from floor to ceiling. Adjustable work surfaces replace standard office desks. Storage areas can be attached to the panels above and below the work surface to optimize space. Wiring is concealed within the panel units. Light fixtures are positioned beneath overhead shelves to illuminate the immediate work surface. As tasks change or as employees move to new positions, the components can be adjusted easily. Bulletin boards, plants, and pictures help to personalize individual work stations.

Advantages. What are the advantages of an open-office plan? In addition to the flexibility just described, space is saved, energy is conserved, and remodeling costs are reduced to the minimum.

An open-office plan saves about 15 percent of floor space per worker compared to an office layout of stationary walls. Also, it makes better use of vertical space above the work surface. Cabinets, files, and shelves can be hung on the panels. In this way wall space (that generally is not used

Furniture in an open-plan system is designed to be taken apart easily and moved as conditions warrant change.

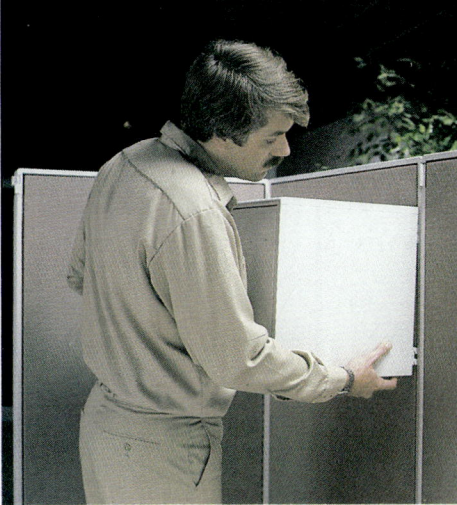

FIG. 10-1 OPEN-OFFICE PLAN An open-office plan is designed to facilitate the flow of work.

in fixed-wall offices) substitutes for floor space that would ordinarily be used for file cabinets or bookcases.

Energy is saved because the panels do not extend from floor to ceiling as permanent walls do. This saves on heating, lighting, and air conditioning costs. There is much better airflow, and the main overhead lighting can be diffused over the entire area. Energy costs are reduced up to one half that of a traditional office plan.

Compared to offices with permanent walls, open-plan offices cost about one tenth of the price to construct. To remodel a fixed-wall office costs from $20 to $50 per square foot; for an open-plan work area it costs only about $4 per square foot.[3] The time required to rearrange an open-office plan is only a fraction of the time it takes to remodel traditional offices. Open-plan offices use permanent walls mainly for just the outer walls of a large work area.

Disadvantages. The open-plan system is not a utopia, for it can have problems which must be addressed. The initial reaction of an employee who is relocated from a private office to a work station in an open area is a feeling of lost job status. Artistic decor and attractive plants can alleviate this problem somewhat.

Open-plan offices are not as soundproof as private offices, so employees must contend with a higher noise level. For this reason the surface materials of ceilings, walls, panels, and floors should be sound absorptive.

Other problems involve security and privacy. There is no way to lock one door to secure all parts of a work station. Also, without a completely enclosed work area, employees do not have the privacy needed for quiet concentration and for confidential conversation. Thus, many companies have both private offices and open-plan offices so that the environment accommodates each worker's needs as well as the work flow.

Proper Layout. The best layout design takes into consideration various factors of the work area. The personal characteristics of employees, the type of work they perform, communication needs, and the interrelationship of work areas in processing information should all be considered.

Individual Work Stations

In a traditional office the worker must adjust to the standard desk, chair, file cabinet, and bookcase. This concept assumes that all workers

---

[3]Hy Bomberg, "Open Plan—Flexibility for the Future," *Management World* (December, 1981), p. 17.

ergonomics science that fits the work place to the person

modular components can be quickly assembled, taken apart, and rearranged

Top: A copy holder is one type of modular component.

Bottom: A swivel turn-table allows two work stations to have access to one terminal.

are the same size, perform similar work, and do not change job functions. Office furniture and equipment vendors now support a new concept—making sure that furniture and machines fit the individual worker's needs.

This science that fits the work place to the person is known as **ergonomics**. The Louis Harris survey found that productivity increased by as much as 17 percent when work stations were designed to meet the needs of the users.[4] As Figure 10-2 shows, the specific needs of word processing secretaries, authors or users, and executive managers differ.

Modular Components. Flexibility for easy change is important in offices containing word processing equipment, for technology keeps altering equipment capabilities and sizes. As machines change, the physical space required for the equipment and the worker's tasks are likely to change also.

Work station parts that can be adjusted by height, length of reach, and angle are responsive to workers' needs. Parts that can be quickly assembled, taken apart, and rearranged are said to be modular. Then as the needs of the workers change or as machines are replaced by newer machines of a different size, the parts can be added, removed, or relocated.

Some examples of modular components include the following: Shelves and vertical dividers can be positioned at the right, at the left, or in the center of the panel support. Whether the worker is left-handed or right-handed, the components can be arranged for convenience. A copy/work holder can be pulled out for use, adjusted for the correct height and angle, and then folded back out of the way when not in use. Work surfaces and seating can also be adjusted.

Shelves and storage units can be hung from panels above or under the work surface. Not only does this arrangement better utilize space, but it also allows for unhampered arm and leg movement.

Keyboards can be located on free-standing tables, lowered shelves, tilted shelves, or in pullout drawers. The pullout drawer is convenient for executives who use the terminal intermittently rather than continuously throughout the day. The open-plan system enables expensive equipment to be shared. For example, a stand that bridges two work stations can support a visual display terminal on a swivel turntable in a lazy Susan or carousel fashion.

Work Space. Each work station needs to provide sufficient privacy for one to concentrate on work, use the telephone, and confer with another person on a confidential basis. Yet there should be enough openness to allow adequate supervision and interaction with others.

---

[4]Harold M. Emanuel and Steve Saunders, "Plugging Into the Open Office," *Today's Office* (June, 1983), p. 29.

CHAPTER 10 Preparing the Environment 273

Secretarial/Specialist Work Station

Author/User Work Station

**FIG. 10-2
VARIATIONS IN WORK STATION NEEDS**
The needs and activities of the employee should determine the layout of the individual work station.

Executive Manager Work Station

The amount of space one needs depends upon the nature of the work being performed and the equipment being used. Design experts recommend at least 70 square feet for an administrative support work station that does not include a personal computer; about 80 to 90 square feet would be needed for one that includes a personal computer. A word processing specialist who uses larger and noisier equipment needs about 90 to 100 square feet. At least 6 feet should be allowed between workers. Supervisors are usually located near the entrance of a large work area, where they are accessible to both the word processing users and the support personnel. Depending upon the type of work performed and the need for conference space, most authors and supervisors need a minimum of 150 square feet.

Built-in Wiring and Light Fixtures. An open-plan office eliminates ugly cords which also can be hazardous to office workers or visitors. Wiring is housed in the panels. Wherever panels join, connectors snap into place to complete the electrical circuits. The ducts or cableways that carry electrical wiring around an office are called **raceways**. Raceways can accommodate the wiring for terminals, dictation equipment, and telephones.

Open-plan systems can also include light fixtures right above the worker's task. This localized light, called **task lighting**, is designed to illuminate the immediate work surface. The light fixtures are generally mounted under shelves or attached to panels.

raceways cableways that carry electrical wiring around an office

task lighting localized light above the worker's task

In an open-office plan, wiring is housed in the panels surrounding each work station.

Task lighting illuminates the immediate work surface.

Visual Display Terminals

Of growing concern to office environmentalists has been the effect of visual display terminals (VDTs, of which the CRT is most common) on operators. A major study by the National Institute for Occupational Safety and Health (NIOSH) revealed a link between the use of VDTs and the number of operator complaints. According to this study, productivity could be increased 25 percent by solving VDT-related problems.[5] The questions to be answered include: (1) Do VDTs affect health? (2) What causes physical discomfort? (3) What can be done to protect operators from VDT problems?

Health Effects. Research by NIOSH indicates that VDTs do not threaten health because of harmful radiation. However, there is evidence of other health problems. Word processing secretaries who operate terminals most of the working day complain of blurred vision, tearing, double imaging, burning and throbbing eyes, and headaches. Such

---

[5]Channer, *op. cit.,* p. 54.

eyestrain adversely affects eyesight. Muscular pain in the neck, shoulders, and back leads to discomfort. This causes the operator to become frustrated, irritable, and depressed.

Factors That Cause Discomfort. The factors which cause eye problems include glare, reflections, poor contrast between the screen's background and its images, and character flicker (images that appear to move or blink). Some operators shift their posture to reduce glare, which can cause backaches. Another factor which leads to morale and performance problems is stress. Stress is caused not only by eyestrain, but also by the operator's perception of the job and the length of time spent viewing the screen without a rest break.

Protecting Operators from VDT Health Problems. Various methods of avoiding or preventing VDT health problems exist. Frequent work breaks should be taken. One recommendation is that employees have at least one 15-minute break for every 2 hours of work at a terminal.

Careful planning of light fixtures will avoid glare and unwanted reflections. It is better to have several low-intensity fixtures that diffuse light evenly rather than one or two bright ones. Supplementary lights which are adjustable should be made available.

The application of ergonomics to word processors can be seen in antiglare screen filters, adjustable keyboards that are separate from the screen, palm rests, and both brightness and contrast controls. As screen brightness is increased, the glare becomes less annoying and the clarity of characters improves.

A VDT screen should adjust vertically, tilt, and swivel. The papers which the operator reads while keyboarding should be at a height and distance similar to that of the display. The keyboard should be about 27

A palm rest is an example of the application of ergonomics to the design of a work station.

CHAPTER 10   Preparing the Environment   277

VDT health problems can be reduced if the operator's work station is designed properly.

inches from the floor. The slope of the keyboard should be between 5 degrees and 15 degrees for the most comfortable typing.

Seating is especially crucial for the operator who sits at a work station for many hours each day. Proper seating can alleviate backstrain, neckstrain, and headaches. The chair should allow for change of posture while providing adjustment for back and seat heights as well as tilt control. The seat should be positioned so that the operator's eyes are level with the top of the screen. The operator will then be looking down at an angle of about 10 degrees to 20 degrees, which should prevent reflections from the ceiling.

CLIMATE OF THE WORK AREA

Neither humans nor machines can function adequately in an environment that has extreme temperature and humidity levels or polluted air. Proper heating, ventilation, and air conditioning (abbreviated HVAC) are crucial. Although a temperature range of 65-75 degrees F (18-24 degrees C) is considered acceptable, a stable 68 degrees F (20 degrees C) is preferred. Humidity should be within the 40 to 60 percent range; a steady 50 percent is recommended. Air circulation and cleanliness also need to be controlled. Air movement of 25 feet per minute is appropriate. Many problems occur when these factors exceed the limits.

Temperature

Equipment, software (magnetic media), and supplies (ribbons, print elements, and paper) deteriorate when subjected to high temperatures. Warping of magnetic media results in distorted recordings. In addition, abrupt changes in temperature cause undesirable expansion or contraction of materials. Heat combined with pressure can cause the oxide coating on magnetic media to peel off.

Humidity

As humidity rises, the magnetic media and printer paper absorb moisture and change dimension. In turn, disk drives malfunction, rubber rollers get sticky, and printers jam. At the other extreme, low humidity allows static electricity to build up. Static electricity can cause logic errors, memory loss or alteration, wipeout of screen display, and even permanent damage to the circuits. Also, electrical shocks can be transmitted to the operator.

When temperature and humidity exceed the limits, equipment fails and the life of the machine is shortened. Service calls also increase. In fact, should the user fail to provide the environmental conditions specified by the manufacturer, the equipment warranty can be invalidated. Software and supplies need to be stored in cool, dry places. Each word processing center or work area should have its own thermostatic controls as well as a hygrometer, so that proper temperature and humidity levels can be maintained.

A hygrometer aids word processing personnel in keeping track of humidity levels.

Air Circulation and Cleanliness

Polluted air containing dust and tobacco smoke particles is hazardous to the eyes, nose, throat, and lungs. The effect on word processing equipment is equally harmful. Unclean air reduces the life of disks/diskettes and wears down the recording heads of the machines. Static attracts the dust and smoke particles to the media. The dust then mixes with the machine's oils and scratches the recording/storage media. When the recording surface is damaged, data errors can occur.

Company officials can use various methods to assure proper air circulation and cleanliness as well as proper temperature and humidity levels. Air conditioners are used to filter the air and lower the temperature during warm periods. Humidifiers and dehumidifiers help control the amount of moisture and dryness. These devices may be part of the heating system or may be purchased separately.

CHAPTER 10 Preparing the Environment

ELECTRICAL POWER

In a word processing environment there are many machines for which power must be provided. Among them are word processors, printers, dictation equipment and transcribing units, telephones, and possibly photocopying machines and an OCR scanner. Before any machine is installed, the specific power requirements should be obtained from the manufacturer. The user must be sure that these requirements are met.

Adhering to the vendor's specifications keeps the warranty from being invalidated because of user negligence. In a word processing environment there should be enough electrical expansion capability to provide an uninterrupted flow of electricity. Those who plan for the environment also should allow for future needs.

Basic Recommendations

Many equipment problems can be traced to inadequate planning for electrical power. Vendors and consultants offer suggestions on how to avoid electrical power problems. Some of the basic recommendations for electrical power include the following:

1 Once voltage requirements have been obtained from the manufacturer, there should be enough power (total amperage) provided for the most demanding piece of equipment.

2 Receptacles for word processing machines (power cords with three-prong plugs) should be properly grounded.

3 Word processors should have dedicated lines, which means that they should not share a power line with a transcribing unit or any other office machine.

4 For multistation systems that connect terminals by telephone line to the central processing unit, that telephone line should be accessible only to word processing terminals. It should not be shared with extension phones. Should someone pick up an extension to a line that is tied into a CPU, the CPU is likely to cut off the connection. The system is sensitive to interference, which can cause good text to be transmitted as garbled characters.

5 The number of telephone lines, extension numbers, and phones must be decided before construction or remodeling begins.

6 Each work station should be equipped with three to five outlets. Adequate outlets must be provided should any work station need to accommodate a word processor, a printer, a transcribing unit, and/or a telephone.

7 The type of outlets (wall, floor, or panel) and the location of the

wiring (panel, wall, ceiling, or floor) should be decided before construction or remodeling commences.

8 Wires, cords, and cables should be hidden as much as possible. One reason is that people can easily trip over such obstacles and not only hurt themselves but also harm the equipment. In addition, open cords are unattractive to the environment. Many of the modern furniture systems provide for wiring needs through the use of raceways in panels as shown in Figure 10-3. Once a panel is plugged into a floor or wall outlet, the outlets on the panel are live.

9 Precautions should be taken to prevent power line disturbances, including static electricity.

Power Disturbances

electromagnetic interference power line disturbances

power surge sudden increase in voltage

Many electronic equipment problems stem from power line disturbances, also known as **electromagnetic interference**. The display screen might flicker, data can be lost, and circuit components can become damaged, causing equipment to break down. One of the most common dangers is a **power surge** (also called a **spike** or a **transient impulse**). A power surge is a sudden increase in voltage that enters a computer or word processor through the power line.

A power surge can be induced by lightning, static electricity discharges, or inductive kicks that are produced by turning on or off a major electric motor on another circuit in the building. A power surge can also occur when electrical service is restored after having been cut off; an enormous wave of voltage is likely to have built up.

Power surges are destructive. However, they do not affect standard motor-driven machines as seriously as they do computers and word processors (products of solid-state technology). Fluctuations in voltage can seriously affect word processors, for they have critical threshold operating voltages. Common problems include alteration of text, erased memory, false logic, and destroyed circuitry that must be replaced by new components.

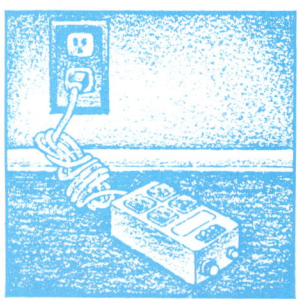

surge suppressor monitors voltage and suppresses abrupt surges

voltage regulator maintains line voltage within a prescribed range

Various protective devices are available that can monitor the voltage and suppress abrupt surges. These devices are known as **surge suppressors** or **transient suppression devices**. Another protective device is a **voltage regulator**, which maintains line voltage within a prescribed range. As variations of incoming power occur, the regulator steps voltage up or down to maintain the prescribed range.

Static Electricity

Static electricity discharges are used when two materials come together and then separate; for example, footsteps (shoes) on a carpet.

CHAPTER 10   Preparing the Environment   281

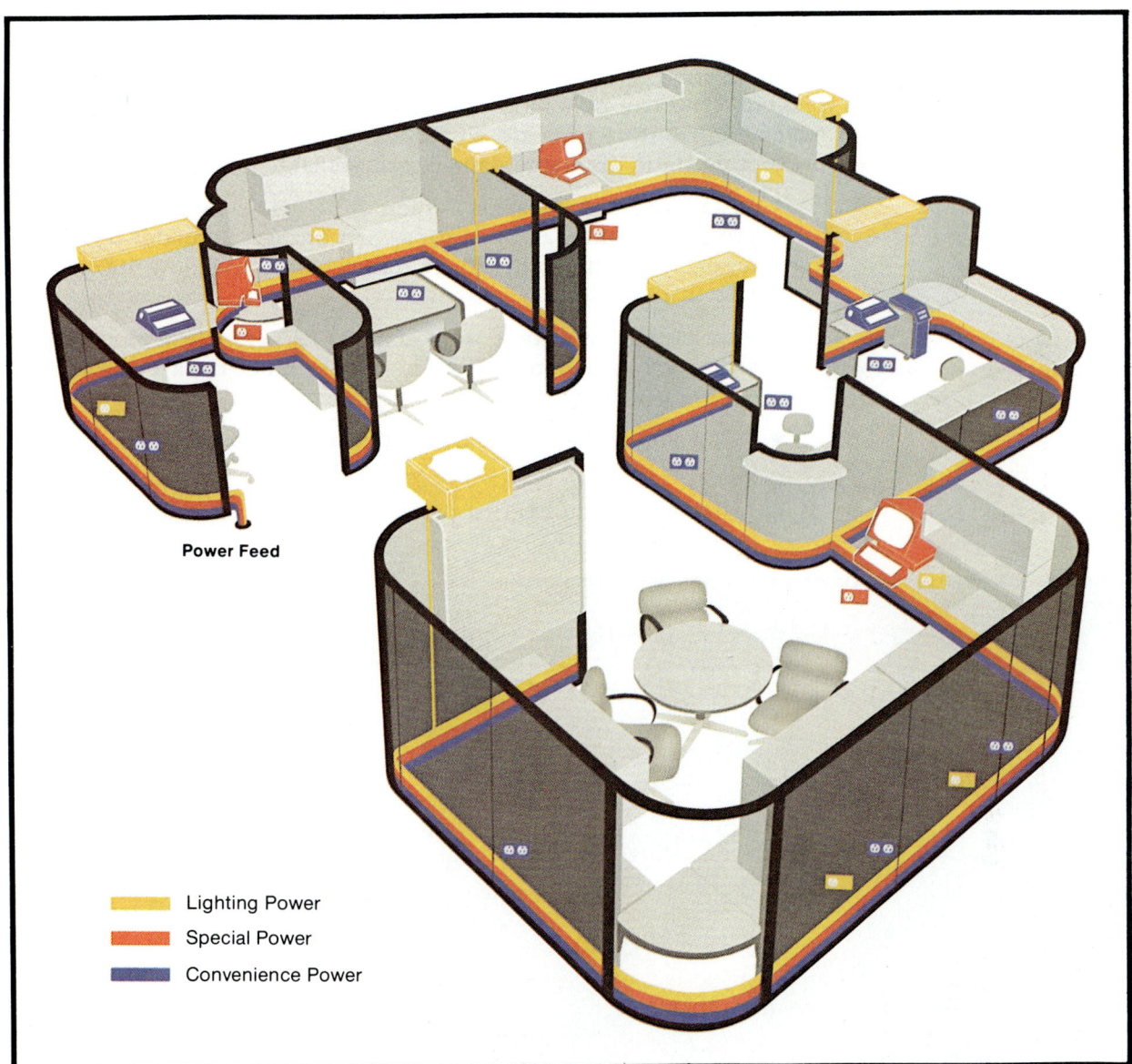

FIG. 10-3
AN ELECTRICAL POWER SYSTEM
Most of the wiring for a work station can be contained within the panels of the work station itself.
(Courtesy of Haworth, Inc.)

The transfer of electrons from one surface to the other results in an imbalance of electrons, which in turn causes a discharge.

A discharge of 1,000 volts can cause problems with word processors. Yet most people cannot feel a discharge of less than 1,500 to 3,500 volts. The average charge accumulated on a person walking across a vinyl tile floor is 4,000 volts; across a carpeted floor, 12,000 volts.[6]

---

[6]Robert J. Kunz, "In-House Consultant," *Words* (April-May, 1982), p. 34.

Materials such as carpet, fabric, and rubber hold charges for a long time. As poor conductors, they add to the problem of static electricity. Problems increase as the air gets dryer and humidity drops below 50 percent. One can conclude that carpeting and low humidity are the major contributors of static electricity discharge. Several methods of preventing static discharge damage are available:

- Installing antistatic mats, which are electrically conductive and grounded, under an operator's chair or directly under the equipment. These mats can reduce static charges to below 500 volts in less than a second.

- Purchasing antistatic (or grounded) carpets. Grounded carpets are woven with conductive fibers that reduce the average level of static discharge.

- Using antistatic spray on the carpet and furniture surrounding the equipment.

- Installing a humidifier to prevent air dryness and to maintain 50 percent humidity.

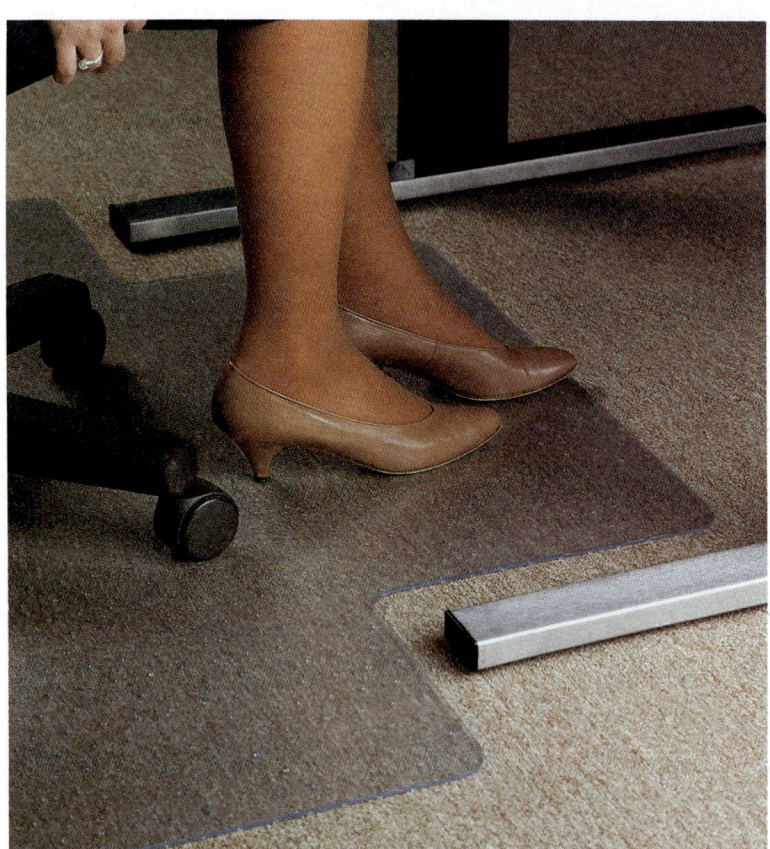

An antistatic mat protects sensitive equipment by reducing the strength of static charges.

CHAPTER 10   Preparing the Environment

LIGHTING

Proper lighting is essential for all aspects of word processing. Work that involves viewing display screens and proofreading is strenuous under the best conditions. Without the needed quantity and quality of light, employees suffer from eyestrain, headaches, and stress. The discomfort causes workers to become less productive and to make more errors. Then job satisfaction and morale decline.

The amount of light that one needs depends upon the type of work that is being done and upon the employee. Running errands and meeting in a conference do not require as much light as keyboarding, reading, and proofreading. Visual display terminals complicate lighting plans, for glare from improper lighting is a severe annoyance to operators. Another consideration is the age of the employee. The aging process of the human eye results in significant changes in visual ability which lead to lower visual performance. Many older workers need more and better light than younger ones to perform the identical task.

The factors to consider for proper office lighting include: quantity and quality of light, types of artificial lighting, and direction and location of lighting. The goals are to provide the right amount and kind of light, as well as to save energy and overhead costs.

Quantity and Quality of Light

Since each affects the other, quantity and quality of light must be discussed together. The quantity (amount) of light is expressed in footcandles (fc) and is measured by an instrument called a light meter. A **footcandle** is the amount of light produced by a standard candle at a distance of one foot. For word processing functions experts recommend a minimum of 150 fc. This assumes that the quality of the light provides 150 fc of visibility.

footcandle a measurement of the quantity of light

Should the quality of 150 fc be poor, the lighting may have the effectiveness of only 80 fc. The quality of light pertains to the intensity, reflectance, brightness, or usability of light. It is measured by **foot-lamberts**. Factors which cause quality to decrease include glare, shadows, and veiling reflections. Glare is a harsh brightness which occurs when an unshielded light source is in or is reflected into the field of view. **Veiling reflections** occur when the light fixture is ahead of or directly above the work station, as shown in Figure 10-4. Light bounces up from the task surface, such as shiny paper, and into the viewer's eyes, causing sections of the material written on the paper to appear washed out and difficult to see. Veiling reflections reduce the contrast between the words and the paper or screen, which lowers visual performance.

foot-lambert a measurement of the quality of light

veiling reflection occurs when light bounces off task surface; written material becomes difficult to discern

Types of Artificial Lighting

Most offices must rely on some type of artificial lighting, since sunlight (natural lighting) is not likely to be evenly available to each work

FIG. 10-4
VEILING REFLECTIONS
Overhead lighting which shines directly down on the work area causes veiling reflections.

station throughout the working hours. Artificial lighting is available in three basic types of bulbs or lamps—incandescent, fluorescent, and high-intensity discharge (HID).

Some office fixtures use incandescent bulbs, which are commonly used in household lamps. However, fluorescent lights are most widely used in offices. Although a fluorescent tube initially costs more than an incandescent bulb, it ultimately costs less and is more energy efficient. Fluorescent lights give more light per watt, emit less heat, and cost less to operate than incandescent bulbs. Fluorescent lamps provide about two thirds of the light produced in the United States.[7]

A more recently developed light fixture is the high-intensity discharge (HID) lamp. HID lights give up to 50 percent more light per watt than fluorescent lights, but the quality of the light makes objects appear to be discolored. The mercury lights used in some parking lots and on streets are examples of HID lights, under which the colors of one's skin

---

[7]Will S. Fisher, "Selecting the Best Lighting for Your Work Environment," *The Office* (December, 1982), p. 69.

and clothes are distorted. To be usable in the office, HID lights are being further refined.

Direction and Location of Lighting

In the traditional office, most of the lighting comes from ceiling fixtures which cast light directly downward. A more recent concept is to provide indirect light from two locations—the ceiling and the immediate work station. In this way both the quality and the quantity of light can be provided most efficiently at the lowest cost. Let's examine lighting in terms of its direction and location.

The direction of light coming from above is either direct, indirect, or some degree in between. **Direct lighting** casts most of the light downward from the light fixture. This kind of light spreads uneven light that causes shadows, creates glare on paper, and makes annoying reflections on visual display screens. In contrast, **indirect lighting** directs most of the light upward to the ceiling and walls, from which the light is more evenly reflected to all parts of the work area. Thus, the chances of glare or shadows are reduced. However, an office with numerous high partitions will have some shadows regardless of the type of lighting. Examples of direct and indirect lighting are shown in Figure 10-5.

The location of light fixtures can be the ceiling and upper walls, the work station, or a combination. The trend is to combine the two sources of light so that about one third comes from the ceiling and upper walls and two thirds comes from the work station. Light fixtures that are built

direct lighting casts most of the light downward

indirect lighting most of the light is directed upward and reflected off walls and ceiling

FIG. 10-5
DIRECT AND INDIRECT LIGHTING
A well-lit office area should have both direct and indirect light sources.

ambient lighting
illuminates the general office area

A task/ambient lighting system is designed not only to increase the efficiency of light, but also to reduce the consumption of energy.

into the upper part of the work station (usually mounted under overhead shelves) to light specific work surfaces provide task lighting. Light fixtures that illuminate the general office area provide **ambient lighting**. Ambient light fixtures may be mounted at the ceiling, suspended from the ceiling, or placed on the top of furniture panels. The term task/ambient lighting means that task (local) and ambient (general) lighting have been combined.

A task/ambient lighting system is designed to increase lighting efficiency and reduce energy consumption. Brightness should be reasonably uniform over the task area. Up to 50 percent less energy is used for task/ambient lighting than for conventional overhead systems. Should one employee be working late, only a few fixtures need to be turned on. Local controls, such as wall switches in a lighted space, permit users to turn on only the light fixtures that are needed.

Proper maintenance of light fixtures includes regular fixture and lamp cleaning, replacement of all lamps in a large area at the same time, and early lamp removal. As lamps are used, the light output declines

while energy consumption remains the same. Fluorescent lamps should be replaced after they have been in service for about 70 percent of their rated lives.

Electronic devices are available to aid in energy and cost savings. Where fluorescent lights are used, there should be no annoying hum from the fixtures. The new electronic fixtures provide more light for less energy than the traditional ones; they reduce air conditioning loads and offer extended lamp life. Electronic dimming systems can sense the amount of daylight available and adjust the artificial lights to hold the light levels at the desired minimum value.

COLOR TREATMENT

Both at home and in the office color affects the mood and influences the physical comfort of people. Color and lighting need to complement each other to create a positive and satisfying environment. Lighting systems, with decreased use of direct ceiling light fixtures, require surfaces of good reflection that create a pleasant soft color. Color is a visual communication which gives meaning to spaces.

Effects of Color

Color theory is built on the relation of color to color with subtle contrasts being the theme. Color schemes should accommodate all surfaces—ceilings, walls, floors, and work stations. The new color schemes reflect a need for peace and tranquillity in the office. As opposed to the abruptness of harsh shades, more pastels are used in the new color schemes.

Each of the following basic colors has certain effects on people. These effects depend upon the shade of the color and how it is used.

- **Red**—Red creates feelings of physical warmth and stimulates creativity. It is appropriate for areas where people spend short periods of time, such as a reception room or a cafeteria. Over long periods of time red can be overstimulating and can cause tension, nervousness, eyestrain, and headaches.

- **Yellow**—Yellow is perceived as a cheerful, warm color, provided that the tone is soft and the shade is light. This friendly color is good for rooms that have windows facing the north, where there is little sunlight. It has the highest retention rating of all colors. Light shades of orange have similar effects.

- **Blue**—Blue is a cool, relaxing color that calms the emotions and the effects of stress. For areas where people do continuous, detailed work that may cause tension, blue is appropriate. It is also used for work areas that have windows facing the south, where sunlight is bright. However, overuse of blue can cause sluggish behavior to the point of depression.

- **Green**—Green is also perceived as a cool color that has a calming effect on emotions. Because it does not cause abnormal reactions and offers a pleasant contrast to other colors, green is sometimes referred to as the equalizer. Green is a popular, easy-to-live-with office color.

- **Black, Brown, and Gray**—These colors create somber feelings of fatigue and decrease the perception of light and space.

- **White**—White increases the perception of light and space. It has no negative reaction to workers.

The number of different colors that can be combined effectively is usually limited to three. More than three predominant colors in a work area have a choppy, overstimulating effect. Also, such a color scheme lacks continuity.

Choosing Colors

The proper selection of colors depends upon such factors as the amount of space involved, the type of work being performed, the length of time spent in that area, and the kind of lighting used. Colors cause people to perceive an area to be larger or smaller than its actual size. Dark colors and tones make an area seem smaller, while light colors can make small work areas seem larger.

Work that involves creative composition and conference discussion can be enhanced by accents of bright, stimulating colors. On the other hand, intense keyboarding and proofreading require cool, soft, and light tones.

The length of time that people spend in a reception area, a conference room, a hallway, or a cafeteria is relatively short. Thus, the designer can use bright, vibrant colors and darker shades. However, work areas in which people spend six to eight hours should be in pastel colors of light shades.

The ceiling, walls, floors, and work surfaces should complement the lighting by providing the proper reflection and contrast. Ceilings and upper walls should have light shades to help reflect light and nonglossy surfaces that reduce glare. In contrast, dark shades absorb light and glossy surfaces increase glare.

The work surface should be a medium shade to provide some contrast to white papers. A nearly white surface blends too easily with paper and makes it difficult for the worker to distinguish the paper from the background. A dark surface offers too much contrast and causes eyestrain. The surface should have a low (30 to 35 percent) reflective value (unlike a glossy surface) to avoid unfriendly glare. Medium shades are also recommended for flooring.

The proper selection of colors is an important aspect of the office environment.

ACOUSTICAL CONTROL

The science that deals with the production, control, transmission, reception, and effects of sound is called **acoustics**. Thus, acoustical control involves keeping the noise or sound level of the office to a minimum.

acoustics science that deals with sound

Word processing centers are susceptible to various types of distracting, unpleasant noise. Printers run intermittently, telephones ring, transcribing machines click as controls are operated, and workers sometimes converse about a team project. Open work areas are especially conducive to noise problems. It takes 20 percent longer to do work under distracting noisy conditions than to do the same work under reasonably quiet conditions.

Measuring Sound

The volume of sound is measured by **decibels**. The human ear has a hearing range of 0 to 130 decibels (dB). However, the nervous system

decibel a measurement of the volume of sound

begins to react at 70 dB, and long exposure to noises over 70 dB may impair hearing. Noise is considered anything over 70 dB.

Most word processing printers produce between 65 and 85 dB of noise, with the average printer producing 72 dB.[8] The noise in a work area of word processing printers without noise control could climb to 100 dB. Environmental experts recommend that office noise be no more than 65 dB.

How Noise Affects People

Excessive noise can be a hazard to health, can cause people to become irritable, and can decrease productivity (with increased error rates). Working under noisy conditions requires more energy than working under quiet ones. Both concentration and decision-making ability are challenged. A soft, continuous sound is not as disruptive as intermittent sounds. Of course, any type of noise becomes more bothersome as its volume increases. Voice communication is likely to be inaccurately received, and confidentiality is lost.

Ways to Reduce Noise

To reduce noise and keep it at a minimum level, various techniques are used. Every effort should be made to avoid unpleasant noise so that maximum productivity and human comfort can be achieved.

Layout. Designing work areas according to work flow decreases the amount of walking, which reduces traffic noise. Those who often work together on projects are positioned within talking distance to avoid excessive phone calls and walking. Work areas with noisy machines should be located away from those persons who need quiet for concentration. However, this is not always possible in a word processing center because the printers are generally located near the word processing terminals.

Separation of Work Stations. In open-plan office areas, workers generally share at least one common panel or screen. These partitions should be curved to reduce the reflectance angle and acoustically treated to muffle sounds.

Equipment Design. Manufacturers of word processors, printers, and other office machines are making machines that run more quietly. As electronic circuit panels replace mechanical parts, noise is being reduced significantly.

---

[8]David Duke, "Acoustical Enclosures Muffle Printer Noise," *Word Processing and Information Systems* (April, 1982), p. 39.

CHAPTER 10 Preparing the Environment 291

Acoustical Enclosures. As an optional device, acoustical enclosures are hoods that are placed over printers (or parts of printers) to muffle sound. They can reduce noise to about 59 dB. Should most of the printer be enclosed, the acoustical sound cover should be equipped with a fan to circulate and cool the air within the enclosure, because printers generate heat.

acoustical enclosure
hood placed over a printer to muffle sound

An acoustical enclosure reduces the noise generated by a piece of equipment.

Printer Pad. A printer vibration pad (mat) can help reduce the vibration noise between the printer and the stand on which it is placed. Some pads are designed to allow proper air flow and to help prevent creeping (gradual movement) of the printer.

Electronic Sound Masking. An electronically generated sound can be installed and tuned to mask unwanted noises. This continuous sound is evenly distributed so that it can be heard but is not distracting. Another option would be to play soft music, which also muffles sound. However, it is difficult to select the type of music that all workers appreciate, and music can create an atmosphere that is too relaxed, especially for creative work.

Ceiling, Wall, and Partition Materials. Materials that are selected for ceilings, walls, and partitions should be sound absorptive. Materials differ in their ability to absorb sound. Soft, porous materials such as cork, fabrics, and fiberboard absorb sound. On the other hand, hard, nonporous surfaces such as concrete, plaster, and glass reflect sound, allowing it to bounce and magnify.

Flooring Materials. When compared to tile, wood, or marble, the type of floor covering that best absorbs sound is carpeting. Both the padding and the carpet backing should be made of material that allows air to pass through. Also, the materials should meet the acoustical rating requirements.

Office Covering Ratings

Commercial office coverings can be rated according to their ability to absorb sound and to lessen sound. Two common ratings are the noise reduction coefficient and the noise isolation class.

noise reduction coefficient a measurement of a material's ability to absorb sound

Noise Reduction Coefficient. A common rating is noise reduction coefficient (NRC). The higher the NRC, the greater the material's ability to absorb or muffle sound. An NRC rating of .95 means that the material absorbs 95 percent of the sound that hits it. Some minimum NRC ratings for office surfaces are as follows:

Ceilings	.75 or higher
Partitions	.70 or higher
Walls	.80 or higher
Carpeted Floors	.20 or higher

noise isolation class quantifies the speech privacy potential of a system

Noise Isolation Class. A newer method of measuring noise reduction capabilities is the noise isolation class (NIC) for primary speech frequencies. This rating quantifies the speech privacy potential of a system. An NIC rating takes into account all factors of the environment. It guides the user in deciding what is needed in the way of partitions, carpeting, and ceilings based on the amount of background masking sound within the work area. For example, a perfect ceiling would have the same capacity to weaken the severity of sound as the open sky; its NIC rating would be 23. A furniture system with an NIC rating of 21 could reduce sound by about 21 dB between work stations, providing the other components had good sound masking qualities. Figure 10-6 shows how panel systems are designed to include sound control.

You are now aware of the major considerations involved in planning a word processing environment. Each has an impact on the ability of people and machines to function efficiently. With a properly planned environment the people, machines, and procedures are enhanced so that maximum productivity can be achieved.

CHAPTER 10   Preparing the Environment   293

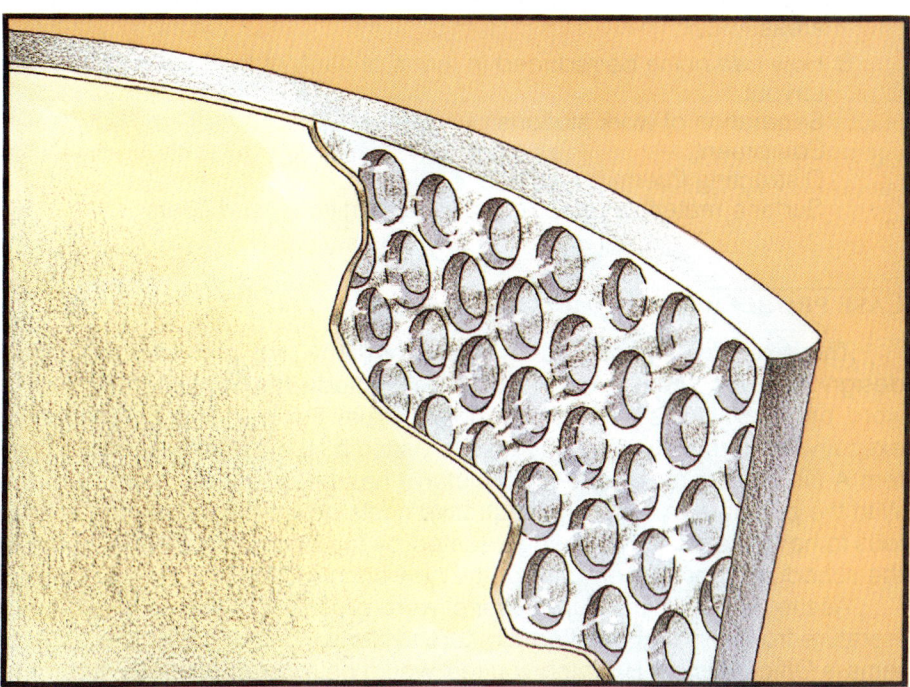

FIG. 10-6
ACOUSTICAL CONTROL
Work station panels can be designed to absorb sound and reduce noise.

DISCUSSION QUESTIONS AND CASE PROBLEM

DISCUSSION QUESTIONS

1. Why is environment important enough to be emphasized as one of the four parts of a word processing system?
2. What are six major areas to be considered in planning the working environment? Who should participate in the planning?
3. If you were designing a word processing operator's workstation, what elements would you recommend to avoid VDT-related problems?
4. What is the ideal climate for a word processing system?
5. For uninterrupted electrical power and dependable machine operation, what devices would you suggest using?
6. Describe the lighting system that would give the right amount of light with maximum usability and would be most economical in terms of energy and cost.

7 Explain three characteristics of effective color treatment for work areas.
8 How can noise be reduced in terms of each of the following factors?
Layout
Separation of work stations
Equipment
Distracting intermittent noise
Surface materials of ceilings, walls, partitions, and floors

CASE PROBLEM

The executive managers of your company are planning the office design for a new construction, which will include the implementation of a word processing system. Memorandums from the planning committee of executives inform you that of the offices visited by the committee, Office System A (illustrated by an attached picture) has been chosen as the model. With the pressure to keep administrative costs down, the committee is anxious to have the current building vacated by the beginning of next month—the scheduled completion date of the new construction.

As the recently hired supervisor of word processing, you have reviewed literature from vendors of office furniture systems. One of the illustrated systems is Office System B, which you feel would be a better office environment

Office System A

CHAPTER 10 Preparing the Environment ───────────────────────────────── 295

Office System B

than Office System A. You decide to make an appointment with the planning committee chairperson to discuss some major concerns that you have for the word processing system.

1. What are some basic managerial errors in this case?
2. Why does Office System A appear to be inadequate?
3. What appropriate environmental factors are evident from the illustration of Office System B?
4. What other factors would need to be considered?
5. How would you convince the chairperson to reevaluate the plans?

Chapter 11 Developing the System Controls

CHAPTER OBJECTIVES:

Explain the purpose of procedures for controlling a word processing system.

Identify the five goals of processing paperwork in a word processing system.

Recognize how procedures for control are needed for both administrative support services and correspondence support (document preparation) services in a word processing system.

Describe each of the ten basic procedures used to control a word processing system in terms of (a) what the procedure is, (b) why it is important, and (c) how to apply it.

For information to be accurate and timely, it must be processed in the most efficient way possible. Machines have been invented and continually improved to become sophisticated tools. Competent people have the intelligence, skill, and desire to produce quality work. To enhance the capabilities of both people and machines, a word processing system must be guided by efficient procedures.

Without well-developed, modern procedures a word processing system is slow and costly. Management expects a word processing system to surpass the efficiency record of traditional office systems. As technology advances to produce more sophisticated tools, procedures must advance also. Procedures determine the speed at which a task can be

CHAPTER 11 Developing the System Controls

done, the amount of effort involved, the wear of the equipment, the quality of the completed document, and the satisfaction of the worker. In essence, procedures are the system controls.

Compared to traditional office systems, word processing systems are developed to process paperwork more quickly, more accurately, at lower cost, with less effort, and with improved quality. Figure 11-1 further defines each of these goals.

GOALS OF WORD PROCESSING

To process paperwork:

More Quickly	Greater speed; increased production rate
and	
More Accurately	Fewer errors; better proofreading
to give	
Improved Quality	Professional print; no signs of error correction; better composition; more personalization
with	
Less Effort	Physical: Minimum of keystrokes; simple formats; no retyping of correct text; avoidance of proofreading correct text
	Mental: Avoids unnecessary decision making
at	
Lower Cost	The least expense

FIG. 11-1
WORD PROCESSING GOALS
The procedures for a word processing system are developed to accomplish these five goals of word processing.

The procedures that guide a word processing system are developed to accomplish those five goals most directly and smoothly. Common procedures include: logging work, measuring production, setting standards, establishing priorities, scheduling turnaround, maintaining quality printout, standardizing formats of documents, managing media files, writing office manuals, and training personnel. These procedures are illustrated in Figure 11-2, and each is described in the following sections.

**FIG. 11-2
CONTROL PROCEDURES**
Procedures are the system controls. Therefore, they must be designed to allow a system to run smoothly and efficiently.

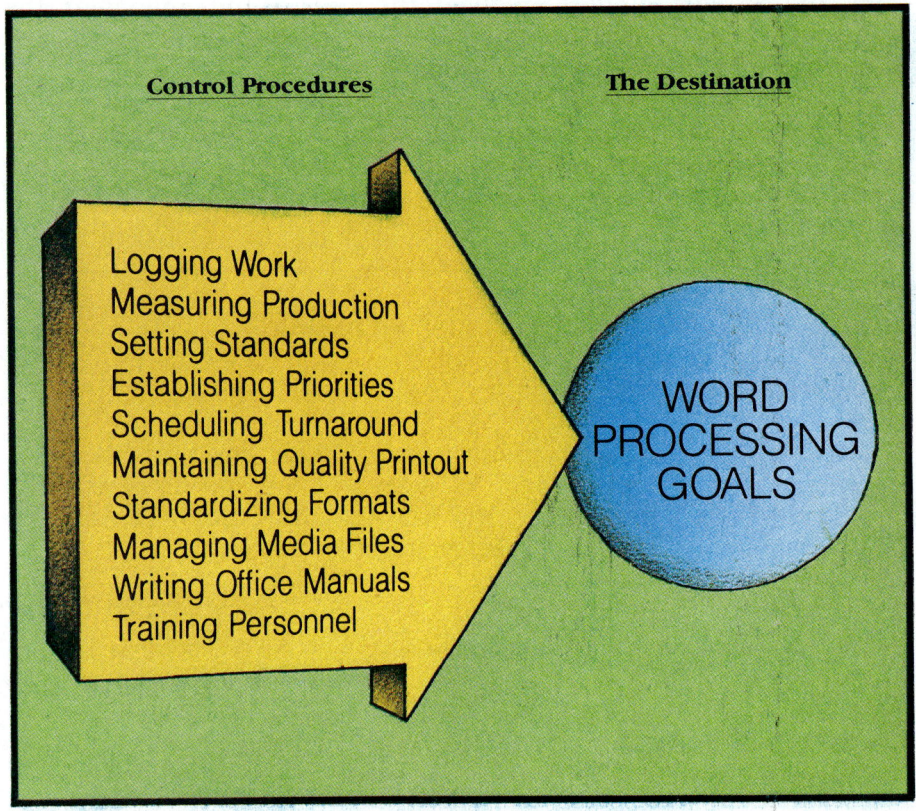

logging recording facts about work as it enters and leaves a work area

LOGGING WORK

Logging is the act of recording facts about work as it comes in and goes out of a work area. Each member of the office support staff might maintain a daily log sheet, or one sheet might be used for logging the work of all of the office support personnel.

Log Sheet

The information that is commonly recorded on a log sheet for a word processing center includes:

1 Date and time received

2 When it is needed (indication of priority)

3 Dictation recorder number and/or cassette number

4 Magnetic media file and/or document label (name)

5 Author's name

CHAPTER 11 Developing the System Controls 299

6 Department of the author

7 Name of person to whom document is to be sent; the addressee

8 Work request number

9 Type of document—letter, memo, report, statistical, form

10 Origin of document—dictation, longhand, rough draft, prerecorded

11 Quality of copy—rough draft or final copy

12 Time completed

13 Number of minutes used

14 Number of lines, pages, or units produced

To enhance the capabilities of both people and machines, effective procedures must be developed.

The content of log sheets varies from company to company. Log sheets should be designed to record only meaningful information. The time and effort used in filling out a log sheet should be kept to a minimum. An example of a log sheet is given in Figure 11-3.

FIG. 11-3
LOG SHEET
Log sheets should contain only meaningful information.

DATE	TIME IN	DOC ID	DOCUMENT NAME	AUTHOR'S NAME	DEPT	TYPE OF DOC	INPUT FORM	OUTPUT FORM	DIFFICULTY	TOTAL LINES	UNITS	ERRORS	TIME OUT	TOTAL MIN
1-16	8:30	W51	ACC-RPT	Lewis	02	L M (R) S	D (L) P R	(FC) RD	F L (O) R S T	110	220		9:20	50
	9:25	TAPE B-03	MKT-BRO	McQueary	10	L M (R) S	(D) L P R	FC RD	F L (O) R S T	198	198	1	10:45	80
	11:00	W54	ACC-ST2	Lewis	02	L M R (S)	D (L) P R	(FC) RD	F L (O) R (S) T	80	200		11:55	55
	1:00	TAPE R12	Brown	Cunningham	07	(L) M R S	(D) L P R	(FC) RD	F L (O) R S T	32	32			
	"	"	Lopez	Cunningham	07	(L) M R S	(D) L P R	(FC) RD	F L (O) R S T	35	35			
	"	"	Stelts	Cunningham	07	L (M) R S	(D) L P R	(FC) RD	F L (O) R S T	28	28		1:40	40
	1:45	TAPE B06	INS-JAN	Lydick	03	L M (R) S	(D) L P R	(FC) RD	F L (O) R S T	179	179	1	2:30	45
	2:35	TAPE B09	EXEC-CF	Carlberg	01	L M (R) S	(D) L P R	(FC) RD	F L (O) R S T	224	224		3:30	55
	3:45	W65	ACC-RPT	Lewis	02	L M (R) S	D L (P) R	(FC) RD	F L (O) R (S) T	120	60		4:10	25
	4:15	W68	ENG-STT	Nguyen	09	L M (R) S	D (L) P R	FC (RD)	F L O R S (T)	108	216		5:05	50
	5:05	W73	COM-4	Sturgeon	06	L (M) R S	D L (P) R	(FC) RD	F L O R S (T)	36	54		5:30	25
						L M R S	D L P R	FC RD	F L O R S T					
				TOTALS						1150	1446	2		425

WORD PROCESSING SERVICES LOG   Specialist **D. Anderson**

TYPE OF DOCUMENT
L Letter
M Memorandum
R Report
S Statistical

INPUT ORIGIN
D Dictated
L Longhand/Shhd
P Prerecorded
R Rough Draft

OUTPUT FORM
FC Final Copy
RD Rough Draft

DIFFICULTY FACTOR
F Form Document = 0.5
L Longhand/Shhd Dict = 2.0
O Original Dict = 1.0
R Revision = 0.5
S Statistical = 2.5
T Typed Rough Draft = 1.5

No. of Documents _11_
Total Units _1446_
Total Errors _2_
Error Percentage _.14_
Total Minutes _425_
UPM (Units Per Minute) _3.40_

Proofread by _Jane Grushka_
Comments
01-84(01)

Work Request

A work request form, as shown in Figure 11-4, is used for work that is not originated by machine dictation. The author may submit a manuscript in longhand form, a rough draft of a speech, or a request to have a prerecorded form letter sent to various names and addresses. Work request forms also are used for work that must be further processed by another office system, such as phototypesetting or reproduction services.

Some work request forms are designed to include both the author's and the supervisor's instructions as well as the office support personnel's logging data. This type of form is also known as a **job ticket**.

Why Work Is Logged

Log sheets that are easy to maintain and accurately kept are functional. They serve two basic purposes:

work request form used for work not originated by machine dictation or work to be further processed

job ticket a type of work request form

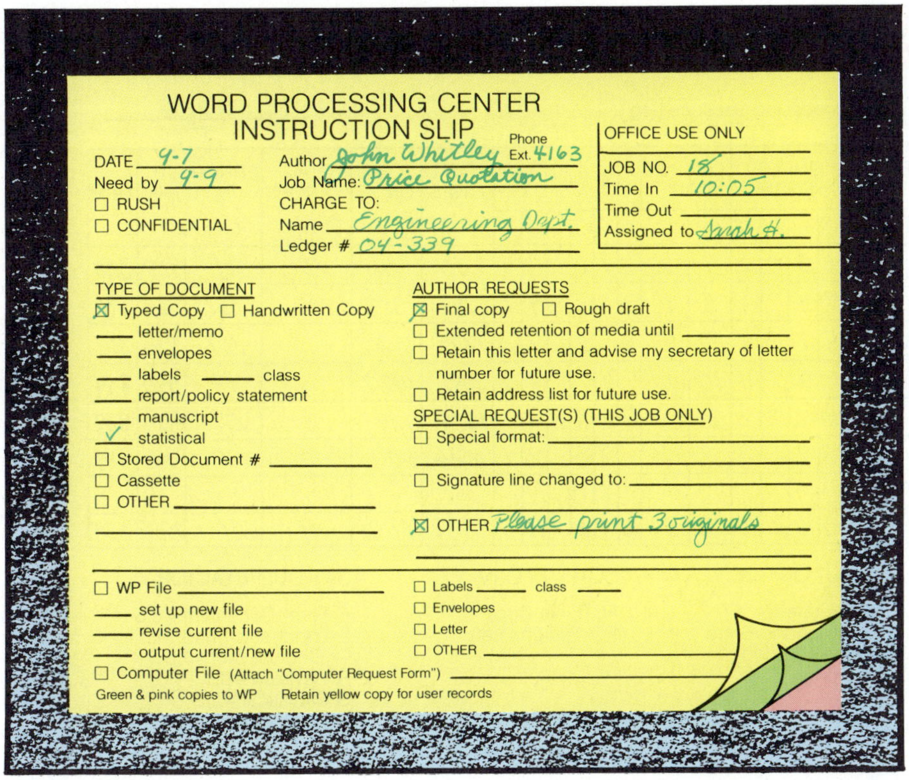

CHAPTER 11 Developing the System Controls   301

FIG. 11-4
WORK REQUEST FORM
Work request forms should be filled in carefully and should contain complete instructions.

- When someone inquires about the status of a job, the supervisor can quickly trace and retrieve the document at any phase of production. For example, the author may have decided to add a table to a report; or perhaps the date and time of a meeting had to be changed suddenly.

- Log sheets are used for recording production data that is compiled and summarized onto production reports. Daily totals may be summarized onto weekly, monthly, quarterly, and/or annual reports for management. Figure 11-5 shows how production data from the word processing services log can be totaled and summarized.

MEASURING PRODUCTION

How do employees and management personnel recognize growth patterns? How much more efficient is a word processing system since new technology has been implemented? Can the company justify the cost of adding personnel? These and other questions can be answered most easily when records are kept on the amount of work produced by

SECRETARY	# OF DOC	TYPE OF DOC				INPUT FORM				OUTPUT FORM		DIFFICULTY						TOTAL LINES	TOTAL UNITS	TOTAL ERRORS	ERROR %	TTL MIN	UPM
		L	M	R	S	D	L	P	R	FC	RD	F	L	O	R	S	T						
D Anderson	11	2	2	5	2	6	3	0	2	9	2	1	6	1	2		1	1150	1446	2	.14	425	3.40
E Edwards	12	3	3	2	4	7	4		1	8	4	3	3		4		2	1283	1388	3	.22	420	3.30
A Hofer	16	10	2	2	2	5	1	5	5	14	2	6		6		2	2	1310	1380	1	.07	430	3.21
R Knoell	10		6	4		4		6	10		4				4	2		1185	1427	2	.14	440	3.24
M Vollmer	22	16	4	2		11	2	7	2	20	2	7	2	7	6			1308	1349	1	.07	430	3.14
A Young	8		6	2	3	2		3	7	1			2	3		2	1	1096	1256	0	.00	360	3.49
TOTALS	79	31	11	23	14	32	16	12	19	68	11	16	9	25	7	14	8	7332	8246	9	.11	2505	3.29

CONTROL SUMMARY of Word Processing Services Log Date January 16

TYPE OF DOCUMENT
L Letter
M Memorandum
R Report
S Statistical

INPUT ORIGIN
D Dictated
L Longhand/Shhd
P Prerecorded
R Rough Draft

OUTPUT FORM
FC Final Copy
RD Rough Draft

DIFFICULTY FACTOR
F Form Document = 0.5
L Longhand/Shhd Dict = 2.0
O Original Dict = 1.0
R Revision = 0.5
S Statistical = 2.5
T Typed Rough Draft = 1.5

UPM = Units Per Minute

FIG. 11-5
CONTROL SUMMARY
This control summary totals and summarizes the production data found on the log sheet shown in Figure 11-4.

each employee. The production data must be summarized to provide meaningful information for management.

How performance is measured—whether formal (objective by measuring and compiling statistics) or informal (subjective such as by observation)—varies from company to company. Some word processing managers have relaxed on the accuracy and degree to which statistics are kept. They feel that too much time is spent on the measurement process and that some of the data is ignored by top management. On the other hand, there are managers who feel that measuring production is vital to the success of their operation. Let's examine basic reasons why companies measure production and then note the methods of actually measuring work.

Reasons for Measuring Production

Most word processing systems measure the work of office support services. However, it has long been felt that managers' productivity

CHAPTER 11 Developing the System Controls 303

could not be measured due to the nature of their work. Since 1980 there has been increased concern about measuring managerial productivity, even though it may not be as easy to measure as the work of the office support staff. The following reasons for measuring production relate to the performance of the office support staff:

1. By comparing monthly and quarterly reports of the current year with previous years, supervisors have facts about trends to present to management. A monthly report is shown in Figure 11-6. From this information, growth patterns can be noted and long-range plans can be made. Examples of information that might be meaningful to management would include: average turnaround time for correspondence, amount of work produced for each department, amount of machine dictation given by each author, proportion of original dictation compared to revision work or repetitive playback of prerecorded documents, and the average number of times a document is revised.

CENTRAL PROPERTY AND CASUALTY COMPANY
WORD PROCESSING CENTER TOTALS
For the Month of: __March__

		March	Feb
ORIGINAL KEYBOARD LINES		110,076	110,598
LINES REVISED		4,716	2,455
VARIABLE LINES		15,782	15,360
LINES PRE-RECORDED	REVISED	22,019	20,105
	FORMS	52,078	56,918
TOTAL LINES TYPED		204,671	205,436
		TOTAL PAGES	TOTAL PAGES
		8,187	8,217

FIG. 11-6
MONTHLY REPORTS
The data in a monthly report is compared to data in monthly reports from previous years to determine patterns and trends.

Methods of measuring performance vary from company to company.

2 From production records the supervisor can calculate the average time it takes to perform a certain type of task. This helps the supervisor schedule work, estimate the turnaround time, and set standards (procedures that are described later in this chapter).

3 When production records are used, supervisors have an objective basis upon which to evaluate personnel. From that basis, salary increases, promotions, and bonuses can be justified; and employees can be assured that they have been treated fairly.

4 The production records justify not only the acquisition of new equipment, but also the type of equipment needed. For example, if a high percentage of applications requires text processing and only a small percentage involves data processing, the selection of a dedicated word processor is justified.

5 Production records provide a basis upon which user departments can be charged for the work produced, which is known as a charge-back system. The charges are usually based on the quantity of work produced and/or on the amount of time used.

6 Major problems within the work flow can be detected from production records. This alerts the supervisor to determine causes so that solutions can be enacted before problems become more serious. Figure 11-7 gives some examples.

7 The addition of personnel (temporary, part-time, or full-time) can be justified through the use of production records.

8 Production records are needed for budgeting so that operating costs can be kept to the minimum, thereby maximizing profits.

Problem	Determining Causes and Solutions
Authors who give the least amount of machine dictation	Does the nature of their work not require machine dictation? Have they been trained on how to dictate? Do they need help in learning to delegate routine tasks?
Slow and inaccurate transcribers	What are their attendance records? Have they had any health problems? Do they need more training? Should they be retained beyond the probationary period?
Increased turnover of office support personnel	How competent is the supervisor? Is the environment adequate? Is there a visible career path with advancement opportunities?
Peak periods (that involve a large amount of work to complete within a short time)	Are they temporary? Should temporary help be hired? Does the growth pattern justify hiring another part- or full-time employee?

FIG. 11-7
USING PRODUCTION SUMMARIES TO DETECT PROBLEMS
Production summaries allow supervisors to monitor work and detect problems before they become too serious.

Measuring production not only encourages efficiency, but also improves the quality of a word processing system. It is important that personnel understand the reasons for measuring production so they can appreciate the benefits. A good supervisor will try continually to improve work methods so that there is economy of motion, time, and paperwork.

Methods of Measuring Production

The tasks of office support personnel vary in difficulty, and not all are easy to measure. Document preparation and administrative support are unique in the way each is measured.

Document Preparation. The work produced by word processing specialists can be measured by counting lines, pages, or units. To count pages one must decide what is the average page and then adjust the count for those that are longer or shorter than average.

Still another factor is the degree of difficulty involved. Any of the following factors can affect the difficulty of producing a document:

- **Type of Input**—original dictation vs. prerecorded text
- **Method of Input**—machine dictation vs. longhand

- **Type of Equipment Used**—electronic typewriter vs. display standalone word processor
- **Characteristics of the Document**—2-column vs. 5-column table, light vs. heavy revision, centered vs. blocked headings, blocked vs. indented text, underscored vs. nonunderscored text, and so forth

Thus, measuring document production becomes quite complex. A fair measurement must take into account the difficulty of the task but should not be so complicated that measurement itself takes an inordinate amount of time.

Some companies measure on the basis of units. Two letters of equal length may be counted as follows: Letter A transcribed from machine dictation = 4 units; Letter B played back from prerecorded text (a form letter) = 1 unit. Figure 11-8 shows how one company counts pages and adjusts the count according to difficulty.

FIG. 11-8
MEASURING DOCUMENT PRODUCTION
To be fair to all employees, measurements of document production should be adjusted according to the difficulty of each document.

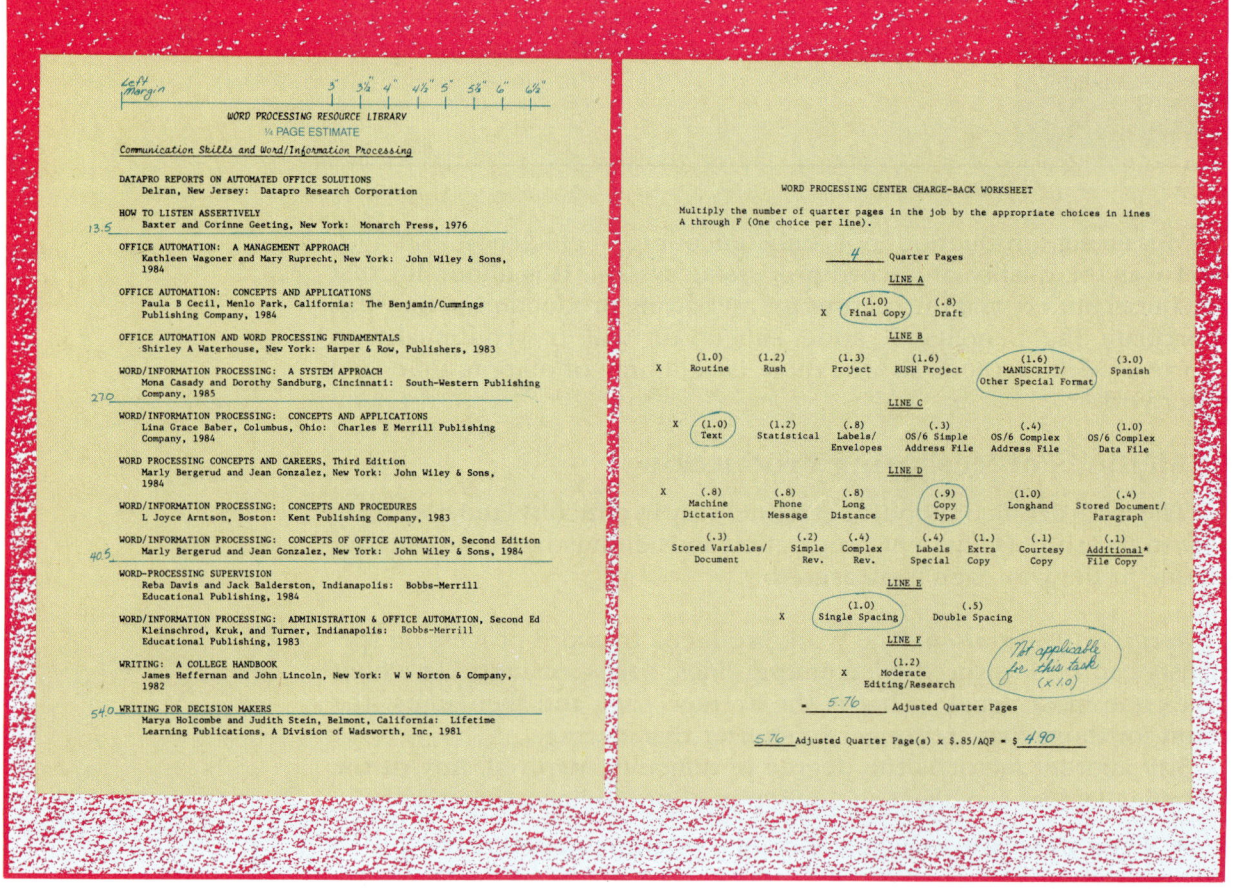

The one-page document of a manuscript (a bibliography) measures four quarter pages. The source was a typed sheet (copy type) from which the operator could easily produce a final copy of text. Notice how the adjusted quarter pages were determined.

Administrative Support. Two ways to measure the work produced by an administrative support secretary are stroke count and time count. **Stroke count** involves marking a stroke for each task, whereas **time count** involves totaling the time spent on the activity. For example, one could record a stroke mark for each phone call that is placed or received; or, one could total the minutes spent during each phone conversation.

Time count generally is used for long, infrequent tasks such as composing routine letters. On the other hand, stroke count generally is used for short, frequent tasks such as photocopying. Devices such as auditrons (counters) that can be inserted into photocopying machines to automatically count the number of copies run facilitate stroke count measurements.

In choosing a method of measuring work, one should design it so that a minimum of effort and time is needed. When measurement processes require too much time, they lose some value.

stroke count   keeping track of productivity by counting the number of tasks performed

time count   keeping track of productivity by totaling the time spent on each task

SETTING STANDARDS

Having kept production records for at least four months, the supervisor can begin to develop standards. A standard is a grading scale or yardstick by which the productivity of various workers can be compared.

Here is how one company developed standards based on line counts. The work of all eight word processing specialists was measured for four months. Instead of adjusting line count according to the difficulty of the task, the supervisor rotated difficult, average, and easy assignments so that each specialist had about equal proportions of easy and difficult work. Total lines were divided by total days; this subtotal was then divided by eight (the number of specialists). The result was 1,100 lines. Therefore, the standard rate of production for document production was set at 1,100 lines a day per operator. The specialist averaging 1,200 lines a day demonstrated above-average productivity; the one producing only 700 lines was below average. In administrative support, an example of a standard would be making six flight arrangements (reservations and tickets) per hour.

An average production rate is a good standard only if all the workers are measured under the same conditions and are doing their best during the period of measurement. As any condition changes, such as equipment replacement, standards must be revised by collecting new data. No universal standards have been established because there are so many

standard   scale by which productivity of workers can be compared

variables not only within one industry but among different types of businesses and professions. Among the variables are the procedures that have been developed, the organization of support services, the type of equipment used, and the nature of the work produced. Thus, each company has to keep production records upon which to base its own standards.

ESTABLISHING PRIORITIES

Many word processing systems use a first-in, first-out order of processing work. However, several requests for various types of tasks may be submitted at the same time. It is not likely that all of the tasks are equally urgent. To treat the authors fairly and to guide the word processing specialists in deciding the order of production, priorities must be established. By having the authors help prioritize categories of tasks according to the order in which they would expect them to be produced, the supervisor has their support in distributing work.

Items that are processed first are not necessarily more important than other items. All work is important to both the author and the company. However, for effective communication and efficient scheduling, certain tasks must be processed before others. This is known as the order of urgency. Figure 11-9 shows an example of establishing priorities of document processing (correspondence support) and of mail processing (administrative support).

priorities tasks to be completed before other tasks so the most urgent work is done first

Since not all tasks are equally important, priorities must be established.

Document Processing (CS)	Mail Processing (AS)
1 Rush requests—documents that must be prepared within one hour	1 Rush requests—mail to be sent by private carrier, registered mail, special delivery, etc.
2 Machine dictation—original dictation of letters and memorandums	2 Sorting and delivering outgoing mail before a.m. pickup or before p.m. pickup
3 Revisions, rough drafts, and short reports	3 Sorting and distributing incoming mail
4 Form letters and mailing list updates	4 Preparing for correspondence to be answered—annotating, getting materials from files, and filling out work requests
5 Long reports and projects	5 Dictating routine correspondence
6 Archiving (transferring text from temporary onto permanent storage)	6 Photocopying documents
7 Duplicating and deleting functions	7 Filing correspondence and reports
8 Updating records and cross-referencing	8 Filing brochures and periodicals

FIG. 11-9
ESTABLISHING PRIORITIES
For effective communication and efficient scheduling, a list of priorities should be established.

A record of the rush requests submitted by each author is usually kept by the supervisor. An above-average number of rush requests from one person might indicate a need for help in organizing work, managing time, and delegating tasks to administrative secretaries.

Each company has to establish its own priorities, because situations vary. Among the variables would be the type of business, the organization of office support services, and the available equipment.

SCHEDULING TURNAROUND

Once priorities have been established, every effort is made to get the work done and returned to the author within a certain time. This is known as scheduling turnaround. Time goals help the office support staff to know what is expected of them. By providing efficient service, the support staff can feel a part of a successful team (with the authors) in promoting good public relations for the company.

Many authors appreciate knowing how soon they can expect work to be done. In fact, they are impressed when word processing and administrative support services surpass the speed by which a traditional secretary would typically perform either function.

Time goals are referred to as turnaround time or turnaround goals. However, turnaround has a unique meaning to each of the following:

- **To the Company**—From the time a document is created and goes through the necessary revision to the time it has been completed in final form and is ready to be mailed or filed.

- **To Word Processing Services**—From the time a work request or dictation enters the center to the time the document has been processed and leaves the center.

- **To the Author**—From the time the author finishes dictating or preparing a work request to the time the document comes back from the center.

For the examples of established priorities given in Figure 11-9, the turnaround goals of secretarial services might be like the ones shown in Figure 11-10.

FIG. 11-10
TURNAROUND GOALS
To provide efficient service and effective scheduling, turnaround goals must be established for the priorities listed in Figure 11-9.

Categories of Document Processing Tasks (CS)	Turnaround Goal
Rush requests (1-2 pages)	1 hour
Original dictation (1-2 pages)	3 hours
Revision and rough drafts (1-5 pages)	4 hours
Short reports (1-3 pages)	4 hours
Form letters; mailing list updates	6 hours
Reports and projects (4-9 pages)	8 hours
Reports and projects (10+ pages)	24 hours
Archiving, duplicating, and deleting documents	24 hours
Updating records and cross-referencing	48 hours

Categories of Mail Processing Tasks (AS)	
Rush requests (special mail services)	½ hour
Sorting and delivering outgoing mail before pickups	½ hour
Sorting and distributing incoming mail	½ hour
Preparing for correspondence to be answered	1 hour
Dictating routine correspondence	2 hours
Photocopying documents	2 hours
Filing correspondence and reports	3 hours
Filing brochures and periodicals	8 hours

Scheduling turnaround aids both office support personnel and authors.

For turnaround goals to be met, there must be an efficient way for work to enter a center and to be delivered back to the authors. The authors send work to the center through the dictation lines, by company mail (delivery service), by telephone, or by a personal visit. For each of the latter three, a work request generally would be prepared. In companies that have large centers, completed work might be routed to the authors every hour or two by personal delivery. Some supervisors rotate this task among the word processing specialists so that they become acquainted with the authors for whom they work.

MAINTAINING QUALITY PRINTOUT

To assure that each document is printed with accuracy and with a professional appearance, quality control techniques are applied. Main functions of quality control include proofreading and monitoring the printer.

Proofreading

To err is human, and each person involved with the production of a document can at one time or another make a mistake. The error could be made during dictation, transcription, revision, or printing. However, the recipient of the document is usually more critical than empathetic about finding errors. Errors not only reflect unfavorably on the author

Careful proofreading involves reading a document at least two times—once for content and once for mechanics.

but also can scar the image of the company. While each step of the production process should include proofreading, the printing step is the last chance for an error to be detected before it leaves the word processing area.

In many word processing centers each document is proofread after it has been printed. The proofreader might be a lead word processing specialist, a proofreading specialist, or the supervisor.

Word processors that have built-in dictionaries (application software) help by bringing misspelled words to the attention of the operator. However, the misspelled word is not corrected automatically by all systems; the operator must then key the correction. Also, a dictionary does not catch errors in grammar (*have* vs. *has*), word usage (*principal* vs. *principle*), decimals (*$1.00* vs. *$100.00*), numbers (*47'* vs. *37'*), punctuation (; vs. ,), or capitalization (*may* vs. *May*). Only an alert proofreader can prevent such errors from being exposed to the reader.

Careful proofreading involves reading the document at least two times—once for content (Does it make sense?) and once for mechanics (Are word divisions, grammar, spelling, and punctuation correct?). In addition, a document that includes references (names, addresses, and amounts) should be checked against the sources. Reading for content will alert the proofreader to the omission of a word, phrase, or line. The author's intended text should not be altered unless a specific request was made to do so. The earlier in the processing cycle that errors are caught, the fewer will be the number of revisions. In turn, the cost of the document can be kept at a minimum.

Monitoring the Printer

In a small word processing facility each operator typically controls one printer and initiates printing action as needed. However, in larger word processing configurations one or more printers are shared by many terminals. A high-speed printer for rough draft quality might be part of the configuration. One person might be assigned to monitor the printers (especially common in systems that have standalone printers), or the operators might initiate their own printing.

Printers that require manual paper insertion (inserting by hand one sheet at a time) necessitate the presence of the operator. The options of feeding continuous forms or single sheets of paper automatically save time because they do not require the presence of an operator once the printing function begins. However, even printers with automatic devices should not be left unattended. They should be monitored frequently to be sure they are working properly.

Cautions. The quality of print is lowered by various problems or acts of neglect. Among them are the following:

1 Uneven insertion of paper (improper alignment)

2 Inserting a sheet of paper with a staple (ruins a print wheel)

3 A worn-out or broken print wheel (uneven impressions cause parts of letters to be lighter than others)

4 A worn-out platen (causes ribbon wear, paper slippage, and type damage—misalignment or embossed characters)

5 Improper selection of pitch (for example, using a 12-pitch print wheel when the printer is directed to print 10-pitch)

6 Worn-out power and feed rolls (affect the speed and quality of printing)

7 Using poor quality ribbons (results in fuzzy, uneven print)

8 Incorrect insertion of a new ribbon

9 Using embossed envelopes (may not feed well through the printer)

10 Electronic failure (may result in a sudden alteration of text)

Form Tractors and Sheet Feeders. In setting up form tractors and sheet feeders, special care is needed. Note the following suggestions:

- Make sure the paper rides tight against the platen.
- Position the paper source correctly for smooth feeding.
- Set the tension at the proper level (forms impression control).
- Avoid using paper that is much heavier or lighter than 20 to 25 pounds.

Handling Print Wheels. Print wheels are delicate and should be handled with extreme care. The life of a print wheel can be maximized by following these recommendations:

1 Store print wheels in cool, dry places.

2 Handle the hub only; do not handle the spokes.

3 Store print wheels in containers that will protect the spokes from bending.

4 Clean print wheels; use mild soap and water (or rubbing alcohol) and a soft toothbrush.

5 In mounting a print wheel, make sure it is aligned properly and seated firmly.

6 Set the impression control at its lowest setting that will still give an even, sharp, and dark impression.

7 Do not use metal and plastic wheels interchangeably on printers.

STANDARDIZING FORMATS OF DOCUMENTS

Allowing each author to request customized formats for the various types of documents being originated does not support the goals of a word processing system. In fact, having to produce various formats for one type of document is slower, less likely to be accurate, and less professional looking than using one standard format. In addition, it takes more physical and mental effort and results in a higher cost to produce the document.

Prior to typing, the word processing specialist must use decision-making time to check or recall the specific style preferred by that author. Should the specialist get confused and choose the wrong format, the document must be revised, which adds keystroking time. Inconsistent formats used by a company communicate a lack of organization, which conveys less than a professional image. Both procedures manuals and training programs are unnecessarily long in order to explain and illustrate each format. Should several specialists be working on a multipage document that involves interfacing systems, coordination of the project is difficult. As time and labor increase so does the cost of the task.

Most word processing centers have developed standard formats for letters, memorandums, outlines, reports, and tables. A 1983 study of 74 companies that have had word processing equipment for at least 12 years revealed that 86 percent standardize the formats of their documents.

Benefits of Standardization

In contrast to customizing or varying the formats of documents, standardizing formats offers many benefits. Both decision-making time (mental effort) and keystroking time (physical effort) are reduced. The possibility of choosing an incorrect format is eliminated, for only one format is used for that type of document. Consistency increases the professional appearance of documents and, consequently, the image of the company.

Work flow is easier to coordinate, especially as word processing interfaces with other systems. Letters that are produced by merging computer master files with word processing text and then scanned for automatic sorting at the postal system are easier and less costly to produce if all three systems are compatible in format standards. A document being phototypeset is easier and faster to process if the source document (recorded on a word processor) is submitted in a format similar to that of the proposed typeset copy.

The trend is toward more blocked and simplified formats in order to enhance both human and machine capabilities. The reason is simple, yet interesting. One of the reasons word processors were invented was to facilitate the revision process. Yet on even the most sophisticated display word processors, the most difficult task is revision.

The more centering, tabulating, indenting, and punctuation within a document, the more complex is the revision process. For example, unnecessary periods not only require extra keystroking but also retard revision. On some word processors one can highlight an entire sentence by touching the period (terminal punctuation mark), which is time saving. By limiting the use of periods to decimal punctuation and terminal punctuation marks, both keystroking and revision are faster. Thus, efficient formatting limits the inclusion of features that retard revision or add to keystroking.

Objectives of Standardizing Formats

The following objectives in developing standard formats support word processing goals:

- Keep the amount of keystroking to a minimum.
- Avoid unnecessary centering, tabulating, indenting, and punctuating.
- Include as much text on a page as possible without making the page too full; use space wisely in order to minimize the amount of paper used.
- Be consistent within a document as well as among various types of documents.
- Be functional so that a particular feature of the format serves more than one purpose.
- Be compatible with other information processing subsystems.

The business letter (Figure 11-11), memorandum (Figure 11-12), outline (Figure 11-13), and the tables shown throughout this chapter all meet the objectives cited. Certain features of each are emphasized in the following sections.

Letter. The modern simplified letter shown in Figure 11-11 is functional and progressive. Its format has these advantages:

1 Keystroking and decision making are minimized.

    a All letters have the same margin settings and dateline position.
    b Blocked format eliminates tabulating.
    c Unnecessary periods after abbreviations and numbered items are eliminated. The inconsistency of periods in some abbreviations (such as 8 p.m., Mrs., and Blvd.) but not in others (such as 80 wam, 35 cps, ABC Corporation, and TROY NY 12180) is eliminated.
    d The military-style date eliminates the comma and separates numbers for easy reading.

2 The letter address is functional for using window envelopes.

    a By typing the date on Line 12, touching return 3 times, and beginning the letter address on Line 15, the typist can position the letter address for a standard window envelope.
    b Window envelopes save addressing envelopes and prevent letters and envelopes from being mismatched.

CHAPTER 11 Developing the System Controls 317

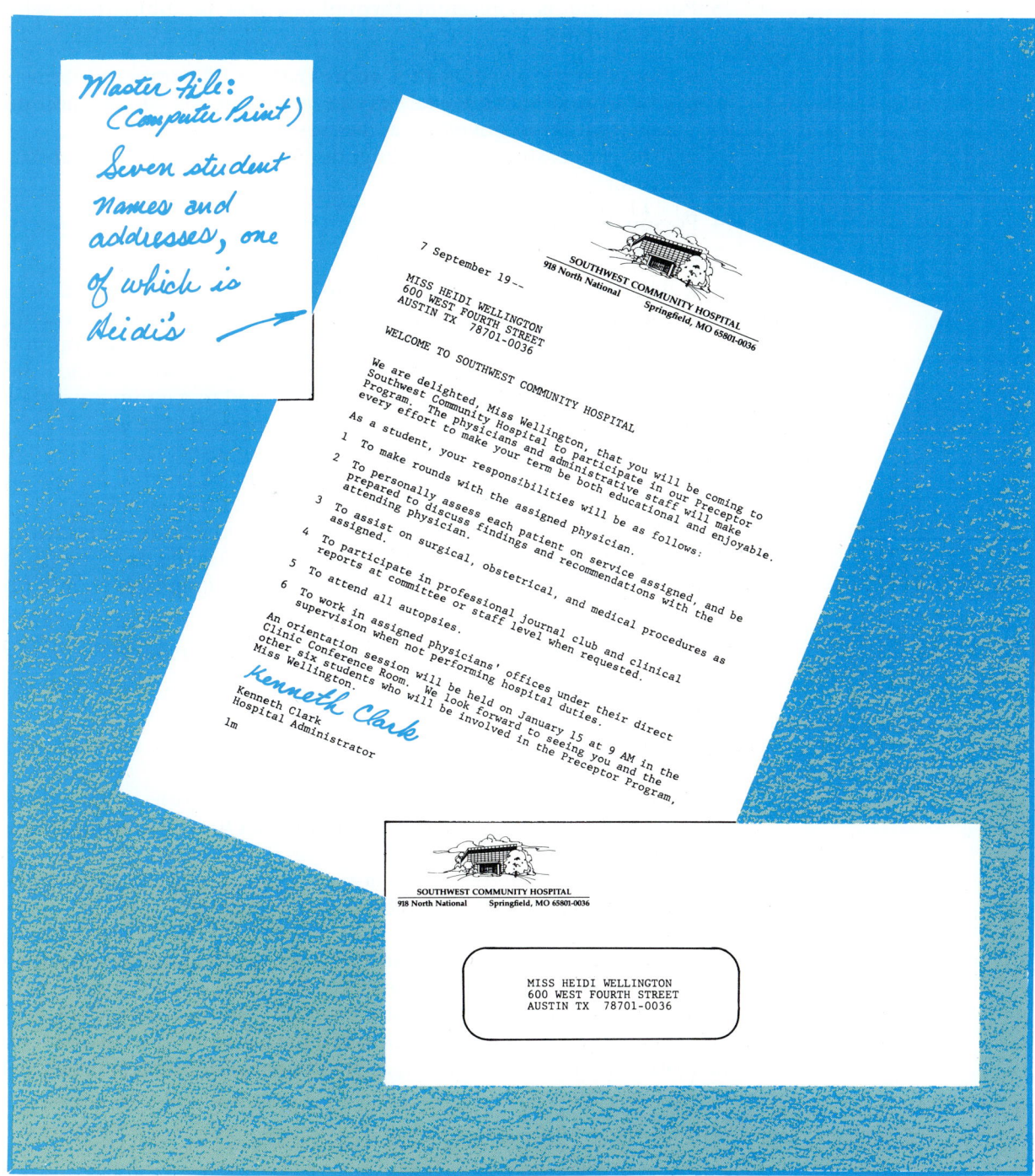

FIG. 11-11
MODERN SIMPLIFIED LETTER

3 Punctuation is consistent throughout and is compatible with other systems.

    a There are no periods after abbreviations or numbered items.
    b The United States Postal Service recommends all caps and no punctuation in envelope addresses.
    c Data processing master files generally omit periods after abbreviations.

4 Personalization is enhanced, which increases the "you approach" and goodwill of communication.

    a The name of the addressee is used in the beginning and near the end of the body, as though the letter writer were speaking to the addressee in person. This replaces the salutation and complimentary close of other letter styles. Also, it avoids the inappropriate "Dear" for letters addressed to a company rather than to a person and/or those that express bad news.
    b The informal, friendly touch is important, especially in this day of advanced technology. People want to be treated as human beings with feelings rather than as impersonal numbers.
    c The author's name is in initial caps, while the addressee's name in the letter address is in all caps. This applies the psychology of effective written communication that says emphasis should be on the reader rather than on the writer.

5 The subject line is functional as an aid to all personnel.

    a The author can capture the reader's attention and identify the theme of the message.
    b The administrative secretary finds it easier to file, retrieve, and sort correspondence.
    c The word processing specialist can assign a title to the document (which is explained in the next section, Managing Media Files).
    d The recipient of the letter knows the purpose of the letter without having to read through several paragraphs.

Memorandum. Many of the points cited about the modern simplified letter apply to simplified memorandums. In addition, the unnecessary words *to, from, date,* and *subject* are omitted. This not only saves keystroking time but also eliminates the need to align the type (print) with those words. Memorandums often apply the more informal approach of addressing the recipient by first name. The simplified memorandum is shown in Figure 11-12.

Outline. In a simplified outline, periods are omitted after the numbers and letters. By omitting periods the typist saves keystroking and

CHAPTER 11   Developing the System Controls 319

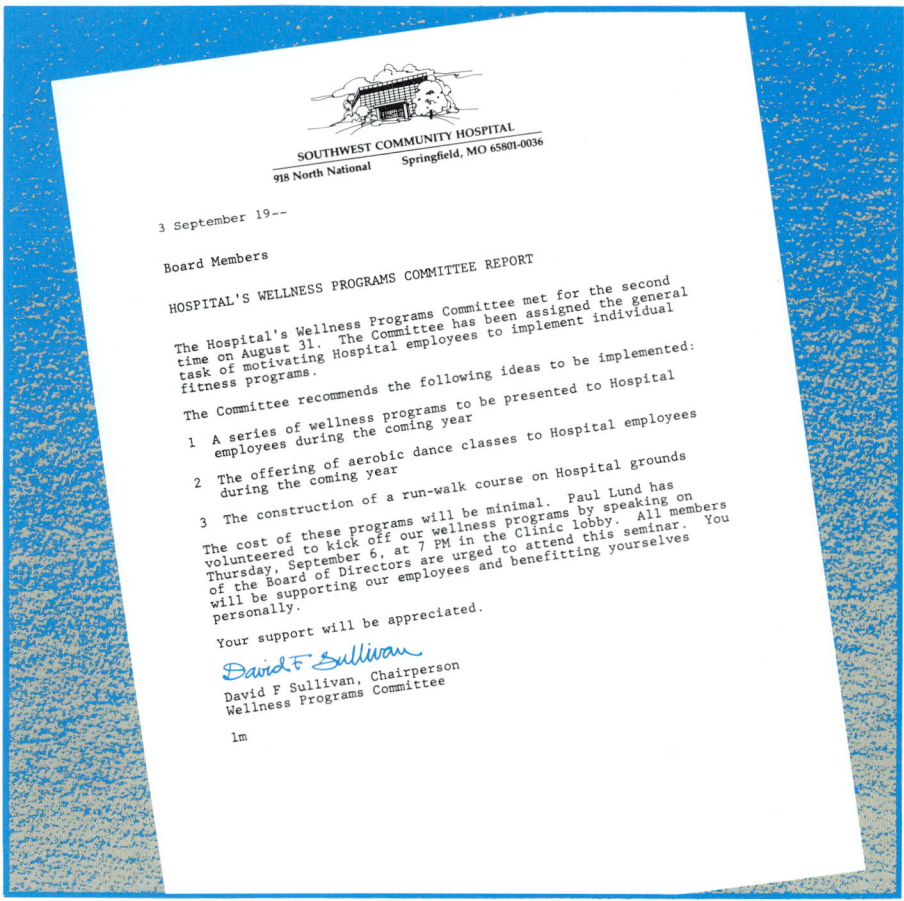

FIG. 11-12
MODERN SIMPLIFIED
MEMORANDUM
As in the modern simplified letter, the capitalized subject line allows for easy filing and retrieval of the document.

space (and therefore maximizes the amount of text to the page). Without the numerous periods, the document has a clean and neat appearance that is easy to read as illustrated in Figure 11-13.

MANAGING MEDIA FILES

As information continues to explode, the number of documents produced increases to the point that file management becomes extremely important. How can one document among possibly 150 that were produced in one day be located? In the administrative support area, one would go to the file cabinets (or shelves) to retrieve a paper copy or a microfiche card. In the correspondence support (document production) area, one would go to the magnetic media files to retrieve a diskette or to access hard disk storage. Just as paper files have to be filed

FIG. 11-13
MODERN SIMPLIFIED OUTLINE
Periods are omitted in this outline format to save keystroking and space.

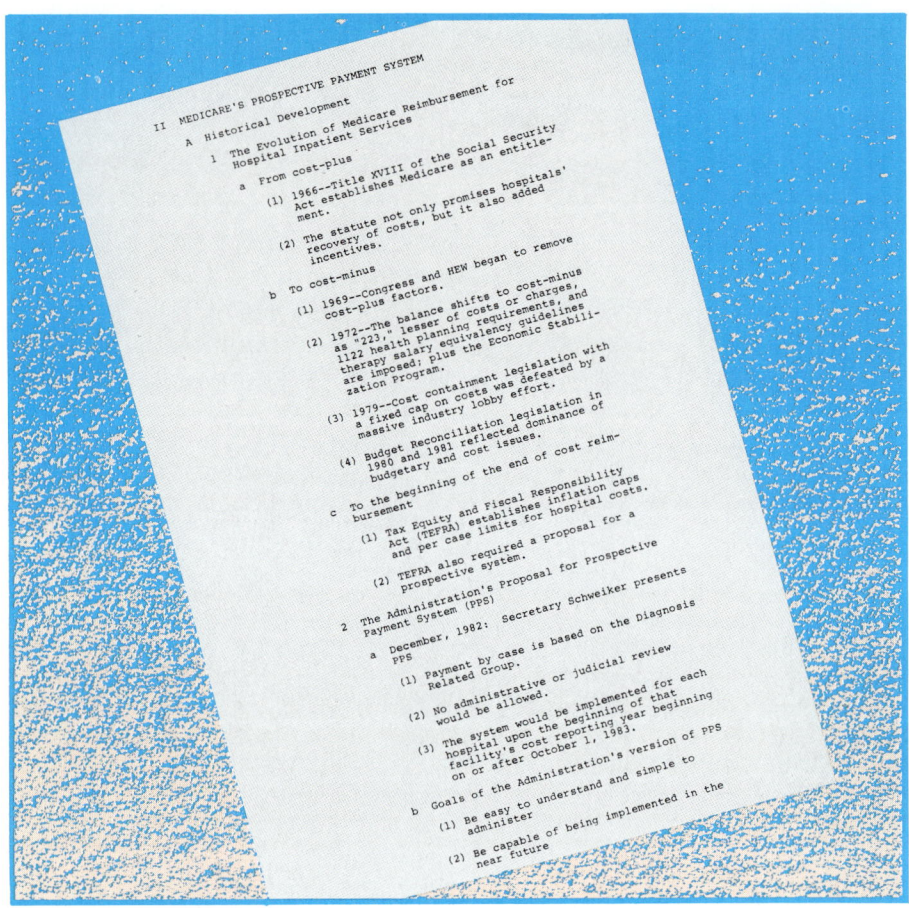

according to a system, so do documents that are stored on a diskette or disk.

Diskette Media

Most standard diskettes can store about 75 pages (not 75 documents, for each document might have two or more pages). Should the work area have 50 diskettes, there would be 3,750 pages to manage.

As a document is recorded on a word processor, it is either automatically given an identification number by the machine, or the operator assigns a **label** (or name) by keying that word or number. This depends on the brand of equipment. However, for all word processors the space for an identification number or label is generally limited to no more than ten characters.

Another space, which is longer, allows the operator to give the document a description or **title**. This could be the addressee's name or the

document label name of a document

document title short description of a document; longer than a label subject line of a letter; it could be the title of a report or table. Calling up the index of documents (Volume Table of Contents) onto the screen enables the operator to review the labels and descriptions of all documents that have been recorded. The index can be printed, as shown in Figure 11-14, and filed with the diskette.

index of documents gives labels and titles of all documents that have been recorded

Disk Media

Since hard disks have the capacity to store volumes of pages, storage is divided into more manageable areas. Just as a city is divided into blocks, which are subdivided into resident lots with respective house numbers, hard disks have a similar address system. The disk is the "city" which is divided into smaller units called **directories** or **libraries** (depending on the vendor's vocabulary)—the "blocks." Each directory or library then contains a number of documents. Just as one residence address might house several occupants, one document address (label or name) might have several pages.

directory/library unit of storage on a hard disk; can store a number of documents

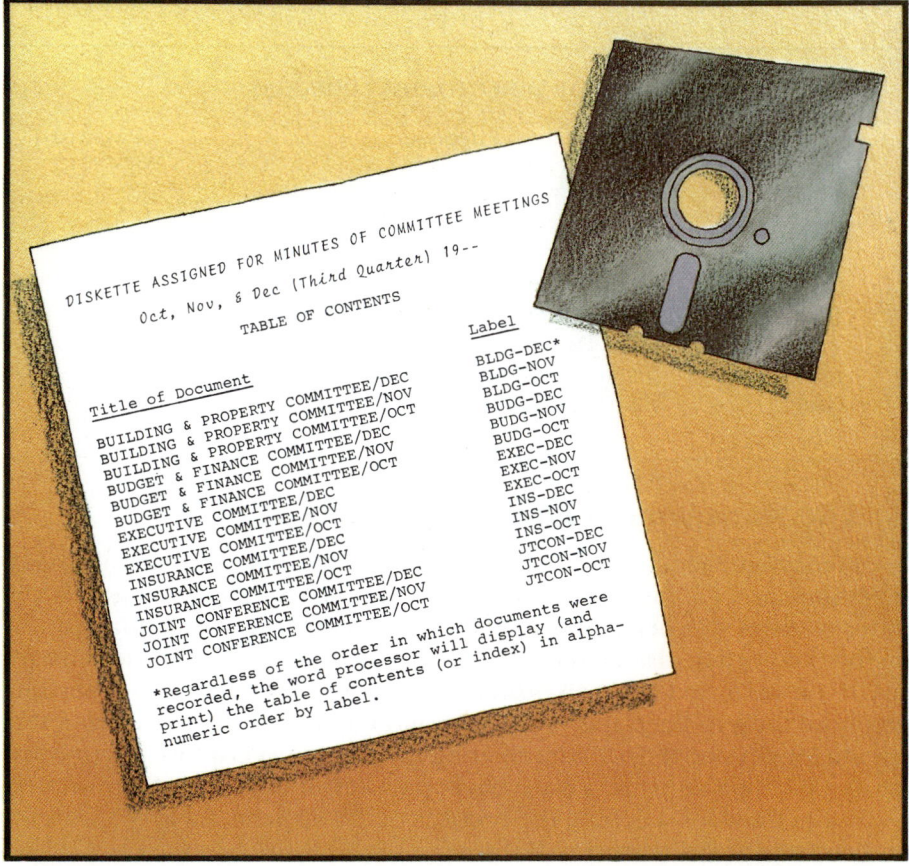

FIG. 11-14
INDEX OF DOCUMENTS
The index of documents lists both the title and the label for each document that has been recorded.

password security feature; allows limited access to a directory/library

The act of labeling and adding a descriptive phrase is the same for hard disks as for floppy diskettes. What is unique to a hard disk is managing the directories/libraries. Each directory/library might contain what one would typically file on one diskette. The directory/library must be set up with a code (short label); on most systems codes are limited to no more than three or four characters. In addition, the directory/library can be protected for confidentiality with a **password**. Only the operators who know the password can access that respective directory/library.

A potential hazard of passwords occurs during emergency situations when an authorized operator is not present. For example, a document could have been sent to a printer without completing the command to have it printed. To power down the system (turn it off) requires accessing the directory/library code and clearing the printer, for which the password must be known. Thus, a record of directory/library codes and their respective passwords must be maintained by a responsible lead word processing specialist as well as the supervisor of the system. An example of a directory/library cross-reference file is shown in Figure 11-15.

FIG. 11-15
DIRECTORY CROSS-REFERENCE FILE
In case of emergency, a record of the password for each directory file should be maintained by at least two competent individuals.

INDEX OF DIRECTORIES/LIBRARIES

Directory Name	Purpose	Password
ACC	Accounting Department	
ANN	Annual Report	
BDD	Board of Directors' Meetings	
COM	Minutes of Committee Meetings	RDM
COR	Correspondence (letters and memos)	
LEG	Legal Department	LDT
MKT	Marketing Department	
NAA	Name and Address File	

File Management Functions

Managing media files includes many functions. Among the major functions are: (1) assigning document labels, (2) composing descriptions or titles, (3) designing and setting up the format of standard documents and other master files, (4) deciding which types of documents are to be recorded on each diskette or directory/library, (5) determining how long to keep the recordings, (6) deleting the documents that are no longer needed, (7) duplicating files onto diskettes for other operators, (8) duplicating files onto backup diskettes (to protect against possible loss), and (9) keeping the records of the Volume Table of Contents of diskettes and directories/libraries.

CHAPTER 11 Developing the System Controls — 323

File management procedures are vital to the control of information. Each word processing system is unique, which means that the magnetic media file system must be custom designed. Points to consider when setting up a magnetic media file system are:

- The paper file system of your company
- The type of business
- The brand and model of word processing equipment
- The length of time recorded documents must be saved
- The organization of word processing services—center, minicenter, or single-person operation
- The number of authors and/or departments being served

Proper Care of Magnetic Media

Magnetic media are quite sensitive to mishandling. Improper care causes errors, data loss, warpage, and premature wear. The following procedures will ensure accurate recordings and maximum life span of diskettes:

1. Do not bend or fold diskettes.
2. Do not stack diskettes or stack materials on top of diskettes. Too much weight on a diskette causes warpage.
3. Do not touch exposed areas of diskettes with your fingers. Skin oils attract dust and other foreign particles. Handle the diskette only by the plastic jacket.

A diskette should be handled only by its plastic jacket.

4 Do not eat, drink, or smoke while handling or using diskettes.

5 Store diskettes in the protective envelope when not in use. They should be stored vertically (standing on their edges).

6 Store diskettes in cool, dry places. Keep chemical solvents away from the storage area. Avoid direct sunlight and radiators.

7 Do not lay diskettes on top of a terminal, CPU, or printer—devices that generate heat (causing warpage) or that are magnetic fields (causing text to be altered or destroyed). Do not place magnetic objects near the diskette.

8 Do not write on the jacket of a diskette when the diskette is inside or on the identification label or index after it has been attached to the diskette. The pressure of writing with a ballpoint pen or pencil can scratch the diskette. Use a felt-tip pen only. It is better to prepare the label and index before attaching them to the diskette.

9 Use pressure-sensitive labels with nontransferable adhesive. Do not add layers of labels. Do not use erasers.

10 Do not use alcohol thinners or cleaning fluids to clean diskettes, nor should they be placed near diskettes.

11 Do not attach rubber bands or paper clips to the diskette.

12 Date the labels when media are first used. Replace frequently used diskettes at least every two years.

Pencils and ballpoint pens should not be used to label a diskette. Only felt-tip pens should be used.

CHAPTER 11 Developing the System Controls

WRITING OFFICE MANUALS

Have you ever been in one of these two situations? (1) You are learning to operate a new machine by wading through a training manual, and you cannot find the answer to the problem you are experiencing. (2) As a new employee in a company, you are performing a task for which you need help. Since there is no procedures manual, you interrupt another worker to get help or you incorrectly guess how it should be done and make a mistake. Both of these situations can be avoided by well-written, functional manuals.

Types of Manuals

Office manuals come in three varieties—reference manuals, procedures manuals, and training manuals. A **reference manual** gives information that is frequently sought. An example would be a compilation of the form letters that are stored on magnetic media. A **procedures manual** gives step-by-step instructions and illustrations on how to perform a task, such as transcribing a letter or dictating a two-column table. A **training manual** explains how to operate a machine, such as a word processor or a dictation machine.

reference manual gives information that is frequently sought

procedures manual gives step-by-step instructions on how to perform a task

training manual explains how to operate a machine

Who uses office manuals? As you can imagine from the examples given, office manuals are needed by all types of word processing personnel—authors, administrative secretaries, word processing specialists, and supervisors. Office manuals should be customized and designed according to the needs of the company. One company's manual might combine reference guides, instructions on how to operate equipment, and procedures for performing a particular task all within one booklet. Another company might print information that is needed by all personnel of the company in one reference manual. The contents of the reference manual might include the company organization chart; names, room numbers, and telephone extension numbers of personnel; standard formats of documents; established priorities; turnaround goals; and media retention schedules.

Purposes of Office Manuals

Office manuals help employees do their work correctly, efficiently, and uniformly. New and temporary employees do not have to interrupt others as often with questions. Should the production of a long document be shared by several people or offices, consistency is directed. Office manuals aid in training employees and shorten the length of training sessions. When people know how the company expects them to perform, morale is maintained. A well-designed, composed, and formatted manual has a positive effect on the quality and quantity of work produced. Office manuals also help supervisors delegate tasks, measure work, and write job descriptions.

Techniques for Producing Effective Office Manuals

Why are some manuals never used? Why is it difficult to find needed information in these manuals? A manual that is organized illogically, written in paragraph format, and presented without helpful illustrations will hardly be used. Employees do not have time to dig for the information, and they are frustrated when they cannot find the help they need. The following techniques are applied by writers who produce functional office manuals (with emphasis on procedures manuals and operator's training manuals):

1. Design it to be packaged in a loose-leaf binder with:

    a. Section dividers
    b. Table of contents with page notations
    c. Page numbers: 1.1, 1.2, 1.3, 2.1, 2.2; or 1a, 1b, 1c, 2a, 2b (for ease of updating and revising by inserting or deleting pages)

2. The cover should be attractive, bright, and durable; it should be easy to locate the manual on a desk or shelf.

3. Arrange information in logical steps and break down each task into manageable learning segments.

4. Write in outline form and/or playscript (see Figure 11-16). Use short phrases rather than complete sentences.

5. Use clear, concise language; use active verbs.

6. Add flowcharts, illustrations, and work samples. Position the illustrations on the same pages as the verbal information. Pictures also help to break up long stretches of words.

7. Show sample forms filled in with the proper information rather than blank.

8. Use a standard format. Once users become familiar with the style, they can locate information quickly.

9. Keep a record of distribution—who received the manual and when. As updates or revisions occur, they can be distributed to the right people promptly.

Office manuals should be periodically reviewed and revised. The users should be invited to make suggestions for improving each revision.

TRAINING PERSONNEL

Training programs exist for many of the same reasons as procedures manuals. They help employees to learn about the company and to perform their tasks with accuracy, consistency, and efficiency.

CHAPTER 11 Developing the System Controls

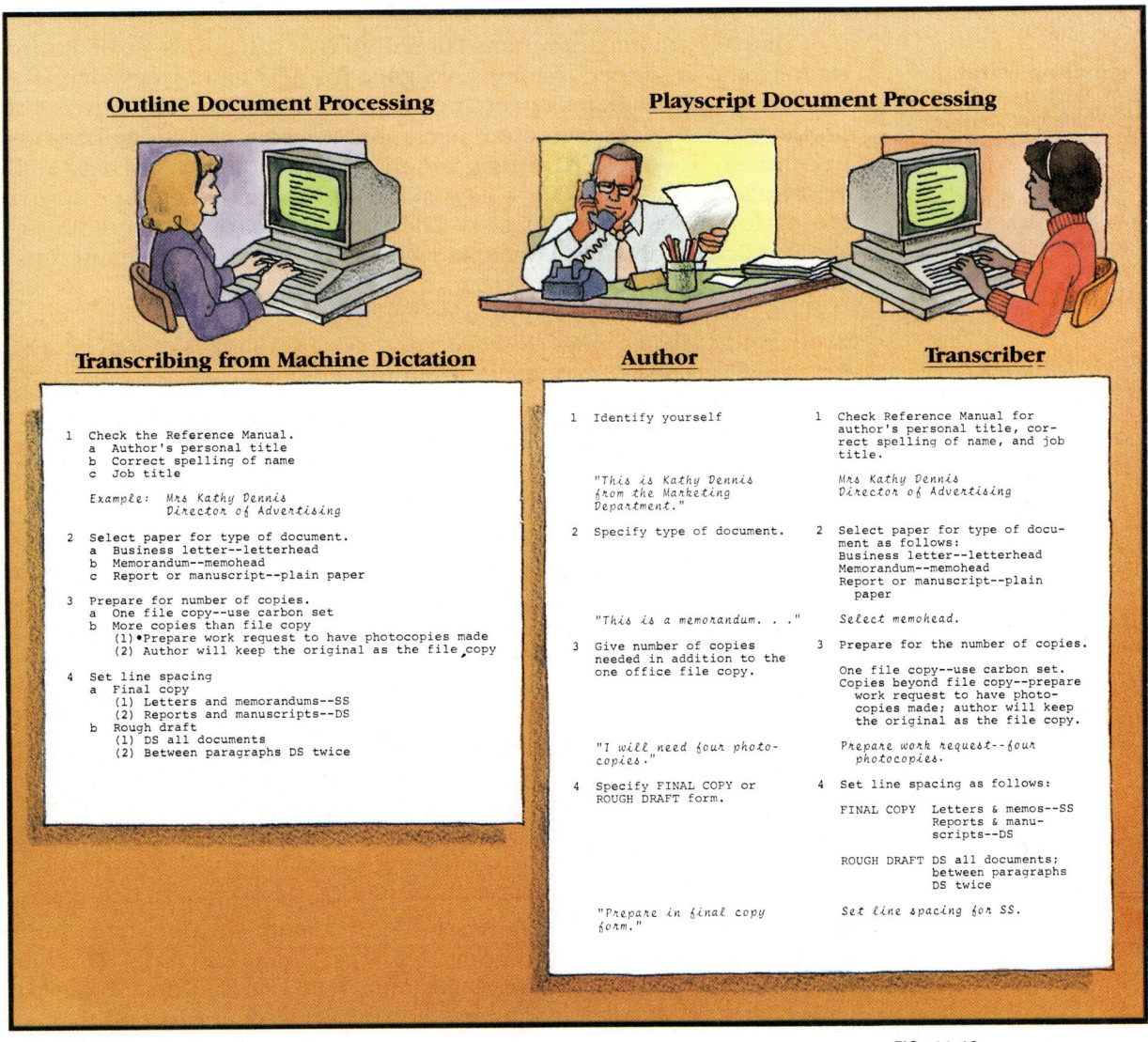

FIG. 11-16
OFFICE MANUALS
To be effective, an office manual should be set up in either an outline format or a playscript format.

Why are training programs important? Learning is much faster and more successful for the student when a teacher is present than when the student has to stumble through a book alone. Even the best designed and written procedures manual cannot be relied upon to do the teaching. A procedures manual assists in the training process and serves as a handy reference after training. As office technology continues to develop, new systems must be introduced. The nature of one's job is likely to change, and personnel must learn to use the new equipment as quickly as possible. Training is an ongoing function.

Types of Training Programs

Company training programs fall within two categories—orientation training and in-service training. Designed for new employees, **orientation training** programs cover such topics as company objectives, the products or services marketed, personnel policies, and fringe benefits. In contrast, **in-service training** programs teach employees (new and/or regular) how to operate a new machine, do a new task, or improve the performance of an old task. The programs also teach employees about office automation concepts (work flow, time management, integration of systems, and so forth).

Orientation training can be directed to a large group about as effectively as to a small group. However, in-service training is more effective for a small group of homogeneous employees.

orientation training programs for new employees to acquaint them with company policies and procedures

in-service training for all employees; teaches them how to do a new task or how to do an old task better

The Trainees and Trainers of In-Service Programs

All levels of personnel from top executives to entry-level employees can benefit from in-service training, as shown by Figure 11-17. In many word processing centers specialists are cross-trained. For each task that is performed within a group, at least two people are trained to do that task as experts. Should one person be absent, the other expert would be able to cover. Cross-training helps personnel learn new tasks, which prepares them for promotions.

The trainers might be departmental supervisors. Some companies have in-house trainers whose job is solely to conduct training programs. Resource people from colleges, universities, and vocational schools might be brought in to teach particular topics. Outside consultants might perform training as part of the implementation process. Employees might be sent to a public or private institution that offers a course on the needed topic(s).

Vendors are limiting the amount of personal training they will supply with the purchase of equipment. Most vendors charge for training additional personnel beyond one operator per workstation. Teacher-led training is being replaced by self-paced instructional materials (books, tapes, slides, and diskettes). Thus, the ability to conduct in-house training is important.

How to Train

Training sessions should be held in a location that is away from the trainees' work stations. Full attention can then be directed to learning. An effective trainer utilizes the following techniques so that trainees not only learn the concept or skill but also enjoy the experience:

1. Prepare the trainee to be ready and willing to learn.
   - Set up goals that are achievable.
   - Create an interest in the topic.

CHAPTER 11 Developing the System Controls 329

PARTICIPANTS	POSSIBLE TOPICS
Authors	Operating dictation equipment Dictating by machine Organizing work and managing time Preparing work requests Using proofreader's marks to indicate changes Submitting priority documents
Word Processing Supervisors	Promoting teamwork Developing procedures manuals Training personnel Evaluating employees Preparing production reports Conducting staff meetings
Administrative Support Secretaries	Preparing documents to be microfilmed Processing the mail Receiving and transferring telephone calls Organizing the work station Dictating routine correspondence Preparing work requests
Word Processing Specialists	Operating new word processors Reviewing language mechanics Acquiring technical vocabulary Formatting documents Managing media files Logging work and summarizing daily production

FIG. 11-17
IN-SERVICE TRAINING
Discussion topics for in-service training programs are determined by the nature of the participants' jobs.

- Show how the trainee will benefit from learning the task or operation by relating it to the job.
- Go from simple to complex applications, providing a constant challenge.

2 Teach the right way first.
- Know your subject matter—how to do the task or operate the equipment.
- Prepare a lesson plan.
- Present material in a logical, step-by-step sequence.
- Keep learning segments short; cover only one or two points or features at a time.
- Do not bluff or guess if you do not know an answer.

3 Make learning experiences vivid.
- Use emphasis in voice and gestures; show enthusiasm.
- Demonstrate each step that the trainee is to do: (1) Tell what is

going to be learned, (2) show how it is done, and (3) have the trainee do it.
- Illustrate with visual aids.
- Use the procedures manual and/or prepare handouts so that trainees have a means of reviewing.
- Use examples from your company's work to enhance the transfer of training to the job.

4 Provide purposeful repetition.
- Repeat important points in several ways.
- Summarize frequently.
- Provide trainee application; have the trainee do it.
- Give additional practice assignments.
- Utilize quizzes that cover the main points; this reinforces the information for the trainee and gives feedback to the trainer.

5 See that the learning experience is satisfying to the trainee.
- Assure that each person will attain some measure of success.
- Teach on the level of the trainees; use terms and examples they understand.
- Fit the application to the needs of the trainees.
- Praise improvements. Be generous with praise.
- Use individual charts so the trainees can monitor their own progress.

A successful training program dispels fears, shows employees how the new concept or skill will help them, and convinces them that the new way is superior to the old way.

You have studied ten procedures that lead to efficient, cost-effective word processing systems. Only with system controls can people and machines perform at their maximum potential.

DISCUSSION QUESTIONS AND CASE PROBLEM

DISCUSSION QUESTIONS

1 What general purpose do procedures for control serve in a word processing system?

2 Compared to a traditional office system, how should a word processing system process paperwork? Give five goals.

CHAPTER 11 Developing the System Controls 331

3 Do each of the ten procedures for control apply only to document preparation functions? Qualify your answer.

4 Why might the cost of a 200-word letter be $7 in one company but $14 in another company?

5 Identify five techniques of formatting that enable one to produce a document most efficiently.

6 For each of the ten procedures for control used in word processing systems, give one reason why that procedure benefits the system.

CASE PROBLEM

The following situations can occur easily in offices that do not have well-developed procedures for control. For each situation, what is the basic procedure that should be developed to prevent the problem?

a Two authors approach a document specialist at the same time with work. Each wants a document typed right away.

b A letter to a potential customer is printed at a slant and has a misspelled word; it is mailed with this appearance.

c An author phones the word processing center to see if the report being typed has been finished. The supervisor does not know who was assigned the job or if it has been done yet.

d Office support personnel are scolded for not getting more work done on the new word processors. The support personnel fear the machines and are frustrated because it takes so long to fumble through the vendor's training manual.

e Management will not approve either the purchase of new word processors or the hiring of additional personnel, for there are no facts upon which to base a decision.

f A prerecorded form letter cannot be found on the diskette.

g Office support personnel fill out work requests in different ways; some do not know how to number them, so they guess incorrectly.

h Without knowing when to expect their work to be done, authors frequently contact the word processing supervisor to see if the job is done yet. Word processing specialists are inconsistent in getting certain tasks done within a certain time.

i Some office support personnel feel that salary increases are unfair; evaluation of office support services does not seem to relate to the quantity or quality of work performed.

j An entire letter has to be retyped because the document specialist misjudged the length of the letter and forgot that this author uses a different letter style.

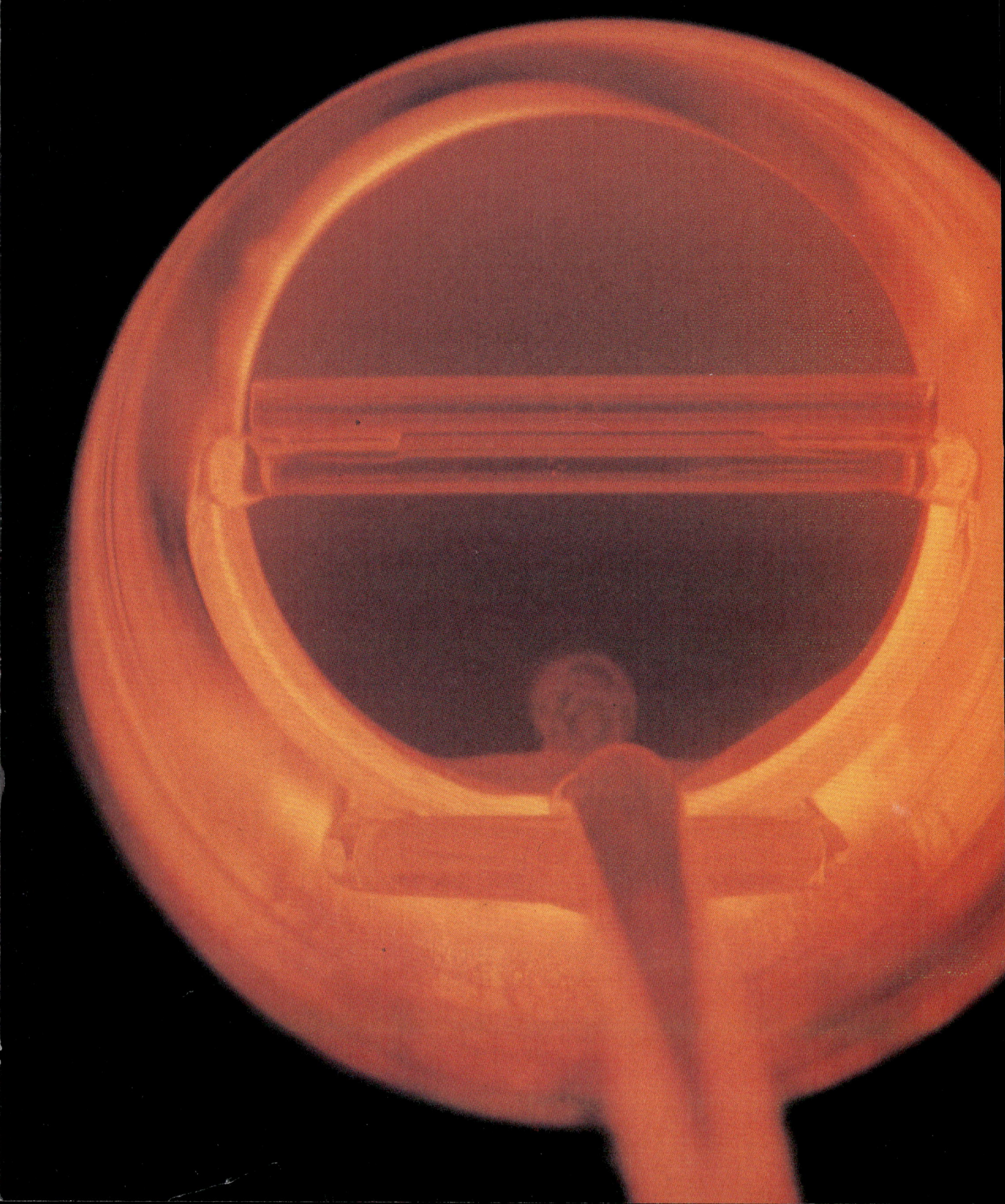

Part 4
INFORMATION PROCESSING IN ACTION

Chapter 12 Managing the System

CHAPTER OBJECTIVES:

Name four basic responsibilities of a word processing manager.

Explain the word processing manager's roles in serving each of the three groups of people within the company.

Describe ongoing functions of a manager after implementation of the system.

Identify effective techniques of supervising word processing personnel and working with users and upper management.

The success or failure of a word processing system pivots on the manager (supervisor). In addition to having a thorough knowledge of word processing concepts, this individual should be able to get along well with all levels of personnel and should be a good leader. The manager is a liaison person who sees that the work of the authors is processed efficiently by the word processing specialists. Because the position involves coordinating and supervising, it may have the title of manager, coordinator, or supervisor of word processing (or of administrative services).

First, this chapter will review the responsibilities of the manager. For those responsibilities that have not been discussed in this book previously, a more detailed coverage is given. Then, the qualities and techniques of effective management will be discussed.

RESPONSIBILITIES OF THE MANAGER

Since a word processing system could be centralized (a large center), partially decentralized (minicenters), or totally decentralized, a manager's role could vary from one company to another. However, the basic responsibilities would include:

1 Developing and modifying procedures

2 Selecting and maintaining machines and software

3 Designing and improving the environment

4 Coordinating people
   a Supervising word processing specialists
   b Assisting authors
   c Reporting to upper management

From the list you should note four key words—*people, machines, procedures,* and *environment*. Yes, effective management coordinates the four basic parts of a word processing system. In this chapter there will be more emphasis on working with *people*, since many of the other responsibilities have already been introduced.

Developing and Modifying Procedures

Upon implementation of a new system, certain procedures are developed (as described in Chapter 11). However, as conditions change the procedures must be modified. Every attempt must be made to improve machine utilization and to increase employee productivity. Also, the word processing manager must work in cooperation with other subsystem managers for efficient information processing.

Two major problems that offices face are (1) the unnecessary proliferation of paper and (2) accumulated text on disks (or diskettes). As businesses grow, the amount of data and text to be processed grows. As the automated machines become more sophisticated, they can very easily duplicate and store more information on disks or diskettes. They can also produce paper documents so quickly that in many cases extras are prepared. Unnecessary extras add to the burden of processing mail, reading the mail, filing, and storing paper.

Managing Media Files. A strict document retention schedule should be established so that old documents are either erased (deleted from the disk or diskette) or transferred to a diskette for storage. Even the diskettes onto which text has been archived (stored) need to be on a retention schedule. Perhaps after two years the entire diskette can be erased and prepared for reuse. Another management responsibility is maintaining top security (confidentiality) of documents.

Managing Paper. Three management functions relate to controlling the amount of paper used and the time spent processing it. They include selecting and stocking supplies, designing and printing forms, and reproducing documents.

A word processing manager has four basic responsibilities: (a) coordinating people, (b) designing and improving the environment, (c) developing and modifying procedures, and (d) selecting and maintaining machines and software.

In word processing, a minimum number of paper weights and sizes should be used. The ideal situation would be to have one standard letterhead, one high-quality bond paper to match the letterhead in color and weight (for second pages of correspondence and for reports), a lower quality plain paper for rough drafts, and possibly onionskin paper for copies. Many companies choose to have the department name as part of the letterhead. Thus, the company must stock as many letterheads as there are departments. To include names of company officers and their titles (such as C. P. Lane, Vice President of Marketing) on the letterheads means that whenever there is change of personnel, the stock of that letterhead must be discarded. This practice not only wastes paper but also wastes time and effort in changing letterheads for the printer (especially for automatic sheet feeders). Another problem is that the printer may have to be adjusted whenever the size or weight of paper changes.

Envelopes, too, should be stocked to include only a minimum number of sizes and weights. Because envelopes have two to four thicknesses of paper within each as they feed through a printer, the printer often has difficulty processing envelopes. Window envelopes save the time and effort of addressing envelopes. They are becoming more popular for sending correspondence and forms (including checks).

Decisions made about the design and printing of forms should take into consideration the typewriter or printing device used to fill in the forms. In addition to keeping the size and weight of the paper standard, other features should be considered. For lines that require two or more positions for fill-ins, the positions should be arranged so that only a few tab stops throughout the form would be needed. In Figure 12-1 you can see how much easier and faster it would be to fill in the form on the top. Throughout an entire form there should be standard line spacing so that the operator can set the line spacing for single spacing, 1 1/2 spacing, or double spacing and not have to change it.

Any decisions about the color of the paper should take into consideration the photocopying process. White is always safe; however, colored paper helps forms to stand out for quick retrieval. Of the various colors available for stock, certain colors and shades (such as yellow and gold) do not photocopy clearly without shading the copy.

Forms should be dated so that old stock is not mistaken for new stock. Should a form include an address to be inserted in a window envelope, the position should enable a standard window envelope to be used if possible (so that special stock does not have to be ordered). You can see how word processing, photocopying, and typesetting systems must work together for functional forms management.

On some word processors, form-writing software is available, which eliminates the use of preprinted forms. The standard text and the fill-in text are merged on the screen and then printed at the same time on plain paper.

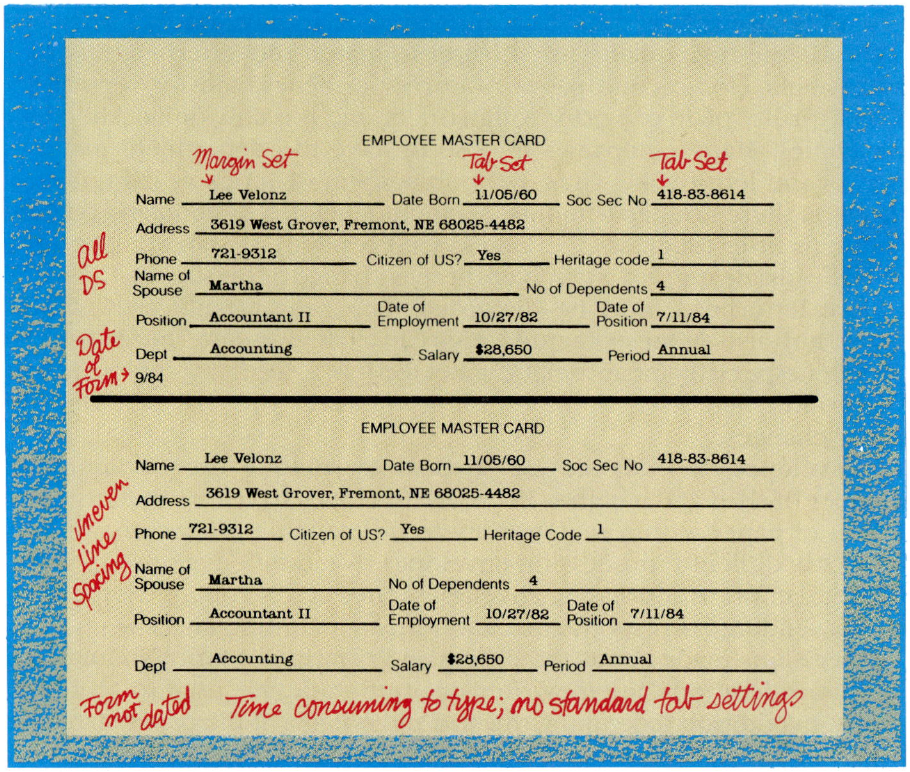

FIG. 12-1
DESIGNING A FORM
Office forms that need to be filled in should be designed to have standard line spacing and a minimum number of tab stops.

Reproducing documents may come under the direction of a word processing manager, especially in a decentralized layout of support services. Even in companies that have centralized but separated word processing and reproduction services, the word processing manager is involved. Every effort should be made to avoid unnecessary paper copying. The manager should encourage users to request copies for only the people who need them. For example, a meeting of 11 members, of whom 2 were absent, would necessitate only 3 copies of the minutes. A functional agenda enables those present to add discussion and decision notes. After the meeting, the filled-in agenda serves as a future reference to those who attended the meeting. Then the only people who need a copy of the minutes would be the chairperson (for the permanent files) and those who were absent. For the rest of the members a copy would be made only upon request.

Another photocopying waste is the time spent waiting in line at the copier. As Chapter 5 explained, the company could have an attendant operate the photocopier, thus eliminating the problem. In companies that do not have a full-time person to operate the photocopier(s), the manager of each department using the equipment should train at least two operators. In addition, a procedure needs to be developed to accommodate priority copying and to eliminate time wasted while employees wait in line at the copier. Ways to overcome the problem might be for the employee to: (1) check the number of people in line and the nature of their tasks; if there are two or more people or if the person at the copier is doing a long task, return to his or her work station; (2) anticipate delay and take other work (for example, proofreading) that could be done while waiting; and/or (3) accumulate several photocopying jobs (batching work) before making a trip to the copier.

Selecting and Maintaining Machines and Software

As Chapter 9 discussed, equipment selection is done when a system is implemented. This is only the first step of managing machines. The word processing manager has continual responsibility for keeping inventory and service records, maintaining and servicing machines, and reevaluating them (including software) in terms of meeting company needs.

Keeping Inventory and Service Records. As soon as a machine is delivered, an inventory card or sheet should be established for it. On one side would be the complete description of the machine—name; brand and model; serial number; company inventory number (shorter and easier to see than the serial number); date of purchase or lease agreement; purchase price or monthly leasing fee; date of installation; name, address, and phone number of the vendor; and names of a salesperson, a marketing support representative, and a service/repair person (including the addresses and/or phone numbers only if different from the vendor's). The installation date is necessary information, since the warranty period (normally 90 days) begins at that time. During the warranty period the vendor replaces or repairs defects without charge.

On the back side of the card or on the lower part of a sheet should be a record of service calls and repairs. If the equipment is under service contract, the amount of the monthly or annual fee should be listed. Otherwise, the cost of each service call should be recorded. Also, a record should be kept on how soon the service person responded to a call. An example of an inventory and service record is shown in Figure 12-2.

Maintaining and Servicing Machines. By properly maintaining equipment, the manager will have to make fewer requests for service and the life of the machine can be extended. The first precaution is to read the operator's manual carefully and to follow the instructions that are given. Upon reporting a machine malfunction to a service person, the person requesting service should expect to be quizzed about the nature of the problem. This is the service person's screening step—to determine whether it is a machine problem or an operator error which caused the machine to do something unexpected.

FIG. 12-2
INVENTORY AND SERVICE RECORD
An inventory and service record should contain complete information about a piece of equipment, including model number, serial number, and history of repair.

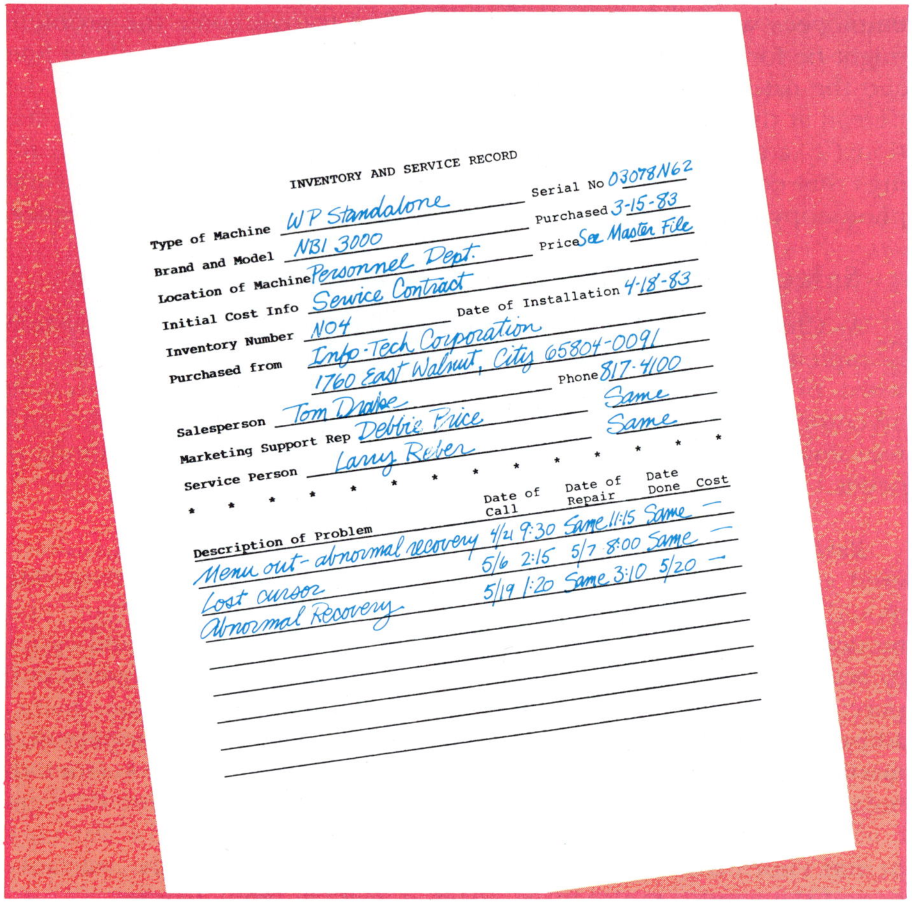

INVENTORY AND SERVICE RECORD

Type of Machine WP Standalone — Serial No 03078N62
Brand and Model NBI 3000 — Purchased 3-15-83
Location of Machine Personnel Dept. — Price See Master File
Initial Cost Info Service Contract
Inventory Number N04 — Date of Installation 4-18-83
Purchased from Info-Tech Corporation
1760 East Walnut, City 65804-0091
Phone 817-4100
Salesperson Tom Drake — Same
Marketing Support Rep Debbie Price — Same
Service Person Larry Reber

* * * * * * * * * * * * * *

Description of Problem	Date of Call	Date of Repair	Date Done	Cost
Menu out-abnormal recovery	4/21 9:30	Same 11:15	Same	—
Lost cursor	5/6 2:15	5/7 8:00	Same	—
Abnormal Recovery	5/19 1:20	Same 3:10	5/20	—

Warranties are contingent on proper use of the machines in accordance with the manufacturers' instructions. The warranties may be voided if the environment is not up to recommendations (as described in Chapter 10), if the user mishandles the equipment, or if repairs are made by an unauthorized third party.

Printers are especially vulnerable to misuse. Dropping a paper clip, spilling a beverage, or allowing dust and small pieces of paper to accumulate within the printer can result in serious damage. Any of these conditions can cause moving parts to become clogged and not work properly. Machines should be wiped with a damp, static-free cloth at least once a week. They should be covered when not in use. In addition, smoking should not be allowed in the machine areas. The manager is responsible for seeing that the work area and the equipment are kept clean and neat. Whatever is not accomplished by regular custodial services might be assigned to word processing personnel on a rotation basis.

When turning on a word processor, the operator should wait two or three minutes to give the unit a chance to warm up. The electrical plug should never be pulled while the machine is in operation. Important text might be lost, or the disk system could be damaged.

Reevaluating Equipment and Software. As work loads increase and production records justify the addition of new equipment, the manager must reevaluate the entire system. Can the current machines be updated with new software? Should the current machines be retained and new ones added? Should the current machines be replaced by faster, more sophisticated machines? In any event, the manager must first compile from production records the facts that justify what is needed. With top management's approval, equipment is then selected. Equipment selection may require an adjustment of procedures, environment, and personnel.

Designing and Improving the Environment

Assuming that the word processing environment was initially designed properly, the manager then is responsible for maintaining and improving it. Work areas can be personalized by employees through the use of bulletin boards, artwork, and plants. The employees should be given the opportunity to select these items and to care for them.

Should worker complaints or machine repair records indicate that the environment is not conducive to efficient work, the manager must initiate action. It is more difficult to correct something (for example, to install air conditioning or change the wiring) after the office is occupied than before. Thus, every effort should be made to plan the environment properly in the beginning.

Adding or replacing equipment often requires rearranging the work area. Only in offices where the word processing area was initially planned with extra space in the event of expansion is it easy for the manager to redesign the work area. In most cases, unfortunately, one has to squeeze more machines and people into an area that has no room for expansion. Obviously an open-office area equipped with modular furniture and partitions is easier to rearrange than a fixed-wall office area with standard office furniture.

Employees should be invited to give suggestions for improving the environment, for environment has an influence on job satisfaction. The manager can then evaluate the ideas and involve the employees in implementing worthwhile ideas.

Supervising Word Processing Specialists

As a manager/supervisor of word processing specialists, you would be expected to do the following:

1 Organize support services and design career paths.

2 Determine job titles and write job descriptions.

3 Interview and approve applicants for hiring.

4 Evaluate employees.

5 Provide job enrichment.

6 Conduct orientation programs and staff meetings.

7 Handle complaints and problems.

Since Items 1 through 4 are covered in Chapter 13, they are merely introduced here. We shall now discuss in greater detail Items 5 through 7, the responsibilities of a manager once the system has been implemented.

Providing Job Enrichment. A competent manager provides the incentive that motivates employees to work to their optimum potential. Realizing that not all people respond to the same motivational techniques, the manager should initiate various ones. Managers should also remember that career goals differ among people.

One way of motivating employees is by charting their daily or weekly performance and discussing the results.

One motivational technique is to have the specialists chart their individual performance daily and/or weekly. For example, a chart might include lines or pages produced and number of errors found. Individual charts should be kept privately by the word processing specialist (and manager). A similar type of chart could mark the performance of a team of workers on a weekly basis; this chart could be placed on the bulletin board.

Each week the top producer could be acknowledged by announcing an "employee of the week" in the company newsletter. The "employee of the month" could be presented a gift certificate, a plant, or a cash bonus. Offering the group a picnic or luncheon for reaching a certain performance level (pages per month, minimum errors) might motivate team effort. Charts, awards, and publicity are effective motivators, for most people like to be winners. It is important to reward outstanding performance so that the incentive and morale of those workers will not drop.

Cross-training is a technique that has a dual purpose. It enables employees to learn new tasks, and it assures the manager that in the event of an employee absence there is a backup person to perform that task or function. Cross-training might occur within one work area or department, whereby the employee is trained to perform another function. (For example, a document production specialist might learn to do an administrative support function.) Or, the employee might cross over to another department. Learning new job functions provides some challenge and variety of work; the more an employee knows about all the departmental functions of the company, the better are that person's chances for advancement. Having at least two people able to perform any job function helps the manager distribute work evenly during peaks and valleys, as well as cover all job functions in the event of employee absences.

Other incentives that some companies offer are profit-sharing plans and options to purchase company stock. These incentive programs help employees develop loyalty to the company.

Special times of the year, such as holidays, the end of the fiscal year, or the renewal of contracts afford excellent opportunities to acknowledge an employee's contribution to the company. Some companies give cash or gifts. Regardless of whether or not a token gift is given, the manager should compose an individual letter of appreciation to each employee. An example is given in Figure 12-3.

Conducting Orientation Programs and Staff Meetings. The manager should conduct orientation programs and staff meetings to keep lines of communication open and to inform employees about new advancements. These group meetings should be planned so that they are functional and utilize a minimum amount of time.

In smaller organizations, it is likely that only one person might join

**FIG. 12-3
EMPLOYEE RECOGNITION
MESSAGE**
A letter of appreciation is a good way for a supervisor to acknowledge an employee's contributions.

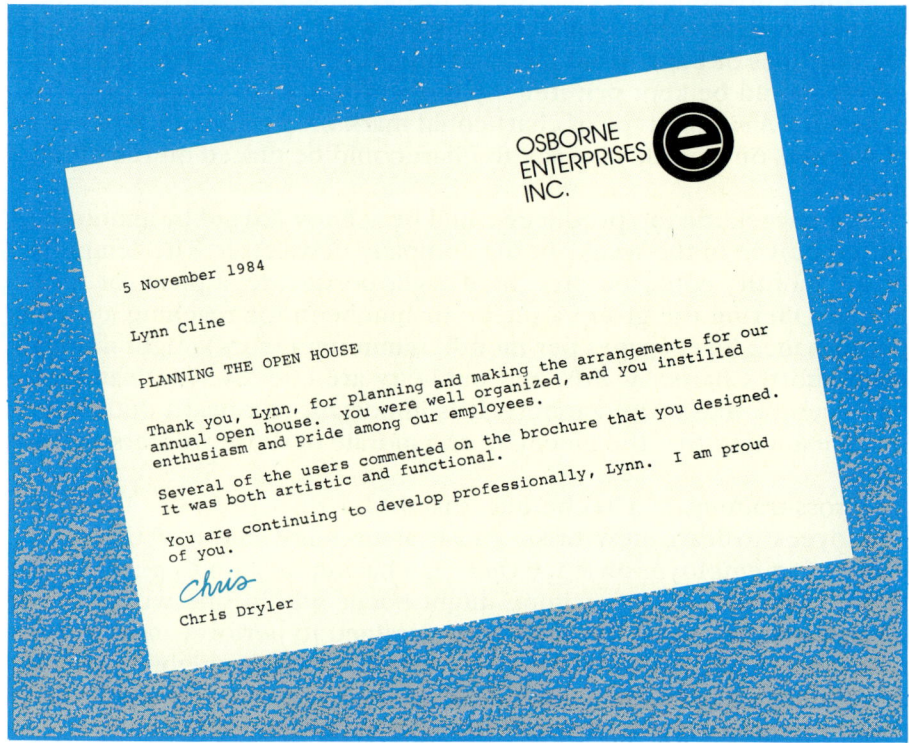

the office team at a time. Too often that individual learns the job responsibilities and procedures in a hit-or-miss fashion. The manager should have a standard list of items to explain and demonstrate to new employees. Of course, reference manuals, procedures manuals, and operator's training manuals are helpful.

Staff meetings are scheduled either on a regular monthly basis or on a flexible basis to be called when needed. Whichever the case, the supervisor should prepare an agenda, as shown in Figure 12-4. An agenda provides a map that allows the meeting to stay on schedule and to proceed in a logical manner. The blank lines enable participants to fill in decisions. Information to be announced that employees must retain as a reference (for example, Item 5 in Figure 12-4) should be included in the agenda. This functional design enables the document to serve two purposes—as an agenda and as informal minutes of the meeting. Should an employee be absent from the meeting, the supervisor merely photocopies a filled-in agenda for that employee's information; no other photocopies are needed.

Staff meetings should not be scheduled during peak periods, such as mornings, Mondays, and Fridays. A Tuesday, Wednesday, or Thursday following the afternoon outgoing-mail deadline might be a good time. In a meeting, positive information should be given before problems are

CHAPTER 12   Managing the System   345

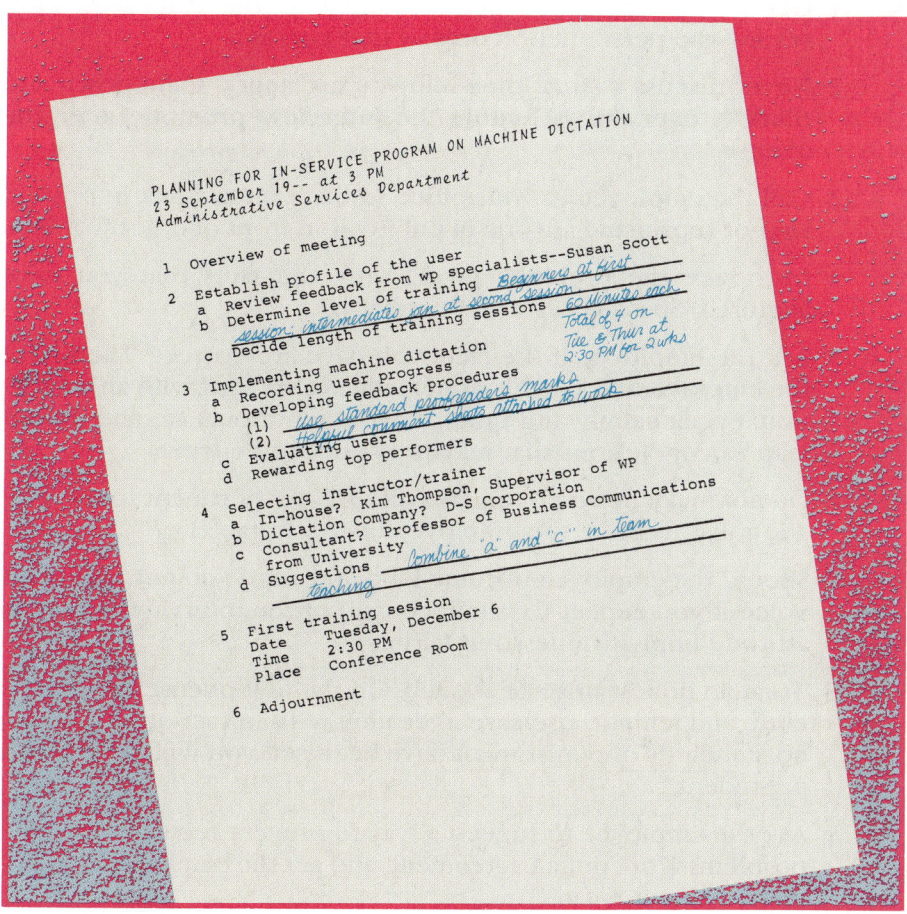

FIG. 12-4
AGENDA
An agenda should always be prepared and distributed before a meeting so that the meeting can proceed in a logical fashion.

presented to be discussed. The meeting should also close on a positive note. A staff meeting should start on time and end on time; it should take no longer than 50 minutes.

Three ways to lower morale are to allow a meeting to drag on, to accent on the negative rather than the positive, and to delegate an unrealistic amount of work to subordinates. There is a difference between involving people in discussions to get their ideas and delegating responsibilities that should be done only by the manager. Managers must distinguish between what to delegate and what to do themselves.

Handling Personnel Problems. There are occasions in any office that require a supervisor to reprimand an employee. In a word processing system, examples might include excessive absences, below-standard productivity, frequent personal phone calls during work periods, personality clashes with other workers, or theft of company supplies. The following steps are suggestions for handling employee problems:

1. Get facts as evidence before talking to the employee; also, review the personnel records of that person.

2. Never discuss a situation while you are angry. Calm down and think it over, but schedule the interview promptly after the offense.

3. Call the employee to your office so that you can talk in private. Do not reprimand anyone in public or in front of other workers.

4. Introduce the problem, giving only the facts that you have acquired. Speak quietly and cordially.

5. Ask the employee if the facts you have are correct. Then have the employee explain his or her side. Never start with an accusation. Speak calmly and quietly; avoid emotionalism and do not leap to conclusions that may prove not to be true.

6. Do not make personal remarks that are not pertinent to the situation just to make the employee uncomfortable.

7. Should the employee become loud and angry, do not raise your voice if you expect to retain control of the interview. Let your attitude imply firmness but fairness.

8. Treat an honest mistake as such. On the first offense, be considerate and lenient. Use care in dealing with infractions for which no standards of punishment have been set; you will be setting a precedent.

9. Ask the employee to suggest a way to prevent recurrence of the problem. Work out an agreement, and get the employee's confirmation that it is fair.

10. Assure the employee that your reaction is based on helping the company achieve its goals; it is not based on a personal like or dislike of the employee.

11. Schedule the employee for a progress review in about a month.

12. Assure the employee that you will make every effort to help him or her overcome the problem and that you have confidence in the employee's ability to correct the problem.

13. Record the incident and the interview in the employee's file.

14. At the follow-up interview, the employee's performance should be reviewed. If performance has improved, be sure to commend the employee. If the problem has continued, punitive action should be taken.

Minor infractions would not involve a formal 14-step plan. Instead, they would merely involve giving constructive criticism. Constructive criticism requires tact so that the receiver gets the message but at the same time feels that the manager is trying to help. Before attempting to give criticism, the manager can set the stage for acceptance by first praising the employee on something that has been done well. Figure 12-5 shows right and wrong ways to give criticism.

Wrong Way	Right Way
You are making entirely too many errors. Did you even proofread this letter?	When you proofread this letter, did you read it twice—once for content and once for mechanics?
You have too many misspelled words in this report. Did you even recognize that they might be misspelled when you typed them? After this, please check your dictionary or you will pay for your carelessness by having a low production rate.	You are to be commended for getting this report done within an hour. However, there are several misspelled words to be corrected. Were you confident of the spelling when you typed those words, or were you unsure? By checking the dictionary, you will catch them early in the process and increase your net production rate.
Here is another loose tape that you did not put away. Do you realize that it might have the president's dictation on it? If you don't start being more careful, you will never have a chance for a promotion.	You certainly have accomplished a variety of tasks today. Has this tape been transcribed? Every tape has important dictation; we would not want to lose someone's letter because of carelessness. Please follow through by putting away the tapes as soon as you have finished transcribing them.

FIG. 12-5
CONSTRUCTIVE CRITICISM
A supervisor must use tact when correcting employee problems. The comments should be helpful and positive.

Assisting Users

The word processing manager's function in relation to users is to see that their word processing needs are fulfilled with accuracy and efficiency. The manager serves a three-way function: salesperson, monitor, and teacher.

As a salesperson, the manager must continually sell the word processing system concept to users. Those who formerly had private secretaries but who now are served (along with other users) by a team of specialists are likely to resist change. They may feel a loss of status by no longer having a private secretary. They may resist changes in procedures. Such negative ideas should have been prevented by the initial stages of the feasibility study and by the implementation of the system.

However, selling the word processing concept is more than a one-time task; it takes continual effort to show enthusiasm for the system and to motivate users to cooperate.

The best way to sell users on the word processing system is to provide word processing services that are equal to or better than those provided by a private secretary. The progress of the system should be presented to users in such a way that they understand how the system has already benefited them.

Other techniques can be used to develop positive attitudes about word processing services. Some managers invite small groups of users to a conference room near the word processing center. Upon being welcomed and treated with refreshments, they are given an orientation to word processing services. In addition to being shown various ways that word processing has helped others in the company, they are given a tour of the facility so that they have a better understanding of how it operates. In companies that have small centers, the same approach can be used by taking one satellite group at a time. The manager needs to keep a record of all users who have attended these sessions to avoid omitting anyone. New people hired by the company should also be invited to tour the facilities as soon as their needs are determined.

Another selling technique is to initiate awards for "boss of the month" or "dictator of the week"; recognition for outstanding work gives users incentive to continue providing high-quality input. An award system often encourages employees.

Users usually are asked to help in establishing priorities so that they are involved in design procedures. They are then more likely to feel that

Left: If users are given a complete tour of and orientation to word processing facilities, they will most likely develop positive attitudes toward the services provided.

Right: Recognition of outstanding users motivates them to continue providing high-quality input.

they are being treated fairly. Sharing production records with users is another way to prove to users that "the new way works."

As a monitor, the manager must watch input carefully. By keeping records of authors' methods of input, the manager can detect whether machine dictation is used enough. If transcribers are having difficulty reading the author's longhand or understanding machine dictation, the manager must develop individual group in-service training sessions for both the transcribers and the authors. In this capacity the manager is a teacher. A helpful comment sheet, as shown in Figure 12-6, can be attached to work that is returned to authors. Users also may need to be encouraged and shown how to delegate work.

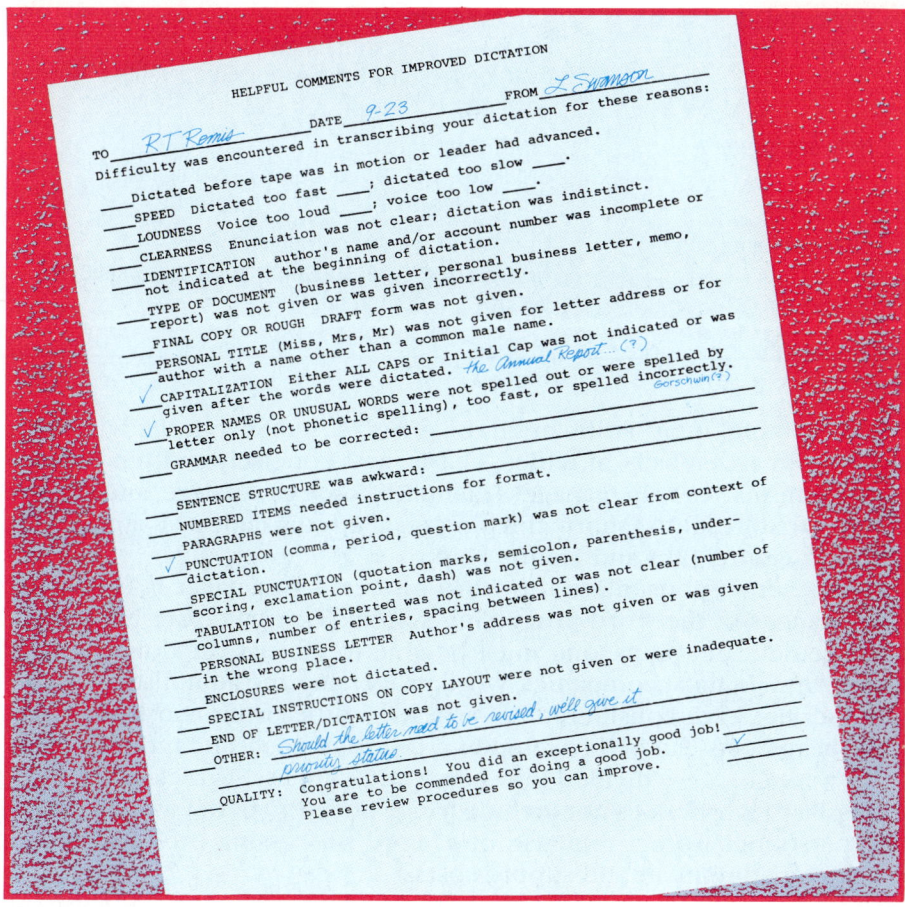

FIG. 12-6
IMPROVING DICTATION
A comment sheet is often used to aid authors in improving their dictation skills.

Reporting to Upper Management

Of prime interest to upper management is the cost-effectiveness of the word processing system. To make any decisions, upper management relies on meaningful information that includes summarized facts. Word processing managers should never approach upper management to request anything (such as additional personnel, a higher salary base for specialists, new equipment, or environmental changes) without having done their homework. Figure 12-7 gives examples.

FIG. 12-7
REPORTING TO UPPER MANAGEMENT
A request should never be presented to upper management unless the persons making the presentation have facts to verify the information.

Request	Required Information and Facts (Comparing This Period With Last Period)
Additional personnel	Number of overtime hours spent Use of temporary help (hours and pay) Production totals
Higher salary base for support personnel	Turnover rate Follow-up or exit interviews Average regional salaries for comparable positions
New equipment	Production totals Breakdown of production by type of task Repair records of current equipment
Environmental change	Number of worker complaints Number and type of equipment service calls Vendor's recommendation

Meaningful information might be given in person, but the wise manager summarizes facts in tables, charts, and concisely written reports. These summaries help managers compare, forecast, analyze, and control (rather than react to) short- and long-term circumstances. Examples are given in Figure 12-8 and Figure 12-9.

Another responsibility of a word processing manager is to manage the finances of the word processing system. To participate in financial management decisions, one must be able to discuss the dollar flow of the system. In most companies, word processing and administrative support services are considered "overhead" in the profit and loss report. Overhead costs can be broken down to direct costs and indirect costs.

Direct costs are divided into salary and expense. Direct salary is the raw salary (which does not include fringe benefits) of the word processing personnel. Direct expense of a word processing production unit would be equipment and supply costs.

Indirect cost is usually labeled overhead or general and administrative cost. This category includes:

- Depreciation of the building
- Fringe benefits

CHAPTER 12   Managing the System ─────────────────────────────────── 351

FIG. 12-8
BAR CHARTS
Bar charts allow upper management personnel to make immediate comparisons of information.
(Courtesy of American National Property and Casualty Company)

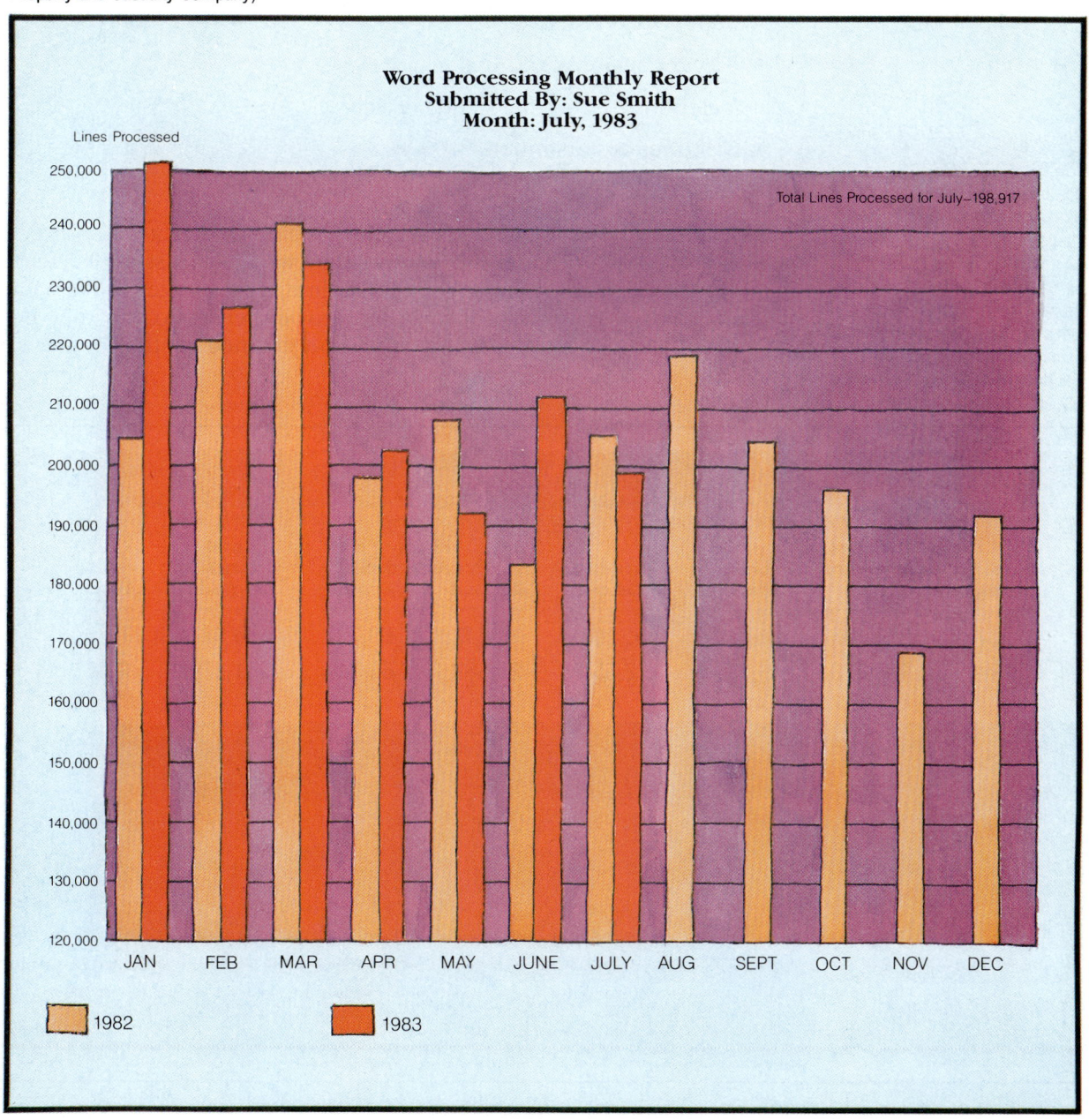

- General office supplies (not word processing equipment supplies)
- Insurance (property and liability)
- Office space rent
- Postage and mailing expense
- Supervisory salaries
- Taxes (business and real estate)
- Telephone equipment and service
- Training of personnel
- Utilities

A profit and loss statement is a sheet on which all direct and indirect costs are balanced with income generated by word processing services. The statement usually contains separate columns for budgeted data versus actual cost. The supervisor must monitor expenses so that they do not exceed the budget allocation or can be justified by the increased

FIG. 12-9
MONTHLY REPORTS
Monthly reports to be presented to upper management personnel should contain only the pertinent information, such as totals. If the managers need to see the statistics of which the totals are comprised, they will ask for them.
(Courtesy of American National Property and Casualty Company)

WORD PROCESSING MONTHLY REPORT
CENTER TOTALS
FOR THE MONTH OF JULY, 1983

Month	Original Keyboard Lines	Lines Revised	Variable Lines	Lines Prerecorded Revised	Forms	Total Lines Typed	Total Pages
July	96,686	4,624	11,993	19,847	65,767	198,917	7,957
June	100,823	5,870	12,557	25,582	66,747	211,579	8,463

WORK EVALUATION

Month	Corr.	Dict.	Forms	Policy Issue	Reports	Printing	Data Processing	Word Processing	Total
July	34,684	42,323	32,058	6,037	50,420	75	272	33,048	198,917
June	34,048	53,490	31,102	5,167	45,333	210	1,248	40,981	211,579

Cancellations for July—172

Supervisor's Comments About These Charts: The **Center Totals** show that fewer lines were produced in July than in June. In comparing **Work Evaluation**, you will note that more lines of correspondence were produced in July than in June. Yet fewer lines were dictated. It is apparent that more authors need to be trained or retrained to dictate correspondence by machine.

amount of production. If the company has a charge-back system, the cost of doing work for each department is calculated and charged to that department.

PSYCHOLOGY OF WORKING WITH PEOPLE

Being a liaison person, the word processing manager should be able to work with all levels of personnel within the company. The three main groups are the employees being supervised, the authors of the system, and upper management. Let's discuss some effective ways of working with each of the groups.

Personnel Who Are Supervised

When workers have respect for the manager's technical knowledge about procedures and equipment, they are reasonably sure that the system has direction and that it is operating with efficiency. When workers have an attractive and functional environment, they are comfortable and are content that their health is not endangered. When workers have a competent manager, they not only have support, but they are motivated to want to perform at their maximum potential.

Managing people, therefore, involves more than technical knowledge; it requires an understanding of applied psychology. The principles are so basic that you might think anyone with common sense would know and practice them. Yet they are the ones most often ignored by many managers.

Listening to Employees. Several studies have been done by Dr. Ralph Nichols, a noted authority on communication skills. Many of these studies indicate that the most frequently listed trait of a successful supervisor by employees is, "I like my boss; he/she listens to me."

When workers know the supervisor cannot or will not listen to a complaint or a problem, they cease trying to approach the supervisor. Instead, they are likely to gather together and discuss the problem away from the supervisor. This can ruin morale. The complaint might be a viable one and by solving it the system may be improved. For example, the transcriber may be having difficulty understanding the dictation of a particular author. This situation might bring to light a misunderstanding or lack of knowledge about the system. An example would be an employee not understanding why work is measured—thinking that the only reason work is measured is to pressure workers and to punish them for errors.

Upon hearing a suggestion from an employee, some supervisors appoint that individual to a committee to do something about it. While some workers like to become involved, others may feel that another

Before assigning tasks, a good word processing manager makes sure that the work load is distributed evenly.

assignment is an unfair distribution of the work load or that it is the supervisor's job to handle the problem. These workers, perhaps the ones with the most initiative, then cease giving helpful suggestions.

A manager must listen carefully, be receptive to suggestions, and be ready to explain situations that result in misunderstanding. The individual who approaches the manager with a problem or suggestion deserves a response. Involving workers in solving problems may be appropriate, but it should be distributed fairly.

Acting on Suggestions. Some supervisors hear and even listen to complaints in a gracious manner. But when the employee leaves, these supervisors have no intention of acting on the suggestion. Of course, the employee's suggestion could have been a poor idea or one that is not feasible, in which case the supervisor should substitute a better suggestion.

What would you think of managers who neither accept employee suggestions nor act on any of them? This type of manager communicates, "I know how to manage; my ideas cannot be improved; and I will run my office the way I want."

Those who are closest to a task that involves a problem may develop the best way to solve the problem. By acting on good suggestions from workers, managers can improve the system and also open lines of communication that will encourage any employee to offer a suggestion from time to time. Better yet, the worker who offered the suggestion should be acknowledged, even if the suggestion cannot be implemented.

Commending Employees. When an employee consistently performs above average, that person deserves to be commended. When any task is performed especially well, the employee appreciates knowing that the supervisor noticed. Supervisors can become so swamped with work that routine good work goes unacknowledged. Sometimes supervisors place more emphasis on finding mistakes and reprimanding workers than in looking for reasons to commend them.

Praise should be sincere—not just an overt comment. It should be given in front of other workers. In the file of that employee, the date and reason for praise might be noted. Every deserving worker should be praised regularly. Few people ever get enough praise to feel sincerely appreciated by their supervisors. Many surveys of lower- and middle-management personnel indicate that they are seldom if ever acknowledged for outstanding achievement. Managers should realize that frequent, sincere compliments usually result in even more diligent work from an employee.

Managers who suffer from the "Snow White Syndrome" are those who will not acknowledge outstanding work because they do not want anyone else in the department to look better than themselves in the eyes of top management. They might either ignore or take credit for the accomplishments of a subordinate. A good manager stays alert for reasons to compliment subordinates, gives credit where it is due, and gives the employee public recognition when appropriate.

Admitting Mistakes. Managers, too, make mistakes. While no one likes to emphasize making a mistake, an effective manager will honestly admit to making a mistake. If it is done with sincerity, the subordinates will no doubt have empathy and will be eager to help the team correct it. On the other hand, a manager who shifts the blame onto another person, especially a subordinate, will cause all of the subordinates to become resentful and uncooperative.

Being Fair. When employees know that a decision or a work assignment is fair, they are more likely to have the incentive to want to do it well. There are many ways that a manager can demonstrate fairness. For example, challenging jobs can be rotated with routine jobs so that no one employee has only the routine work. The exception might be in a small center that has only two word processing specialists, one of whom is an entry-level person just learning the job. The manager likely will begin training this person with the easier, more routine jobs until the individual's performance is up to standard.

As you will recall from Chapter 11, one reason for keeping production records (assuming the work measurement system is fair—allowing for difficulty of the task) is to help determine salary increases. Such salary decisions appear to be fairer and more objective than those that are based purely on subjective evaluation by the manager. When rewards and promotions are unrelated to the quality or amount of work done, morale drops.

Motivating Individual and Team Effort. By being enthusiastic and by pitching in to help the team on occasions of peak work periods, the manager can inspire the team. The manager's example by dress, grooming, work organization, professional growth, and personality has a big impact on the motivation of the team.

A competent manager encourages professional growth among the workers. One way to achieve this goal is to delegate assignments. There is a delicate line between accepting one's management responsibilities and delegating work to subordinates. The appropriate tasks to delegate are those that do not involve management action, decision/policy making, disciplinary power or authority, and work with superiors. Examples of appropriate tasks to delegate include: totaling log sheets, gathering data, and assisting new operators.

Other ways to motivate the team would be for the company to pay for their membership dues and seminar fees in professional organizations. The company might also pay for continuing education at public or private post-secondary schools or colleges/universities.

Users of Word Processing Services

The users may be at the same level of the organization chart as the word processing manager; yet some could be positioned higher or lower. In most situations the word processing manager should treat them all as equals, as other managers.

One way that a word processing supervisor can encourage cooperation and team effort with this group is to show empathy for their problems. The manager should keep in mind that each person on the organization chart has had unique experiences. The reason that some authors shy away from using dictation equipment might be because they were never taught how to dictate in school, or because they were criticized about their dictation skills. This information is helpful in designing in-service training programs for authors.

Periodically, the word processing supervisor should have a private conference with each user. At that time the manager should ask for feedback about word processing services and carefully listen to complaints and suggestions. At the same time, the manager might see ways by which the user could be better assisted. In these conferences each user should be commended about something. What an easy but simple way to build team effort!

One way that a word processing manager can encourage cooperation from users is by showing empathy for any problems they may be experiencing with word processing services.

Upper Management

Employees in upper management positions should be treated more formally than those on the same level as the word processing manager. Middle managers should realize that top managers are not experts in every facet of the business. As problems are relayed to top management, word processing managers should present the facts in a concise, informative way. The wise word processing manager will be ready to explain at least two possible solutions for each problem.

For a supervisor to convince any potential user to use word processing services, there must be evidence of upper management support. This means that upper management personnel should set an example by using word processing services in the most efficient way. How unfortunate it is to see traditional secretarial systems in the administrative offices of schools that are teaching modern word processing concepts and skills in the classrooms. The same irony can be seen in companies in which top management uses a traditional secretarial system but expects

A word processing manager can communicate effectively with top management by using the you approach.

middle- and lower-management levels to use the word processing system. Thus, a word processing manager must apply tact, diplomacy, and enthusiasm in obtaining top management support.

Two techniques that usually are effective in communicating with top management are (1) giving them praise for their accomplishments in the company and (2) applying the you approach by pointing out how the word processing system is benefiting them in reaching corporate goals. The positive approach is especially appreciated by those who are burdened with corporate problems and challenges on a daily basis.

Managing a word processing system certainly requires many qualities. The word processing manager determines how well people, machines, procedures, and the environment accomplish word processing goals. How important it is that this person have technical knowledge, a pleasing personality, and leadership ability.

DISCUSSION QUESTIONS AND CASE PROBLEM

DISCUSSION QUESTIONS

1. What are four basic responsibilities of a word processing manager?
2. Why is a word processing manager considered a liaison person? Identify three groups of people the word processing manager serves.

CHAPTER 12 Managing the System 359

3 Once implementation of a word processing system has taken place, is the manager done with the basic responsibilities of machines, procedures, and the environment? Qualify your answer.

4 Which of the three groups of people within a company is it most important for the word processing manager to commend?

5 Why might a senior secretary with outstanding word processing skills not be qualified to be a word processing manager (or supervisor)?

CASE PROBLEM

Steve is manager of a six-person word processing center staff. The center had been experiencing excellent production turnaround for the past year until the last few weeks. When Steve checked his production records, he noted one newly created user department was receiving poor turnaround. In addition, he had received several complaints from these users that their work had been received with many errors. The personnel department had informed him that this same user group had requested their own secretarial position to provide quicker and more accurate typing service.

Steve met with his staff and discovered that no one was anxious to assume responsibility for this user group's input. The staff members complained that the work was always delivered in hard copy format, the handwriting was difficult to read, the users were unavailable for assistance, and their requests included demanding deadlines. Steve had not had an opportunity to meet with this user group, since the group had been established while he was on vacation.

Steve's objectives in managing the word processing center are to ensure quality work and good turnaround, to prevent unnecessary company hiring, and to establish good user rapport. In addition to meeting the needs of users and top management, Steve strives to maintain a supportive climate for the word processing staff.

1 Does Steve have responsibilities to this user group? What are they?

2 Does Steve have responsibilities to his word processing staff? What are they?

3 What responsibility does Steve have to the company for his department's operation?

4 What steps can Steve take to rectify these problems and recover his department's previously good reputation and record?

Chapter 13 Staffing a Word Processing Department

CHAPTER OBJECTIVES:

Identify five criteria for an open career path.

Write a job description for a word processing position.

Assemble facts to justify equitable word processing salaries.

Describe the word processing manager's function in hiring new employees.

Explain the features of an organized orientation program.

Describe the process of evaluating employee performance effectively.

Why do some companies have higher turnover rates than do others? Why is the morale lower for some groups of specialists than it is for others? Does the presence of word processing equipment in a company indicate an open career path (one with opportunities for advancement)? These and other questions will be answered in this chapter as concepts of staffing a word processing department are presented.

Staffing a department involves designing career paths, analyzing jobs, determining job titles, writing job descriptions and specifications, establishing a salary scale, interviewing applicants, planning the orientation, and evaluating employee performance. These tasks are likely to be the responsibility of the word processing manager or supervisor in cooperation with the personnel director.

DESIGNING OPEN CAREER PATHS

In some companies the path of those employees pursuing word processing careers leads to a dead end. New employees may be so fascinated by the bright and shining word processing machines that they have only surface vision. Once the glamour of the new job wears off, they may become disenchanted to learn that their administrative support counterparts are earning a higher salary. Or perhaps there are only two levels within the job category and no higher position to work toward. Worse yet, imagine the status of a person operating a sophisticated word processor whose job title is Clerk Typist!

In these situations there is hardly a career path; and if it exists, it certainly is not an open career path. The impact of improper staffing results in low morale, many absences, high turnover, and poor production rates.

To offer an **open career path** for word processing and administrative support specialists, a company must meet five conditions. These conditions are first listed and then described more specifically in this chapter.

open career path a way to advance to higher levels or positions of employment

1. A job title and a job description must exist for each word processing and administrative support position.
2. Both word processing and administrative support services must be organized throughout the company with professional supervision for each group.
3. Three or more levels of advancement must occur within each area of specialty.
4. Word processing and administrative support services must have the same number of levels with a salary structure that reflects equal status for comparable word processing and administrative support levels.
5. Management positions must exist that are related to and filled from the word processing staff and the administrative support staff.

The organization chart in Figure 13-1 shows how companies can organize professional office services into groups of specialists.

Some companies organize professional office services into groups of generalists rather than groups of specialists. Generalists have a variety of skills and perform a myriad of tasks, including the operation of word processors or multifunctional terminals. An open career path for generalists would meet the following conditions:

1. A job title and a job description must exist for each office support position.
2. Office support personnel must be organized into groups with professional supervision for each group.
3. Three or more levels of advancement must occur within each group.

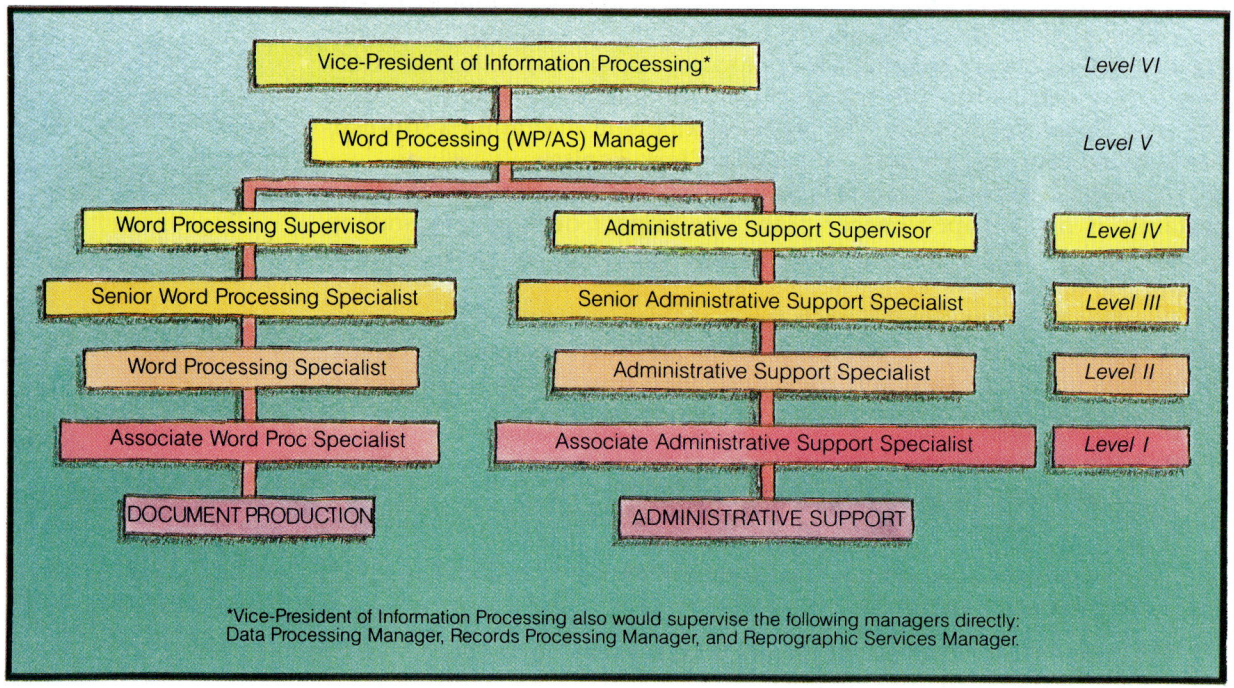

FIG. 13-1
ORGANIZATION OF
PROFESSIONAL OFFICE
PERSONNEL AS SPECIALISTS
This organization chart shows how a company can organize professional office personnel into groups of specialists to create an open career path.

4 The salary structure must reflect equal status for comparable group levels.

5 Management positions must exist that are related to and filled from office support groups.

The organization chart might be like that shown in Figure 13-2.

In this chapter the term *organized* implies that office support personnel have as formal a structure as other employees on the organization chart. They typically serve a group of users and are supervised by a professional. In contrast, traditional secretaries, who serve users on a one-to-one basis, are supervised by the user(s) and generally do not appear on a company organization chart.

Describing Jobs

The more specific a job description is, the more likely it can be filled with a qualified person. Also, the salary scale is more likely to be commensurate with the responsibilities and qualifications of the jobs within the company. The first step toward developing a job description is to analyze the job carefully. Then an appropriate title and description can be developed.

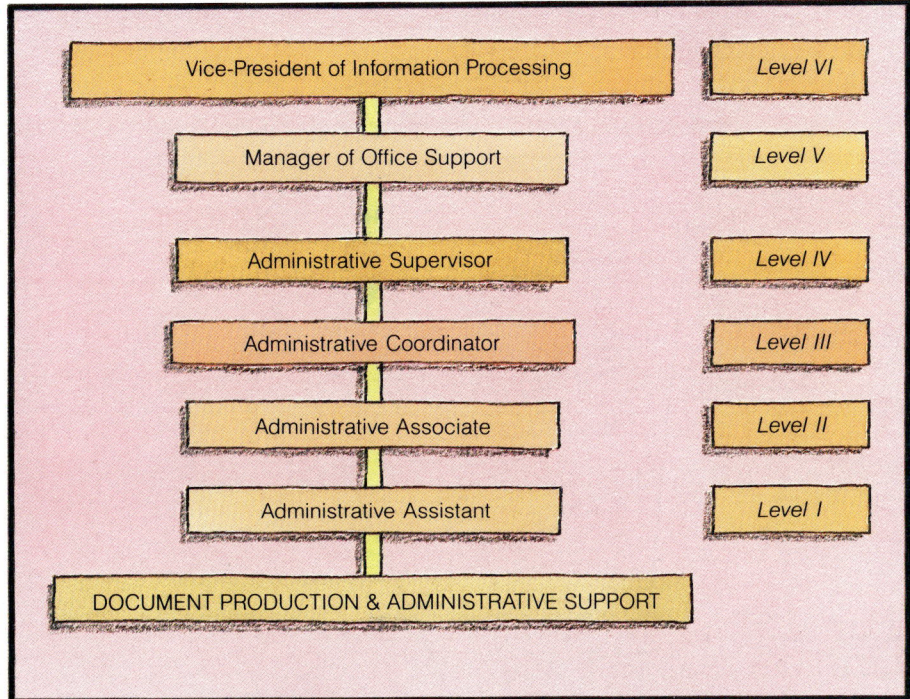

FIG. 13-2
ORGANIZATION OF PROFESSIONAL OFFICE PERSONNEL AS GENERALISTS
This organization chart shows how a company can organize professional office personnel into groups of generalists to create an open career path.

Analyzing the Jobs

A thorough **job analysis** of a word processing position involves studying various factors of the job. The basic factors include: number and types of tasks performed, degree of technical ability involved, number of people (if any) supervised, amount of creativity and initiative required, and extent of confidential information handled.

Once a word processing system has been implemented, each job should be reviewed annually to determine if it has changed. The employees perform a vital role in analyzing their jobs and in assisting with the annual review. The period of analysis (or review) should be about two weeks of a normal work period. Peaks (for example, the first two weeks of April in an accounting firm) and valleys (for example, the two weeks after the end of a term in a university) should be avoided.

During the two-week period, employees keep a record of the types of activities performed and the amount of time spent on each. They also may assist with evaluating tasks in terms of decision making and difficulty. Figure 13-3 shows a job analysis form.

job analysis the act of gathering information and determining basic factors involved in performing a specific job

Determining Job Titles

Job titles for similar positions vary from company to company. Among the most commonly used titles for positions within word processing systems are those given in Figure 13-4.

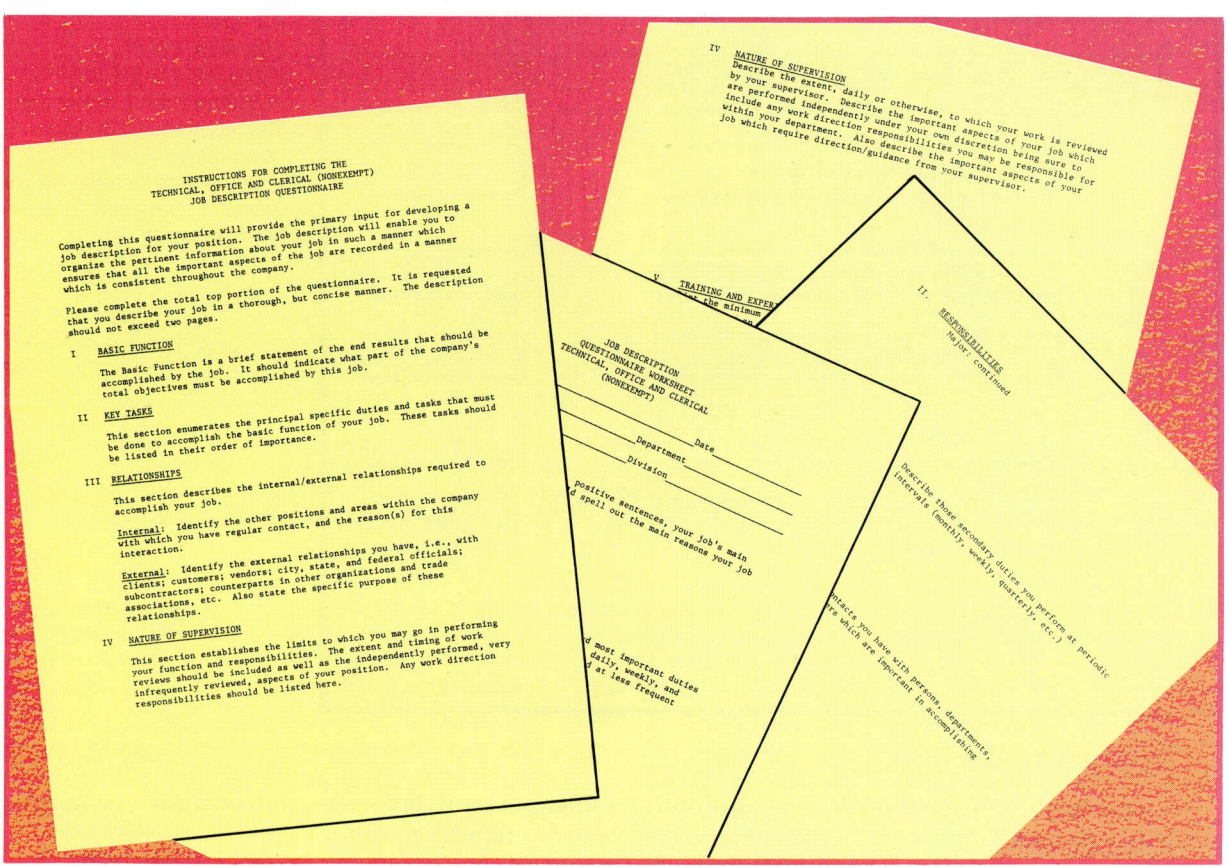

FIG. 13-3
JOB ANALYSIS FORM
Jobs should be reviewed annually to determine if there are any changes to be made in the job description.
(Courtesy of Comserv Corp.)

job description includes job title, level, supervisor, department, basic function, duties, and job requirements

When both administrative support and correspondence support are organized in a company, the hierarchy of positions might be similar to those shown in Figure 13-1. The hierarchy of generalists might be like those given in Figure 13-2.

The job titles that include the words *operator* or *secretary* have been challenged by some authorities. The word *operator* may not imply the high level of technical ability required for the position. Some feel that the title *secretary* implies the use of more professional skills than those used by word processing operators. Thus, a job title not only should reflect the nature of the job but also should give the position appropriate status.

Writing Job Descriptions

From the information acquired by job analysis, a detailed and functional job description can be written. The basic components include: job title, classification or grade level, job title of the person to whom the

CHAPTER 13 Staffing a Word Processing Department

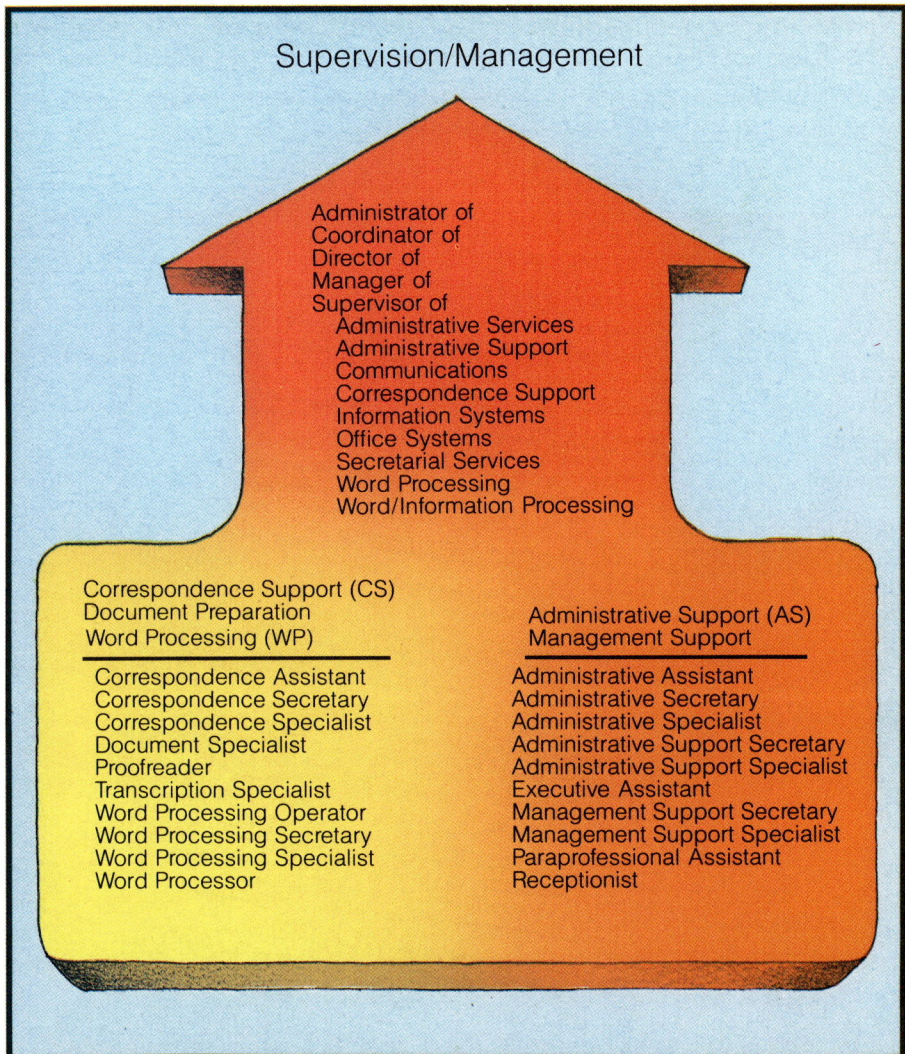

FIG. 13-4
JOB TITLES IN WORD PROCESSING SYSTEMS
Companies use many different titles for similar positions in a word processing system.

individual in that position reports, department or division, basic function of the job, an itemized list of general duties and responsibilities, and minimum job requirements (job specifications).

The minimum job requirements include the skills, education, experience, and any other special demands required for the position (such as the ability to operate certain equipment). This information identifies the prerequisites an applicant should possess to qualify for the position. The qualifications for a position are used to recruit, select, and train employees. In addition, they help employees establish career goals.

Each job description should be dated so that the latest revision is never confused with an earlier edition. The cover page of a group of related job descriptions should chart the hierarchy of those positions. Refer back to Figure 13-1 as the cover page for the job description shown in Figure 13-5. Figure 13-2 would be the cover page for the job description of an Administrative Coordinator given in Figure 13-6.

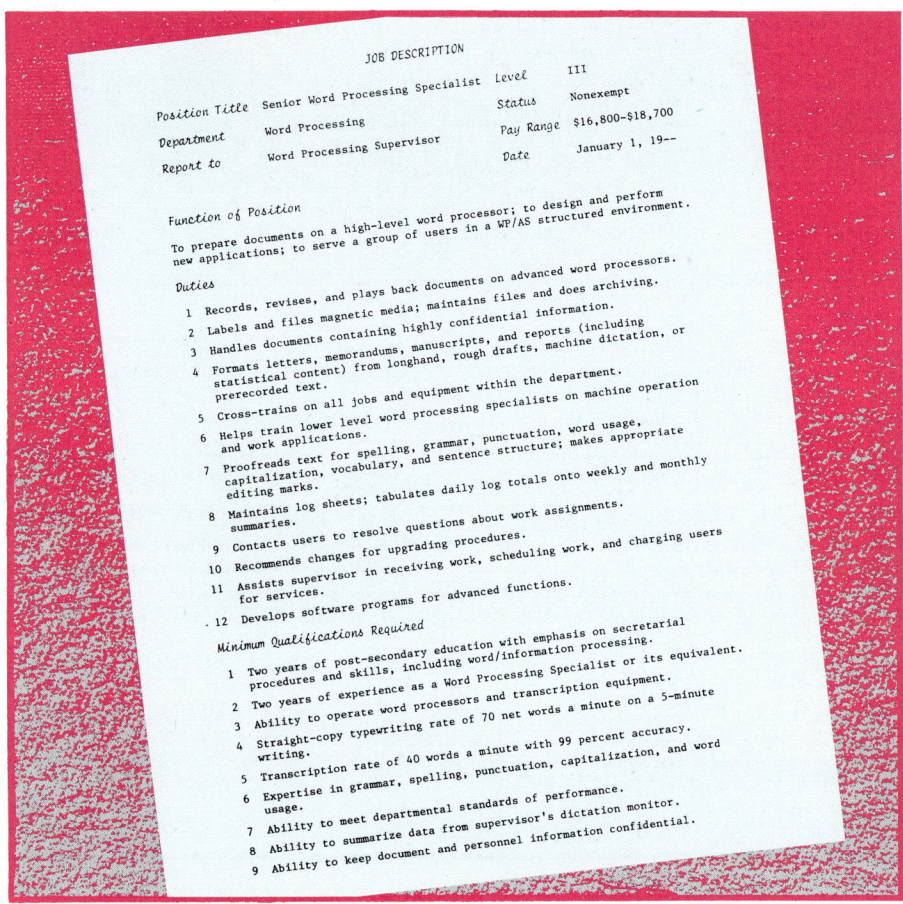

FIG. 13-5
JOB DESCRIPTION FOR A SENIOR WORD PROCESSING SPECIALIST
This job description is for a position in a company that has organized its professional office staff into groups of specialists.

nonexempt worker is entitled to overtime pay for hours worked over 40 during a workweek

exempt worker is not entitled to overtime pay for hours worked over 40 during a workweek

Those positions which entitle the worker to overtime pay for hours worked over 40 during the workweek are referred to as **nonexempt** positions. The positions of Senior Word Processing Specialist and Senior Administrative Secretary are considered to be nonexempt. However, management positions, such as Word Processing Manager, usually are fully **exempt** from the minimum wage and overtime pay requirements of the Fair Labor Standards Act.

CHAPTER 13 Staffing a Word Processing Department

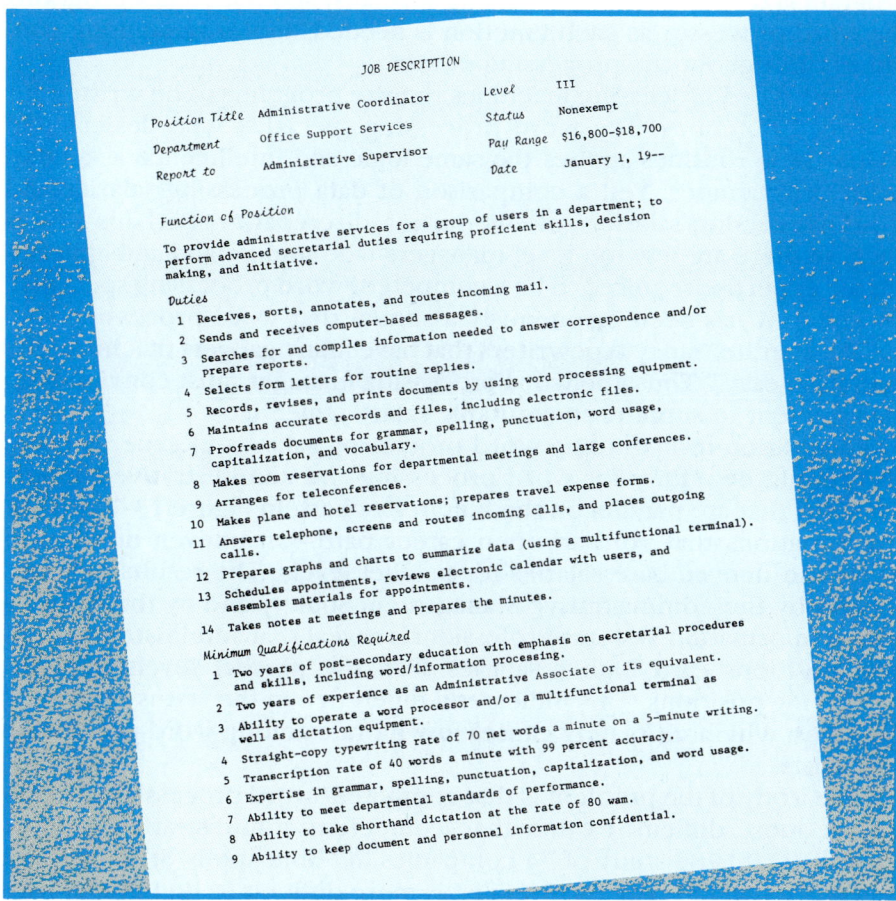

FIG. 13-6
JOB DESCRIPTION FOR AN ADMINISTRATIVE COORDINATOR
This job description is for a position in a company that has organized its professional office staff into groups of generalists.

ESTABLISHING A SALARY SCALE

The establishment of an equitable salary scale for word processing personnel involves several considerations. First, one should be aware of problems that exist within the industry. Facts need to be acquired by the word processing manager and presented to top management to justify equitable salaries. The last step is to determine the base salary for each level and grade within the scale.

Problems of Which to Be Aware

One of the problems that exists in some word processing systems is low salaries for specialists who program word processors. Yes, word processing specialists are the equivalent of computer programmers. The only difference is in the sequence of performing tasks. A computer programmer writes the program before attaching the data on which the program is to run; a word processing specialist spontaneously programs the word processor as each function is needed, and programming continues throughout the processing of text.

Some word processing machines require programs to be written for advanced functions. The word processing specialist who designs and writes these routines applies the same logic and intelligence as a computer programmer. Yet, a comparison of data processing salaries and word processing salaries reveals quite a discrepancy. Perhaps this is because there are few top-level managers who understand and appreciate the expertise required to be a competent word processing specialist. Too often it has been erroneously assumed that word processing specialists operate "fancy typewriters that have many gadgets that make the operation easy." Thus, the word processing manager must convince top management to support an equitable salary scale.

In addition to upgrading word processing salaries in general, there also should be equity for word processing and administrative support positions that are parallel on the hierarchy chart. In Figure 13-7 you see two situations that void an open career path—an uneven number of levels and uneven base salaries for parallel levels. The results of salary surveys by the Administrative Management Society and by the Association of Information Systems Professionals reveal that administrative support positions earn higher salaries than the parallel levels of word processing positions. This indicates a difference in the status of parallel positions, which ultimately causes low morale among word processing specialists.

The irony of the problem is that competent word processing specialists are more difficult to find than competent administrative support specialists. A 1983 study of 74 companies in Minneapolis/St. Paul asked supervisors which type of specialist is more difficult to find. A majority of the supervisors responded, "the word processing specialist." A proficient word processor with expertise in grammar, spelling, punctuation, word usage, formatting, proofreading, and machine operation is the more difficult specialist to find.

Facts to Justify Equitable Salaries

The word processing manager must present facts that prove to the director of personnel and to top management the importance of establishing an equitable salary scale for all support positions. Some points to emphasize include:

1 What are other companies within the region paying for comparable positions? Several professional organizations conduct wage and salary surveys. Among those that report word processing salaries would be the Administrative Management Society, the Association of Information Systems Professionals, and the Dartnell Institute of Financial Research. A local word/information processing

SITUATION A—AN UNEVEN NUMBER OF LEVELS

Level	Administrative Specialists	Word Processing Specialists
5		$360
4		$335
3	$310	$310
2	$285	$285
1	$260	$260

SITUATION B—UNEVEN BASE SALARIES FOR PARALLEL LEVELS

Level	Administrative Specialists	Word Processing Specialists
5	$375	$360
4	$347	$335
3	$328	$310
2	$305	$285
1	$280	$260

FIG. 13-7
JOB LEVELS AND SALARIES
An open career path does not exist in these situations because Situation A has an uneven number of levels and Situation B shows uneven base salaries for parallel levels.

association might have a periodic salary survey, which would be most pertinent.

2 What is the consequence of high turnover rates and the inability to attract competent, qualified applicants? The high costs of recruitment, interviewing, training, and the initial below-average production rates should be emphasized.

3 How critical are errors in document processing? What effect does incompetent work have on the image of a company? Is management willing to pay for quality word processing personnel as well as quality data processing personnel and other information processing personnel?

4 If a company pays the minimum wage for part-time and temporary word processors, management should be informed about such inequity. What types of jobs typically earn only the minimum wage? A comparison will show that even a part-time or temporary word processing specialist is using skills and abilities that are far above the skills required of most workers receiving the minimum wage.

The word processing manager should work with the personnel director in evaluating each word processing and administrative support position to determine the relative value of each job. This means that there must be an estimated or measured worth of each job in relation to other jobs. Factors to consider and weigh would be complexity of tasks, level of skills required, the amount of contact with others, supervision of others, the effect of errors, knowledge of concepts, physical (including visual) demands, and the amount of confidential information handled. Additional factors which influence salaries include work experience, education, the cost of living, the supply and demand of word processing and administrative support workers, government regulations, collective bargaining agreements (if applicable), and competition with similar companies.

HIRING NEW EMPLOYEES

If done carefully, the steps taken to hire word processing personnel can set the stage for a pleasant working relationship and avoid high turnover rates. These steps include recruiting, screening, interviewing, testing, and evaluating applicants.

Recruiting Qualified Applicants

What are the best sources from which to recruit qualified applicants? Who performs the recruiting function? A job opening might result from an employee leaving the company or from the approval by top management of a request for a new employee position. In either case, the word processing manager works with the personnel director, who is primarily

When a new employee is needed, the word processing manager works closely with the personnel director to determine the qualifications necessary for the position.

responsible for filling the position. It is the word processing manager's responsibility to clearly define the kind of employee needed and to suggest sources from which to recruit applicants.

When defining the kind of employee needed, the word processing manager must take into consideration a review of current employees. The manager must analyze the career goals of the employees so that there is the proper mix of employee expectations for career advancement. Also, the stability of the current employees should be estimated. An example will illustrate the point.

Let's assume that the job vacancy (or new position) is a Level II within a six-level hierarchy. If two thirds of the Level II employees aspire to being promoted eventually to supervisory positions and it is not likely that any of them plan to leave the employ of the company, an individual without strong career advancement goals should be recruited. On the other hand, if two thirds of the Level II employees do not have strong career expectations, an individual with promise for promotion to a supervisory level should be recruited. A manager needs to have a proper mix of career-oriented workers as well as noncareer-oriented workers. If not, individual career goals cannot be realized and employees are likely to become dissatisfied.

The personnel director is guided by corporate policies and government regulations in performing the hiring function. The corporate policy might lean toward promoting from within the company or toward hiring from the outside. In the case of the preceding example, the word processing manager would assess the Level I workers to see if one is ready to be promoted to Level II. Should the decision be made to hire from the outside, the personnel director will see that the job vacancy is advertised to assure equal employment opportunities according to government regulations.

The word processing manager can contact sources that are most likely to yield qualified applicants. Among the best sources are business teachers in the local high schools, vocational schools, and community colleges, as well as both public and private colleges and universities. Of course, schools that offer word processing courses are recommended. Most business teachers are not only cooperative but also delighted to help match job openings with qualified students (for part-time or temporary jobs) or graduates (for permanent positions). Another prime source of qualified applicants is the local word/information processing association, where the job vacancy can be announced. Vendors of word processing equipment may know of qualified people who might be looking for a better job. However, care should be taken to be professional about recruitment techniques.

Applicants should be requested to submit an application letter that is accompanied by a data sheet (resume). The applicant will also at some time be asked to fill out the company's standard application form. Upon receipt of these documents, the word processing manager can begin

Before scheduling interviews, the word processing manager must screen all applications received by the company for the position.

screening applicants to determine which ones should be invited to come for an interview.

Screening Applicants

In screening applicants, the word processing manager must keep in mind the duties of the job and the minimum qualifications as expressed on the job description. Most word processing positions, whether emphasis is on document preparation or administrative support, demand a high level of typewriting and language arts skills. Thus, a review of the initial screening instruments would include the following observations:

- **The Application Letter**

    A Appearance
    1. Quality bond paper
    2. Dark, clear type; no smudges or messy corrections
    3. Proper personal business letter style
    4. Inclusion of return address and telephone number
    5. Consistent punctuation (periods after all abbreviations or omitted entirely)
    6. Signature (by pen—not by pencil)

    B Composition and Mechanics
    1. Perfect spelling

2 Proper sentence structure
3 Indirect reference to data sheet
4 Using the name of the addressee in the body
5 Correct grammar, punctuation, capitalization, word usage, and word division
6 Avoidance of words like *all, always, extensively,* and *thorough* that indicate the applicant knows it all
7 Avoidance of negative words that cast doubt, such as *if, hope,* and *trust*

C Relating Education and/or Work Experience to the Job
1 Does the opening paragraph identify the job position for which the applicant is applying?
2 Does the applicant reveal any knowledge about the company? Has the applicant taken the initiative to learn about the company—nature of the job, products or services marketed, etc?
3 Has the applicant identified how he or she can specifically serve the company?
4 What characteristics make this applicant better qualified than other applicants?
5 Does the applicant ask for an interview? Are possible times given?

- **The Data Sheet (Resume)**

A Appearance
1 Quality bond paper
2 Dark, clear type; no smudges or messy corrections
3 Consistent punctuation (periods after all abbreviations or omitted entirely)
4 Design and arrangement of information—Is it attractive? balanced? a demonstration of initiative and creativity?
5 Perfect spelling

B Education
1 How recent is the education?
2 Was a high school diploma and/or college degree earned?
3 What was the major area of study?
4 Was grade point average and/or class rank included?
5 Were specific office administration courses listed?

C Skills
1 Were specific skills listed?
2 Was the ability to operate various office machines included?

D Work Experience
1 What kind of work experience has the applicant had? Does it relate to the position of vacancy?

            2 Were these part-time or full-time jobs?
            3 Were duties and responsibilities described in specific terms? Were accomplishments included?
            4 Was there consistency in verb tense and construction of sentences or phrases?
            5 Do the periods of education and work experience connect? Or, are there obvious gaps with no evidence of activity?
        E References
            1 Are credentials on file at a placement office or employment agency?
            2 Were references listed? If so, were they given with complete names, business addresses, and business phone numbers?
            3 Does each reference obviously relate to the applicant's education or work experience? Or might some references be personal friends, relatives, or the clergy—those not appropriate for a job application?

- **The Application Form**

    A Can the applicant follow directions? Was the form filled out as directed?
    B How detail-minded is the applicant? Was each blank filled in with pertinent information or *not applicable*? Or, were parts left blank?
    C How neat (vs. messy) and professional (vs. lack of professional office administrative skills) is the applicant? Was the form filled in by a typewriter or by longhand? (Unless you specified that it should be filled in by longhand to observe the person's handwriting, the professional applicant would type the information.) What is the quality of the type or of the longhand?

From the suggested points to observe on each document, there are several qualities that are common to all three: accurate typing and correct mechanical skills (grammar, spelling, punctuation, word usage, capitalization, and word division). The question the word processing manager must ask is: "If this is how the applicant tries to impress a potential employer when the person wants a job, how would the person perform once employed and not trying so desperately to impress the employer?"

The next step of the screening process is for the interviewer to check out references and transcripts. Employment agencies and school placement offices at which the applicant has registered can provide a set of **credentials**, which includes reference statements. To obtain an official **transcript** of the applicant's grades, the interviewer would need to ask the applicant to have it sent. Only the applicant can authorize the educational institution to send a transcript. An applicant who takes the

---

credentials information about a job applicant on file at an employment office or school placement office

transcript list of courses completed and grades earned by a student at an educational institution

initiative to have credentials and transcript sent without the interviewer's request demonstrates a keen interest in working for the company. In addition, this saves the interviewer's time and expense of contacting employment agencies and schools for the documents.

Many interviewers telephone references given on the data sheet. In this way they can obtain more specific information about the applicant's performance as an employee and/or as a student than might be given in a written reference. Some employers question the credibility of written references, especially if the applicant chose to have the option of reading them (nonconfidential references). Telephoning references is also faster than waiting for credentials to be mailed.

Scheduling Interviews

Having screened the applicants, the word processing manager would select the most promising candidates and schedule an interview for each. A telephone call followed by a confirmation letter is the normal practice. The applicants who demonstrated proper application procedures and who were rejected at this point deserve the courtesy of an acknowledgment. An interviewer never knows when he or she might need to reevaluate one of the applications, and it is important to project good public relations for the company. Figure 13-8 illustrates the type of letter that should be sent to an applicant to confirm an interview. Figure 13-9 illustrates the type of letter that should be sent to applicants who were not selected for an interview.

After the screening process has been completed, the most promising applicants are scheduled for individual interviews.

Testing for Employment Skills

An employment test for a word processing position should be representative of the basic job tasks. The most common test administered for office jobs is a straight-copy timed writing to determine the applicant's typewriting skill. From this type of test the applicant's gross words a minute rate, errors, and net words a minute rate can be determined. However, straight-copy timed writings are not representative of actual word processing applications, for word processing specialists do little typing from an error-free typed or printed copy. To determine the applicant's command of language arts, proofreading, and decision making, an application test should be administered.

From actual work that has been produced by the company, an application test could be developed that includes:

1. Transcribing a letter from machine dictation
2. Typing one page of a report from a rough draft
3. Setting up and typing a three-column table from longhand

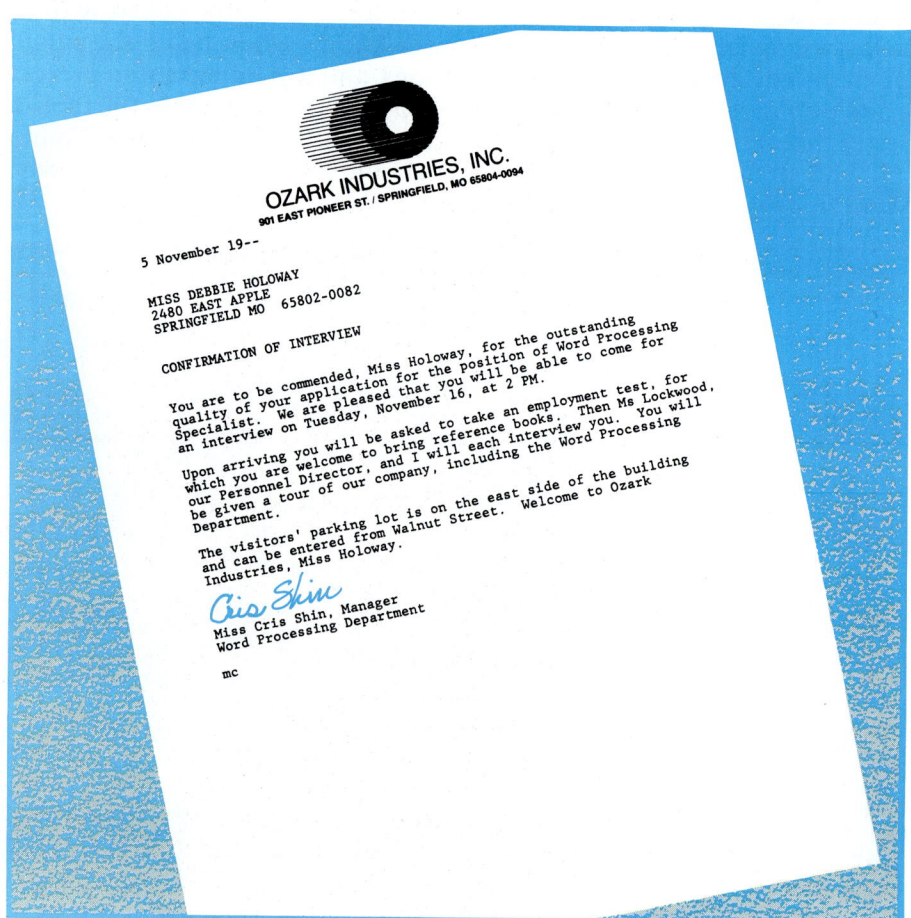

FIG 13-8
LETTER TO CONFIRM AN INTERVIEW
The most promising job applicants should be scheduled for an interview by the telephone. A follow-up letter is then sent by the firm to confirm the date and time of the interview.

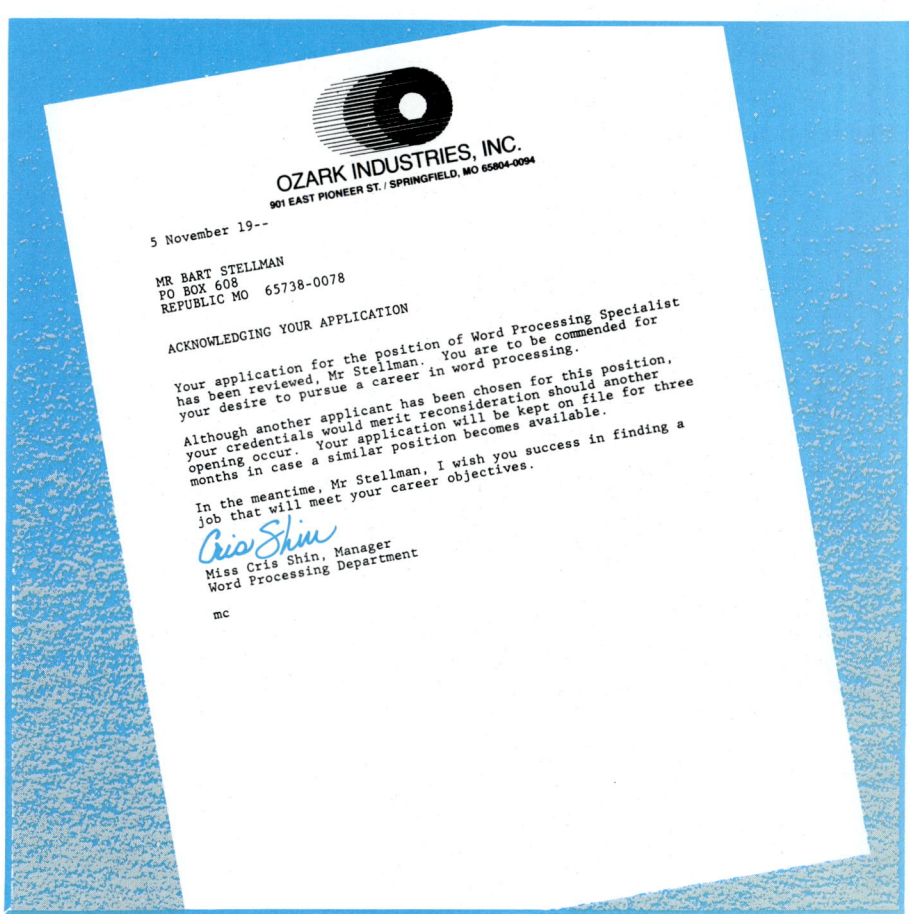

FIG. 13-9
LETTER TO APPLICANT NOT SELECTED FOR AN INTERVIEW
Applicants not selected for an interview deserve the courtesy of being notified of the company's decision.

These three documents involve three common methods of input. Built within the test should be planted grammar, spelling, word usage, punctuation, and thought errors. In this way the word processing manager can observe more than straight-copy typewriting skill. Figures 13-10 and 13-11 give examples from an application test.

This type of test enables the interviewer to determine the applicant's ability to format basic business documents (which involves math calculations) and to apply the mechanics of the English language. Proofreading, of course, can also be observed. The application test can be evaluated on the basis of three elements—the number of minutes used, the number of uncorrected errors, and the usability (mailability) of the three items.

A new method of testing applicants is to allow them to take an application test on a word processor. Certain brands of equipment not only count the keystrokes but also clock the time the operator takes to produce a certain document. For example, the first part of the test might be

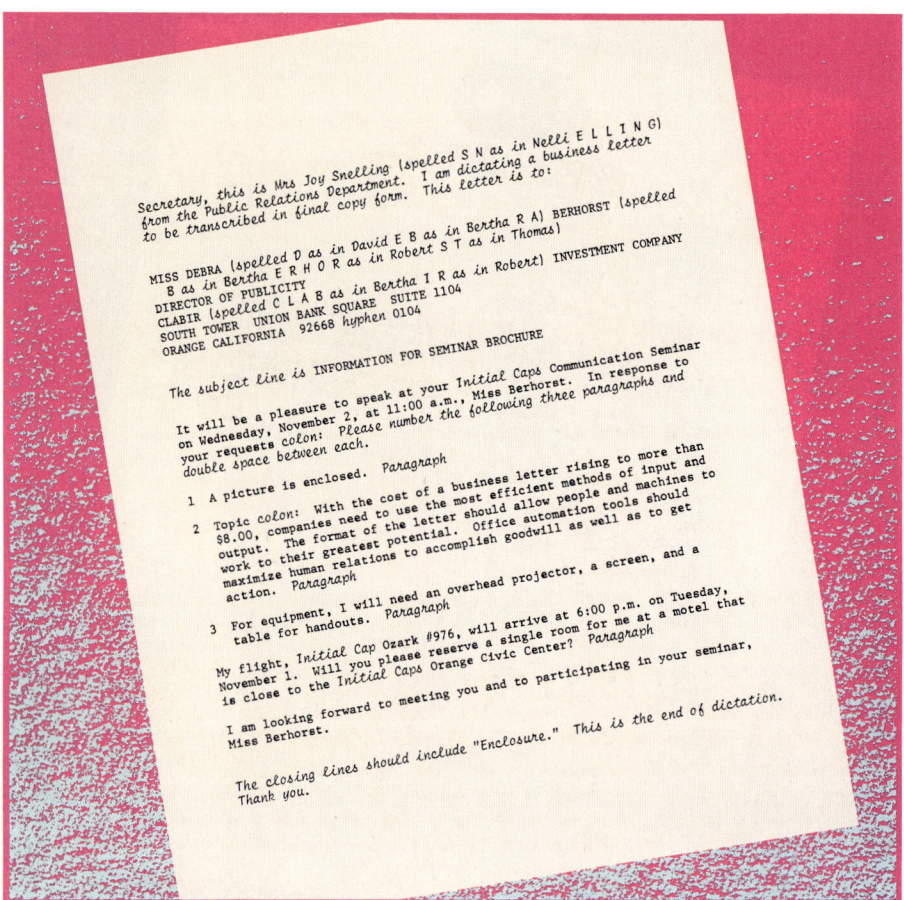

FIG. 13-10
LETTER TRANSCRIPTION
One part of an application test might be an appraisal of the applicant's ability to transcribe a letter from machine dictation.

to record a letter; the source might be machine dictation, longhand, or rough draft. For that part of the test the word processor would display the number of keystrokes and the length of time it took the operator to perform the task. The second part of the exam might be to edit the recording, for which the word processor would display the number of keystrokes and the amount of time involved. Some brands also are equipped with the software program to assist in evaluating the accuracy of the document.

All applicants should be tested under the same conditions (same type of machine, identical instructions, and approval to use reference materials). Then standards of performance can be set against which applicants' scores can be compared. In cooperation with a business teacher, the application test could be administered to a group of students in an advanced typewriting or word processing class. This would

CHAPTER 13 Staffing a Word Processing Department

help the interviewer accumulate enough scores to develop a valid test instrument.

Interviewing Applicants

Prior to the interview, the interviewer should have reviewed the application letter, data sheet (resume), application form, references, and transcripts so that any questions about the applicant's background can be listed. In addition, there would be questions to ask that might reveal the individual's attitude, ability to get along with others, desire to operate machines, and so forth. Examples of questions to ask that might lead to desired information are given in Figure 13-12.

You will note that each of the questions requires more than a *yes* or *no* response; the applicant is encouraged to talk. Since most people do best what they enjoy doing the most, it is wise for the interviewer to get

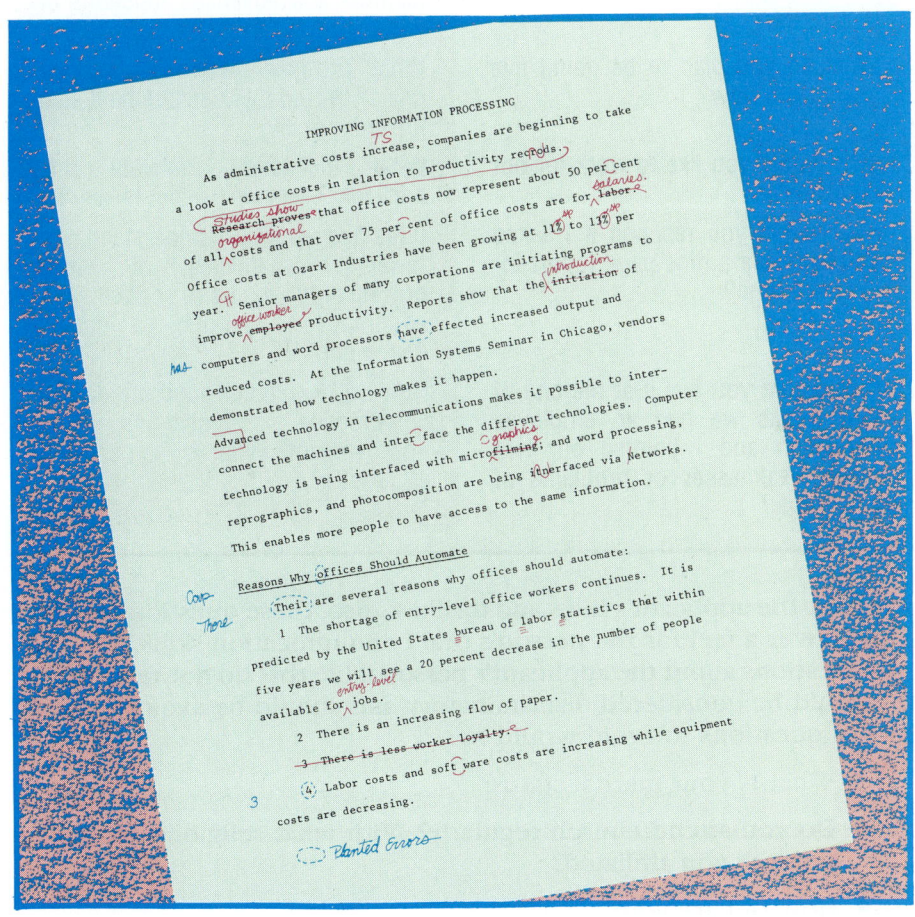

FIG. 13-11
ROUGH DRAFT
Another section of an application test might be an evaluation of the applicant's ability to type from a rough draft.

FIG. 13-12
THE INTERVIEW
A well-designed interview question will force the applicant to give more than just a yes or no answer. However, questions about the applicant's personal life should be avoided.

Question to Ask	Desired Information
What are your strongest abilities and personal characteristics that you would bring to this job?	In what areas does this person have confidence?
What kinds of office tasks do you enjoy the most? What tasks do you least care to do?	In this position, would the person be doing what is enjoyable? Would the person be doing many tasks that are disliked?
If you have a weakness as it would relate to this job, what do you feel it would be?	Is the applicant honest? Does the applicant have a healthy self-concept?
Do you enjoy typing? Do you like to operate word processors? If so, why?	Does the applicant have enthusiasm about the equipment? Would this person use initiative to try new features and advanced functions of the word processors?
What do you plan to be doing five years from now?	What are the applicant's career goals? Would this position be a step toward a goal?
Why would you like to work for our company?	What incentives motivate this applicant? Can we predict loyalty?
How would you respond if I asked you to revise a nine-page report for the third time?	Does the applicant understand the revision capabilities of word processors? Is there desire and endurance to produce a quality document?
How would you feel if at the end of four weeks we had an employee evaluation and I pointed out two major weaknesses or problems of your work?	How well would this applicant accept constructive suggestions for improvement? What is the person's attitude?

a feel for the applicant's likes and dislikes. Also, these questions give the interviewer a feel for the person's oral communication skills.

Questions about the applicant's personal life that do not relate to the job could be considered discriminatory and should be avoided. Examples of questions to avoid would be:

- What is your marital status?
- Do you attend church regularly? With what religious denomination are you affiliated?
- How old are you?

CHAPTER 13 Staffing a Word Processing Department

- Where were you born?
- Of what nationality are your parents?

Having done the homework for the interview, the word processing manager must then plan the order of activities (employment test, interview, and tour) and arrange for the setting. The receptionist should be made aware that the applicant is expected at an approximate time. The word processing manager might ask the receptionist to note the promptness of the applicant's arrival and see how the applicant uses waiting time.

When the applicant arrives, the interviewer should extend a welcome and invite the person to be seated. A small round table for both the interviewer and applicant is better than a large desk that separates the two and communicates an authoritarian atmosphere.

During the interview, the interviewer should give an honest description of the job, including the challenges as well as the rewards. This can be conveniently done during the tour. To present a picture that is too glamorous would mislead the applicant with false illusions. Once the glamour of the new job wears off, the employee is likely to become dissatisfied with the job, thus creating morale problems.

Having asked the prepared questions, the interviewer should ask if the applicant has any questions about the job or the company. Unless these topics have already been addressed, the interviewer should explain the career opportunities, the salary and fringe benefits, and the company's support for professional growth.

The word processing manager should get an idea of an applicant's likes, dislikes, and oral communication skills from the interview.

At the conclusion of the interview, the applicant should be thanked for coming and should be informed about the approximate date that a decision will be made. For most positions the decision should be made within two weeks of the interview.

Evaluating Applicants and Making the Selection

Having administered an employment test and interviewed each of the final applicants, it may be quite easy for the interviewer to make a selection. On the other hand, the candidates might appear to be equally qualified and the choice may be difficult for the interviewer to make.

Narrowing the Choice to One. Assume the choice has been narrowed to two candidates. With a chart similar to the one shown in Figure 13-13, each interviewer (word processing manager, personnel director, and possibly a supervisor or senior word processor) could evaluate each of

FIG. 13-13
RATING CANDIDATES
This chart allows the interviewer to rate candidates in many areas. The best candidate for the position would have the highest total number of points.

RATE THE CANDIDATE *Fred Morriset* ON EACH OF THE FOLLOWING FACTORS BY WRITING THE NUMBER WHICH BEST EVALUATES THAT FACTOR.

Factor	Low 1	2	3	4	High 5
Ability to get along with others on the team					5
Patience and tact in working with users				4	
Acceptance of constructive criticism				4	
Dependable and punctual in attendance					5
Appearance (dress and grooming)					5
Quality of: application letter					5
data sheet (resume)					5
application form				4	
Performance on employment test:					
English skills				4	
speed					5
accuracy and proofreading					5
formatting					5
Ability to handle the pressure of deadlines				4	
Expertise in oral communications				4	
Flexibility in handling interruptions					5
Enthusiasm about and initiative in using word processors					5
Positive attitude					5
References' information				4	
Ability to understand word processing concepts					5
Aptitude for advancement				4	

TOTALS 92
32 60

CHAPTER 13 Staffing a Word Processing Department   383

the two finalists. For each factor a number would be placed in the appropriate column. By totaling the number of points, it would be easy to identify the most outstanding candidate.

In addition, the word processing manager should ask the opinions of the departmental employees who met the applicants. It may be necessary to contact some of the references again to clarify a point in question.

Most word processing managers conclude that if the choice is between a candidate with better English skills versus one with better production speed, the former would be the choice. With additional experience the production speed is likely to improve, but improving one's command of the English language is not as feasible. Attitude is important, for someone with a positive, cooperative, and friendly personality can be trained to improve. An employee with a negative attitude is not easy to train, and that person's influence on other workers can have a devastating effect on production.

Making a Job Offer. As soon as the choice has been made, the candidate should be given the job offer. Either the word processing manager or the personnel director will issue the formal offer, which is usually done by telephone and then followed by a formal letter. The letter will include information such as the starting date, job title, department, immediate supervisor, salary, initial employment requirements (physical exam and parking permit), and announcement of the first orientation session. This formal letter is actually a contract for employment. An example is given in Figure 13-14.

Notifying Other Candidates. It is only proper to promptly notify the candidates who were not selected. The tone of the letter should demonstrate courtesy and appreciation, leaving the door open for possible future employment. See Figure 13-15 for an example.

PROVIDING ORIENTATION FOR NEW EMPLOYEES

To be a new employee of a company is both exciting and awkward. The newness of the environment, the people, and the equipment may be invigorating. But not knowing the basic policies, procedures, and management philosophy can retard progress and be embarrassing. This is another responsibility that is likely to be shared by the word processing manager and the personnel director.

Orientation refers to a carefully planned introduction for new employees to learn about the company in general and about their jobs specifically. Thus, the orientation will no doubt take more than one session.

FIG. 13-14
LETTER OFFERING EMPLOYMENT
Generally a job offer is made by telephone. A follow-up letter confirms the offer and gives the employee any additional information.

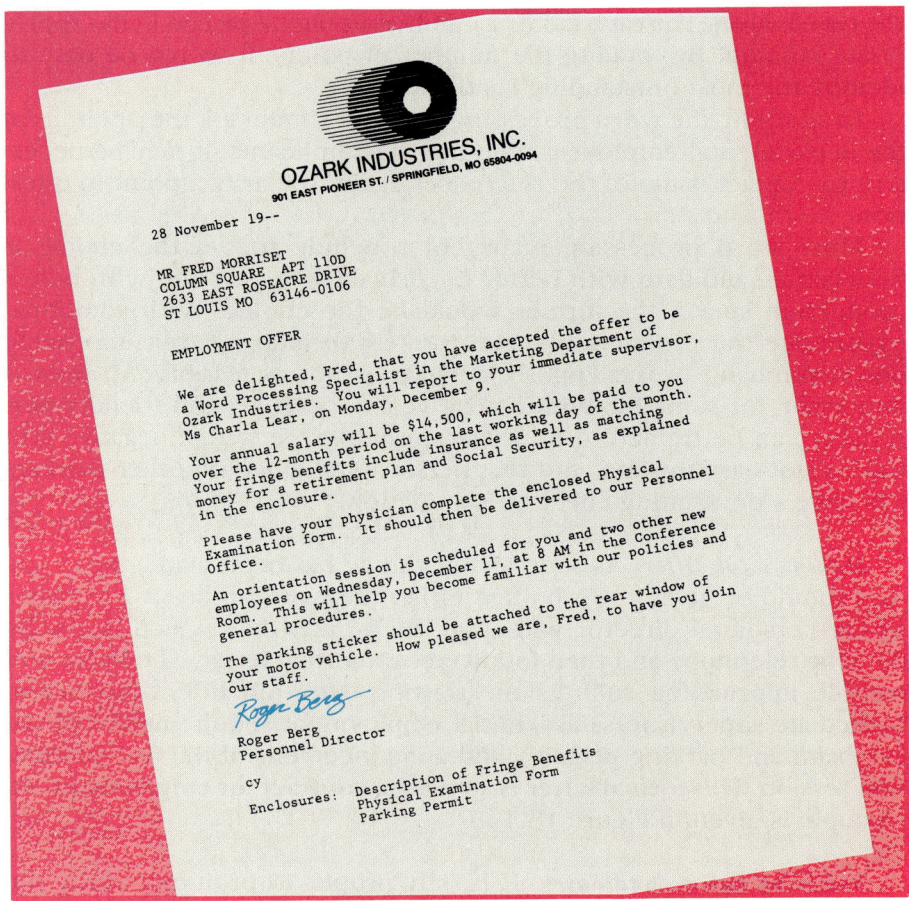

Orientation to the Company

A general session for new employees of all departments would be conducted by the personnel director. Topics that would likely be included would be the following:

History of the company	Educational programs
Organization of personnel	Holidays
Products and/or services marketed	Vacation schedules
Description of customers (or clients)	Dress codes and rules of conduct
Payroll deductions and procedures	Suggestion system
Fringe benefits	Performance reviews
Bulletin board function	Promotion policies
Cafeteria services	Security system
Health and physical fitness programs	Parking policies
Recreational programs	

All new employees should be given a general orientation to the company. This is conducted by the personnel manager.

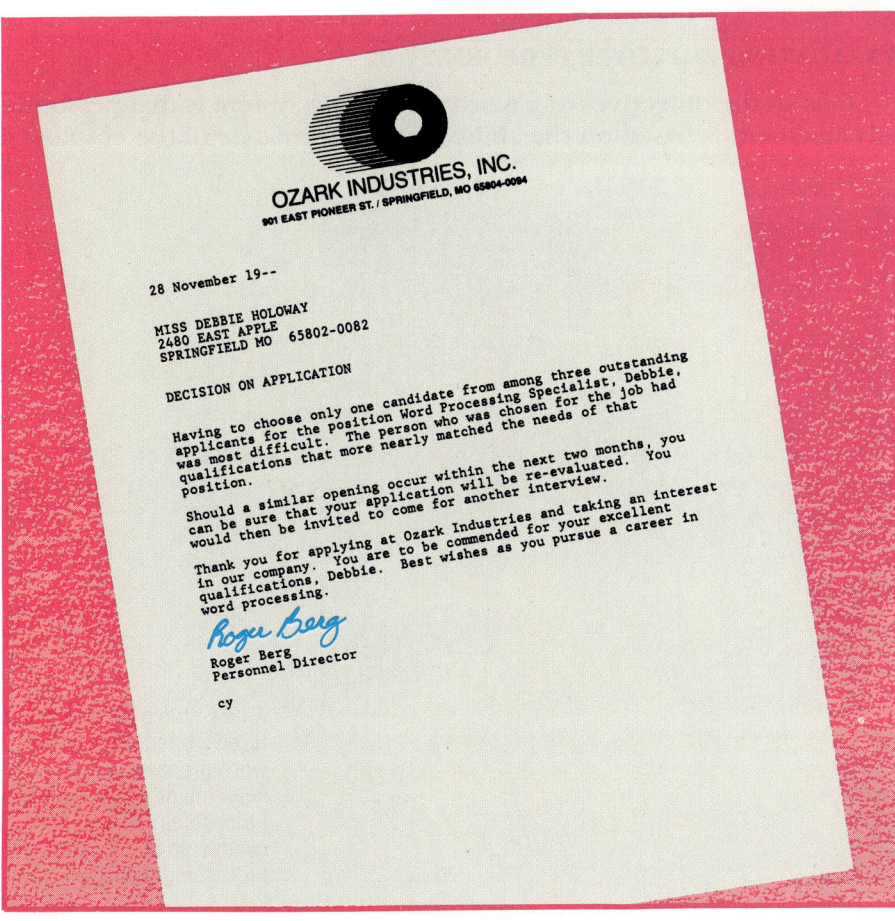

FIG. 13-15
LETTER NOTIFYING CANDIDATES NOT CHOSEN
Applicants not chosen for a position should be notified promptly.

This information is usually printed in an employee handbook for later reference, but it should be presented orally during the general orientation.

Orientation to the Job

The orientation to the job would be conducted by the word processing manager or an assistant supervisor. The orientation period may extend to three or four days so that the new employee has a chance to absorb only portions of the information at a time. To assure that all new employees are thoroughly introduced to the policies and procedures of the department, an **orientation checklist** is recommended. The checklist guides the supervisor in presenting information in a logical order, as shown in Figure 13-16.

orientation checklist
list of items to cover to introduce a new employee to a job

Throughout the orientation program, the supervisor will make note of the areas in which the new employee will need specific training. In-service training then actually teaches the new concepts and skills needed for the job, as described in Chapter 11.

EVALUATING EMPLOYEE PERFORMANCE

One of the objectives of a word processing system is that personnel advancement is based on the ability and performance of the employee.

A new employee also should receive orientation to the word processing department's policies and procedures. This is conducted by the word processing manager.

ORIENTATION CHECKLIST
WORD PROCESSING DEPARTMENT

New Employee _____ Beginning Date _____

Supervisor _____ Ending Date _____

First Day

_____ Describe the basic functions of the job
_____ Explain the word processing cycle (work flow)
_____ Explain hours of work, break periods, and lunch period
_____ Discuss attendance records and requirements (time cards, punctuality, reporting absence)
_____ Introduce to departmental associates
_____ Invite questions from employee
_____ Give employee a copy of each procedures manual to read

Second Day

_____ Go through the procedures manual(s) and explain each part
    _____ Priorities
    _____ Turnaround goals
    _____ Standard formats
    _____ Work requests
    _____ Transcription procedures
    _____ Logging and measuring work
    _____ Quality control procedures
    _____ Replenishing supplies
    _____ Reporting equipment problems
_____ Introduce reference manuals
    _____ Users' names, titles, and phone numbers
    _____ Form documents
    _____ Dictionary, English handbook
    _____ Directory of customers
    _____ Telephone directory, city directory, ZIP code directory
    _____ Mail service
    _____ Telephone etiquette
_____ Invite questions from employee

Third Day

_____ Explain work standards
_____ Describe performance review
_____ Give grievance procedures
_____ Discuss suggestion system
_____ Explain personal mail and telephone calls
_____ Invite questions from employee

FIG. 13-16
ORIENTATION CHECKLIST
An orientation checklist guides the supervisor in presenting important company information and introduces the new employee to company policies and procedures.

This is in contrast to the traditional office system in which a secretary's advancement depends on the boss's position and in which politics often override fairness in promoting office workers.

New employees must be evaluated before the probationary period expires. They may be evaluated at the end of 30 days of work, after three months, and then again at the conclusion of six months of service. Thereafter, employees usually are evaluated annually.

The Evaluation Form

employee evaluation
appraising an employee's performance on the job

To develop a functional **employee evaluation** form, the word processing manager and the personnel director should review the job descriptions of the department. The duties, responsibilities, and minimum qualifications given on the job descriptions should be reflected in the evaluation form. As the form in Figure 13-17 shows, both objective data (for example, average production rate and error percentage) as well as subjective observation (attitude and leadership) should be included.

Conference with Employee

After filling out the performance evaluation form, the word processing manager would have a conference with the employee. During the conference the supervisor would review the evaluation form with the employee. Positive comments should precede suggestions for improvement. Employees are more likely to accept suggestions for improvement if the supervisor has first given facts about marginal or unacceptable performance. In conclusion, the supervisor will ask the employee if the evaluation is accurate and fair, which is verified by the signature of each.

At the end of the interview the employee should feel appreciated for good performance and be motivated to improve. The competent manager knows that by showing an interest in each employee and helping

An evaluation form should be reviewed during a private conference between the word processing manager and the employee.

PERFORMANCE EVALUATION

Name _____
Title _____
Department _____

0 Unacceptable
1 Marginal
2 Acceptable but needs improvement
3 Above average
4 Excellent

FACTORS	DESCRIPTION	COMMENTS	0	1	2	3	4
Attendance	Number of times absent or late to work						
Production Rate	Standards (Lines per Day) Excellent ____ Above Average ____ Acceptable ____ Marginal ____						
Accuracy Rate	Standards (Error %) Excellent ____ Above Average ____ Acceptable ____ Marginal ____						
Teamwork	Works with others in dept. to meet goals and deadlines; voluntarily offers help to others						
Follow Through	Is detail minded to complete a task; follows procedures						
Confidences	Keeps information about work and about people confidential						
Work Organization	Maintains an organized, neat, and clean work station; assembles files and materials in an orderly manner.						
Equipment Operation	Shows initiative in learning new features of equipment; helps maintain machines and reports repairs						
Mechanics of English Language	Uses correct grammar, spelling, punctuation, capitalization, word usage, & word division						
Leadership	Suggests ideas for improving procedures; speaks tactfully with users; helps train others						
Appearance	Is appropriately dressed and groomed						

SUMMARY COMMENTS

1 Major Strengths of Employee _____

2 Significant Accomplishments of Employee _____

3 Area(s) Needing Improvement _____

4 Plan for Meeting Improvement Goal(s) _____

5 Employee's Career Goals _____

6 Significant Comments Made By the Employee During the Conference _____

Date of Completed Evaluation Form _____

Date of Employee Conference _____

Overall Rating _____

Comments _____

Signature of Supervisor/Manager _____
Signature of Employee _____

FIG. 13-17
EMPLOYEE EVALUATION FORM
A well-designed evaluation form takes into consideration the duties, responsibilities, and minimum qualifications of a position.

employees reach individual career goals that the departmental and company goals can also be achieved.

Staffing a word processing department is critical to the overall achievement of departmental and company goals. Without qualified and satisfied workers, a word processing system cannot operate at maximum efficiency. In this chapter you have been made aware of the criteria for open career paths—those that offer promotional opportunities to those who aspire to advance to high management levels. Should you become a supervisor or manager of a word processing system, you have learned the steps and procedures for hiring employees and evaluating their performance.

DISCUSSION QUESTIONS AND CASE PROBLEM

DISCUSSION QUESTIONS

1. What are five obvious characteristics of a dead-end word processing career path?
2. If you were trying to convince top management and the personnel director to increase the salaries of word processing personnel, what facts would you gather and present? Give three.
3. Assume you are a word processing manager. List the steps involved in hiring a new employee.
4. Describe how a word processing manager should provide feedback to the employees about their performance after the evaluation forms have been marked.

CASE PROBLEM

For many years the managers of Surburia Bank calculated their departmental budgets to indicate what their projections of expenses would be for the coming year. The financial department used these figures to determine the bank's overall operating expenses and plans. These budgets were often revised and consolidated with those of other departments. (The budgets of companies are much like your budget of expenses. The goal is to match the income with the monthly expenditures and yet allow some flexibility to purchase new items or plan new methods.)

This year the bank has a new information processing system. The word processing manager developed a program on the word processor for budget production that provides an automatic method for figure entry and consolidation. The tedious tasks of revisions and calculations are cut in half and the figures can be retained indefinitely on magnetic media. Because the word processor is used for input, the job of budget preparation is now delegated to the word processing specialists. The word processing manager has been praised for developing the method but has received no formal recognition.

The department managers are convinced that the "machine" has made the job easier. They are often overheard saying how "easy" budget preparation has become since the days in which they had to perform their "complicated" data processing budget programs. Ironically, the word processing manager is at a salary far below that of the data processing managers, even though the responsibilities and competencies are similar.

1 What steps can be taken to establish an equitable approach to the position of word processing manager?
2 How can the new "programmed" budget process convince upper management of the expertise required for the position?
3 Are there ways in which the word processing manager can enlighten the departmental managers of the programming equivalence between word and data processing?

Chapter 14 Integrating Technologies for Information Processing

CHAPTER OBJECTIVES

Define information processing.

Identify the subsystems of an information processing system.

Describe how word processing relates to each of the subsystems of information processing.

Explain how subsystems are connected for a totally integrated information processing system.

Word processors that are loaded with various software packages and that interface with several other office automation systems play major roles. On the other hand, word processing could be a software package that has been attached to a personal computer and may be a minor function of that workstation. Regardless of its size or status within a company, word processing must be placed in perspective as one of several subsystems that compose an information processing system.

Word processors that are loaded with various software packages and that interface with several other office automation systems play major roles. On the other hand, word processing could be a software package that has been attached to a personal computer and may be a minor function of that workstation. Regardless of its size or status within a company, word processing must be placed in perspective as one of several subsystems that compose an information processing system.

CHAPTER 14   Integrating Technology for Information Processing — 393

INFORMATION PROCESSING

Information is created more quickly and in larger volume than most human beings can comprehend. Available in the forms of data, text, image, and voice, information has grown to such volume that it is considered a resource. Technology has developed tools to help people handle information with accuracy and efficiency. Built with powerful microprocessors, these tools can take on advanced capabilities as well as communicate with each other.

The integration of technologies makes information available to countless users. Information then becomes a resource with such magnitude that it must be carefully managed to achieve the benefits for which it was intended.

In the typical corporation about 10 percent of the information is numerical; the rest is in the form of text, image, or voice.[1] Managing the information resource involves making the right information available to the right people at the right time. An information processing system can be as sophisticated as an integration of various subsystems, or it can be as compact as a workstation. A compact workstation might combine an intelligent printer, a graphics display screen, a telephone, and the access to a local area network.

SYSTEMS WHICH INTEGRATE

Data processing, electronic mail, and the other components of information processing are presented in this chapter. Included in the review of each system is the relationship of word processing to that technology. The means of connecting individual subsystems to build an integrated system are then discussed.

Word Processing

A word processing system is unique in its ability to manipulate text. Editing and formatting functions groom documents so that they represent the company in a most professional way. Companies that have repetitive correspondence need only to key the text once and add the variables. Then they can watch the system play back as many "originals" as needed with only the touch of a finger between playbacks.

A word processor can complete a document cycle by itself. In addition, it is a common input device that feeds text into other office systems such as computers, phototypesetters, and intelligent copiers/printers. With added software, word processors can perform multiple functions—calendaring, graphics, and math calculations to name a few.

---

[1]Kate Barnes, "Integrating MIS and Office Automation: What's Involved," *The Office* (September, 1983), pp. 113-116.

Text captured on a word processor can be immediately printed on paper, stored on magnetic media, or directly transferred to the screen of another word processor or computer terminal. The word processing industry has flourished, for there is a constant attempt to increase the efficiency of processing the mountains of paperwork that exist in businesses today.

Data Processing

A skeleton overview of data processing includes a brief description of the equipment, basic applications, and the significance of software innovations. A more comprehensive discussion of the issues that result from the interfacing capabilities of data processing and word processing is given in Chapter 15.

Equipment. A description of computer equipment might begin with the two basic families or types of computers—analog and digital. **Analog computers**, common to science applications, work with information that has continuous signals. An example would be monitoring the changes in a hospital patient's physical condition. In contrast, **digital computers** work with information that has well-defined signals, such as numerical calculations. Computers that are used for business applications are commonly digital computers; however, voice technology involves analog signals.

A computer system is controlled by a CPU—the brain of the system. The memory houses the programs (instructions) and data (information to be processed) as the CPU uses them. **Peripheral equipment** refers to the pieces that connect to the CPU, which include printers, terminals, storage units, and modems.

Computer systems are broken down by size into three groups—large mainframe computers, minicomputers, and microcomputers. You might think of these as a five-course meal versus a three-course meal versus a snack.

Large computer systems are the "five-course meals." They can have several hundred terminals and sophisticated peripherals attached. The mainframe can simultaneously receive input from many terminals and control various functions. Examples would include controlling communications, keeping records, performing accounting calculations, and monitoring inventory. These systems cost upward of $500,000.

Minicomputer systems perform about the same functions as large computer systems, but they operate on a smaller scale and at a slower rate. They would be considered the "three-course meals." A minicomputer system can support a large number of terminals that can be performing various operations simultaneously. The cost of minicomputers ranges from $50,000 to $400,000.

Microcomputer systems contain the same basic components as their

---

analog computer
processes information that has continuous signals

digital computer
processes information that has well-defined signals

peripheral equipment
pieces that connect to the CPU

CHAPTER 14 Integrating Technology for Information Processing 395

Microcomputer systems perform the same functions as large computer systems on a smaller scale and at a slower rate.

two larger counterparts, but they are limited in capacity and in the number of terminals that can be supported. Compared to the "full-course meals," microcomputers are "snacks." Basically a single-function machine, a microcomputer performs only one operation at a time. The CPU is limited to supporting one to five terminals. Other limitations include a slower printer and smaller storage capacity. These desktop computers generally are self-contained with the ability to operate as standalones or as extensions of minicomputers and large computer systems. Prices range from $1,000 to $20,000.

Applications. The basic data processing applications performed by computers can be divided into three categories—numerical calculations, decision making, and file manipulation. The numerical calculations can be as simple as totaling employee time sheets or as complex as payroll processing. Given decision-making information and raw data, computers can coach management in predicting market trends and designing new products. An example of file manipulation would be keeping track of accounts receivable records, such as purchase orders received, invoices issued, and checks received from customers. The computer can put the records in order and can also sort individual records by type.

A graphic display effectively communicates lists of numeric data.

Software Innovations. The proliferation of creative software packages that can be attached to computers has introduced new menus for information processing. Among the most popular are graphic and word processing packages.

Graphic software allows users to view color graphs, which summarize large volumes of data, rather than viewing detailed numerical columns as illustrated in Figure 14-1. Graphic displays can communicate more effectively than statistical printouts to give managers a quick look at important information. Graphic software is available to computers as well as to word processors.

Word processing software can be attached to a computer of any size, including personal computers. Typical users of word processing software on microcomputers are small businesses that have many functions to be performed. Word processing applications are important but not extensive.

FIG. 14-1
CONVERSION OF NUMERICAL
DATA TO GRAPHIC DISPLAY
Some software packages can convert large volumes of data to graphic display.

Electronic Mail

For medium-to-large corporations with geographically dispersed offices, electronic mail can be a cost-effective management tool. This machine-to-machine method of communication allows messages and other types of information to be sent without moving paper or recording media; the information is sent electronically. Should a paper copy be needed, it is made by the receiver's equipment.

Electronic mail provides a faster exchange of information than public, private, or intercompany mail delivery services. In this case, "faster" means that electronic mail provides immediate or same-day delivery. The number of recipients could be one or more.

As Figure 14-2 shows, word processing is but one technology that can send information electronically. The various technologies that can communicate electronically include:

- Communicating word processors
- Computer-based message systems
- Facsimile
- Intelligent copiers/printers
- Optical character recognition (OCR)
- Telex/TWX
- Voice mail

You will note that all forms of information (data, text, image, and voice) can communicate electronically. Intelligent copiers/printers, OCR, and voice mail are discussed later in this chapter.

Communicating Word Processors. The application of electronic mail that is most appropriate for word processing is that of processing textual material. Examples of textual content would be important messages, reminders, suggestions, and ideas. The document, whether in the format of a letter, memo, or report, is generally short—no longer than one page. However, branch office workstations could each contribute a section of a long report that is finalized at the corporate office.

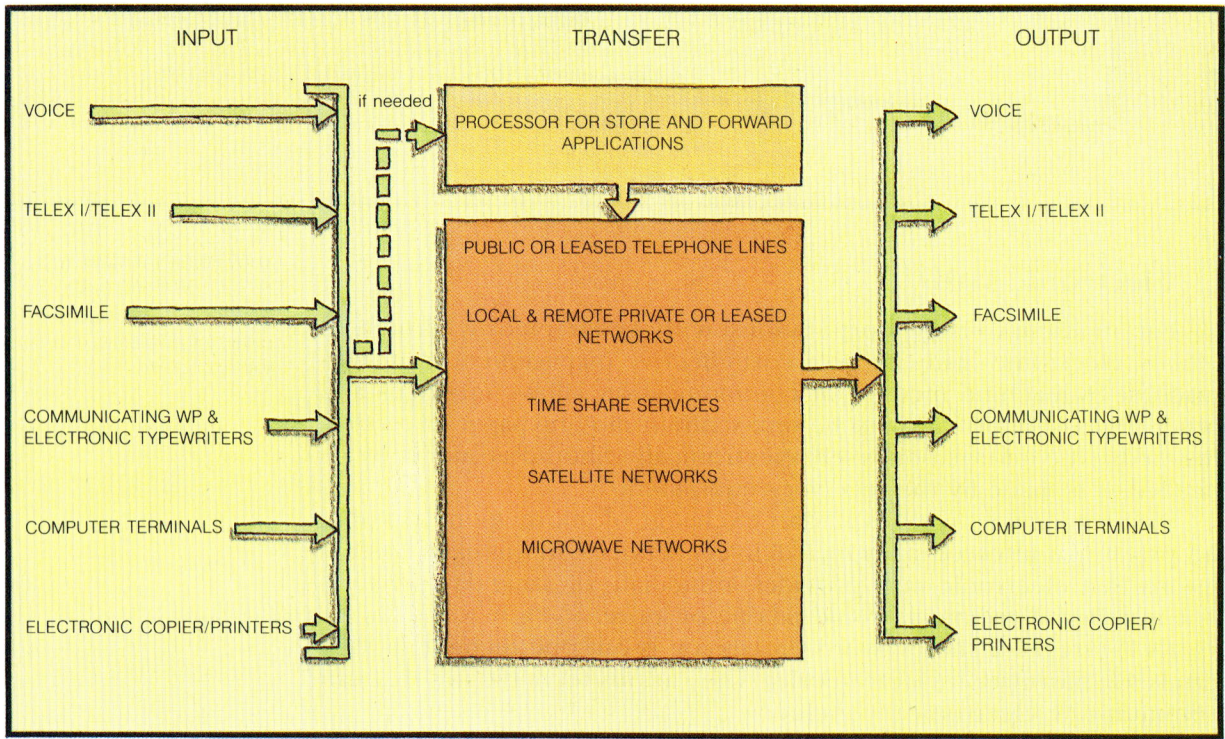

FIG. 14-2
ELECTRONIC MAIL SYSTEMS
There are many technologies that can send information electronically. They are shown as inputs in this illustration.
(Courtesy of Datapro Research Corp.)

Communicating word processors can connect directly with other communicating word processors, or they can be linked to other systems. Examples of machines to which communicating word processors can communicate include OCR scanners, typesetters, and computers. When linked to a computer system, the communicating word processor becomes a computer-based message system.

Computer-Based Message Systems. Since large computer systems are equipped with the power to control many office technologies, they are evolving as the directors of electronic mail traffic. Thus, computer terminals, personal computers, and word processors could be the keyboarding devices. Messages can be either sent immediately or stored and forwarded at a time when transmission rates are cheaper.

Each user must have a sending and receiving device, an electronic mail address (number), a file (electronic mailbox) to contain incoming and outgoing messages, and a directory of user names and addresses. Text-editing functions can be performed only by communicating word processors or by word processing software features attached to a terminal.

Computer-based message systems are available in various forms. Three basic forms are:

- Communicating word processors
- Remote computing services (Users share an off-site computer and pay for the cost of services needed.)
- In-house systems (A company owns its own computer system and communications resources.)

Facsimile. Facsimile has been popular for many years and is one of the most cost-effective means for sending mail electronically. Any image—data, text, or graphic (photographs, charts, graphs, line drawings, and signatures) can be sent. No special document format is required, and little training is needed to operate the equipment.

The basic problem with facsimile has been incompatibility of equipment. Facsimile terminals of different manufacturers generally are not compatible with each other or with other types of communication terminals. However, efforts toward standardization are in progress.

Telex and TWX. Telex and TWX are among the oldest of keyboard-entered communication services. The device used to enter and to receive text is the teletypewriter.

TWX stands for Teletypewriter Exchange Service. When owned and operated by two separate companies, Telex and TWX were in direct competition with each other and were not compatible. Now owned by one company, these two services have resolved the problem of incompatibility. Computer store-and-forward switching systems have been

Facsimile is one of the most cost-effective means of sending mail electronically.

installed to resolve the differences of Telex and TWX codes and transmission speeds.

Telex and TWX offer the advantages of providing domestic as well as international service, immediate or store-and-forward delivery, and relatively low cost. Their disadvantages include relatively slow service (compared to other electronic mail devices), required training to operate the special keyboard, and draft-quality output. Also, the less expensive and older models use paper tape storage media.

The capabilities of electronic mail technologies are expanded by communication networks. These are introduced at the end of this chapter.

Micrographics

As Chapter 6 explained, paper files produced by word processors can be filed in their original form or reduced to microfilm for more compact storage. Word processing and computer output can be filed and retrieved electronically without first committing a document to paper. The electronic filing and retrieval systems that make this possible are COM and CAR.

Computer Output to Microfilm. More and more documents are being created digitally (on disk) from the start by the use of personal computers and word processors. It is not always economical to keep them in paper files or on-line digital storage. Information that is stored in the computer in machine-readable form can be converted to human-readable form on microfilm. COM produces microfilm directly from a computer without printing the documents on paper. Thus, the need for paper is virtually eliminated for every document put on COM.

As each document is keyed into the computer system, it is captured on coded 16mm film automatically. The document is assigned an address (sequential location number) that corresponds to the address of its filmed image in the microimage file. Other key information relating to the document can be entered in computer memory and stored as part of the record in the data base. Microfiche is a common output medium.

Advanced COM equipment can print data on microfilm at a rate of 10,000 pages an hour. Little or no operator intervention is required.

Computer-Assisted Retrieval. To enhance the management and retrieval of microform images, CAR systems have been developed. CAR systems are not limited to controlling information in microform media. They are also used to manage paper-based records. CAR enables the retrieval of a document to be achieved within 30 seconds.

To retrieve a specific document, the operator calls up the address and supporting information on a microfilm reader-printer or a CRT terminal. If a paper copy is required, it can be printed on the retrieval device.

CAR can be interfaced with various office automation components, including word processing media. It can be applied to indexing and managing documents recorded on word processing diskettes. CAR can be used to manage information created on word processors, personal computers, and electronic message systems which input to the company's central computer system. Also, CAR can be applied to indexing and gaining access to documents created by word or data processing where the entire text is output and stored on COM.

The need for paper is virtually eliminated when COM is used.

Applications. Examples of documents that are conducive to COM and CAR include employment records, credit records, financial transactions that require signature verification, library catalogs, customer account files, accounting records, correspondence, court records, technical reports, and legal documents. Documentation is required for birth certificates, drivers licenses, marriage certificates, and death records—documents that are repeatedly used. The filing, storing, retrieving, and reproducing of these documents can best be met by the use of micrographics.

Status of Micrographics in Relation to Other Technologies. Vendors predict increased use of micrographics in the word processing environment. Users, such as airlines, that need immediate, real-time access to data prefer to use a display terminal and retrieve the data from a disk. The fact that the cost of magnetic disks is decreasing offers large-volume storage at a competitive price. The development of optical disk storage provides users the option of more convenient and less expensive storage. The two technologies could even complement each other. The user could file on-line with optical disks and then shift to micrographics for storage.

Optical Character Recognition

Optical character recognition first gained popularity in data processing applications. Common uses included mail sorting, clearing and sorting checks by banks, and processing remittances from customers. For word processing, OCR scanners enable companies to retain secretaries at typewriters for draft copies, while utilizing word processing machines for editing and printing the final copies.

Optical scanners can read characters from typed pages at a rate of about 40 times the manual input rate. Unlike facsimile, that involves only the sending of an image, OCR output can be further processed. Each readable character is transformed into machine-readable language. In this section you will look at applications, equipment, and innovations of OCR as it relates to information processing.

Data Processing and Word Processing Applications. OCR equipment used for data processing generally is faster and more expensive than the scanners used for word processing. For data processing applications OCR involves reading numbers. The interfacing of OCR with word processing requires that text be examined and revised after it is scanned so that there are no errors. In examining textual material, the proofreader must identify both mechanical and content errors. All proofreading by human beings is done "manually."

OCR scanners for data processing react to errors differently than do those used for word processing. When a data processing scanner comes

Unlike facsimile, OCR output can be further processed.

to an unrecognizable character, it usually sends the document to a reject pile rather than make a guess as to what the number might be. OCR scanners for word processing, on the other hand, either make a guess or flag the characters that are unrecognizable. The word processing specialist then must examine the text and edit it for accuracy of mechanics and content.

Word processing applications that involve long, strictly narrative documents (rather than tabular or specially formatted copy) are especially conducive to OCR scanning. Law firms were among the first to utilize OCR.

Equipment Configuration and Features. Three basic parts comprise an OCR scanner—a paper transport, a scanning device, and recognition and output logic. The paper transport accepts one page at a time from the feed stack, advances it through the scanning device, and deposits it in the output hopper. The scanning device scans a line, character by character, across the page. Characters are recognized by their light-absorbing and reflecting qualities. The recognition and output logic analyzes the signals generated by the scanning device to identify the characters being read. It then converts the signals into digital data for output onto compatible media. Some scanners include a video display terminal (VDT) for on-line operation correction.

Text scanned by the OCR is transferred to the word processor in two ways. The scanned text can be recorded on disk (or diskette) and transferred to the word processing system by that means. Or, the scanned text can be transferred on-line and stored in memory, from which it is called up onto the word processor's screen for final editing.

The accuracy of an OCR depends largely on the copy quality. A scanner will not always read a character correctly. Some scanners will replace the unrecognizable character with a special flag character. As text is called up on the word processor's screen, the operator searches for flags and replaces each with the correct character. Scanners that allow for on-line correction involve another method. Coming upon a questionable character, the scanner displays the character on the video screen. The operator can then key in the correct character by using the attached keyboard.

Innovations. The upcoming generation of OCR devices will be able to read unclear (but visible) characters in any type style. They will be many times faster and more accurate than the current models. Also, they will be able to read various paper colors, sizes, and thicknesses. They are programmed to learn new typefaces as they scan text, which will enable them to scan published materials, such as books, magazines, and newspapers. These advanced devices that can read most of the commonly used type styles and combinations of fonts are called omni-font readers.

Advanced OCR readers can scan more than 300 pages an hour. The error rate for well-prepared and clean copy averages well under one error for every 10,000 characters read. On some models the error rate is less than one character substitution per 300,000 scanned characters.[2]

An OCR reader that is connected to a communication network offers options which can speed up electronic mail. For example, one system can automatically send a scanned message in any one of four ways: Telex, TWX, direct-distance dial, or by a store-and-forward service that interfaces incompatible terminals.

Computer terminals of various vendors may not be able to communicate with each other or with a central processor. The more advanced OCR systems can create communications compatibility among numerous diverse and incompatible systems. It is predicted that advanced

---

[2]Peter F. Polizzano, "OCR Scanners: Expanding Horizons for the Office," *The Office* (June, 1983), pp. 116-124.

office scanners will combine the characteristics of both OCR and facsimile. This would enable graphics, logos, and signatures as well as textual and numerical material to be read. OCR scanners also are being incorporated into microfilm technology.

As an input device, OCR depends on the use of paper in the office. As the availability of personal terminals increases and paper output from typewriters decreases, the need for OCR drops. However, the paperless office is not yet here. The continued development of OCR depends on its interfacing with other technologies.

From 60 to 70 percent of the cost of typesetting involves the keying of textual material.

Typesetting

To explain the interrelation of word processing and typesetting, three topics must be discussed. First, the work flow of a typical typeset document from manuscript to distribution is shown. Second, the ways by which word processors fit into the work flow are given. Third, common typesetting terms are introduced.

Work Flow of an All-Text Typeset Document. The work flow of a typeset document can be broken down into many steps. The first step is the initial drafting of the manuscript, which may have been typed by the author or transcribed from the author's dictation or longhand draft. The manuscript is keyboarded and stored on a disk for subsequent typesetting. The output of the material is in galley form.

A galley was originally the frame used to hold the metal letters as they were being assembled for hot type. After they were assembled in the tray, ink was rolled over them and paper pressed on them to get a "galley proof." With modern typesetters, there actually are no galleys. However, many people refer to the first proof of a typeset document as the **galley**.

galley first proof of a typeset document

The galley is cut into pieces and pasted onto pages according to the desired layout; this is known as paste-up. These pages are made into plates. The document is then printed, collated, and bound. Last, the document is distributed to the intended recipients. These steps are charted in Figure 14-3.

Technology is speeding up the process by eliminating or combining some of the steps shown in Figure 14-3. An example is a preview facility, which displays type almost as it will appear in print. The type is displayed in proper size and in its proper location.

An area composition device goes a step further; it allows the operator to work with the material on the screen in its actual position and size without inputting typesetter codes. This device is especially helpful in typesetting business forms, which require complex coding procedures.

Direct-to-plate technology is another advancement that is occurring. Paste-up is beginning to take place on video screens, as is happening in the newspaper industry. By 1990 it is predicted that there will be printing operations in which photographic materials are not used; instead, everything from keyboarding to platemaking will be handled electronically.

Inputting Via Word Processors. As Chapter 5 introduced, text can be transferred from a word processor to a typesetter. If the word processor and the typesetter are compatible, direct interface can be attained in one of two ways: (1) The two devices can be cable-connected or wired through the telephone system, or (2) the word processing diskette can be copied onto the typesetting diskette. In either case, most rekeying is avoided. Only typesetting codes have to be added.

Interfacing word processors to typesetters greatly reduces the rekeying, proofreading, and recorrecting that would occur if the typesetting operator worked from a typed paper document. From 60 to 70 percent of the cost of typesetting involves the keying of textual material. Thus, labor costs are significantly reduced by having the word processor key the material and check it for accuracy. Then it can be transferred to the typesetter.

Classification of Systems. A typesetting system may be a convenience (decentralized) system or a centralized system. In either case word processing machines are likely to interface with the typesetting equipment.

CHAPTER 14 Integrating Technology for Information Processing

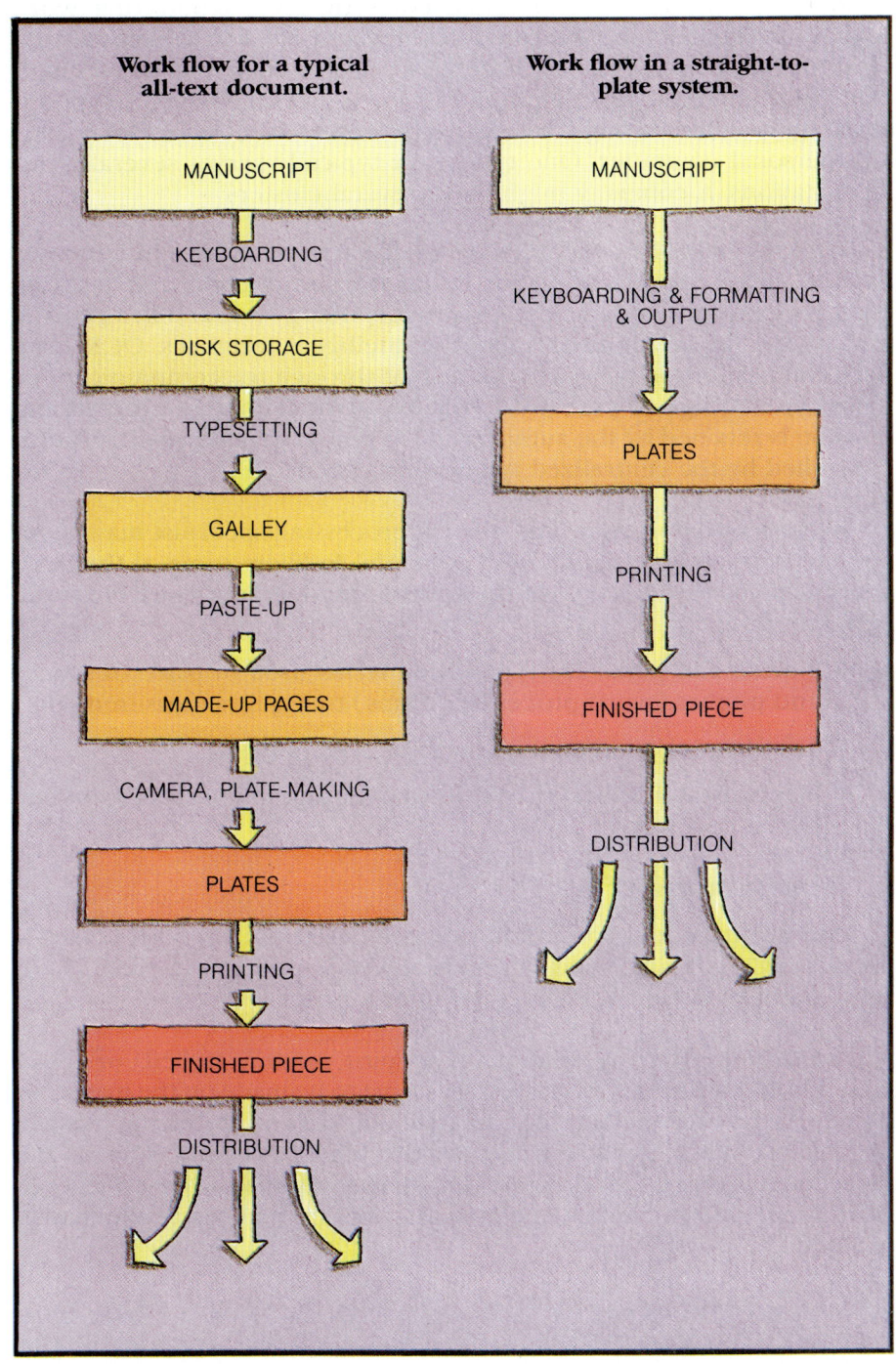

FIG. 14-3
WORK FLOW OF AN ALL-TEXT TYPESET DOCUMENT
As you see from the illustration, there are many steps involved in the production of an all-text typeset document.

Convenience System. A convenience typesetter is a typesetting word processor. The machine is located near the authors, and the typesetting operator keys in the text (directly inputs). A convenience cluster involves the interfacing of an input device to the convenience typesetter. The input device might be a word processor, electronic typewriter, or a personal computer. One typesetter typically serves several input work stations. A company might have several clusters.

Centralized System. In a centralized system the typesetting equipment is located in a central place—the in-house reproduction and printing plant. As expected, the highest level of technology is found in a centralized system. In this configuration, the intelligent terminals, OCR scanners, and word processors are connected through telecommunications to the typesetting equipment. The control of input content, storage, and revision is retained by the author; and the typographic form of output is controlled by the centralized typesetting system.

point measurement from the top of ascending characters to the bottom of descending characters

pica unit of measurement for typeset material

leading adjusting the space between lines

kerning adjusting the space between characters and words

Typesetting Terms. Although a word processing specialist may never operate typesetting equipment, it is helpful to know some of the basic vocabulary when talking with the typesetting operator. Here are some terms to note:

- **Points** and **picas** are typesetting terms used in place of spaces and pitches (word processing terms) to express measurements.
- **Leading** is the amount of space between lines.
- **Kerning** is the process of adjusting the amount of space between letters and words.

Reprographics

The evolution of reprographics has focused on three processes—duplicating, copying, and printing. Word processing relates to reprographics in producing quality input for each.

Duplicating. The preparation of a spirit master, stencil, or offset master is much easier if no corrections have to be made on the master or stencil. As a matter of fact, the most difficult part of producing masters or stencils is making good corrections that will not be noticeable on the reproduced copies. The keyboarding and revision can be done on a word processor with error-free final playback committed to the master or stencil.

Copying. Regardless of the copying process, the quality of the original type affects the quality of the copy. Clear, dark type results in better copies than unevenly shaded, gray type. Another factor is the problem of corrections. Many corrections that are made to an already-typed or printed original are usually noticeable on the copies. A word processor is instrumental in producing letter-quality originals (the corrections having been made before the document was printed) from which professional looking copies can be made.

Electronic Printing. Among the various types of electronic printing devices, the intelligent copier/printer seems to have the most potential for interfacing with other information processing systems. The IC/P can accept digital input from word processors, computers, prerecorded magnetic media, and graphic scanners. The output (either paper copies or digital information) can be produced on site, stored, or sent electronically (a form of electronic mail).

Appropriate users are organizations with several branch offices and large volumes of internal documents. The electronic mail feature is attractive to institutions, such as banks, government agencies, insurance companies, and utilities, that need communications and distributed printing.

Endowed with such sophisticated functions as line justification, page numbering, change of type styles and sizes, and unattended transmission, IC/Ps are competing with other systems. Examples include typesetters, offset duplicators, copiers, and facsimile.

Office automation experts predict that the IC/P will be instrumental in tying together workstations, electronic files, and electronic mail for internal and external office communications. For electronic mail, IC/Ps can be utilized in three ways: (1) wired directly to computers or communicating word processors, (2) linked by communication lines to workstations and other IC/Ps located at remote sites, or (3) interfaced with local area networks.

Impact of IC/Ps on Word Processing. In some companies IC/Ps are replacing daisy wheel impact printers for high quality images of large volumes of text. For word processing systems that must process many forms, IC/Ps are especially valuable. The need to maintain forms inventories and the waste that results when new forms replace obsolete ones are both eliminated. Each form can be digitized and stored electronically and then printed only as needed, which is at the time the filled-in text is keyboarded.

Teleconferencing

Office communications is a broad category which includes sending and receiving telephone calls, writing letters and memos, and participating in conferences and meetings. Communications is an expensive element of office work. Comprehensive management studies reveal that executives spend more time communicating in meetings and on the phone than doing desk work. Further, most face-to-face meetings

Computer conferencing has broad application in word processing environments.

(involving expensive travel and time away from the office) could be handled in less costly ways.

Teleconferencing as a means of exchanging information offers four basic options. These options are computer teleconferencing, audio (voice) teleconferencing, audiographic (audio and image) teleconferencing, and video (slow-scan or full-motion television) teleconferencing. These were introduced in Chapter 1.

Computer Conference. In this option an electronic message system records communications among the participants, each of whom has a display terminal connected to the computer mainframe. Each participant can access, read, and respond to these communications regardless of what the other participants are doing. There is much flexibility because the participants do not have to be at their desks at the same time. The computer system keeps a verbatim log of the meeting, which can be printed if necessary. This teleconference option is especially effective for managing ongoing project activities and for avoiding communication delay caused by different time zones.

Computer teleconferencing has broad application in word processing environments. The conference manager typically distributes an agenda, which includes various topics to which the participants must respond. The participants do their research and then send the responses to the computer. Situations that involve mostly text are usually prepared on a word processor or on a computer terminal directed by word processing software. Text is then transmitted via the computer system.

Participants report that certain problems which formerly would have been tackled by a person-to-person conference can be solved with increased speed and effectiveness via computer conferencing. Issues can be dealt with when they arise, rather than being postponed until the next scheduled face-to-face meeting. Also, more people can participate in decision making because the cost of face-to-face meetings traditionally limits the number of people who are invited to meet.

Audio Conference. An audio conference is a voice-only conference that is actually a conference telephone call. The participants at each site generally are grouped in a room that is equipped with a telephone, audio speakers, and at least one microphone.

Audiographic Conference. In this type of teleconference a medium for transmitting graphics is used in addition to the telephone. The images might be transmitted by facsimile, computer graphics, or electronic blackboards.

Slow-Scan Video Conference. Slow-scan video is an option which is much less expensive than full-motion video. With this option the pictures of the participants are in the form of still poses (or freeze-frame television).

slow-scan video type of teleconference; pictures of participants are in the form of still poses

Full-Motion Video Conference. When it is necessary for participants to see each other, as well as visual aids in live action, a video conference is appropriate. Video conferences are of two basic types—telepresentations and teleconferences (telemeetings).

A **telepresentation** is a one-way video (transmission of the picture) but two-way audio private broadcast. Communication is distributed from one central site to several offices. Typical applications would be press conferences, professional development programs, sales meetings, and shareholders' meetings.

telepresentation one-way video and two-way audio private broadcast

A teleconference involves the participation of people located in their respective offices who interact across the miles as if they were sitting in the same meeting room. In short, it is a two-way, full-motion video connecting all sites. The system may be on the company's own premises or in a public room rented by the hour.

Some companies offer video teleconferencing centers in major cities. The users (companies that cannot afford their own video teleconference system) go to the nearest centers and pay by the hour for the services used.

The choice of a teleconference option depends on the application at hand and the length of the conference. A one-hour teleconference is likely to be less expensive than travel expenses of the participants, including time away from the office. As the length of the conference increases and video equipment becomes necessary, the economic relationship changes.

Voice Processing

Voice processing technology is based on the premise that the fastest way to put a thought into action is to speak it, and the most efficient way to capture speech is to record it. Thus, it is an attempt to interface humans and machines.

As voice processing technology is evolving, two basic forms can be identified—voice messaging and voice recognition. While voice messaging is well developed for business use, voice recognition is still in the beginning stages.

Voice Messaging. A voice messaging system is also known as voice mail (VMX stands for voice mailbox) or as voice store-and-forward. It was designed to replace short memos and phone message slips that can so easily be misplaced and to eliminate telephone tag.

Voice messaging enables vocal correspondence to be accomplished by telephone and computer. To place a call, the caller accesses the voice message system. The system's voice (recorded and stored in digital form) asks the caller to enter his or her code by depressing the buttons on the push-button phone and entering the "mailbox" number of the person to receive the message. Then the caller gives the message by speaking into the phone. When the message is completed, the caller's voice (analog signals) is digitized (converted to data signals) and stored on the computer disk. The stored message can then be recalled, routed, and dispersed just like a piece of electronic mail.

To receive messages, a recipient dials the voice mailbox and gives the code for retrieving messages. Upon searching through the disk, the computer speaks the names of callers who have left messages. The recipient can ask the computer to play back all the messages or just certain ones. The computer converts the digitized voice back to the caller's voice. The recipient can then instruct the computer to erase the message, store it for a later recall, or transfer it to an associate's electronic mailbox for further action.

Voice mail differs from electronic mail in that the message is spoken and heard; with electronic mail, the message is typed and read. A voice message system differs from traditional telephone conversations in that it is a one-way communication, while a telephone conversation is a two-way interactional communication.

Common voice mail applications are situations for which there is a need to act quickly on telephone information. For example, field sales personnel often need inventory, pricing, and delivery information to serve customers promptly. Customers might need fast service on equipment. An executive might need to check with all sales representatives to clear a certain date for a regional meeting.

CHAPTER 14 Integrating Technology for Information Processing 413

Voice messaging systems are gaining in popularity. The main advantages of voice messaging are the following:

1. Eliminates telephone tag
2. Enables caller to make one call that will reach all recipients regardless of difference in time zones—especially significant for international calls
3. Allows the recipients to work uninterrupted on important projects and then accept messages at their convenience
4. Saves time, possible error, and misplacement of short memos

Voice Recognition. Voice recognition (also known as speech recognition) is a technology whereby the computerized system responds to voice commands to perform various functions. While it has been greatly improved for data processing functions, it is not yet practical for word processing functions.

voice recognition
computerized system responds to voice commands to perform various functions

Two systems which involve voice recognition but which have unique meanings are speech recognition and speaker verification. They are distinguished as follows: Speech recognition involves transforming spoken words into a format that can be used by a computer to perform functions. Speaker verification transforms words into digital format and then matches the format (voice pattern) to a preestablished library of voice patterns.

Speaker verification is used when security and confidentiality are needed. For example, an authorized employee speaks into the system,

speaker verification
used to protect confidentiality and to enhance security

Voice processing technology is an attempt to interface humans and machines.

and the system determines if the speaker is actually the person he or she is claiming to be. Common uses include (1) controlling the access to a building, a security area, or confidential files and (2) handling electronic funds transfer.

Voice recognition for word processing functions requires that the computerized processor interpret continuous speech, which is extremely complex, and convert it to a typed/printed page. The sound waves of continuous speech (with its unlimited vocabulary, accents, and individual mannerisms) must be converted into digital impulses. The system then compares those impulses to the digitized sound patterns that have been stored in its memory.

Systems have been developed that are capable of recognizing a limited number of single and distinct sounds, such as letters of the alphabet; numbers; and words such as *yes, no, on,* and *off*. A system that recognizes only single words is known as discrete word recognition. Thus, voice recognition for data processing applications is not only feasible but also expanding in development. It is commonly called voice data entry.

Voice data entry is used for taking inventory, verifying credit, accessing a data base, and processing orders. In placing an order by a sales representative, speaker verification provides the security that assures that only qualified people can enter an order. The transaction is directly with the computer system without intervening steps of order processing and keyboarding. Voice recognition is especially beneficial for voice data entry for these reasons. It:

1. Is more error-free than manual data entry.

2. Reduces the wasted time and motion of manual tasks that require further processing by writing or typing.

3. Assists people performing tasks that require the use of their eyes and both hands. Examples would include sorting baggage, taking inventory, and reporting laboratory results.

4. Is more user-friendly than any keys or functions of keyboard terminals.

5. Allows handicapped people who cannot keyboard to access the computer.

Continuous speech recognition continues to develop with the goal of reaching 99 percent reliability, which would make it usable for word processing. So far, the machines that have been developed are quite limited in their capabilities. They have small vocabularies, restrictive rules for word arrangement, the ability to recognize only a few speakers, and the requirement that words be spoken with exaggerated pauses between them. Certain vendors are building this feature into personal computers and word processors (called listening typewriters).

Voice-actuated typewriters or word processors will not replace human beings. They will need specialists to operate them, to proofread the copy, to make the necessary corrections, and to print an error-free copy.

LINKING SUBSYSTEMS

You have learned about the major office systems that process information. Each has a specific function, but they can join forces to process certain types of information. The rewards of connecting systems include increasing the speed, decreasing the amount of human effort, and lowering the cost of processing the work. At the same time, the amount of information that is committed to paper is kept at a minimum.

The biggest hurdle to jump in connecting systems is overcoming the problem of incompatibility. One way to accomplish the feat is to use a black box (protocol conversion processor) that converts or translates the language of one machine to another, as was described in Chapter 7. More sophisticated approaches are provided by networks, which enable more than two types of machines to communicate. Networks are classified as local area networks, switch and access networks, and wide area networks.

Local Area Networks

As described in Chapter 1, a local area network links various types of machines within a building or adjacent buildings. With the ability to communicate, the dissimilar machines can work together as a team as shown in Figure 14-4. This means that the information that exists in one system can be reused without being reentered into another separate system. All input devices can be connected to one universal system for the exchange and integration of information. Generally the entire system is housed within one building, adjacent buildings, or the same geographic area.

A local area network is composed of a communications facility (for example, a coaxial cable, such as that used for cable television) and interface units that link the computers and terminals to the communications facility. Either a baseband or a broadband design might be used.

Using radio waves, a **baseband communications channel** uses the basic frequency band (instead of higher frequencies) and a coaxial cable. The coaxial cable has one channel, which is like a party line. Many machines have the channel available, but only two can use it at one time. There is no central switching unit to route traffic over the network.

More expensive than a baseband channel, a **broadband communications channel** can handle more advanced applications—including the transmission of voice as well as data and text. The coaxial cable of a broadband design provides many channels per cable. A controller is

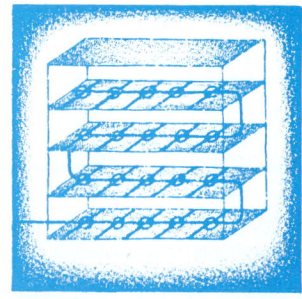

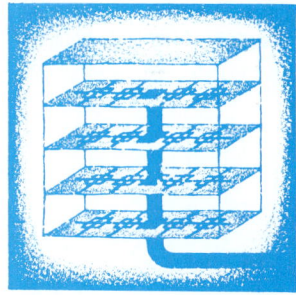

Top: A baseband channel provides a single transmission channel and allows one-way transmission of information.

Bottom: A broadband channel provides a variety of transmission channels and allows two-way transmission of information.

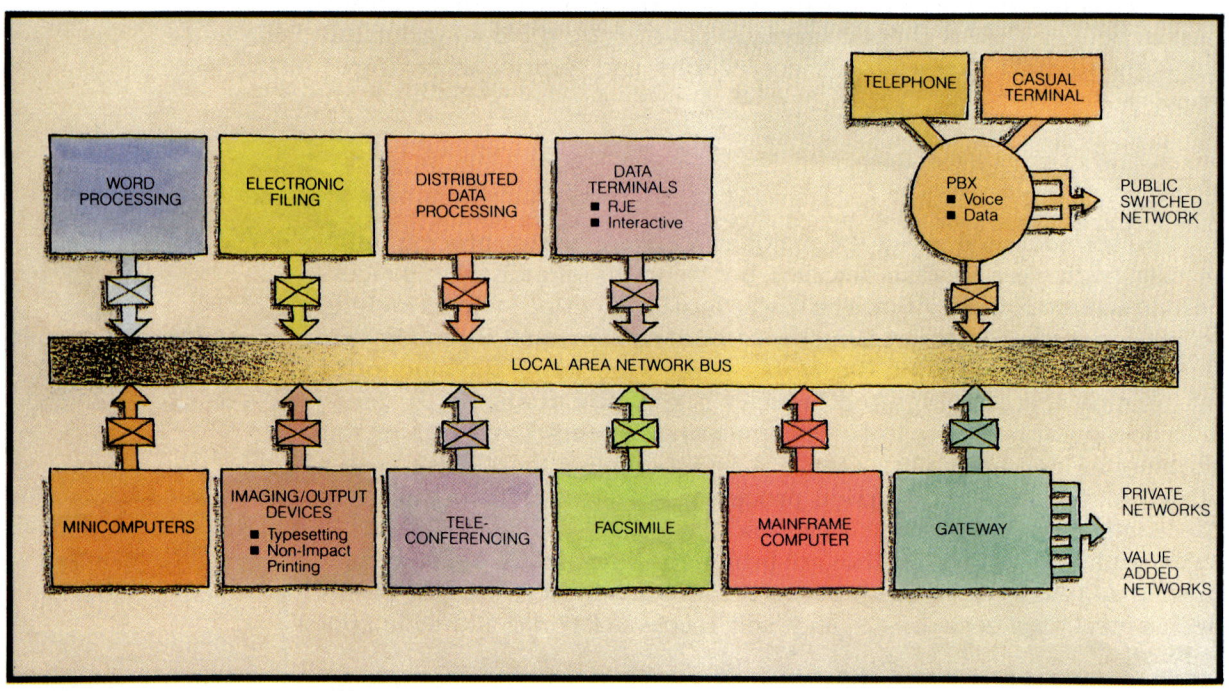

FIG. 14-4
LOCAL AREA NETWORK SYSTEM
A local area network system allows dissimilar machines to exchange information within one universal system.
(Courtesy of Harris Corporation)

used to route traffic for the large numbers of simultaneous users as they share one of many individual channels of the system. Broadband uses the wide bandwidth of radio frequency transmission.

The technology of fiber optics is also being developed. The capacity of fiber optics is so boundless that it goes beyond one's imagination. Instead of using electricity to pass information, this technology sends information in the form of light signals along fine glass threads. Glass fibers can carry a great deal of information at a fraction of the size and weight of metal (such as in copper cables). Another advantage is that light waves are immune to electromagnetic or radio interference, which means that less information is lost than with copper wire. This technology is still in the development stages, and the cost is high compared to other technologies being used.

The communications facility and the interface units of local area networks are purchased by the user. Thus, users must shop for network systems as well as the equipment itself.

Switch and Access Networks

Similar to extension cords, switch and access networks connect LANs to each other or to gateways that open to larger networks. Switch networks are used to speed up the transfer of digital data (used in data processing and word processing systems). Most telephone systems employ analog technology. Digital information must be converted to analog signals before it can enter a public switched network. As you will recall from Chapter 7, special devices called modems are used to convert digital signals to analog signals so that the information can be transmitted by telephone lines.

A multiplexer is a high-speed rotary switcher (a hardware device) that allows a number of different signals to be transmitted over one channel. Thus, it permits several terminals, at various locations, to share a telephone line.

Wide Area Networks

As you will recall from Chapter 1, global connections are provided by wide area networks, sometimes referred to as global networks. Local area networks can be expanded into larger network configurations that enable companies to send information from city to city, across the nation, and to other countries throughout the world. These larger telecommunication networks make use of combinations of telephone lines, microwave radio links, and satellites to send information.

Preceded by a number of more primitive satellites, the first communications satellite for business applications was launched in 1965. Since then, larger and more complex satellites have been launched. Meanwhile, the size and complexity of earth stations have been shrinking. The cost of satellite services in general has been steadily decreasing. Thus, it is becoming more cost-effective to employ them for business uses.

Information processing, composed of many technologies, has grown by leaps and bounds. You have learned about each of the subsystems that performs a special information processing function. Word processing relates to each of its system "associates" in unique ways, but its primary function is text manipulation. For the many subsystems to work together as an information processing team, they must communicate. This link is provided by various types of communication devices that expand into networks.

The result of a successfully integrated information processing system is the fulfillment of certain goals. In contrast to individual subsystems operating independently of each other, a totally integrated system processes information more quickly. Less physical effort is involved, as recreating, rekeyboarding, and reproofreading tasks are eliminated. The cost of processing information is reduced to the most economical means. Accuracy is improved as efforts to eliminate or reduce errors are facilitated. The quality of the output can have the highest professional appearance; or it can be less than letter quality, depending upon the application.

Both managers and office support personnel can work at their most efficient levels without being frustrated and slowed down by interruptions. Paperwork is reduced, for information is not committed to paper

Satellites are one means by which wide area networks can provide global communications.

unless there is a need. In that case, a paper copy can be made at the receiver's end.

A totally integrated information processing system sounds like a utopia. Electronic tools appear to be friendly, and they seem to have unlimited capabilities. However, users have concerns that have developed into issues. They are described in the next chapter to give you a realistic view of the modern business world.

DISCUSSION QUESTIONS AND CASE PROBLEM

DISCUSSION QUESTIONS

1. What are the basic forms of information that are processed by the integration of technologies?
2. Name nine systems that can interface for a total information processing system.

3 How does word processing relate to and interface with CAR, OCR, and typesetting?
4 With which of the electronic mail systems can the receiver get a paper printout automatically?
5 Distinguish between the following types of teleconferences:
   a Computer
   b Audio
   c Audiographic
   d Slow-scan video
   e Full-motion video
6 How can incompatible equipment be linked for a totally integrated information processing system? Include the following terms in your explanation: protocol conversion processor, modem, multiplexer, radio waves, coaxial cable, LAN, wide area network, and satellite.
7 What are five results (achieved goals) of a successfully integrated information processing system?

CASE PROBLEM

Maria Perez is the manager of the information processing department of a large insurance company. Maria's word processing staff is responsible for producing the internal company rule book—the manual that describes the policies and procedures for salespeople. This book is updated each month, which requires that many pages be revised. Prior to the revision, the changes have to be read to be sure that they meet the approval of the state insurance commissioner's ruling for changes.

After being revised by the word processing staff, the pages are verified and then delivered to the typesetting staff for further processing (typesetting and photocopying). When the pages are copy verified, they are photocopied, punched, and distributed to each of the company's 50 branch offices. This step takes about three to four weeks for completion.

The branch offices have been complaining that the long delay to receive information affects the sales to their customers. After receiving the revisions, they must revisit a customer to explain the changes. On occasion, business has been lost because customers question the efficiency and reliability of the company's procedures in processing paperwork.

Top management has asked Maria to investigate alternatives to the present method. Then Maria is to make recommendations that would speed up the delivery of the revised manual to the branch offices.

1 Under the present method, what processes need to be handled more efficiently?
2 What devices could speed up the process?
3 Is there a single piece of equipment that could create efficiencies in several areas? If so, what is it? Describe the resulting work flow.

Chapter 15 Participating in a Total Information Processing System

CHAPTER OBJECTIVES:

Describe issues that have evolved as information processing systems developed.

Identify both the positive and negative aspects of office automation issues.

Distinguish the new roles and organizational structure arising from such a merge.

Develop ways that would better prepare you for the coming changes.

Most people approach their first experience with word processors, electronic workstations, personal computers, and other equipment that makes up the new information processing system with a combination of awe and fear. It is inevitable that the change from using familiar office tools such as pens and pencils, typewriters, dictating machines, and photocopiers could cause some anxiety regardless of what was being changed. However, the seeming complexity of the electronic workstation (whether terminal, communicating word processor, or desktop microcomputer) causes users to be apprehensive. An excellent time for building users' confidence with the new system is during their introduction to the equipment. Careful and thorough explanations during the demonstration followed by assisted, hands-on training can both hasten the user's comfort level and instill enthusiasm.

Making a transition to anything new or different does not always go smoothly without some conflicts and stress. But when the change is in pursuit of crystal-clear improvements, the conflicts and stress can be softened. The transition to a totally automated information processing system also introduces mixed emotions for the participants. Every aspect of office operations is affected—from daily work routines to personnel.

To an office automation professional such challenges are exciting. A successful outcome can be a very rewarding experience for the company as well as for the individual users. The results to be gained from an information processing system are well worth the extra care and concern the team members provide to the user community before, during, and after project implementation. The measure of system success is directly related to the level of users' acceptance, confidence, and daily use of the equipment. It is important for the team members to be aware of potential problems in order to relieve users' fears and replace those fears with positive attitudes.

New users not only must spend time to learn all of the actions and commands that allow them to operate the new equipment, but also must face changes in both office procedures and personal work habits. The new procedures generally result in a redistribution of the power that comes with knowledge. New company organizational structures arise. When word processing was in its infancy, this organizational structure was called a Word Processing Center. Even now, as more individuals reduce their dependence upon the familiar props of office work—pen, pencil, paper, eraser—they face a new office structure. This new organizational structure will no doubt become known as the Information Processing Center. Apprehension is a natural reaction under these circumstances. In order to allay this fear, the planning team should recommend to management that reorganizational changes occur slowly and only after users are comfortable with the system's operation.

Many people who are completely unfamiliar with a computer may be awestruck by its capabilities. Ultimately, the workstation is a little computer. In these individuals' minds, the computer is not a dumb object but a living entity that represents brainpower. Often these people do not understand that the computer can be only as smart as the person who operates it. One good way to provide users with a more comfortable experience during their introduction to the workstation is for a team member to share his or her learning adventure. A thorough training program will help employees utilize these tools to their greatest potential.

To reduce the psychological stress of the employees and yet provide as many efficiencies and cost reductions as possible, companies usually begin their approach to office automation from a proven electronic standpoint—word processing. From this point, the other subsystems of information processing can be phased in slowly to provide user comfort, training, and control.

An information processing system is an integrated collection of subsystems that supports the operation of an office procedure. Typically, it provides a facility by which office workers may communicate in sequencing the steps of the procedure. An information processing system will:

- Support the creation and revision of information.
- Support the storage and retrieval of information.
- Enable limited forms of processing to be applied to information, such as typesetting or graphic illustrations of the textual information.
- Connect the office with the rest of the organization and the outside world in order to share information.

In other words, an information processing system provides an environment and a context in which workers can do office work. Most office work takes the form of information processing, decision making, or interpersonal communication.

When evolving to an information processing system, companies should approach the evolution from one or a combination of needs. These needs are as follows:

- The quality of the *information*
- The needs of the *people*
- The adequacy of the *tools*
- The rationality of the *process*
- The *organization*

Companies which have experienced problems with the quality of their information will select and implement a system that will provide them with information improvements. They will be interested primarily in seeking out equipment that will ensure the accuracy and timeliness of this information. They will want to maintain a central filing system for that information in order to capture only relevant data from a single reliable source. This means that the system also must have a means of organizing, structuring, and indexing the data so that it can be accessible to them by any number of identifiers and from wherever they are located.

Companies which are primarily concerned with satisfying the needs of their employees will select and implement a system that will provide these employees with the right tools. The team members will ensure that the employees receive good training on a system that is fitted with specific applications that will respond to these needs. They will also be concerned that all system devices, such as workstations and printers, fit aesthetically into the working environment so that the employee will feel motivated in using the system.

Companies that are very analytical and cost conscious will select and implement a system wherein the tools can be matched to the tasks by being effectively designed for the tasks; thus, properly used. In addition, the team members will make certain that the system is at the right level of integration so they can maintain a cost effectiveness during current and future growth years.

Companies that have potential users who are very technical and equipment oriented will select and implement a system based on its operating capabilities. The team members responsible for the selection will be concerned that all system components are relatively trouble-free and that information storage is safeguarded against destruction from system failure or theft. They also will select workstations with a keyboard layout tailored to the tasks and easily modified for changes in applications. Each piece of equipment will fill a definite need and can be cost justified alone or as a collective system.

Companies which are involved in reorganizational changes will select and implement a system that is designed to meet its stated goals. The team members responsible for this selection will make certain that the system will be properly structured to operate effectively and appropriately positioned in its environment. Lastly, they will ensure that the system will respond to an individual user's needs as well as to the overall company plans and needs.

The ideal approach to the selection and implementation of an information processing system would be to combine the best of these perspectives into a single approach. However, all companies do not have the same priorities. Thus, the job of system selection and implementation is more complex for the information processing planners. Though the process is complex, it is quite possible to have a successful system installation. The more thorough planners are in their approach and the more aware they are of users' and companies' needs, the more confidence they will have toward making the right decision.

PROBLEMS INVOLVED WITH MERGING THE NEW TECHNOLOGIES

Perhaps nothing in the computer industry has stirred up as much discussion as office automation, which is synonymous with information processing or an integrated information processing system. The technology itself is bewildering. There are doubts of equipment compatibility and true integration still confronting the industry. But the technical issues are only a small fraction of the moral, social, and humanistic questions being raised about the automated office.

As vendors display their many products, businesses search for more efficient pathways to making profits. Technology continues to advance more rapidly than businesses can comprehend. The office worker is

Managers can help office workers accept new technology by expanding their level of understanding.

sometimes lost in the resulting shuffle. The concerns of the office workers are being expressed by labor unions, trade organizations, and the national press.

As you read the issues that follow, it should become obvious how to correct the problems indicated. The users, in describing their problems, are pinpointing areas which should be better planned or avoided in a successful installation. As a team planner, you should develop keen listening skills in order to anticipate potential users' problems and react to them in a positive manner.

Human Issues

To some individuals, office automation is viewed as being quite threatening to office workers. Automated office systems have been accused of taking away jobs, making job functions obsolete (for example, eliminating the need for shorthand, posting machines, etc.), and being the cause of several serious health hazards. Other individuals look at office automation as being the creator of more meaningful jobs or as the salvation for organizations mired in paperwork and suffering from communication breakdown. Proponents of office automation say that it will create greater efficiency and save millions of dollars in the process.

There is enough documentation in the industry to support either viewpoint. But it is clear that office automation is here to stay. Thus, office workers should be helped to accept the new technology by

CHAPTER 15 Participating in a Total Information Processing System 425

expanding their level of understanding. Secretaries, clericals, and typists—groups traditionally without a voice in management decisions—have either embraced the new technology as a welcome aid or have required assistance to improve their job potential with the new equipment. It is also clear that the success of automating the office depends not on the machines themselves, but on how management and the information processing planners handle the implementation, training, and support.

Health Issues

The spokesperson for the National Association of Working Women has expressed concern about the role of the office worker in office automation. Her concerns fall into two categories: the design of the machine and the design of the job. She says that the design of the machine, critical to the health and safety of the worker, is a solvable problem. Nevertheless, it is serious because the problems are not being corrected. CRTs have been accused of causing eye problems, backaches and neckaches, headaches, and possibly birth defects. However, vendors have taken great strides to improve their models and are encouraging companies to provide periodic break periods for their workers.

To avoid VDT-related health problems, workers should be given frequent rest breaks and their work should be varied.

A recent National Research Council report (sponsored by the National Institute for Occupational Safety and Health, NIOSH) absolved CRTs of causing serious eye problems. The report concluded that many of the machines on the market are now ergonomically correct for use. However, there also are individuals and organizations who claim that people are hesitant to use the machines when there is no real cause for their apprehension. They rationalize by citing that no one has demonstrated any long-term ill effects from CRTs.

Job Enhancement Issues

Though the health effects of CRTs continue to generate controversy, the problem that is more easily resolvable for information processing planners is the design of the new jobs. Many people fear that office automation has led to the reorganization of work along the lines of the factory model of the past. The director of the publication *9 to 5* states:

> "Jobs that used to have variety and some exercise of judgment—and I mean even the very low-level clerical jobs—are now being broken down into their smallest possible components. New jobs are being created that repeat one task over and over again."[1]

Promoters of office automation believe better jobs have been created. They argue that, far from being a threat, advances in technology are freeing office workers and allowing them to take on greater responsibility in their jobs. One management training consultant in Lexington, Massachusetts, states:

> "Some people are afraid and intimidated by the technology, but the vast majority love it. It takes away the scut work and gives people time to handle the more challenging projects."

Recent office surveys tend to support the positive outlook for office automation. Kelly Services, the Troy, Michigan, temporary agency, has published "How Office Workers View Automation," a survey of nearly 500 office workers in Fortune 1300 firms. According to the Kelly report, three quarters of the respondents felt their new skills enabled them to exercise greater responsibility. And 90 percent said their new skills improved their overall position on the job. Although one in four said the job had become more routine since the introduction of the new equipment, 94 percent believed the new skills opened up opportunities for advancement.[2]

There are many surveys and individual praises about the positive effects of office automation; however, serious problems are still being

---

[1] "Automation May Increase Discrimination," *Office Administration and Automation* (April, 1983), pp. 32-35.
[2] "In the Industry," *Information and Word Processing Report* (February 15, 1984).

encountered. Several states have introduced bills on CRT safety to their legislatures, and workers' compensation claims have already been awarded. Some office workers have become more vocal about the drawbacks that automation has brought to their jobs.

A billing clerk at a Boston hospital admitted that information is more accessible with the technology, but she said she was unhappy to learn her work is being monitored by the machine she uses. Not informed that such monitoring was taking place, she learned from a monthly report that her output was under scrutiny. "This has pulled me further away from management. It doesn't take into account the 10 million things I do around here," she said.

At a Boston-area travel agency, a reservation supervisor who sits at her terminal all day has developed eyestrain and backaches as well as occasional headaches. She said her job would be impossible without the computer, but more job variance is needed to relieve the monotony. She pointed out that management gave little or no thought to implementation of the technology when it was brought in. Now, because of the vocal response of the employees, management is giving more consideration to the structure of the office.

The NIOSH-sponsored research report, referenced earlier in this chapter, indicated that CRT users report less individual control over their jobs than do nonusers. They report less ability to make decisions and feel less capable of taking actions. In addition, CRT users report less control over the pace of their work—the machine has taken control of the pacing. CRT users also are bothered more by environmental factors, such as design of the work place.

If an information processing system is implemented properly, job enhancement should result.

Job Loss Issues

Though serious job loss is more likely to occur in the future, there is already evidence of the disappearance of many traditional clerical positions. The discontinuation of a position is difficult to monitor. It happens in a piecemeal fashion and tends not to be noticed. Several companies have closed field or branch offices when computers made it possible to recentralize the organization. New kinds of jobs will appear with the new technology, but the key concern is that the displaced workers receive the proper training to get the new jobs.

The new technology affects more than just the support staff. Professionals and managers have raised some of the same concerns about automation as secretaries and clericals. Since office automation usually is phased in through lower positions, middle-management personnel may not face the health issues of the new equipment. However, the role of the middle manager is certainly changing and expanding with the advent of the new technology. Rather than being collectors of data, the mid-level managers will do more analysis of data as the groups under their control expand. There is apprehension, however, that middle managers may be hit by job loss as well.

Though there have been occasions of problems such as these, they should not be considered a natural outcome of office automation. The experts tend to agree that a thoughtful and well-directed implementation of office automation will bring about the desired results. Organizations that report the best results are the ones that involve the end users in the implementation process as much as possible.

The Children's Hospital Medical Center in Akron, Ohio, is an example of user involvement bringing about successful implementation. The task team brought together to direct the automation consisted of the hospital's management engineer, the director of data processing, the director of purchasing, and an experienced word processing user. The word processing user, as it turned out, was the most important member of the team. Only the true operator could evaluate the software in terms of sophistication of features and capabilities, and user-friendliness of the system.

Training and Support Issues

Training and support after a system is installed are also crucial. Companies are reluctant to allow more than one or two people to be out of the office for training at any one time. Having one employee train the others usually does not work. That person is not a teacher and inevitably cannot answer all of the questions. Sometimes management can aggravate the situation by expecting immediate productivity on the new equipment. The result could be increased stress and displeasure with the new technology. Organizations with the most success are those that

Once implementation of a system has occurred, it is crucial that training and support continue.

develop in-house training centers for employees and involve the vendor in consultation and training.

As office automation spreads, the synergy among vendor, customer, and end user will determine the ultimate acceptance and efficiency of the installed system. Efforts to organize office workers continue as labor unions look to the Europeans as examples of what unity can bring to the workplace. In Europe, ergonomics has been an important subject for years. In some countries, especially Scandinavia and Germany, ergonomics is taken so seriously that office workers have actually gone on strike (and won) over poor working conditions. The results of these strikes have made ergonomically designed offices mandatory within many European offices. Hardware, furniture, office environment, and user training/education are listed as the most important factors for employers to consider when creating a satisfactory workplace. Office workers in the United States agree that the technology would be more than welcome as long as their concerns are addressed and corrected.

Organizational Issues

There are important organizational ramifications to consider when merging separate technologies. Information processing is a composite of various subsystems which may or may not be operating as independent departments within the company. The basic subsystems are data processing, records management, word processing, and telecommunications. The newly integrated information processing department may very well cut across some of these organizational lines. In that case, to which department would these personnel report—one of these departments, or will a new department be established?

Publications have long predicted a power struggle among these departments over control of the new information processing system. There are internal political consequences that must be resolved before integration of separate technologies can take place within a company that has strong departmental structures. Without a clear-cut organizational structure, the integrated system could fail simply because it has many more opponents than defenders.

Technical Issues

There are several hardware considerations in planning for a successful merge, especially between word and data processing systems. Word processing systems are highly interactive with the CPU. To avoid excessive drain on the system, most word processing terminals are "smart." As you will recall, this means that the software used for system operation is down loaded into the machine itself. The terminal can interact with the software needs without requesting the CPU to *insert* or *delete* and waiting for a response. Data processing terminals are usually "dumb." They have no workstation memory. These terminals interact directly with the CPU but have fewer reasons for doing so.

Storage requirements also must be considered. Both word processing and data processing vendors are highly optimistic of the number of terminals that can be supported by various CPUs. However, massive manipulation of large documents can create severe problems. Some common examples are: (1) response time degrades for data processing users because the CPU is interacting exclusively for a single word processing user, and (2) some peripherals will not be able to begin their operation because of limited task space.

The need for user-friendly terminals cannot be overemphasized. Data processing terminals have been designed for use by highly trained programmers. Word processing systems, on the other hand, have been designed with the operator in mind. They utilize a normal typewriter keyboard, and function keys are placed where they are easy to use.

Some data processing systems have a hard time handling the variable record lengths of word processing files. In addition, word processing systems often have control codes embedded in the text which the data processing system cannot handle. As software developments continue, these problems will diminish. But they still exist and must be addressed if an integrated system is to be successful.

CHAPTER 15 Participating in a Total Information Processing System — 431

RESPONSIBILITIES OF THE MANAGER OF WORD PROCESSING

Word processing and data processing systems address the same problems from different perspectives. As they are integrated, these differences must be resolved. While the resolution of the differences is not always clear cut, the problems created by them can be readily identified.

Service orientation is the first problem that an organization typically faces. Data processing departments usually operate on strict schedules. Word processing, on the other hand, is traditionally a reactive process. The influx of material cannot be controlled. A word processing system must react to the users' service needs. As a result of this difference in orientation, data processing departments are perceived as being less service oriented than word processing departments.

As integration becomes more common, it will be important for data processing management to recognize the need to be more attentive to users' needs and requirements. Schedules must be more flexible when dealing with textual data; i.e., a contract which has to be signed today or the legal document which must be in court by 4:00 p.m.

As data processing becomes more distributed, these typical standard

As word processing and data processing systems are integrated, managers must be willing and able to resolve the inevitable differences between the two departments.

operating procedures will be replaced by more service-oriented controls. Companies already operating in a distributed environment will have a much easier time adjusting to the changes required by the integration of information processing.

The second likely problem is ease of communications between the users and the servicing staff. Word processing personnel often work directly with all managers and executives when processing their information and communication requests. This daily relationship provides a mutual communication familiarity between the users and the word processing personnel. On the other hand, data processing personnel, particularly programmers and technical support staff, rarely interact with their users. The users' projects are approached from an intensely technical perspective which is extremely difficult for an untrained user to understand. When interaction is required or a project request is made of this department, the system's analyst meets with the users. As a result, many of the staff within the data processing departments are less visible to other departments' personnel and are perceived as being unapproachable.

The third problem, and perhaps the most difficult to solve, is acquiring a thorough knowledge of both the word processing and data processing processes. Many word processing managers have had exposure to data processing without realizing it. They have ventured from text processing to application programs which expand the keyboarding functions. Merge document programs, spelling verifiers, and math packages are but a few of the programs being used by word processors to reduce the repetitive keyboarding and to curb potential errors. In addition, many word processing personnel have experience with data communications between office system devices. They have become familiar with the use of telephone lines, modems, and data processing protocols.

Many data processing managers also have experienced exposure to word processing since many of their data processing staff use a simple word processing application package for their programmers. In large, distributed mainframe systems, programmers commonly send messages to other terminal users. They also have some document formatting tools available on their mainframe computer.

There is a large technology overlap between word and data processing in the office automation arena. The biggest hurdle for integration to clear is that of providing a means for the two areas to communicate with each other—personally and technologically. Much of the terminology used in a word processing system is different from the terminology used in a data processing system. In order to communicate with each other, it is necessary for managers in both departments to speak the other's language. The data processing group should be able to relate to this need, for in developing an application system for users the analyst must be able to speak their language. However, the word processing manager has few experiences from which to draw a good data processing awareness. The successful word processing or data processing manager should learn those terms in order to avoid costly duplications of hardware, software, and manual effort. By broadening the level of knowledge and understanding between the two departments, there is a greater possibility for a successful integration and a general improvement of overall corporate productivity.

New Roles

Inevitably, the information processing manager occasionally will end up as a referee whenever there is a difference of opinion between the merging departments. In addition to the role of referee, the manager also must function as a clearinghouse through which all new ideas, procedures, and equipment purchases are filtered. By maintaining this type of centralized control over the diverse and decentralized departments, the manager can speed up the integration of the various office systems.

The challenge facing the information processing manager is to take a number of different groups and weld them into a cohesive administrative support operation as shown in Figure 15-1. The way management tackles the job will differ from company to company. However, there are some standard procedures that apply in most situations.

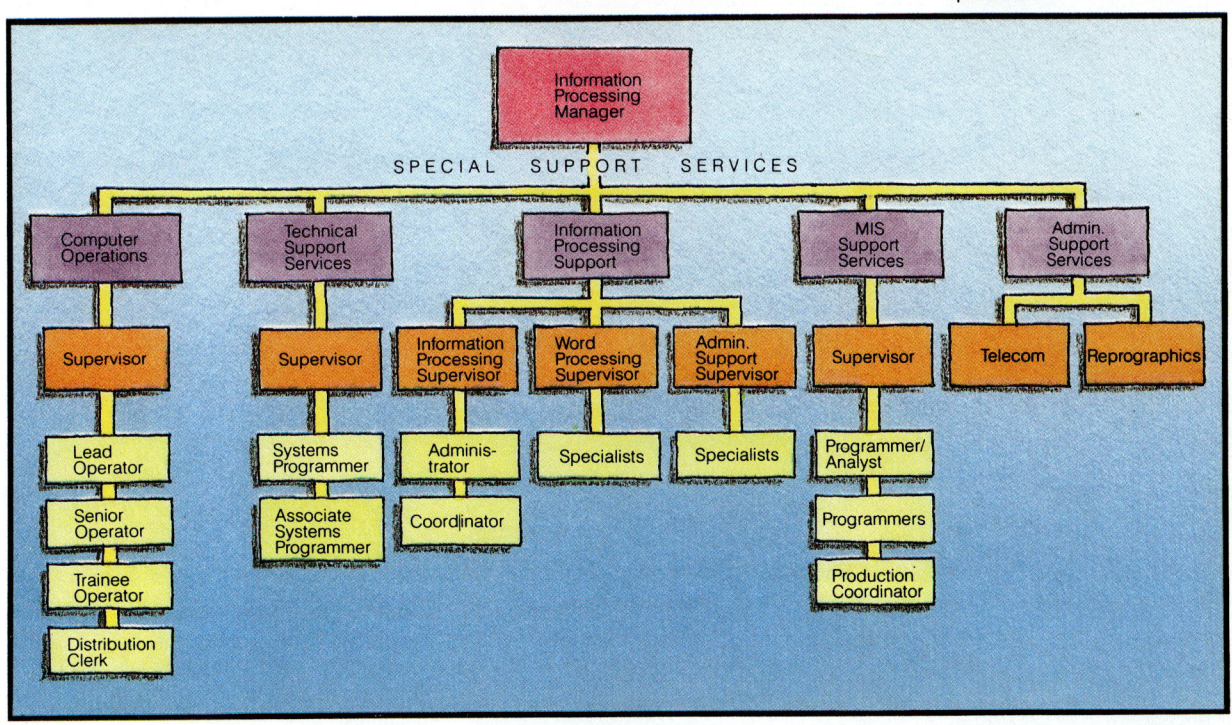

FIG. 15-1
ORGANIZATION CHART
An information processing manager must be able to merge a number of different groups into a cohesive administrative support operation.

The first procedural step is to analyze the needs of the users. The information processing manager should determine what users expect of the support groups and then identify which group can best provide each service. There should be a constant feedback between the users and the support groups to ensure that the level of service is satisfactory.

As a second step, the information processing manager must act as a consultant to the support groups, advising them on how to provide the desired services in the most efficient and economical manner. The manager also must establish performance standards for the groups. Once established, those groups should strive to meet or surpass these performance standards.

As an ongoing procedure, the information processing manager should open lines of communication among the various user departments. Regular meetings will provide a convenient time to share information, establish good rapport and team spirit, and instill enthusiasm. In

A good manager never forgets the importance of the human factor—the interface between people and machines.

addition, the manager should maintain communications and exchange information with other companies that are attempting to integrate their different systems. These external communications will provide the manager with objective views and new ideas.

A sequel to the above procedure suggests that the manager keep abreast of the latest technological advances. This awareness may be gained from outside contacts, periodicals, brochures, conferences, and exhibits. The investment in hardware is substantial to the company. Ideally, each piece of equipment that is in operation today should have the capability to fit into the office of tomorrow. To do this, the information processing manager should have some idea of what shape tomorrow's office will take. With this in mind, hardware selection will be less difficult and integration will be more successful.

The most recurring procedural step for the information processing manager should be that the importance of the human factor—the interface between people and machines—is never forgotten. The increasing integration of hardware systems is bound to have an effect on the organizational structure of the office. The change will be proportional to the equipment integration itself. If the merge is accomplished over a period of years, the resulting change to the organizational structure also will evolve slowly. Preparing people for this change is critical to the success of the system's acceptance and use. Information processing managers should consider this responsibility a high priority.

New Operations

The manager's role is not alone in changing with the implementation of an information processing system. New jobs are created or expanded to provide for greater operational requirements. Two such new positions are shown in Figure 15-2.

As jobs change, new job descriptions need to be written to identify the new duties. Some of these changes expand the scope of the previous word processing position considerably. Often companies will wait until the new position settles into identifiable responsibilities and duties before finalizing the description. A tentative job description with generalized accountabilities may be developed. Some of the expanding responsibilities are as follows:

- Positions require a thorough technical knowledge of office systems including word processing, electronic mail, personal decision support functions, records processing, data storage and manipulation, and telecommunications. In addition, the employees moving to these positions must possess strong analytical abilities in the areas of time and work measurement, as well as in cost and productivity studies.

- The positions require the ability to establish and maintain rapport

FIG. 15-2
NEW ROLES
The positions of administrator and coordinator are new positions created by the implementation of an information processing system.

STAFF POSITION RESPONSIBILITIES

Administrator	Coordinator

• Manages the system operation
  1 Provides first-line troubleshooting
    a host problems
    b C.E. interface
    c user terminal and printer problems
  2 Maintains system libraries
  3 Debugs programs
  4 Responds to user operational problems
  5 Monitors system activity reports
  6 Administers system security
• Analyzes performance of the following:
  1 System use and changes
  2 Measurements and controls
  3 User applications
  4 Work simplification
  5 Communication efficiencies
  6 Needs studies—ongoing
  7 Security and central access
• Develops administrative improvements
  1 Sets uniform standards and procedures
  2 Recommends equipment and work flow changes to achieve greater efficiencies
  3 Mediates between all company offices and departments to avoid unnecessary duplication of work
• Manages the office system coordinator and has overall responsibility for system use and operation; provides backup for the office system coordinator
• Provides training to local and field office personnel
	• Manages the system operation
	  1 Provides first-line troubleshooting
	    a host problems
	    b C.E. interface
	    c user terminal and printer problems
	  2 Installs and moves equipment
	  3 Monitors and maintains the flow of electronic mailways
	  4 Inputs new and changed user profiles and status
	  5 Maintains system libraries
	  6 Debugs programs
	  7 Dumps disks
	  8 Maintains inventory of supplies
	  9 Logs repair activities
	  10 Responds to user operation problems and questions
	  11 Maintains directories
	  12 Monitors disk space
	  13 Maintains system software documentation
	• Assists administrator
	  1 Develops systems procedures
	  2 Coordinates installation
	  3 Recommends improvements to the system
	  4 Serves as a backup in the event of an absence
	• Provides training to local and field office personnel
	• Reports regularly to the office systems administrator

CHAPTER 15 Participating in a Total Information Processing System

with all levels of employees to effect enthusiastic, user-supported facilities.

- The positions must interface heavily with the users. This includes helping users with their day-to-day questions and problems, assisting them with programming and developing new projects, interviewing prospective users to determine the feasibility of using the system, and scheduling the installation of equipment in the user areas.

- Administrators and coordinators are challenged to ensure the most effective utilization of the automated office system. They must anticipate the future hardware and/or software needs of the company and make recommendations which fulfill those needs. Another challenge is to develop and maintain well-trained users.

- In these staff positions, the individuals must keep abreast of new technology and applications in information processing in an effort to keep the office system state-of-the-art. Reading trade magazines and journals, attending equipment showings, and keeping in contact with vendor representatives are fundamental steps. In addition, they should attend professional meetings and exchange business information with other user professionals.

- The administrator and coordinator work with the purchasing department in selecting supply vendors appropriate to the office system equipment operations.

- These positions are responsible for the management and operation of the Office System Control Center—its daily routines, maintenance, user training, and control procedures. Performance and quality control statistics will be established and periodically refined.

Once the job becomes more comfortable, the job description may be altered to contain more specific accountabilities. The process of change will continue until a definite routine is established within the position. Specific responsibilities that can be included for these new positions are defined as follows:

1. Define ongoing system requirements by conducting needs studies, reviewing existing operations, and soliciting companywide input.

2. Determine and recommend appropriate procedures, equipment, and solutions in response to needs analysis data.

3. Communicate with vendors and solicit proposed equipment information as required.

4. Coordinate system implementations including installation, documentations, enhancements, and maintenance.

5 Facilitate system/user education programs.

6 Consult with administrative support personnel in resolving information processing problems.

7 Maintain the office system, ensuring that it performs to standards agreed upon between the user community and the Office System Administration.

8 Provide programming and technical support for the user community (including training) and standards for use on the system.

9 Maintain a high degree of technical knowledge by keeping abreast of the latest ideas, equipment, and methods for office system installations.

10 Maintain a good working relationship with the company's office system vendor by ensuring that all terms and agreements are being adhered to.

11 Monitor the automated office system by recommending and administering changes to improve the efficiency and effectiveness of the system.

As you may have discovered by now, the benefits derived from an information processing implementation can easily affect the entire office system. Up to now, companies have been involved with limited technological improvements to specific groups within the office system, such as those provided by word processing or data processing systems.

The broad scope offered by information processing should influence top-priority positioning within a company. In order to dignify this priority, there must be a centralized plan to give it a well-defined role within the organization and to arrange its implementation. Such planning involves a hard look at the organizational structure and at the goals and functions of the entire system.

PREPARING FOR THE FUTURE

The installation of an information processing system signals only the beginning of future preparation. It is incorrect to consider that the project will be complete by a specific date. An information processing system should continually evolve just as technology continually evolves. It needs to be nurtured during this growth period by concerned, informed administrators. The most appropriate individuals for this continuing attention are the members of the organizational team responsible for developing the original plan and selecting the equipment. Their task is to keep abreast of rapid technological improvements in both products and ideas.

Many different circumstances can influence changes to a system. Among these influences are converging technologies, new and obsolete products, and management/organizational changes which signal new directions. Changing needs require that the information processing system be flexible in responding to these needs.

The Information Age is one of astounding technological advancements. Satellites offer an immediacy of information and a worldwide communication sharing. Businesses are becoming more reliant upon data banks of information to conduct their daily operations. Businesses also will expand administrative operations beyond their office walls with employees operating electronic communicating devices from their homes. In the home, personal computers, computerized appliances, and video discs are changing the way people conduct their lives. Universities offer degrees in computer science for which courses can be accessed through electronic media. Government projects are promoting nationwide automated information systems.

As more and more advancements are made, other needs and their solutions are just around the corner. The perfect information processing system of today will be made obsolete by the ever-changing system discoveries of tomorrow. The more one keeps abreast of the system improvements today, the more likely his or her system will keep pace with tomorrow.

In the Seventies, there was considerable interest in training people for specific jobs during the advent of word processing. A renewal of interest in learning as a discovery is beginning in the Eighties. Training deals primarily with the known; it is the transmittal of knowledge. Learning deals primarily with the unknown; it focuses on the discovery of knowledge. The increasing complexity of the world and the incredible speed with which new occupations and career fields are opening up are bringing pressures on educators to better prepare students to deal with greater fields of interest. Some people must be equipped to become generalists. While specialists are still necessary, the many tasks faced today lie in understanding relationships and in synthesizing information.

Periodicals and Publications

There is a wealth of information to be gained from written materials. The field of office technology has many trade publications which regularly feature articles and columns on information processing or various aspects of office automation. Specific articles may be found which cover word processing, office systems, telecommunications, personal computing, or data processing. Specialized fields, such as education, video, personal computing, and photography, also have trade magazines in which the reader can uncover many references to the variety of information processes. Even the airlines include subject matter dealing with information processing in the periodicals they provide for passengers. The future also holds widespread use of electronic publishing. Until this development becomes more widespread, the written word remains the best source of information.

Many of these periodicals are offered free of charge to those involved in specific fields. There are a few general office publications that provide free monthly copies to interested readers providing the recipients regularly indicate their continuing interest. Some are available on a subscription basis, while others are available with membership in an organization. Vendors also provide a good source for information with their in-house publications and customer information circulars. There are more and more books available on the specific subsystems of information processing such as word processing, facsimile, and micrographics. However, very few books are available today that cover the entire spectrum of information processing.

To maintain a thorough technical knowledge of information processing systems, those individuals responsible for the planning of such systems should constantly review a broad spectrum of publications. In order to accomplish this much reading, the planner would need to devote full time to the project and spend many thousands of dollars annually. To curb the costs and create reading efficiencies, many companies consolidate publication orders, highlight those articles of value, and route them to employees having an interest in those topics.

Clubs, Groups, and Associations

Most businesses encourage their employees to join professional organizations which have special interest groups concentrating on information processing. Many such groups deal with one aspect of the field; others are vendor oriented and deal with a single vendor system. Many of these organizations charge nominal yearly dues. Some companies pay the dues for their employees. These companies view the employee benefits that can be derived from belonging to these organizations as an asset to their business.

Two kinds of groups deal specifically with office automation. One is designed primarily for the executive level of company management—presidents and upper management. History has demonstrated that upper management personnel are more apt to participate in groups which are attended by their peers. These groups host conferences with related businesses and offer consulting services on planning and technical problems facing the top manager. Their annual fees are quite expensive.

The other groups are local and regional professional organizations which are not operated for profit but are designed for information sharing among end users with similar interests. Though they may attract top management personnel, these groups are not limited to a specific level of company management. Their goals are to satisfy the interests of all participants and to provide an awareness of the entire operation of information processing. They accomplish these goals through monthly presentations, reference material, and sometimes annual conferences and exhibits. Their annual dues are modest.

Seminars, Conferences, and Trade Shows

Many local, regional, and national professional organizations offer annual seminars and conferences for those individuals interested in office automation. Included in these conferences are vendor exhibits which are designed to offer the participants a broad perspective of available products.

Some conferences and seminars are developed by consulting groups for profit and advertising purposes—commercial ventures. Others are sponsored by established business and professional organizations, by publishers, or by institutions of higher learning. Many vendors offer periodic seminars and presentations for their customers as a means of improving product proficiency, announcing new offerings, and soliciting additional sales.

Members of business and professional groups and other more experienced users are a good source for advice about which presentations to attend. Those unfamiliar with information processing will benefit from attending one or two presentations that cover the subject in general. Once participants have become more familiar with the offerings, they can become more selective.

Vendor trade shows offer planners an opportunity to see in one

Whether designed primarily for executive-level managers or for all levels of employees, the main goal of many groups and associations is the sharing of information.

place most of the new products for which they could not schedule time or travel arrangements. In addition, planners can compare competitive models and witness multiple demonstrations. Often they will have the opportunity to view equipment not offered within their locality. Trade shows broaden one's product knowledge and perspective.

Talking to Others

Office automation has influenced an infinite number of people from every walk of life. It is unusual to find someone unfamiliar with its concept. An abundance of information can be derived from asking questions, not only from work associates, other planners, and association members but also from neighbors, relatives, and friends.

Among planners, there is a willingness to share new discoveries, to cite the failures, and to applaud the successes. Telephone calls to other users within the limits of professional ethics and good manners are usually met with friendly receptions. Letters, too, normally produce cordial

Managers can nurture the growth and development of an information processing system by keeping in contact and sharing information with others who have implemented information processing systems.

responses. There is no better place to begin talking to others than within a local group or at a conference.

There is no mystery about information processing. A successful installation comes with thorough planning, active involvement of users, and implementation of procedures to use the system effectively. The transition to a totally automated information processing system requires dedication and understanding from all participants. To an information processing professional such challenges are exciting. A successful outcome can be a very rewarding experience for the company as well as for individual users. The results to be gained from an information processing system are well worth the extra care and concern the team members provide to the users before, during, and after project implementation. The measure of system success is directly related to the level of users' acceptance, confidence, and daily use of the equipment. The magic comes with a good approach, an open mind, and an infectious desire to improve.

The decade of the Eighties is a time of startling and rapid change in many companies. Information processing planning teams have a special challenge. They not only have to understand the effects of change, but they also must introduce change in a way that will help their companies to survive, to grow, and to gain a competitive edge.

When these planning teams learn about the trends and issues in office automation, they must look beyond the technology itself. Larger goals and objectives must be considered. Long-term visions for the organizations must be created which accommodate operations ten years into the future.

Many organizations have introduced some form of information processing technology. These range from centralized computer systems that handle many basic accounting functions to word processing systems in which specialists process documents and perhaps maintain electronic calendars. Some departments have their own systems to handle word and data processing. Also, there is a growing number of personal computers being used—some that can communicate to the central computer and to local systems and some that cannot. In the field of communications, there are telephones, electronic mail, and links to the central computer systems. There even exists a network of leased voice and data lines. Much of this has occurred over the past five years. The aim has been to achieve two main objectives:

- First, companies wanted to take advantage of the new technology and the cost savings anticipated from the improved price/performance of new systems.

- Second, companies wanted to make a dent in the productivity problem in order to cost-justify these systems. These companies measured marginal gains and assumed that if a system could handle more information faster, then it must be good.

However, as company planners worked toward these objectives, they uncovered new findings. They learned that when the true potential of this new technology is tapped, the process of work itself is changed. For example, when an office system can handle multiple functions and at the same time allow the ordinary user to transfer information between separate activities, then the work process has changed. Looking at another situation, when two separate departments can coordinate their needs and share information, then suddenly the process itself has changed.

The planners also realized that *more* information is not necessarily *better* information. When 5 memos are replaced with 25 memos, productivity has not necessarily increased. The original objective of increased productivity introduced a wide variety of measurements within companies which emphasized quantities rather than quantity/quality results. Thus, only marginal gains in productivity were attributed to the new technology because companies were experiencing added costs due to the increased quantities.

The information processing planners finally learned that the true advantage of the new technology is flexibility for change. Moving with changes in the technology provides the ability for improved customer service, better and consistent product quality, and timely, accurate information for decision makers. The advantages are not limited to cost savings and improved productivity. They are strategic. Implemented correctly, this new technology can allow a company to change its impact on the market, improve profits, and chart its future position.

Therefore, when it comes to a discussion about information processing systems, the perspective of upper-level management has to be focused on the long-term strategy of the business. It is the responsibility of the information processing planners to clarify that focal point. In doing so, the planners also must identify the major trends in business and technology in order to respond to new challenges in creative and effective ways. Some new trends can be identified in the following examples:

- Technology will continue to become less expensive, faster, and easier to use. Microprocessors, laser disks, fiber optics, digital switches, and better and more advanced human interfaces will play a major role in new developments. Voice and image processing will take their rightful positions next to word and data processing in fully integrated office systems. Rather than new hardware, companies will be using software as the predominant new developmental tool.

- There will be vastly improved communications capabilities due to an accelerating merger of communications with office systems and data processing.

CHAPTER 15 Participating in a Total Information Processing System — 445

- Information planners will be facing a more knowledgeable and a more demanding user group—users who perceive that they can be more effective in their jobs with better information systems and users who are leading the charge in the acquisition of personal computers.

- There will be a continual growth in the quantity of information available to us—information generated from within an organization and information available from outside sources; i.e., reports, memos, surveys, newspapers, and magazines. The list of available information will be endless, and the information overload will continue to be a very real problem. It will become more difficult to handle and extract meaningful information from these growing sources.

- There will be a need for worldwide communication networking since many companies will be expanding to compete with both domestic and foreign competitors. There will be factories, warehouses, laboratories, and sales and service offices scattered in many locations, and the information generated by these businesses has to be made available quickly and easily.

- Management will begin to understand that information systems can and must be used to gain a competitive advantage. The office will have to be managed with clear-cut goals, operating plans, business strategies, and performance plans because office automation is a business enterprise—not a technological expedition.

The question most information processing planners are asking is, "How can organizations put technology to good advantage to meet every requirement of every organization?" The new information processing manager should be concerned with what can be done today to prepare for a change in process and the introduction of new and better technology.

There will be as many answers to this question as there are organizations. It is unlikely that any single vendor will be able to meet every requirement of every organization. However, one thing is certain: To handle the vast changes that are coming and to bring systems and communications to the user in an effective way, the information planners and the selected vendors must have a strong understanding of office systems, data processing, and communications. Together, users and information processing planners must form a partnership that will not only integrate the separate systems effectively, but do it in such a way that the company will recognize the new technology as a valuable resource.

After reading this chapter, you should have learned of the complexities of merging the new technologies. Making a transition to anything new or different will not be without some conflicts and stress. You also should have discovered the problems and pitfalls to avoid in the transition to an information processing system. However, when company management, the users, and the planners are in agreement that the change will provide everyone beneficial improvements, a smoother, trouble-free implementation is possible. You should have gained an insight into the new roles and organizational structure arising from such a merge. Most importantly, you should have learned how to better prepare yourself for the coming changes.

DISCUSSION QUESTIONS AND CASE PROBLEM

DISCUSSION QUESTIONS

1. Give an example of a problem associated with each of the following issues in the merging of new technologies:
   a. Human issues
   b. Health issues
   c. Job enhancement issues
   d. Training issues

2. Cite an example that illustrates how the new technology actually improves each of the issues listed in Question 1.

3. Does the issue of job loss affect only a certain category of the office work force?

4. How does the role of the word processing manager differ from that of the information processing manager?

5. What are five things you can do to prepare for the changing future of office automation?

CASE PROBLEM

Peter worked in the purchasing department of his company for three years. His job involved placing orders, comparing costs, and tracking information. In addition, each month he billed the various departments for their purchases. It was very tedious and time-consuming work, but he enjoyed it. He rarely missed a day of work. Often, he needed to ask the department secretary to assist him on the projects in order to meet his end-of-the-month deadlines.

Ten months ago, his work was computerized. Peter now calls up the necessary information from his workstation, places inquiries to the system, and prints information for both billing and accounting purposes. He never has had to request help from the secretary nor does he have to interface with user departments to clarify orders. He meets all of his deadlines.

The new workstation did not alter his working environment, his job description, or his salary. He still has the same furniture and the same lighting schemes. Peter admits his work is far easier, even though the company has expanded operations. However, he complains of headaches and has applied for job openings in other departments. He misses work quite frequently, so the personnel department is apprehensive about placing him elsewhere.

1 What problems could be affecting Peter's performance?
2 Could these problems be caused from the use of the workstation?
3 How could Peter's job be reconstructed to improve it?

Glossary

acoustical enclosures Hoods that are placed over a printer (or parts of printers) to muffle sound.

acoustic coupler A small device that indirectly converts data signals to and/or from tones; much simpler in design than a modem.

acoustics The science that deals with the production, control, transmission, reception, and effects of sound.

adapter A device that allows a dictator to use another size of cassette in a recording device.

ambient lighting Lighting used to illuminate the general area surrounding the work space. In contrast, task lighting means the illumination of the specific work area.

analog computer A computer which processes information that has continuously variable physical signals, such as temperature and sound.

analog signal Variable wave lengths, such as voice waves, used over telephone lines.

aperture card A small card containing one or more microfiche frames. Each frame has an identifying code (printed or keypunched) which permits rapid and accurate access to the information.

applications software Programs provided by the vendor which allow users to perform tasks without having to write the programs themselves. Examples of such tasks are data processing, spreadsheets, graphics, or word processing.

archiving Transferring documents from hard disk storage to floppy disk or magnetic tape for permanent storage.

asynchronous transmission A mode of transmission in which data is transmitted a character at a time and preceded and followed by start/stop bits. Operators must be on opposite ends of the line at the same time to complete transmission.

audiographic conference A teleconference in which the use of the telephone is combined with an electronic means for exchanging data, text, or graphics.

audio teleconferencing A teleconference in which each member is connected by and participates by telephone.

baseband communications channel A type of communication cable which provides a single channel (allowing only one signal to be sent at a time) for data transmission.

baudot The most common language or code used in the transmission of information.

bisynchronous transmission See synchronous transmission.

black box Any electronic device that automatically translates signal flows from one message protocol to another protocol.

boilerplate documents Documents created by combining address lists and other variables on one diskette with standard text that is stored on another diskette.

Boolean logic The computerized logic of word processing that recognizes words by spaces and special control characters. It differs from data processing logic in which binary arithmetic is employed.

broadband communications channel A type of communications cable which provides a variety of channels (allowing more than one signal to be sent at a time) for data transmission. Data can be transmitted in two directions at the same time.

bubble memory A storage technique that uses magnetic fields to create regions of magnetization on a crystal sheet. When data is stored in these regions, small bubbles appear, each bubble representing digital information.

buffer storage Temporary storage within a device that consists of a few lines or less.

cassette A recording/storage medium in the form of a magnetic tape packaged as a reel-to-reel cassette.

centralized word processing approach A word processing design in which all of the equipment is centrally located in one area. This approach provides for a more controlled supervision over cost, employees, equipment, and procedures.

coated-paper copier A copier that uses a process in which the image of the original is projected directly onto the charge-sensitive surface of the copy paper.

coding Making an indexing decision on a document by highlighting or writing.

commercial printing When typesetting services are provided by an outside vendor.

communicating word processors Word processing machines that talk to each other by exchanging typed words and have a wide range of text-editing capabilities.

compatibility The ability of one machine to share with or communicate information to another machine.

computer-assisted retrieval (CAR) A method of indexing microfilm images by a computer for rapid retrieval.

computer-based message system (CBMS) A form of electronic mail whereby a person can key in a message on a computer terminal and have it stored in the memory of the computer. The recipient can have it displayed as well as printed by keying in on a terminal.

computer conferencing A type of teleconference in which the participants communicate by keyboarding on computer terminals.

computer output to microfilm (COM) The process of converting documents recorded on computer media directly to microfilm.

continuous speech recognition Voice recognition technology whereby the computer can convert the flow of words without distinct pauses to printed form.

credentials Information (including reference statements) about a job applicant that is on file at an employment office or school placement office.

daisy wheel printer An electronic impact printer which uses interchangeable print wheels. These print wheels usually print faster than the ball element.

data base The huge storage capacity within the computer system that enables important information about customers, sales, employees, and so forth, to be stored.

data processing The manipulation (such as calculating, merging, or sorting) of numbers by a computer system to produce statistical information.

dataset See modem.

data signal Structured pulses that move data across special data lines or into computer formats. This is in contrast to analog signals, which have variable wave lengths.

decentralized word processing approach A word processing design in which equipment is scattered in various areas throughout the company. This approach provides for a more reactive, responsive, and less structured environment which can be tailored to individual users' needs.

decibel A measurement of the volume of sound.

demodulation The process of readjusting (converting) analog signals back to their original form (data signals).

developmental planning The vehicle used to convince top management that there is merit to be gained in planning the implementation of a new project. Developmental planning occurs before top management has given approval to a project plan.

digital computer A computer which processes information in the form of well-defined and distinct signals that can be coded numerically, such as numbers and words.

digital data Discrete on/off pulses representing bit patterns of information.

digital signal See data signal.

digital voice exchange (DVX) An automated voice store-and-forward system that allows users to create and send digitized voice messages via telephone.

direct lighting When most of the light is cast directly downward from the light fixture.

direct lithography A process of duplicating which images the paper between a plate cylinder and an impression cylinder.

directory A unit of storage on a hard disk that has the capacity to store a number of documents.

discrete media Recording media that must be physically loaded into the recording device prior to dictation and removed from the recorder for transcription.

discrete word recognition Voice recognition technology whereby the computer can convert single distinct spoken words (such as *on* or *off*, *yes* or *no*, numbers, or letters) to printed form.

disk crash See head crash.

display standalone A single-station system with a keyboard, storage facility, a printer, and a CRT display screen.

distributed logic system A multiterminal system that distributes the logic (computing power) of the central computer to individual work stations whereby peripherals and sometimes the storage facilities of the central system are shared.

distributed word processing center See decentralized word processing center.

distribution step The step within the word processing cycle which involves sending (transmitting) documents to the recipients.

document label The name of a document that serves as its identification on the diskette or directory of a hard disk.

document title A short description of a document that is recorded on a disk/diskette. A title is longer than a label.

dot matrix printer A printer that uses a print head with pins in which characters are formed by a grid or a series of matrix dots.

double density diskette A diskette in which the Mylar (or other chemical) coating of the diskette is altered in such a way that it stores twice the amount of data as is stored on a single density diskette.

double density, double sided diskette A diskette in which twice the amount of data may be stored on both sides of the diskette.

double sided diskette A diskette in which both sides of the diskette may be used for storing data.

down loaded When operating instructions are transferred to a workstation or printer allowing it to function without having to access the CPU.

dual-spectrum copier A machine which uses a copy process that requires two separate types of paper. Light is used to create an image on an intermediate paper. Then the intermediate is used to produce an image on the final copy paper by means of heat.

dumb terminal A terminal that depends on the CPU for logic.

electromagnetic interference Disturbances in the electrical power line which can cause the display screen to flicker, data to be lost, and the circuit components to become damaged.

electronic file cabinet The systematic storage of information within a computer system for easy access and retrieval; a data base.

electronic filing The combination of micrographics and computer systems (COM and CAR) to capture, index, store, and retrieve information.

electronic mail Sending information over a distance by electronic means.

electronic typewriter A sophisticated, electronic machine (a step above electric typewriters) that permits limited storage and manipulation of text to be keyboarded and printed from the same device.

electrostatic copying A copier which uses a process by which the reflected image of an original document is converted into a static charge that is used to attract toner-imaging material to the surface of the copying paper.

electrostatic printer A nonimpact printer that uses a technique wherein an image is formed by a light source, translated through data stored in the system, and then reformed through a photoconductor by static charge onto paper.

employee evaluation The act of appraising an employee's performance in fulfilling the duties and responsibilities of a job.

endless loop Recording media in a long and continuous loop that is accessible to either the dictator or the transcriber but is not physically handled.

environment That which surrounds a person, including air, light, color, sound, furniture, and fixtures.

ergonomics The study of the relationship between people and machines with the goal of designing furniture and machines to meet the safety and comfort needs of the worker; the science that fits the work place to the person.

exempt A type of job position which does not entitle a worker to receive overtime pay for hours worked over 40 during the workweek. Management positions usually are exempt.

facsimile (FAX) An exact copy of a document; the process or result by which images (typed copy, graphs, signatures, pictures, etc.) are scanned, transmitted electronically, and reproduced on paper.

feasibility study A way of determining the practicality of implementing a study's objectives.

fifth-generation typesetting A typesetting process which uses lasers and digitized fonts to produce images on nonphotographic paper.

file management Determination of the archival, retrieval, and backup procedures for both word processing systems and total office information systems.

first-generation typesetting A typesetting process which mechanized the manual methods of pouring molten lead into type slugs and then casting the slugs onto a line of type.

flexible diskette A recording/storage medium that consists of a continuously rotating, magnetic-coated Mylar disk enclosed in a protective envelope.

floppy disk See flexible diskette.

footcandle The amount of light produced by a standard candle at a distance of one foot.

foot-lambert A measurement of the quality of light which pertains to the intensity, reflectance, brightness, or usability of light.

fourth-generation typesetting A typesetting process which uses laser scanning and digitized fonts to produce images on photographic paper.

full-motion video conference A teleconference in which conference members at distance points have the ability to see and hear each other.

galley A typesetting term which originally described the frame used to hold the metal letters as they were being assembled for hot type. Since this process is no longer used, galley now refers to the first proof of a typeset document.

gigabyte Represents one billion bits of storage.

global networks See wide area networks.

hard copy The completed paper document.

hard disk A rigid, random-access, magnetic recording/storage medium that has a high storage capacity.

hardware All of the physical parts of the equipment; i.e., the keyboard, the printer, and the disk drive.

head crash When the read/write head of the disk (diskette) storage device malfunctions causing damage to the disk head itself, the disk platter, or the Volume Table of Contents and results in a loss of stored information.

hot type casting See first-generation typesetting.

impact printer Generates characters by stamping or inking an impression through a ribbon with a character slug, element, or hammer needle.

implementation planning The actual project activities that occur after top management has given approval to the project.

indexing Determining the caption or title under which a document would most likely be found. This also includes cross referencing under other possible titles.

index of documents See Volume Table of Contents.

indirect lighting When most of the light is directed upward to the ceiling and walls from which the light is more evenly reflected to all parts of the work area.

information float Information that waits to be processed by the postal service or that has to be re-created or rekeyed.

information processing See office automation.

in-house printing When all the typesetting steps are performed within the company (rather than by a commercial printer).

ink jet printer A nonimpact printer which sprays ink electrostatically across the paper to form individual print characters.

input step The step within the word processing cycle which involves entering words; the act of originating thoughts or ideas using words.

in-service training Programs which teach employees (new and/or regular) how to operate a new machine, do a new task, or improve the performance of an old task.

intelligent copier/printer (IC/P) A copier/printer that has some logic and can perform printing functions.

job analysis The act of gathering information and determining the basic factors involved in performing a specific job.

job description A written description of a job that includes job title, classification/grade level, supervisor, department, basic function, list of general duties and responsibilities, and minimum job requirements.

job ticket A work request form that includes both the author's and the supervisor's instructions as well as the secretary's logging data.

kerning A typesetting term which describes the adjustment of space between characters and words.

keypad meter A device used to monitor copier usage. It can be either a key or a coded card that when inserted into the copier unlocks the copier for use and tallies the number of copies made.

leading A typesetting term which describes the process of adjusting the amount of space between lines.

library See directory.

local area network (LAN) A means of linking various types of machines within a building or within several buildings that are close to each other.

logging The act of recording facts about work as it comes in and goes out of a work area.

Mag Card A An electronic office typewriter with an auxiliary magnetic card device that provides for text keyboarding, internal text manipulation, and printing from the same device. It then records the text onto magnetic card media.

Mag Card I An early mechanical standalone that could capture up to one page of text on a single magnetic card. Revisions were limited to changes that could be made within a single line on the card.

Mag Card II An early mechanical standalone that could merge information contained on two separate magnetic cards. It also had a buffer storage for editing.

magnetic card A recording/storage medium that is the size of a computer card and is coated with magnetic material.

Magnetic Tape Selectric Typewriter (MTST) The first word processor that used a single-reel, magnetic tape cartridge for text storage.

mechanical standalone An electric typewriter that has been modified to include some computerized edit and logic capabilities. This machine also has an auxiliary magnetic media recorder which allows the operator to store completed text.

megabyte Represents one million bits of storage.

message switching system A computer storage and control device that can be attached to an on-premise telephone system.

microfiche A transparent sheet of film or a card containing multiple microimages. The fiche usually is coded and identified for easy retrieval and reading.

microfilming The act of recording tiny photographs (microphotographs) on film.

microform The end product produced by the process of microfilming documents. Microfilm, microfiche, aperture cards, micro-thin jackets, and ultrafiche are all examples of microform.

micrographics The science of photographically reducing documents to a fraction of their original size onto film.

microprocessors Wafers of silicon on which integrated circuits are built. These "chips" contain the basic logical circuits of a computer.

mission statement A general statement issued by a company's upper management to its employees that provides guidelines and goals for their coming year's work plans and objectives.

modem A device used to convert data signals into analog (voice) signals for transmission over ordinary telephone lines. Another modem at the receiving end of the transmission converts the analog signals back into digital form. A modem also is called a dataset.

modular components Parts that can be quickly assembled, taken apart, and rearranged.

modulation The process of adjusting the wave length or measurement of any incoming data signal and passing it on across lines for transmission in the form of an analog signal.

multiterminal word processing system A word processing system with many work stations that share the computing power, printers, and sometimes storage facilities of the central computer system.

Noise Isolation Class (NIC) A rating for office systems that takes into account all factors of the environment and indicates their potential to provide speech privacy (reduce sound).

Noise Reduction Coefficient (NRC) A rating for materials that indicates their ability to absorb or to reduce sound. The higher the rating, the greater the ability to absorb sound.

nonexempt A type of job position which entitles the worker to receive overtime pay for hours worked over 40 during the workweek.

nonimpact printer Forms images onto paper without impact on a ribbon. The character shapes are stored in the system memory and released by a special imaging mechanism onto the paper.

nonsynchronous transmission See asynchronous transmission.

nonvolatile The capacity of a disk to retain information even in the event of a power loss.

office A place where administrative functions, such as consulting, recordkeeping, and clerical work, are performed for an enterprise or organization.

office automation The use of electronic tools to increase office productivity and reduce costs.

off-line When the operator of a device is not actually connected to the communication line while creating a document.

offset duplication A duplicating technique that uses an intermediate medium to produce images.

offset lithography A duplicating technique where impressions are made "offset" from a plate to an intermediate and then to a page.

open career path A way to advance to higher levels or positions of employment.

open-office plan The flexible, modern approach to office planning which combines modular furniture and open office layout. Workers are separated by panels, partitions, or screens, instead of by permanent walls. Also called open-plan system or open-office landscaping.

operating system software The instructions that command the various electronic parts of the equipment to function in a certain way. This software engages the hardware to accept the instructions of the applications software.

optical character recognition (OCR) Reading (scanning) typed or printed data and/or text electronically and converting it to the recording medium of another machine so that it can be further processed.

optical (laser) disk A developmental storage device that uses lasers to optically scan information and then store it.

orientation checklist A list of items (policies and procedures) to cover during a program that introduces a new employee to a job.

orientation training Programs for new employees which cover such topics as company objectives, the products or services marketed, personnel policies, and fringe benefits.

output step The step within the word processing cycle which produces typed (printed) documents by using word processing equipment.

password A security feature that is available on some models and brands of word processors. Only with the secret password can one access the diskette or directory.

peripheral equipment Pieces that connect to the CPU, which include printers, terminals, storage units, and modems.

personal computer A standalone, multifunctional system usually purchased by the private (home) user for personal applications.

photoconductivity A process that places an image on paper by exposing the image to a light source and reproducing it much the same as would a copier.

phototypesetting The process by which the professional type that you see in books, brochures, forms, directories, advertisements, and newspapers is created.

pica A unit of about 1/6 of an inch used in measuring typeset material.

plain-paper copier A copier that employs an electrostatic copying process which uses plain paper to accept the toner image from the charge photoconductor.

point A typesetting term used to express measurement from the top of an ascending character (*b, d,* or *l*) to the bottom of a descending character (*g, j,* or *y*).

power down Turn the system's power off.

power surge A sudden increase in voltage that enters a computer or word processor through the power line.

priorities Tasks to be completed before other tasks so that the most urgent work is done first. In a word processing system, the order in which tasks are to be completed is determined so that the most pressing work is done first.

procedures Guidelines for office activities which are developed to help control the management of work flow, personnel, and the operation of the word processing system.

procedures manual A guide which gives step-by-step instructions and illustrations on how to perform a task.

PROM chip A small computer chip placed within a machine that contains preprogrammed operating instructions.

proportional spacing Spacing between words and lines is adjusted to compress or expand characters for special effects.

protocol The preliminary negotiation or exchange that takes place before transmission between two communicating units.

raceways The ducts or cableways that carry electrical wiring around an office.

random access Text that is stored on a storage medium in a random order.

read only memory A solid-state memory for programs that is inflexible and cannot be altered.

read only storage A type of storage in which the surface of the recording medium cannot be reused or written over.

recirculating document handler An automatic document feeder that refeeds original documents into a copier for repeated exposures.

records management system The manner in which records of business information are organized, retrieved, and stored within companies.

reference manual A guide to information that is frequently sought.

reproduction step The step within the word processing cycle which involves duplicating or photocopying documents.

reprographics Reproduction or duplication of documents.

revision step The step within the word processing cycle which involves changing and/or correcting the text. Also known as editing.

second-generation typesetting A typesetting process which composes text on film through the use of movable optic assemblies and flash lamps.

serial access Text that is stored on a storage medium in sequential order.

shared-logic system A multiterminal system which shares the logic (computing power) of the central computer system.

shared resource system A multiterminal system where several workstations share printers, disk files, OCRs, and other equipment.

slow-scan video A teleconferencing option by which the pictures of the participants are in the form of still poses (freeze-frame television).

smart drawer storage Storage devices for microforms that provide controlled filing for sequential coding and promote easy retrieval.

smart terminal A terminal that receives a portion of the CPU logic and stores it in its internal memory.

software The program or written instructions for the hardware.

speaker verification A voice recognition system that determines if the speaker is actually the person he or she is claiming to be. Used to protect confidentiality and enhance security.

speech compression The act of removing long pauses from speech. On dictation machines (with this feature) long pauses during dictation are removed.

speech recognition See voice recognition.

spike See power surge.

standalone word processor A single-station system with a keyboard, storage facility, and a printer that does not share the resources of a central computer system.

standard A grading scale or yardstick by which the productivity of various workers can be compared.

storage step The step within the word processing cycle which involves filing the hard copy (paper document) and/or the magnetic medium (for example, diskette).

stroke count A method of measuring work which involves marking a stroke for each task as it is performed.

surge suppressors Various protective devices that can monitor the voltage coming through an electrical line and suppress abrupt surges of power.

synchronous transmission A mode of transmission in which data is transmitted in blocks of characters. Control settings usually are planned in advance so transmission can be nonstop. This mode of transmission commonly is used for sending batches of information.

system utilities Methods that reduce the amount of unused storage space on a disk.

tab card See aperture card.

task lighting Localized light that is designed to illuminate the immediate work surface.

telecommunications Communicating electronically over a distance.

teleconferencing The meeting of at least three persons at two or more locations by telephones and other electronic devices.

telepresentation A one-way video and two-way audio private broadcast.

teletypewriter A typewriter-like device that can "talk to" a similar device by typed words. These machines do not have text-editing capabilities.

thermal copier A copier which uses heat-sensitive paper and only carbon-based (pencil) originals to produce images. Through the use of infrared lights, the image absorbs the light and increases its temperature. The increased temperature darkens the sensitive copy paper and creates a reproduction of the original.

thimble A small, electronic print element for impact printers shaped like a thimble.

third-generation typesetting A typesetting process which uses electronics and internal logic to generate characters through the use of CRT screens.

time count. A method of measuring work which involves totaling the time spent on the activity.

time-sharing word processor A word processing workstation that via communication lines can access other computer systems and use their application programs.

traditional office An office that does not adjust to changes in the marketplace.

training manual A guide which explains how to operate a machine.

transcript A list of the courses completed and the respective grades earned by a student at an educational institution.

transient impulse See power surge.

transient suppression devices See surge suppressors.

turnaround time The elapsed time between the submission of a job (such as a word processing document) to an operator and the return of the results.

turnkey system A single outside supplier is contracted to plan and implement an information processing system and to supervise its operation until the office staff has the capacity to keep it running efficiently.

ultrafiche A microfiche that has been refined through a miniaturization process to produce more than ten times the data on a single frame. Also called ultramicrofiche.

veiling reflections Annoyances that occur when light from a source directly above and in front of a viewer bounces off the task surface and into the viewer's eyes.

voice input system (VIS) A method of input that allows an author to dictate into a computer which has a bank of identically stored words and which in turn prints out the message automatically. Also known as speech recognition or voice recognition technology.

voice message system (VMS) A communication aid that enables a person to speak into a telephone device and have the voice message stored in a computer system. When the recipient accesses the computer, the message will be played back. Also known as voice mail.

voice-operated relay Causes the recording tape to halt when the author stops talking and to start advancing again when speech resumes.

voice recognition A technology whereby a computerized system responds to voice commands to perform various functions.

voice store-and-forward See voice message system.

voice teleconferencing See audio teleconferencing.

voice verification See speaker verification.

voltage regulator A protective device that maintains line voltage within a prescribed range.

Volume Table of Contents Identifies the location of each document that has been stored on a disk by pointing to the position where the text can be found. If damaged, the information on the disk becomes inaccessible.

wide area networks Telecommunications networks that make use of combinations of telephone lines, microwave radio links, and satellites to send information.

Winchester disk A type of hard disk that allows dense data storage. It is sealed within a filtered enclosure so that the disk and the read/write head are protected from damage.

word processing The efficient processing of text.

work area A place where employees are grouped to perform related functions.

work flow The general processing of information in an office.

work request form A form upon which authors or principals ask for and describe work they need to have performed.

Index

A

acoustical control, 289-292
acoustical enclosure, defined, 291
acoustical panels, 292-293
acoustic coupler, defined, 180
acoustics, 289-292
adapter, defined, 60
agendas, illustrated, 345
air circulation, 278
ambient lighting, 286-287
American Standard Code for Information Interchange, 180
analog computer, defined, 394
analog signal, defined, 180
antistatic mat, 282
aperture card, defined, 146
application, letter of, 371-373
application form, 374-375
applications software, 98
archiving, defined, 141
ASCII. *See* American Standard Code for Information Interchange
asynchronous transmission, defined, 168, 182
audio conference, 20, 411
audiographic conference, 20, 411

B

baseband communications channel: defined, 415; illustrated, 415
baudot, defined, 179
bisynchronous transmission. *See* synchronous transmission
black box, defined, 179
boilerplate document, defined, 82
Boolean logic, defined, 178
box files, 134
broadband communications channel: defined, 415; illustrated, 415
bubble memory, defined, 91
buffer storage, defined, 77
built-in wiring, 274
business, costs of, 28
business reply mail, 162

C

cable routing: overhead, 248; plastic troughs, 247-248; raised floor, 248
CAR. *See* computer-assisted retrieval
career paths, 360-362
cassette: defined, 89; types of (illus.), 60
CBMS. *See* computer-based message system
centralized typesetting system, 408
centralized word processing approach, 256-257
certified mail, 161
checklists: environmental conditions, 251; file management, 261; floor plan design, 245; power and cabling, 247; word processing checklist, 257; work flow procedures, 259
clericals, 27
cluster systems, 86-87
coated-paper copier, defined, 105
coaxial cables, 415
coding, defined, 132
COD services. *See* collect on delivery services
collect on delivery services, 163
color, in the office decor: choice of, 288; effects of, 287-288
COM. *See* computer output to microfilm
comment sheet, illustrated, 349
commercial printing, 111-113
communicating word processor, 22, 68-69, 398-399; as an input method, 68-69; defined, 22
communicating workstation. *See* communicating word processor
compatibility, 11-12, 36, 38, 178-179; defined, 178; illustrated, 179
competition, in the marketplace, 28
computer-assisted retrieval, 19, 147-148, 401
computer-based message system, 21-22, 171-173, 399; defined, 21; illustrated, 173
computer conferencing, 20, 410-411
computer output to microfilm, 19, 147, 400-401
computers: mainframe, 394; microcomputer, 394-395; minicomputer, 394-395; personal, 83-84
constructive criticism, illustrated, 347
continuous speech recognition, 73, 414-415
control summary, illustrated, 302
convenience copiers, 103
convenience typesetting system, 408
copying, survey analysis of, 214
copy machines: cost of, 119-121; options on, 113; print quality of, 116, 408-409; speed and volume of, 116-118; types of, 103-106
copy/work holder, illustrated, 272
corporate management team, 30
costs: direct, 350; indirect, 350, 352; overhead, 350
CP/M 80, 98
cross-referencing, 132
cross-training, 343. *See also* training
CRT. *See* visual display terminal

D

daisy wheel printer, 92
data base, defined, 13
data collection, 207-210
data processing, 12-14, 394-396
dataset. *See* modem
data sheet, 373-374
data signal, defined, 180
decentralized word processing approach, 257-258
decibel, defined, 289
demodulation, defined, 180
design specifications, 223-224, 235
developmental planning, defined, 192
dictation, 58-66; advantages of, 58-59; problems of, 59-60; uses of, 58-59
dictation equipment: central systems, 62-63; desk top units, 61-62; portable units, 61; recording media, 64-65; special features, 66; supervisor's console, 64; transcriber's unit, 65-66
digital computer, defined, 394
digital data, defined, 16
digital signal. *See* data signal
digital voice exchange, 169-171
direct costs, 350
direct lighting, 285-287; defined, 285; illustrated, 285
direct lithography, defined, 107
directory, defined, 321. *See also* library
discrete media, defined, 64
discrete word recognition, 73, 414
disk crash. *See* head crash
diskette media, 320-321
disk media, 321-322
disks, storage capacities of: flexible diskettes, 89; hard disks, 90; Winchester disks, 90-91
disk storage, 140-144, 244
display standalones, 80-83
distributed logic system, defined, 87
distributed word processing approach. *See*

461

decentralized word processing approach
distribution of text, problems with, 151-154
distribution step, of word processing cycle, 52
document assembly. *See* boilerplate document
document label, defined, 320
document title, defined, 320
dot matrix printer, 93
double density diskette, defined, 89
double density, double sided diskette: defined, 89
double sided diskette, defined, 89
down loaded, defined, 86
dual-spectrum copier, defined, 105
dumb terminal, 85, 430
duplicating, 408
DVX. *See* digital voice exchange

E

E-COM service, 165
electrical power, disturbances in, 279-282
electromagnetic interference, defined, 280
electronic file cabinet, defined, 19
electronic filing, defined, 19
electronic mail, 21-22, 193, 397-400, 409, 412; benefits of, 166-168; characteristics of, 168; defined, 21; illustrated, 398; types of, 168-177
electronic mailbox, 22, 399
electronic message systems, types of, 168-177. *See also* electronic mail
electronic printing, 409
electronic sound masking, 291, 292
electronic typewriter, 77-78
electrostatic copier, defined, 108
electrostatic printer, defined, 96
employee evaluation: defined, 388; illustrated, 389
EMS. *See* electronic mail
enclosure, acoustical: defined, 291
endless loop: defined, 64; illustrated, 65
environment: and personnel involvement in, 267-268; changes in, 267; defined, 266; design and improvement of, 341; effect on productivity, 267; importance of, 266-268; problems of, 267
environmental factors: checklist, 251; dirt and dust, 252-253; humidity, 251; lighting and acoustics, 253-254; static electricity, 253; temperature, 250-251
equipment: evaluation of, 235-241; preparation for installation, 249-250; selection of, 223-224, 235-241
ergonomics, 272, 429
evaluation: of equipment, 235-241; of job applicants, 382-383; of personnel, 388-389; rating job applicants (illus.), 382

exempt, defined, 366
Express Mail services, 164

F

facsimile, 21, 175-177, 399; defined, 21; illustrated, 176
FAX. *See* facsimile
feasibility study, 206-220
fiber optics, 416-444
fiber optics copier, 105-106
fifth-generation typesetting, defined, 110
file management: checklist, 261; defined, 260; functions of, 322-323
file manipulation, 395
file requisition slip, illustrated, 133
files, types of, 134-135
filing: problems with, 125-127; survey analysis of, 214
filing methods: centralized, 130; decentralized, 130
fire protection equipment, 246
first-generation typesetting, defined, 108
flexible diskette, defined, 89
floor plan design, checklist, 245
floppy disk. *See* flexible diskette
footcandle, defined, 283
foot-lambert, defined, 283
form tractors, 314
fourth-generation typesetting, defined, 110
FTE equivalent. *See* full-time employee equivalent
full-motion video conference, 21, 411-412
full-time employee equivalent, 211

G

galley, defined, 406
glare, 253, 283
global network. *See* wide area network
graphic display, 396, 397

H

hard copy, 129, 130-135
hard disk, 89-91; defined, 89; quality control, 142-143; storage devices for, 143-144; Winchester disk, 90
hard dollars, 212
hardware, 97-98
head crash, defined, 86
hexidecimal values, 180
high-cost copiers, 120-121
hiring: evaluating applicants, 382-383; interviewing applicants, 379-382;

making a selection, 382-383; recruiting applicants, 370-372; scheduling interviews, 375; screening applicants, 372-375; testing for employment skills, 376-379
hot type casting, defined, 108
humidity, 278
hygrometer, illustrated, 278

I

IC/P. *See* intelligent copier/printer
impact printers, types of, 92-95
implementation planning, 241-264; defined, 192; environmental factors of, 250-254
incompatibility. *See* compatibility
indexing, defined, 132
index of documents: defined, 321; illustrated, 321
indirect costs, 350, 352
indirect lighting, 285-287; defined, 285; illustrated, 285
information: electronic retrieval of, 140-149; forms of, 5, 9; impact of, 8-11; manual retrieval of, 130-140; methods of storing, 128-149; storage and retrieval problems of, 125-127
Information Age, 177, 439
information float, defined, 9
information processing, 393, 423-430; as it affects word processing careers, 24-25; basic principals of, 6; changes in, 9, 11; factors contributing to changes in, 187-192; subsystems of, 11-22
in-house printing, defined, 17
ink jet printer, 95-96
input, 50-74; comparison of methods (illus.), 59; determining the best type of, 74; step of the word processing cycle, 50
input, types of: communicating workstation, 68-69; longhand, 53-54; machine dictation, 58-66; OCR, 69-72; rough draft, 54-56; shorthand, 56-58; voice recognition, 72-73; work request, 66-68
inputting, via word processors, 406
in-service training: defined, 328; illustrated, 329
insured mail, 162
integration of systems, 393-415, 432-433. *See also* office automation or information processing
intelligent copier/printer, 16, 106, 409; as a reproduction option, 106; defined, 16
interviewing, 210, 379-382; applicants for an opening, 379-382; discriminatory questions, 380-381
interviews, scheduling of, 375

Index

J

job analysis: defined, 363; illustrated, 364
job description, 435, 437-438, 361, 362-366; defined, 364; of an administrative coordinator (illus.), 367; of a word processing specialist (illus.), 366
job enrichment, 342-343
job fulfillment, 205-206
job loss, 428
job ticket, defined, 300
job title, 361, 363-365

K

kerning, defined, 408
keypad meter, defined, 121

L

label. See document label
LAN. See local area network
laser disk. See optical disk
laser printer, illustrated, 97
lateral filing cabinets, 135
leading, defined, 408
letter, modern simplified, 316-318
letter of application, for a job, 371-373
library, defined, 321. See also directory
lighting: ambient, 286; direct (illus.), 285; direction and location of, 285-287; HID lamps, 284-285; indirect (illus.), 285; quantity and quality of, 283; task, 286; types of artificial, 283-285
lithography: direct, 107; offset, 106-107
local area network, 23-24, 415-416; defined, 23; illustrated, 416
logging work: control summary (illus.), 302; defined, 298; why it is done, 300, 301
log sheet, 298-300
longhand, 53-54; illustrated, 53; reasons for using, 54; why to avoid, 54
low-cost copiers, 119-120

M

machine dictation. See dictation
machines: evaluation of, 341; inventory and service records of, 339-340; selection and maintenance of, 339-341. See also equipment
Mag Card A, defined, 79
Mag Card I, defined, 79
Mag Card II, defined, 79
magnetic card, 88-89
magnetic media: care of, 323-324; filing and retrieval problems of, 137; quality control, 138, 140; types of files for, 137-138
Magnetic Tape Selectric Typewriter, defined, 78
mail delivery systems: electronic mail, 165-177; intracompany, 154-159; public and private, 159-165
Mailgram, 163
mail handling, survey analysis of, 213-214
mailroom, design procedures for, 155
mainframe computer, 394, 432
manager, responsibilities of, 334-353, 431-438
managerial staff survey, 208-209
manuals, office: procedures, 325; reference, 325; training, 325-326
mechanical standalones, 78-80
media, 98; disk, 321-322; diskette, 320-321
media files, management of, 319-324, 325
medium-cost copiers, 120
megabyte, defined, 90
memorandum, modern simplified, 318-319
merging text. See boilerplate documents
message switching system, 168-169
microcomputers, 394-395
microfiche, defined, 146
microfilm: cartridges or cassettes, 145; micro-thin jacket, 145-146; roll film, 145
microfilming, 18
microform, defined, 144
micrographics, 18-19, 144-149, 400-402; advantages of, 144-145; applications, 402; common forms of, 145-148; defined, 18; disadvantages of, 145; status in relation to other technologies, 402; storage devices for, 148-149
microprocessor, defined, 9
micro-thin jacket, 145-146
minicomputers, 394-395
mission statement, defined, 31
mobile mail unit, electronic, 158-159
modem, 180-181, 182
modern simplified letter, 316-318
modern simplified memorandum, 318-319
modern simplified outline, 318-319, 320
modular components, defined, 272
modulation, defined, 180
MS/DOS, 98
MTST. See Magnetic Tape Selectric Typewriter
multiterminal systems, 84-87

N

networks: local area, 23-24, 415-416; switch and access, 416-417; wide area, 24, 417

NIC. See noise isolation class
noise: effect of, 290; reduction of, 290-282. See also acoustics
noise isolation class, defined, 292
noise reduction coefficient, defined, 292
nonexempt, defined, 366
nonimpact printers, 95-96
nonsynchronous transmission. See asynchronous transmission
NRC. See noise reduction coefficient

O

objectives, defining, 192-193
OCR. See optical character recognition
office, defined, 26
office, traditional: problems of, 26-29
office automation, 9, 423-430. See also information processing or integration
office manuals: producing, 326; purposes of, 325
off line, defined, 175
offset duplication: defined, 106; illustrated, 107; types of, 106-108
offset lithography, 106-107
open career path, defined, 361
open-office landscaping. See open-office plan
open-office plan: advantages of, 269, 271; defined, 269; disadvantages of, 271; illustrated, 270; proper layout of, 271
open-plan system. See open-office plan
open-shelf filing system, 134
operating system software, 98; 100
optical character recognition: and data processing, 402-403; and word processing, 402-403; as an input method, 69-72; benefits of, 70-71; defined, 15; equipment, 403-404; illustrated, 69; innovations, 404-405; problems, 72; process of (illus.), 15
optical disk, 91-92
orientation: programs, 260-264, 343-345; to the company, 384; to the job, 386; training (defined), 328. See also training
orientation checklist: defined, 386; illustrated, 387
outline, modern simplified, 318-320
outline format, illustrated, 327
output, 76-100
output equipment; multiterminal systems, 84-87; standalone word processors, 77-84; time-sharing word processors, 87-88
output step, of word processing cycle, 50
overhead costs, 350

Index

P

paper, management of, 335-339
password, defined, 322
paste-up, 406
peripheral equipment, defined, 394
personal computers, 83-84
personnel: handling problems of, 345-347; health hazards, 424-426; management and training of, 260; organization of, 254-258, 429-430; organizing meetings, 343-345; supervision of, 353-356
photoconductivity, defined, 96
photocopiers. *See* copy machines
phototypesetting, defined, 16. *See also* typesetting
pica, defined, 408
plain-paper copier, defined, 105
planning, preliminary steps of, 192-201
playscript format, illustrated, 327
point, defined, 408
power and cabling checklist, 247
power disturbances, 280
power down, defined, 86
power surge, defined, 280
printer pad, 293
printers, 92-96, 313-314; impact, 92-95; non-impact, 95-96
printing, commercial, 111-113
printing elements, 92-96, 314; handling of, 314; illustrated, 92
priorities: defined, 308; illustrated, 309
procedures: defined, 258; development and modification of, 335-339
procedures manual, defined, 325
production: measurement of, 301-307; methods of measuring (illus.), 306; reasons for measuring, 302-305
profit-sharing plans, 343
PROM chip, defined, 93
proofreading, 311-313
proportional spacing, defined, 16
protocol, 182-183, 432

Q

quality control: of hard disks, 142-143; of magnetic media, 138, 140

R

raceways, defined, 274
random access, defined, 89
read only memory, defined, 96
recirculating document handler, defined, 118
recording/storage media, 64-65, 88-92; discrete, 64; endless loop, 64-65
records management system: defined, 128; objectives of, 128, 138, 140
reference manual, defined, 325
registered mail, 162
reproduction options, 103-113, 115
reproduction step, of word processing cycle, 52
reprographics, 102, 408-409
Request for Proposal, 223-235
resume, 373-374
revision step, of word processing cycle, 51
RFP. *See* Request for Proposal
ROM. *See* read only memory
rough draft: illustrated, 55, 379; potential problems of, 55-56
rotary files, 134
routing slip, illustrated, 131

S

salary: establishing a scale, 367-370; job levels (illus.), 369; problems of which to be aware, 367-368
satellites, 417
scheduling/calendaring, survey analysis of, 214
second-generation typesetting: defined, 108; illustrated, 110
serial access, defined, 90
shared-logic system, 85-87
shared resource system, defined, 87
sheet feeders, 314
shorthand, 56-58; advantages of, 57; disadvantages of, 57-58
sign-off sheet, 131
site, preparation and layout, 241-250
slow-scan video conference, defined, 411
smart drawer storage, defined, 148
smart terminal, defined, 85
Snow White Syndrome, 355
soft dollars, 212
software: defined, 97; innovations in, 396; selection and maintenance of, 339-341; types of, 97-100
sound, measurement of, 289-290
sound masking, electronic, 291, 292
speaker verification, 413-414
special delivery services, 161
special handling services, 161
speech compression, defined, 66
speech recognition. *See* voice recognition
spike. *See* power surge
staff meetings, 343-345
standalone word processor: defined, 77; display, 80-83; mechanical, 78-80; types of, 77-84
standardization, of documents, 314-319; benefits of, 315-316; objectives of, 316-319
standards, 307-308
static electricity, 280-282
storage, of hard disks, 140-144
storage and retrieval: of hard copy, 130-135; of magnetic media, 137-140
storage capacity, defined, 88
storage devices, for paper, 133-135
storage step, of word processing cycle, 52
strategy plan, illustrated, 194
stroke count, defined, 307
study plan, designing a, 206-207
supervising, 341-347
support personnel survey, illustrated, 208
surge suppressor, defined, 280
survey forms, 206-220; analyzing, 211-212; distributing, 208-209; reporting results of, 217-220; summarizing, 217
suspension system files, 134
switch and access networks, 416-417
swivel turntable, illustrated, 272
synchronous transmission, defined, 168, 182
system maintenance, 260
system operations, 260
system utilities, defined, 141

T

tab card. *See* aperture card
task lighting, 274, 286
team analysis approach, 197-200
team member chart, 199
telecommunications: defined, 22; illustrated, 23
teleconferencing, 20-21, 193; 409-412; audio teleconferencing, 20; audiographic teleconferencing, 20; computer conference, 20; defined, 20; full-motion video conference, 21
telephone tag, 152-153
telepresentation, defined, 411
teletypewriter system, 21, 173-174
Telex, 173-175, 179, 399-400, 404
temperature, 278
terminal, dumb, 85, 430
terminal, smart: defined, 85
text, distribution problems of, 151-154
textual report, illustrated, 195
thermal copier, 104-105
thimble, 92
third-generation typesetting, defined, 110
time count, defined, 307
time-sharing word processing system, 87-88
title. *See* document title
traditional office: defined, 27; problems of, 26-29

Index

training, 205, 326-330, 428-429, 438; how to, 328-330; in-house, 429; in-service, 328; orientation, 260-264, 328; types of, 328; vendor-provided, 328, 429
training manual, defined, 325
transcriber's unit, 65-66
transcription, of a letter (illus.), 378
transient impulse. *See* power surge
transient suppression device. *See* surge suppressor
transmission modes: asynchronous, 182; full-duplex, 181; half-duplex, 181; simplex, 181; synchronous, 182
tub files, 134-135
turnaround, 32-33; illustrated, 310; scheduling of, 309-311
TWX, 9, 173-174, 399-400, 404
type ball, 92
typesetting, 16-17, 108-111, 405-408; as a reproduction option, 108-111; centralized system, 408; convenience system, 408; types of, 108-111
typewriters, voice-actuated, 415
typing, survey analysis of, 215

U

ultrafiche, defined, 146

V

VDT. *See* visual display terminal
VDT work station, 276-277
veiling reflection: defined, 283; illustrated, 284
vendor, selection of, 239-241
vendor evaluation checklist, 235
vendor trade shows, 441-442
vertical files, 134
visual display terminal: causes of discomfort, 276; health effects, 275-276; protection from health problems, 276-277
VMX. *See* voice mailbox
voice-actuated typewriters, 415
voice input system, defined, 72
voice mail. *See* voice message system
voice mailbox, 412
voice message system, 22, 412-413
voice-operated relay, defined, 66
voice processing, 412-415
voice recognition, 22, 72-73, 413-415; as an input method, 72-73; defined, 22, 413
voice store-and-forward. *See* voice message system
voltage regulator, defined, 280
Volume Table of Contents, 90, 142, 321; defined, 90; illustrated, 321
VTOC. *See* Volume Table of Contents

W

warranties, 340
wide area networks, 24, 417
Winchester disk, defined, 90
word processing, 12, 297-298, 393-394, 431-438; control procedures (illus.), 298; defined, 12; goals of (illus.), 297; manager responsibilities of, 431-438
word processing cycle: distribution step, 52; illustrated, 51; input step, 50; output step, 50-51; reproduction step, 52; revision step, 51; storage step, 52
word processing system, composition of: environment, 45-46; machines, 43-45; people, 41, 43; procedures, 45
word processors, standalones, 77-84
work area, 268-278; climate of, 277-278; defined, 268
work flow, 27, 209-210, 215-217, 260, 405-407; analysis of, 215-217; defined, 27; illustrated, 216, 407; of an all-text typeset document, 405-406
work flow procedures, checklist, 259
work plan development, 201-202
work request: as an input method, 66-68; defined, 300; illustrated, 67, 301
work space, 272, 274
work stations, variations in, 271-274

Photo Credits

Cover Photo: ©1982 Joel Gordon

I Part Opener: Reproduced with permission AT&T Bell Laboratories

- 12 Photo courtesy Steelcase Inc.
- 13 upper right: NCR Corporation
- 14 left: Courtesy of Lundy Electronics & Systems, Inc.
  upper right: Courtesy of Lundy Electronics & Systems, Inc.
  lower right: NCR Corporation
- 15 Courtesy of CompuScan, Inc.
- 19 left: NCR Corporation
  right: Courtesy Eastman Kodak Co.
- 20 Photo Courtesy of Satellite Business Systems
- 29 Photo courtesy of Haworth, Inc., Holland, Michigan
- 30 Courtesy of Squibb Corporation
- 32 Photo—Merck & Co., Inc.
- 42 upper left: Photo courtesy Steelcase, Inc.
  upper right: Photo—Merck & Co., Inc.
  lower right: Courtesy of Xerox Corporation

II Part Opener: Storage Technology Corporation ©1983

- 61 upper right: Courtesy of Lanier Business Products, a Harris Company
  lower right: Courtesy of Dictaphone Corporation, Rye, NY
- 62 Courtesy Dictaphone Corporation, Rye, NY
- 63 Courtesy of Lanier Business Products, a Harris Company
- 68 Courtesy of CPT Corporation
- 71 The Western Union Corporation
- 73 Photography courtesy of Sydis, Inc.
- 79 Courtesy of International Business Machines Corporation
- 81 left: Courtesy of Wang Laboratories, Inc.
  right: Courtesy of International Business Machines Corporation
- 85 NCR Corporation
- 86 Courtesy of Wang Laboratories, Inc.
- 94 top: Courtesy, Datagraphix, Inc.
  lower left: Courtesy of Xerox Corporation
- 104 Canon U.S.A., Inc.
- 112 Photo courtesy Varityper
- 114 Courtesy of Xerox Corporation
- 119 Courtesy of International Business Machines Corporation
- 135 Photo courtesy All-Steel
- 136 bottom: Kardex Systems, Inc.
- 139 both photos: Ring King Visibles, Inc.
- 140 Ring King Visibles, Inc.
- 146 Courtesy, Datagraphix, Inc.
- 147 3M Company
- 156 AFI/Addressograph Electronic Addressing Systems
- 160 both photos: U.S. Postal Service
- 163 U.S. Postal Service
- 164 U.S. Postal Service
- 167 AMP Inc.
- 170 Courtesy of Wang Laboratories, Inc.
- 189 HUD photo
- 191 upper left: American Petroleum Institute
  lower left: American Petroleum Institute
  right: Courtesy Southwest Forest Industries/ photographer Paul Fusco
- 193 Photo courtesy All-Steel
- 196 Photo courtesy All-Steel
- 204 Photo courtesy All-Steel
- 213 Photo courtesy of Haworth, Inc., Holland, Michigan
- 225 All Comserv photos
- 228 All Comserv photos
- 231 All Comserv photos
- 242 Photo courtesy All-Steel
- 243 both photos: Photos courtesy Environetics
- 254 Photo courtesy Steelcase, Inc.
- 268 Photo courtesy All-Steel
- 269 Photos courtesy All-Steel
- 274 Packard Industries Officenter 2000 Series
- 276 Wright Line Inc., Worcester, Massachusetts
- 277 Photo courtesy Steelcase, Inc.
- 282 Wright Line Inc., Worcester, Massachusetts
- 286 Photo courtesy of Haworth, Inc., Holland, Michigan
- 289 Photo courtesy Steelcase, Inc.
- 291 Gates Acoustinet, Inc.
- 304 Photo courtesy of Kellogg Company
- 311 Photograph courtesy of Hewlett-Packard Company
- 312 Photo courtesy All-Steel

IV Part Opener: Storage Technology Corporation ©1983

- 336 right photo: Photo courtesy ITT Corporation
- 342 Photo—Merck & Co., Inc.
- 372 ©William James Warren/West Light
- 381 ©1984 Sepp Seitz/West Light
- 385 Honeywell
- 395 NCR Corporation
- 396 Photo courtesy Hewlett-Packard Company
- 403 Dest Corporation
- 405 Photo Courtesy Compugraphic
- 418 Courtesy TRW, Inc.
- 434 Courtesy of Xerox Corporation